SOVIET RELATIONS WITH LATIN AMERICA
1918–1968

SOVIET RELATIONS
WITH LATIN AMERICA
1918–1968

A Documentary Survey

Edited by
STEPHEN CLISSOLD

Issued under the auspices of the
Royal Institute of International Affairs
OXFORD UNIVERSITY PRESS
LONDON NEW YORK TORONTO
1970

302/17

Oxford University Press, Ely House, London W.1

GLASGOW NEW YORK TORONTO MELBOURNE WELLINGTON
CAPE TOWN SALISBURY IBADAN NAIROBI DAR ES SALAAM LUSAKA
ADDIS ABABA BOMBAY CALCUTTA MADRAS KARACHI LAHORE
DACCA KUALA LUMPUR SINGAPORE HONG KONG TOKYO

SBN 19 214982 2

Printed in Great Britain by
Ebenezer Baylis and Son, Limited
The Trinity Press, Worcester, and London

Contents

Preface and Acknowledgements

The documents included in this volume have been drawn from a wide range of Soviet and Latin American sources, some of them readily accessible, other —particularly those taken from Comintern and Latin American Communist sources—less so. For most of the articles published in the Soviet daily press I have relied on the translations furnished (with permission) by the *Current Digest of the Soviet Press*, published weekly by the American Association for the Advancement of Slavic Studies at the Ohio State University. Where I have found an official English version of a document (e.g. in the Comintern, and some Cuban, publications), I have used it in preference to translating directly from the original. In a few cases, where such a text is fuller than the printed version or the latter has proved unobtainable, I have worked from broadcast monitoring reports or official press releases, for which it has not always been possible to give an attribution.

All short explanatory footnotes accompanying the text of the documents have been added by the Editor. In the Introduction the footnotes (indicated by the letters of the alphabet) are mainly confined to source references; longer Supplementary Notes (indicated by numbers) are appended at the end of the Introduction (pp. 60 ff.).

In order to provide an immediate link between the text of each document and the relevant section of the Introduction, a reference to that page is given in parentheses, in italic type, beneath the title of each document, and at the end of each title in the List of Documents and Extracts. In the text of the Introduction, figures in parentheses in bold type refer to the number of the relevant documents or extracts reproduced here.

I am indebted to a number of colleagues and friends for their help in obtaining the documents or commenting on the Introduction. I am particularly grateful to Mr Andrés Bande, and to Dr Boris Goldenberg, who has given me the benefit of his unrivalled knowledge of the history of the Latin American Communist Parties. I should also like to thank Mr Humphrey Higgins for his assistance in tracking down a Russian literary allusion, and the staff of the Royal Institute of International Affairs, particularly Miss Elaine Arrowsmith and Mrs Lydia Bott of the Press Library (the latter for help in transliterating Russian names), and Miss Rena Fenteman, who checked many typescript copies against the originals. A special debt of gratitude is due to Miss Hermia Oliver for her invaluable collaboration in preparing the manuscript of this book for publication.

The scope of Soviet relations with Latin America is expanding rapidly and offers a fruitful and important field for further study. It is hoped that the documents assembled in this volume—incomplete as they must be—and such deductions as I have drawn from them will assist other investigators to undertake more detailed research into the relations between the Soviet Union and individual Latin American countries and into different facets of Soviet policy towards the Western hemisphere.

London, 6 August 1969   S.C.

Abbreviations

AFP	US Dept of State, *American Foreign Policy, Current Documents.*
ann.	annex.
APRA	*Alianza Popular Revolucionaria Americana.*
CC	Central Committee.
CDSP	*Current Digest of the Soviet Press.**
CPSU	Communist Party of the Soviet Union.
Dok. Vnesh. Pol.	*Dokumenty Vneshney Politiki SSR* (1957–).
ECCI	Executive Committee of the Communist International.
El Movimiento. . .	Comintern, S. American Secretariat, *El Movimiento revolucionario Latino-Americano: versiones de la primera Conferencia Comunista Latino-Americana, Buenos Aires, 1929.*
FRUS	*Foreign Relations of the United States, Diplomatic Papers.*
GAOR	*General Assembly Official Records.*
Inprecorr	*International Press Correspondence* (ECCI periodical).
LNOJ	*League of Nations Official Journal.*
Martínez de la Torre, *Apuntes . . .*	R. Martínez de la Torre, *Apuntes para una interpretación marxista de historia social del Perú* (Lima, 1947-9). 4 vols.
PSP	*Partido Socialista Popular.*
PURS	*Partido Unido de la Revolución Socialista.*
Relatorio	*A insurreição de 27 de novembro: Relatorio do Delegado E. Bellens Porto, Policia Civil do Districto Federal, Rio de Janeiro, 1936.*
RILU	Red International of Labour Unions.
SCOR	*Security Council Official Records.*
UNCIO	UN Conference on International Organization, San Francisco, 1945, *Documents* (London, 1945–55).

---

* Published weekly by the American Association for the Advancement of Slavic Studies at the Ohio State University. Copyright 1958, 1959, 1960, 1961, 1962, 1963, 1967, 1968, by permission.

List of Documents and Extracts

Note: Italic figures in parentheses denote page references to the Introduction.

III. WAR, COLD WAR, AND PEACEFUL COEXISTENCE

1. LATIN AMERICA

INTRODUCTION[a]

I Antecedents

Tsarist Russia and Imperial Spain

THE King of Spain's domains in the New World and the empire of the Tsar of All the Russias had seldom impinged upon one another. Peter the Great once considered, and rejected, a madcap scheme for the conquest of Spanish America.[b] More serious had been the threat that the Russians, pushing south from Alaska, might establish trading posts along the Pacific coast of North America which would ultimately threaten New Spain and other Spanish possessions.[c] It was this fear that, in 1789, led the Viceroy of Mexico to order the founding of a Spanish settlement at Nootka Bay which in turn alarmed the British Government and became a *casus belli* between Spain and Britain. Three years before this incident, Francisco Miranda, the Precursor of Latin America's independence movement, had arrived at the court of Catherine II and sought to enlist Russian support against the Spanish crown for his dreams of emancipation.[d] But Russia showed little sympathy for the Creole cause and was tardy in recognizing the independence of the ex-colonies who feared that the Tsar might help Spain to restore the *status quo*. The prospect of Russian encroachments down the Pacific coast of North America continued to alarm the new rulers of Mexico, as they had the Viceroys,[e] and did not completely fade until Russia sold Alaska in 1867.

---

[a] Throughout the Introduction, bold-type figures in parentheses refer to numbers of documents or extracts reproduced in this volume.

[b] I. Zabelin, 'Proyekt zavoyevaniya Ameriki, podanny Petru Velikomu', *Moskvityanin*, i (1851), pp. 121–4, quoted by L. A. Shur, in *Latinskaya Amerika v proshlom i nastoyashchem* (Moscow, 1960), p. 341.

[c] See Enriqueta Vila Vilar, 'Los Rusos en América', *Anuario de estudios americanos*, xxii (Seville, 1965), pp. 569–672.

[d] V. Miroshevsky, 'Ekaterina II i Miranda', *Istorik-Marksist*, no. 2, 1940, pp. 125–8.

[e] In a report presented to the Supreme Governing Junta of the Mexican Empire on 29 December 1821, the Commission for Foreign Affairs wrote of the Russian settlements that 'their proximity is fraught with danger. Should their maritime enterprises continue, they could gain possession of Upper California, thereby not only causing the loss of that most rich and fertile country but endangering the equally fertile provinces of Lower California, Sonora, Ostimuri, and the two Primerías. These adventurers must be stopped. The spark which is not put out at once will later grow into a blaze' ('Un Programa de política internacional', *Archivo diplomático histórico* (Mexico, 1932), no. 37, p. 23).

Russian immigration

During the course of the nineteenth century, some Russians did establish themselves in Latin America but as legal immigrants, not interlopers. Most settled in rural areas of Brazil and the River Plate countries.[a] But although, during this period too, the first diplomatic, economic, and cultural links were forged (1),[b] relations between Latin America and Russia remained slight. This was to bring the Soviet Union both advantages and disadvantages. It justified their claim that, unlike Spain, France, Britain, and the United States, Russia had no imperialist record or designs to live down in this area. But it also meant that, when they did begin to take an interest in it, the Soviet leaders were ignorant of Latin America and consequently prone to misjudge its problems.

Marx and Lenin on Latin America

Nor had the founders of Marxism-Leninism themselves much specific, or even always reliable, guidance to offer so far as Latin America was concerned. Marx had written an essay on Simón Bolívar (2) based largely on the memoirs of a disgruntled French soldier of fortune, whose distorted and unflattering view of the Liberator coloured official Soviet writing until the mid-1950s.[1] He had a poor opinion of Spaniards, and a still poorer one of Latin Americans, whilst Engels told him frankly that he believed the Mexicans could only benefit by coming under the tutelage of the United States.[c] Lenin had declared that the South American republics, specially Argentina, were no more than neo-colonies, technically independent, but commercially bound fast to Britain (3)—a view which, with Wall Street replacing London as the chief instrument of economic imperialism, still remains the standard Soviet picture. Lenin himself had little knowledge of Latin America, but he spoke with two delegates representing the Mexican Communist Party at the 2nd Comintern Congress in 1920. One of them has recorded[d] that

Lenin was not interested in the socialist movement in Mexico. He realised that it was bound to be very rudimentary. But he was interested in the masses of the people in Mexico, in their relation to the United States, whether there was a strong opposition movement to the United States.

[a] A fresh stream of immigrants followed after the First World War. These were mostly Russians and Ukrainians from territories forming the new Polish state and also exiles fleeing from the Bolshevik Revolution (see below, p. 33).

[b] The first scientific expedition was organized in the 1820s by Gregori Ivanovich Langsdorf (1774–1852), who had been sent to Brazil as Russia's first Consul-General. The expedition collected valuable ethnographical data but produced little published work of scientific value, since Langsdorf contracted a fever which permanently impaired his brain.

[c] 'The Spaniards are indeed degenerate. But a degenerate Spaniard, a Mexican—that is the ideal! All the vices of the Spaniards—boastfulness, grandiloquence, and quixoticism— are found in the Mexicans raised to the third degree' (letter to Engels, 2 Dec. 1847, *Marx-Engels Werke*, xxvii (Berlin, Dietz Verlag, 1963), p. 417). Engels commented (ibid. xxix. 280) that 'in America we have witnessed the conquest of Mexico and are glad of it. . . . It is in the interests of its own development that henceforth Mexico should be placed under the tutelage of the United States. It is in the interests of the development of the whole of America that the United States, in taking possession of California, gains control of the Pacific Ocean.'

[d] 'Manuel Gómez', probably a pseudonym for Charlie Phillips, in *Survey*, no. 53, Oct. 1964.

The other[a] adds that Lenin told him that

there were more urgent revolutionary tasks which must have priority. It would be a long time before revolution could succeed in the New World. Conditions might mature in the near future. But American imperialism was on the alert to intervene as it had done in the past.

II The Comintern Period

Comintern interest in Mexico

During the early years of its existence, the Soviet Union had, indeed, too many other pressing preoccupations, and too high hopes of speedy revolutionary outbreaks elsewhere, to spare much thought for Latin America. The first emissary to that area—whether representing the Comintern or the Commissariat for Foreign Affairs it is hard to say, since the functions of those two bodies were not then clearly differentiated—was Mikhail Borodin, whose mission seems to have been primarily to finance the Soviet trade delegation, then short of funds in the United States, and also to assist any Communist activities likely to distract the United States from possible intervention against the Soviet Union.[2] After arriving in Mexico in 1919, Borodin got into touch with the young Indian nationalist, M. N. Roy, whom he converted to Marxism. Through Roy, Borodin was able to meet President Venustiano Carranza, who is reported to have expressed interest in the possibility of establishing relations with the Soviet Union;[3] the prospect of a substantial purchase of Mexican henequen may have helped secure Borodin a friendly hearing.[b] With the Russian's encouragement, Roy persuaded a wing of the small Socialist Party to declare itself Communist and then left for Moscow, together with Charles Phillips, an American Communist, to present the declaration at the 2nd Comintern Congress.

Phillips returned to work for a time in Mexico, where he was joined by two delegates from the Comintern, the veteran Japanese Communist Sen Katayama and a young Italian-American, Luis Fraina. Neither appears to have achieved much. Katayama left after a few months, and Fraina returned to the United States and defected from the Communist ranks after difficulties with the Mexican Communists over the use of funds in the 1923 elections. The Comintern attempted to prescribe in detail the tactics to be followed by the Mexican Communist Party (12), but the latter, under the pressure of events, took decisions which Moscow disapproved of and forced to be reversed. Carranza had been overthrown in 1920 and succeeded by General Álvaro Obregón. The choice for

---

[a] M. N. Roy, *Memoirs* (Bombay, 1964), p. 346.

[b] Carleton Beals, who was himself involved in the early Mexican Communist movement, states that 'Borodin had convinced Mexican representatives abroad that Russia was prepared to buy enormous quantities of henequen for her harvest fields, and so secured a Mexican diplomatic passport to arrange for its purchase and negotiate for recognition' (*Glass Houses: Ten Years of Free-lancing* (New York, 1938), p. 45).

the latter's successor lay between his nominee, Plutarco Elías Calles, and the right-wing General Adolfo de la Huerta. The Communists first favoured de la Huerta, then switched to Calles. Though they had even gone so far as to give the Obregón–Calles side armed support when de la Huerta attempted a coup, instructions were received from the Comintern that the new Calles administration should be opposed and his influence with the people undermined (**18**).

In the meantime, Moscow had been putting out feelers through its mission in Germany for the establishment of diplomatic relations with the Mexican Government. Obregón was interested in the development of trade with the Soviet Union, but hesitated to commit himself to the full diplomatic relations on which the Russians insisted.[a] On 30 July 1924 the Mexican Ministry for Foreign Affairs announced that since Mexico recognized the right of each country to choose whatever form of government it deemed suitable, the Government 'finds no obstacle to renewing relations with Russia'. On 20 August President Kalinin addressed a note to President Obregón requesting *agrément* for Stanislas Pestkovsky as the first Soviet Minister to Mexico. Pestkovsky duly presented his credentials to the Mexican President on 7 November 1924.

The establishment of a Legation in Mexico City was hailed in Moscow as a success for Soviet foreign policy and the preliminary for an extension of Soviet influence throughout the Western hemisphere. G. V. Chicherin, the Commissar for Foreign Affairs, addressed the Comintern Executive Committee in glowing terms on the popularity of the Soviet Union in Mexico and the enthusiastic welcome accorded everywhere to the Soviet Minister (**13**).[4] His statement prompted a tart reminder from Calles, who had succeeded Obregón as President of the Republic, that the Soviet Government must not abuse the diplomatic privileges granted it in Mexico for the purposes of propaganda and political intrigue.[b] The Soviet Legation hastened to explain in a communiqué to the press that Chicherin's words must have been misreported or misunderstood. He had not for a moment wished to imply that Mexico might be construed as a pawn of Bolshevism; 'neither he nor his government had ever pretended to make use of the influence of the Mexican government nor of the labour organisations to develop any specific policy'.[c] Mexican irritation over the Chicherin statement was understandable, since it provided ammunition for those circles in the United States which were ready to depict Mexico as a hotbed of Bolshevism. Allegations to this effect made at the end of 1926 by Under-Secretary of State Olds and, in a much publicized statement on the following 12 January, by Secretary F. B. Kellogg, were vigorously rebutted by Calles, who insisted that Mexican policies were in no way influenced by those of the Soviet Union or conceived in Communist terms.

Pestkovsky and Mexican labour

If the advent of a Soviet mission in Mexico proved an irritant in that country's

[a] *Dok. Vnesh. Pol.*, vi (1923), no. 283, p. 478 & no. 288, p. 486.
[b] *Excelsior* (Mexico City), 2 Mar. 1930.
[c] Beals, p. 338.

relations with Washington (which had not yet decided to establish diplomatic relations with Moscow), the course of Mexican-Soviet relations themselves were far from smooth. Even before the arrival of the Soviet Minister, Moscow had unwittingly offended the susceptibilities of the country's most powerful labour leader, Luis N. Morones, head of the *Confederación Regional Obrera Mexicana* (CROM), by refusing him admission to the Soviet Union whilst on a tour of Europe. Pestkovsky's tactless cultivation of extremist elements and rival labour groups alienated CROM still more and drew from that body a firm though politely worded protest (**14, 15**). The Mexican Government protested more sharply still when a contribution of $25,000, said to have been raised by the Red Trade Union of Railway Workers in Moscow, was paid into the fund organized to assist the Mexican railway workers who had come out on a strike which Morones, now Minister of Labour, was attempting to break with the help of CROM.[a] By the end of 1926 Pestkovsky had been recalled and replaced by Mme Aleksandra Kollontay.[5]

Mme Kollontay

The new Soviet Minister—a woman of charm and intelligence—appears to have taken a different view of her functions. In a statement attributed to her in Berlin before leaving to take up her Mexican appointment, Mme Kollontay observed:

I hope to demonstrate that the modern diplomat's job is strictly business and commercial and not concerned with intrigues and society gossip that characterized pre-war diplomacy. The diplomat should also scrupulously refrain from propaganda or mixing in the internal affairs of the country to which he has been accredited. The great task ahead of me is the advancing and the perfecting of commercial relations between Russia and Mexico.[b]

Mme Kollontay returned to the same theme of closer trade relations when presenting her letters of credence to President Calles on 24 December (**16**). In a subsequent interview with the President she also expressed the hope that the differences which had arisen between CROM and the Soviet representatives would be overcome (**17**). Little progress had however been made towards either of the two objectives referred to by the time Mme Kollontay left Mexico a year and a half later.

In its relations with Mexico, Moscow was attempting to follow two incompatible policies. On the official level—for Mme Kollontay appears to have given her assurances in good faith[c]—there was the attempt to improve relations with the Government of President Calles and his successor Emilio Portes Gil, and with its chief labour organization, CROM. On the unofficial level—through the Mexican Communist Party, which followed, though not always as obediently as was required of it, the line laid down by the Comintern—there

[a] *Dok. Vnesh. Pol.*, x (1927), p. 594; Beals, p. 340.
[b] *Excelsior*, 2 Mar. 1930.
[c] President Portes Gil declares that 'so long as this lady was in charge of the Soviet Legation our relations with that country were extremely cordial and we never had the slightest grounds for discord with her Government' (*Quince años de política mexicana* (1941), p. 373).

was the attempt to penetrate and control CROM, or if that were not possible, to supersede it, and an ambivalent attitude towards the Calles Government of supporting it against the Right whilst undermining, radicalizing, and ultimately overthrowing it. With regard to CROM, efforts were first made to secure its adhesion to Aleksandr Lozovsky's[a] Profintern, the Red International of Labour Unions (RILU)[b], and when these failed, a rival body called the *Confederación Sindical Unitaria de México* (CSUM) was launched. But if the Communists were too weak to make much headway in the field of labour, they had a considerable following amongst the peasantry, specially in the state of Vera Cruz. There the peasant leaders Manuel Díaz Ramírez and Ursulo Galván were also members of the Presidium of the Peasant International (the Krestintern). In Durango state another peasant leader, Guadelupe Rodríguez, was a Communist who had been in Moscow in 1927 for the tenth anniversary celebrations of the October Revolution. The testing time for these peasant organizations came in March 1929 when a right-wing revolt broke out against the Government of Portes Gil, who had been elected President in place of the murdered Obregón. The Peasant Leagues put their armed forces into the field and helped the Government to quell the revolt.

Comintern directives for a rising

The Comintern strongly disapproved of these tactics, and the leadership of the Mexican Communist Party was obliged to send directives to the peasant leaders instructing them to turn their arms against the Government and fight an action on two fronts with a view to precipitating social revolution. Galván refused, and was ultimately denounced and expelled from the Party. Rodríguez attempted to carry out the directives and issued a revolutionary May Day proclamation urging the peasants to seize land and the workers to take over the factories.[c] He was caught by the local military commander and summarily executed.

Following the execution of Rodríguez, the Comintern issued a manifesto inciting the Mexican people to all-out war on the Portes Gil Government. When the 1st Congress of Latin American Communist Parties met in Buenos Aires in June 1929 the Mexican delegates were taken to task by the Comintern spokesmen for the tardiness of their Party in exploiting the recent emergency (19). The congress records state that 'Suárez', who was the chief delegate of the Mexican Communist Party at this Congress,[d] advocated tactics which were even more extreme than the official line of the Comintern. 'The Party must wait no longer to put into effect the proletarian revolution in our country', he

---

[a] Pseud. of Solomon Dridzo.

[b] *Inprecorr*, 18 Feb. 1926.

[c] *El Machete* (organ of the Mexican CP), 8 June 1929. The Mexican police confiscated the entire edition of *El Machete* containing instructions for the armed rising, and was able to arrest most of those to whom the incitement to revolt was addressed. (Diego Rivera, 'Lo que opina Diego Rivera sobre la pintura revolucionaria', *Octubre* (Mexico), no. 1, 1925, quoted in R. García Treviño, *La ingerencia rusa en México* (Mexico, 1959), p. 191).

[d] According to García Treviño (p. 95), Suárez was the pseudonym of the famous muralist, D. A. Siqueiros.

insisted. 'The only solution for our Party is to take up arms and organize an armed rising, thus preventing our militants from being killed with impunity.'[a] If the rising was suppressed, he urged that the rebels should take to the hills and organize guerrilla resistance.[b] He even demanded that resistance should begin without waiting for the lengthy process of organizing a disciplined Communist Party, and raised the question of whether the Party would not further its ends by a well-timed *attentat*. Both these proposals were dismissed as erroneous by the Comintern spokesman, but more than ten years later, when the help of the Mexican Communists was sought in liquidating the exiled Trotsky, it was to such action that Moscow turned.[6] As a means of tightening up discipline in the Mexican Party, from which a number of leading Communists had only recently been purged on Moscow's insistence on charges of deviation,[c] it was agreed at the 1929 Congress of Latin American Communist Parties that a Subsecretariat of the Comintern should be set up in Mexico.

Rupture of relations

With the Mexican Communists committed to militant opposition to the Government, official relations between the Soviet Union and Mexico came under increasing strain. Mexican protests (**21**) against the hostile tone of the Soviet press and the subversive incitements of the Comintern (**20**) were brushed off with bland assurances that the Soviet Government had no control over the Soviet press and nothing whatever to do with the 'completely autonomous international organization' known as the Comintern (**22**). Relations continued to deteriorate. The Soviet Legation in Mexico, now under the charge of Mme Kollontay's successor, Dr Aleksandr Makar, was accused by Portes Gil of furnishing funds, propaganda, and instructions for attacks on the Government.[7] Communist-instigated demonstrations were staged in a number of foreign countries in protest against alleged persecution of 'progressives' in Mexico. Mexican démarches in support of the Chinese Government in the latter's dispute with the Soviet Union embittered Soviet-Mexican relations still further. Before handing over to his successor, General Pascual Ortiz Rubio, Portes Gil decided that the moment had come to break off relations with Moscow (**25**). In January 1930 Dr Makar was informed that the Mexican Government considered that diplomatic relations with the Soviet Union were at an end and he was soon afterwards forced to leave the country. The Mexican Government also withdrew its own mission from Moscow, and expelled the remaining Soviet diplomatic and commercial representatives from Mexico.

Mexico's action in breaking off relations was an unexpected rebuff for Moscow. Maksim Litvinov referred to it in terms more of sorrow than of anger, protesting that the Mexican Government had no real grounds for complaint and was acting under imperialist pressure: 'we can therefore only express our

[a] *El Movimiento*, p. 182.

[b] Ibid., p. 183.

[c] The muralist Diego Rivera, who had been made much of in Russia a year or two previously and was later to be Trotsky's chief protector and friend in Mexico, states that he was amongst those purged on Manuilsky's instructions (*Octubre*, no. 1, 1925, quoted by García Treviño, p. 191).

sympathy with the Mexican people in this affair' (24). The Russian press put the matter more crudely. Mexico, which in any case 'does not carry much weight' in the international world, had no real national independence and was simply being manipulated by American capitalists (23).

Soviet activities in Argentina and Uruguay

In South America, Soviet interest had at first been primarily directed towards the countries of the River Plate. On several occasions, Moscow declared its readiness to enter into diplomatic relations with Argentina and the other republics (4, 37). Only Uruguay, attracted by the prospect of developing valuable trade links with the Soviet Union, reacted favourably to these advances and established diplomatic relations in 1926. On 21 August the Uruguayan Foreign Minister sent a telegram to Maksim Litvinov, Acting People's Commissar for Foreign Affairs, declaring that the Uruguayan Government, 'anxious that diplomatic relations be resumed between the two countries, recognizes the USSR as a *de jure* Government'.[a] A Soviet commercial office was established in Montevideo the following year,[b] but it was not until 1933, when the world economic depression had forced Uruguay to make every effort to secure new markets for her exports, that the Uruguayan Government decided to exchange permanent diplomatic missions 'in view of the increasing trade relations between Uruguay and the USSR'. In reply to this communication, V. Krestinsky, the Acting People's Commissar for Foreign Affairs, expressed the Soviet Government's agreement to exchange missions and 'to enter into negotiations for the purpose of concluding a trade treaty between USSR and Uruguay'.[c] Argentina and the other South American countries, allegedly as the result of British pressure (38),[d] declined to agree to renew diplomatic relations, but in December 1927 the Argentine Government authorized the establishment of a branch of Yuzhamtorg (41), a Russian agency set up for the purpose of developing trade with South America.[e] Some expansion of trade, mostly with Argentina and to a lesser extent with Uruguay, followed (6, 9), but in fluctuating volume and with a great preponderance of Soviet imports over exports.[f] It was hoped in Moscow that a similar expansion of trade with other South American countries would follow, and would also lead to the establishment of diplomatic relations with them. However, in July 1931, the Argentine police raided Yuzhamtorg headquarters and suspended its activities (42). Though charges of dumping and 'wild fabrications regarding the links between Yuzhamtorg and Communist activities in the countries of Latin

[a] *Dok. Vnesh. Pol.*, ix, no. 238, p. 393.

[b] *SSSR i Latinskaya Amerika, 1917–67* (Moscow, 1967), p. 84.

[c] Leonard Shapiro, *Soviet Treaty Series* (Georgetown UP), ii, 75.

[d] *Dok. Vnesh. Pol.*, x, 595. Argentina's official reason for not renewing relations was that the Soviet authorities had attacked the Argentine Legation in St Petersburg and refused to make amends (38).

[e] An account of this organization and of its operations is given by A. P. Malkov and V. M. Marchenko, 'Deyatelnost Yuzhamtorga', *Novaya i noveyshaya istoriya*, no. 4, 1968, pp. 82–8.

[f] This is clear from the table shown on facing page.

America' were indignantly rejected on the Soviet side, it would seem that Yuzhamtorg did to some extent serve as cover for the transmission of funds to the Comintern's South American Secretariat.[8]

Arraignment of Uruguay at the League of Nations

After its suppression in Buenos Aires, Yuzhamtorg moved its headquarters to Montevideo. Although, two years later, President Gabriel Terra suspended the Constitution and took some repressive action against the Uruguayan Communist Party, relations between Moscow and Montevideo continued for a time without major friction. According to a later statement by Litvinov at the League of Nations (32), the only difference arising in this period was over the Uruguayan Government's wish to deport a Russian-born anarchist whom the Soviet Union refused to receive—a difference which Litvinov claimed President Terra had indicated he would be prepared to overlook 'if we would buy two hundred tons or so of Uruguayan cheese'. At the end of 1935, however, following a rising in Brazil which the Brazilian Government declared had been instigated by the Comintern and secretly financed through the Soviet Legation in Montevideo,[a] the Uruguayan Government decided to suspend relations with the Soviet Union (26–30). Moscow at once retaliated by cancelling all trade transactions with Uruguay and winding up Yuzhamtorg (31). The Soviet press savagely attacked the Uruguayan Government for its subservience to Brazilian pressure (30) and a complaint was lodged with the League of Nations on the grounds that Uruguay had violated her obligations as a member of the League by breaking off relations on the pretext of groundless accusations. After a spirited debate in the League Council, the dispute was concluded by the passing of an anodyne resolution (32–5). Though the Soviet press did its best to pass this off as a diplomatic victory (36), it could not be disguised that the USSR had lost her last diplomatic foothold in Latin America.

Comintern links with Latin America

The rupture of diplomatic relations with Mexico and Uruguay left Moscow with the Comintern network as virtually its sole contact with the countries of

Note [f] *cont.*

(000 rubles)

Year	Soviet exports to Argentina	Soviet imports from Argentina
1923–4	—	4,674
1924–5	—	37,099
1925–6	3	36,304
1927	1,157	89,672
1928	2,737	29,836
1929	12,947	98,928
1930	12,864	60,522

(*Source: SSSR i Latinskaya Amerika*, p. 83.)

[a] See below, pp. 18–19 and docs 49–55

Latin America. Nor was this network as tightly woven, or its individual links as strong, as Moscow would have wished. In Mexico, the most promising base for the expansion of Soviet influence throughout Central America and the Caribbean, the Communists had proved too unruly and too much weakened by internal faction to become a serious factor in national politics. Nevertheless, in the early 1920s, they were instrumental under Comintern guidance in founding or directing Communist Parties in Cuba, Guatemala, and elsewhere. As a reinforcement to, or perhaps as a check on, the activities of the Mexican Communists, the Communist Party of the United States was also entrusted with special responsibility in the same area.[a] In South America, the chief base for the Comintern's activities was the River Plate area. After the 3rd World Congress in 1921 the Comintern had accepted the Argentine Communist Party's application for affiliation, and, after the 5th World Congress, had requested it to set up a special bureau for South America, the *Secretariato Sudamericano de la Internacional Comunista*. This seems at first to have been run in a rather arbitrary fashion by the Argentine labour leader José F. Penelón.[b] After his expulsion from the Argentine Communist Party, the Secretariat was reorganized and placed under the control of Vitorio Codovila, a Communist of Italian extraction who was to prove one of Moscow's foremost representatives in Latin America for some forty years. Under his direction the South American Secretariat, through its publications, its 'open letters' and secret directives, the intervention of its 'instructors' in the affairs of the Latin American Communist Parties, and the meetings which it periodically organized for the same (8), remained Moscow's most effective instrument in Latin America for more than a decade.[c]

The 4th and 5th Comintern Congresses

When the Comintern held its 4th Congress in 1922, Latin America was given slightly more attention than before. A member of the Executive was charged with special responsibilities for the area,[d] and there were Latin Americans amongst the delegates. One of these was Luis Emilio Recabarren, the well-known Chilean labour leader. Though the Comintern had succeeded in founding and directing the small Communist Parties of Latin America, it had so far failed to command the allegiance of any Latin American of real stature and political following. Recabarren, it seemed, might play this role. He virtually controlled the powerful Chilean Workers' Federation and had founded the

---

[a] The decision to charge the United States CP with this function was taken at the 6th enlarged plenary session of ECCI on 15 March 1926.

[b] See p. 13.

[c] The S. American Secretariat organized its 1st Congress of Latin American CPs in Buenos Aires in June 1929, and published the proceedings. The 3rd Congress is said to have been held in Montevideo in October 1934 and has been only scantily reported. No reports whatsoever appear to be extant for the 2nd Congress, which seems to have been held, also in Montevideo, in 1931 or 1932 (*Inprecorr*, no. 41, for 1935, p. 1074). See also p. 18, note c.

[d] J. Degras, ed., *The Communist International, 1919–43, Documents,* i: *1919–22* (1956), p. 455. He was a Swiss, Edgar Woog, working under the name of 'Stirner', who later became a leading figure in the Swiss Labour (Communist) Party.

Workers' Socialist Party which he later persuaded to seek affiliation to the Comintern and to change its name to that of the Chilean Communist Party. On his return to Chile, Recabarren published a number of laudatory articles about the Soviet Union, but at the end of 1924—either disillusioned by his experiences in that country or in a fit of depression at the course events were taking in Chile—he committed suicide.[a] Amongst the delegates to the 5th Comintern Congress two years later was another outstanding Latin American, Víctor Raúl Haya de la Torre, founder of the *Alianza Popular Revolucionaria Americana*, whom the Russians hoped to win over. Haya de la Torre, however, decided against co-operation with the Communists, and APRA developed as a movement independent of Comintern influence. The Soviet leaders whom Haya de la Torre met at this time—amongst whom were Lunacharsky, Frunze, Trotsky, and Chicherin—showed little real interest in Latin America or understanding of its conditions.[b] Lozovsky, the head of the Profintern, showed rather more interest in Latin America (**47**), kept up a friendly correspondence with Haya de la Torre, and took advantage of the presence in Moscow of a number of Latin Americans who had been invited to attend the celebrations in honour of the tenth anniversary of the October Revolution (1927) to promote the formation of a Communist-sponsored labour organization for Latin America, the *Confederación Sindical Latino-Americana*.[c] Political relations with the Latin American Communist Parties were handled through the Comintern's 'Latin Secretariat', which also covered France, Italy, Spain, and Portugal. It was not until 1929 that a separate Secretariat for Latin America was set up in the Comintern headquarters.[9]

The 6th Comintern Congress, 1928

The 6th Comintern Congress paid more attention than had previous Congresses to the revolutionary potentialities of Latin America. 'South America', declared Bukharin in his opening speech, 'is for the first time widely entering the orbit of influence of the Communist International.' Outlining events in that area, he declared that America was elbowing out British imperialism, and national and agrarian revolutions promised to turn into social revolutions (**5**). The 'Theses' drawn up at the end of the Congress exhorted Latin American Communists everywhere to step up activities against 'the landlord regime and imperialism' and called on them to co-operate in this task with the petty bourgeoisie, though they 'may not under any circumstances politically subordinate themselves to

---

[a] Recabarren's relations with the Comintern remain obscure. It seems probable that a man of his forceful character and independent views would not take kindly to obeying directives from abroad. Some distrust of his 'reformist' and bourgeois tendencies are certainly expressed in Comintern and Soviet publications (see *Otchet ispolkoma Kominterna* (Moscow, 1925–6), p. 325).

[b] 'I have the general impression that they know little or nothing about conditions in our America. Chicherin, the Commissar for Foreign Affairs, put a number of questions to me about Mexico, but many of his questions showed that he knew little about a country with such interesting social problems' (Haya de la Torre, *Nuestra América y el mundo* (Lima, 1961), pp. 158–9).

[c] *Inprecorr*, 17 Oct. 1927. The founding congress did not take place until May 1929 in Montevideo.

3

their temporary ally' (7). They should demand outright expropriation of large estates, confiscation of foreign and domestic capitalist enterprises, the repudiation of the national debt, better working conditions for labour, the arming of workers and peasants, the conversion of regular armies into militias, and 'the establishment of the Soviet power of the workers, peasants, and soldiers'. For the first time at a Comintern Congress delegates from a large number of Latin American Communist Parties were present and were given the floor. The Comintern, declared the Brazilian delegate, had sadly neglected Latin America up to now. 'We hope', he concluded, 'that it is not going to lose interest, and that it will help us in developing our Communist Parties, which are still small, into real mass parties.'[a]

The 1st Latin American Communist Congress

The Comintern did its best not to disappoint these hopes. The following year, 1929, two important gatherings were organized in Latin America under its auspices: a constituent Congress for the *Confederación Sindical Latino-Americana* in Montevideo, from 18 to 26 May,[b] and the 1st Latin American Communist Congress in Buenos Aires, from 1 to 12 June. Lozovsky, representing the Profintern, presided over the first, Codovila, representing the South American Secretariat and Jules Humbert-Droz,[c] under the name of 'Comrade Luis', representing the ECCI, over the second. The Buenos Aires Congress was attended by 38 delegates from 14 Communist Parties in Latin America, the United States, and France, as well as by representatives of the Comintern organizations.[d] The line laid down by Moscow was that of the extremist intransigence of what is known as the 'third period' (1929–35). The Latin American Communist Parties were enjoined to pursue militant revolutionary tactics and to have no truck with pseudo-progressive Governments or with reformist Socialists or bourgeois nationalists. The political situation and the role of the Communists in the major countries were reviewed, and the debates give us some idea of the scope and nature of the Comintern's work during the 1920s. In addition to the situation in Mexico, to which reference has already been made, developments in Argentina, Colombia, Peru, and the Central American and Caribbean areas received special attention.

Comintern objectives in Argentina

Moscow attached special importance to the development of a strong Communist movement in Argentina and Uruguay, since these countries were a

[a] *Inprecorr*, 8 Aug 1928, p. 819.

[b] See *El Trabajador Latino-Americano* (Montevideo), official organ of the *Confederación Sindical Latino-Americana*; *Crónica sintética del Congreso Sindical Latino-Americano*, year 2, nos. 17–18, June–July 1929, pp. 51–74.

[c] See below, p. 62, note 9.

[d] The countries represented were Argentina, Brazil, Bolivia, Colombia, Cuba, Ecuador, El Salvador, Guatemala, Mexico, Panama, Paraguay, Peru, Uruguay, and Venezuela. The absence of delegates from Chile was attributed to 'the recrudescence of the white terror' in that country (see *El Movimiento . . .* for a full account of the proceedings).

main source of food for Great Britain, whom the Soviet Union still suspected of preparing to launch another 'imperialist war' against her. The control of labour in the River Plate was therefore seen as a means by which any warlike initiative on the part of Britain could be paralysed. The Argentine Communists, who had transformed their International Socialist Party into the Argentine Communist Party in 1920, had however been weakened by schisms both of the Left and of the Right. Moscow chose to back the group led by Vitorio Codovila and Orestes Ghioldi whose immigrant origin may have been regarded as an important factor in the event of any divergence between Soviet and Argentine interests. They received Comintern backing for the purge of a rival Left faction in 1926 (40), and for the more serious expulsion of a Rightist group under the experienced Argentine Communist leader Penelón in the following year. That the issue was less one of ideology than of readiness to champion the presumed interests of the Soviet Union regardless of the cost to the Argentine working class is clear from the frank admissions made by an Argentine delegate to the Buenos Aires Congress:

At the time of the raid on Arcos House in London, and on the Soviet Embassy in Peking, etc., the South American Secretariat launched a manifesto with the justified slogan: 'Not a bushel of wheat nor a pound of meat for the imperialist armies in their struggle against the Soviet Union.'

Penelón strongly opposed this on the grounds that it was not 'feasible' and that 'only feasible slogans should be launched', and that 'the worker organizations are weak'. What is more, he alleged that its application, by restricting exports, would bring down the workers' wages. 'That is why they would not understand the slogan. . . . Penelón had no faith in the revolutionary capacity of the masses.'[a]

Colombia—failure to exploit strikes

A good deal of attention was devoted at the 1929 Latin American Communist Congress to the widespread strikes which had occurred the previous year in the Colombian banana plantations (44), and to analysing the failure of the local Communist leaders to turn them into a nation-wide revolutionary movement. According to one delegate who had been a prime mover in the strikes, these had led to disturbances which had cost the lives of over 1,000 men, women, and children. The Colombian delegates to the Congress blamed Comintern headquarters for ignorance of Colombian geographical and political realities and for failure to send adequate instructions. They claimed that they had never received the Open Letter sent by the Comintern and had only read it later in the journal published by the South American Secretariat (45). The Comintern spokesmen excused themselves by explaining that

in Moscow, the following occurred. One delegate gave a fantastic account of the armed movement which was on the point of breaking out and of the subjective and objective conditions for revolution which obtained in Colombia.

---

[a] Speech by Ghitor (Orestes Ghioldi) (*El Movimiento* . . . p. 377

Then another arrived and gave us a report that differed completely from the first; later, a third comrade arrived who gave us particulars quite at variance with the previous ones. With such contradictory reports, no comrade can think that the Comintern could have done more than it did for the movement, for these unreliable reports which we received made it impossible to assess the situation in Colombia properly.[a]

A Comintern agent who had been sent to Colombia at the time but who seems to have carried little weight, pointed out that the Colombian Communists were hampered by having no party of their own, but had to work through the *Partido Socialista Revolucionario*, 'which had nothing in common with a Communist Party'.[b] Some leaders of that party did indeed switch their political allegiance to the powerful Liberal Party. After the 1929 Latin American Congress, the Comintern decided that the Colombian Communists must be disciplined and what remained of the *Partido Socialista Revolucionario* turned into a reliable Communist Party, and it sent delegates to Colombia to see that this was done.[c]

Directives to Peruvian Communists

Several factors complicated the development of a Communist movement in Peru. One was the existence of Haya de la Torre's APRA, which Moscow had at first hoped to bring under its control, and despite repeated rebuffs, courted afresh when Popular Front tactics were introduced in the mid-1930s.[d] Another was the outstanding influence exercised amongst the Peruvian Communists by the brilliant Marxist writer José Carlos Mariátegui, whose analysis of Peru's basic Indian problem smacked in Moscow of 'populism'[e] and whose tactics of founding a Socialist Party, which it was proposed to control by means of a

[a] Ibid., p. 198.

[b] Ibid., p. 127. This agent was a Frenchman called Rabaté (working under the assumed name of 'Austine'), who had been sent to Colombia to represent the Profintern. He claimed that the Colombian comrades should therefore have taken it for granted that he was also acting for the Comintern.

[c] The Comintern representative chiefly responsible for this work in 1930–1 was Joseph Zack Kornfeder, a leading member of the United States CP. In a statement made in 1951 to a subcommittee of the Judiciary Committee to investigate internal security, Kornfeder claimed that he 'succeeded to organise a very loose, inefficient, socialist political party in Colombia and make out of it a Communist Party' (Hearings, 82nd Congress, 1st & 2nd sess., Washington, 1951, p. 865).

[d] See above, p. 11. Haya de la Torre states (*El Anti-imperialismo y el Apra* (Lima, 1961), pp. 46–7) that in the correspondence which took place between them in the 1920s, Lozovsky had not raised any objection to the existence of APRA as a separate organization, though he had criticized it for including intellectuals. Lozovsky referred to this correspondence with Haya, whom he described as a 'good element and a very honest man', in his speech to the 4th Profintern Congress at Moscow in 1928 (**47**). A renewed approach to APRA was made by the Communists in early 1935, when an open letter was addressed to Haya by the 'Peruvian Delegation, on behalf of the Conference of the Communist Parties of Latin America', urging that APRA should join forces with the Peruvian CP for a campaign of 'national liberation' (*Inprecorr*, 25 May 1935, pp. 593–5).

[e] He was criticized on this score by Miroshevsky, the leading Soviet Latin Americanist of the time (*Dialéctica*, no. 17, 1946). This unfavourable view was later revised (see S. I. Semyonov and A. E. Shulgovsky, 'The role of José Carlos Mariátegui in the formation of the Peruvian Communist Party', *Novaya i noveyshaya istoriya*, no. 5, 1957).

small clandestine Communist Party working within it, seemed highly dangerous. A delegate sent to Moscow in 1927 returned to Peru with a memorandum setting out the Comintern's thinking on this and other subjects **(46)** and the same line was repeated by the Comintern spokesmen at the Buenos Aires Congress.[a] A fuller analysis of the situation in Peru and a renewed directive to proceed at once with the founding of a Communist Party was sent by the Comintern and reached Peru a few days after Mariátegui's death **(48)**. In accordance with these instructions, the Socialist Party was transformed by a majority vote into the Peruvian Communist Party at the end of May 1930.

Central America—Sandino and the Communists

The Comintern seems to have favoured the creation of one Communist Party for all Central America rather than, as at present, separate parties for each individual country. A delegation from the Mexican Communist Party was sent to organize the Guatemalan Communists on this basis in 1925, and a similar operation was carried out in El Salvador in the same year.[b] That these developments were considered in Moscow at the time as of only marginal importance is clear from the admission of the chief Comintern delegate to the Buenos Aires Congress that he was not even aware of the existence of a section of the Communist International in El Salvador![c] The Comintern's main interest in Central America during the late 1920s was centred on Nicaragua, where Augusto Sandino, an officer of the Nicaraguan army, was holding out against the American marines in guerrilla operations which were to last for seven years and to win him the prestige of being the hemisphere's leading 'anti-imperialist' hero. The Comintern made every effort to monopolize the channels of popular support for Sandino and to bring him under their influence. To this end, Agustín Farabundo Martí, the leading Communist organizer in Central America, served for a time as private secretary to Sandino, but left him when it became clear that he stood for a nationalist, anti-imperialist struggle and not a social revolution.[d] In a letter of January 1930 to the Secretary of the Mexican Communist Party, Sandino broke finally with his Communist connections, and was later denounced by the Comintern for his 'treachery'.[e]

The Comintern role in the formation of the Cuban CP

The Cuban Communist Party was founded in 1925 on the initiative of the Comintern, who sent a member of the Mexican Communist Party to Havana

---

[a] *El Movimiento . . .*, pp. 101–3.

[b] Ibid., p. 225.

[c] Ibid., p. 201.

[d] According to Blanca Luz (*Contra la corriente* (Santiago, 1936), p. 53), Martí stated just before his execution in 1932: 'My break with Sandino was not due, as has been sometimes alleged, to differences of moral principles or contrary norms of conduct. I declined to return with him to the Segovias mountains since he was unwilling to embrace the Communist programme which I stood for. He had raised only the flag of independence, of emancipation, whilst my aim was social revolt.'

[e] *Inprecorr*, 24 Mar. 1933.

for that purpose.[a] The leading spirit in the new party was a dynamic young student leader, Julio Antonio Mella. The Russian cargo ship *Vatslav Vorovsky* happened to be in Havana at the time, and Mella swam out to it through the shark-infested waters to present the crew with a Cuban flag and invite them to send representatives to the meeting.[b] They appear to have declined the invitation, but to have sent messages of solidarity and a red flag in return. Mella's independent character and penchant for theatrical gestures appear to have led to differences of opinion with the more Comintern-orientated members of the new Party, which included a group of recently arrived Jewish immigrants from Central and Eastern Europe.[c] Arrested for organizing strikes, Mella went on a seventeen-day hunger strike in prison which stirred public opinion in Cuba and led to his release and exile in Mexico, where he worked for the Mexican Communist Party, of which he eventually became for a time the Secretary-General.[d] Here Mella's forceful and independent character led again to clashes with the Party, causing his expulsion, recantation, and readmission.[e] His assassination in the streets of Mexico by a gunman in the service of the Cuban dictator Gerardo Machado cut short the career of a revolutionary *caudillo* whose like was not to be seen again on the Cuban scene until the appearance of Fidel Castro three decades later.

Chile—bolshevization of the Party

The Chilean Communists were not represented at the Buenos Aires Congress. Their absence was officially attributed to 'the recrudescence of the white terror' in their country.[f] It may also be explained by the failure of the Comintern to bring the Party fully under its control. After the untimely death of Recabarren, leadership had passed to Manuel Hidalgo, under whose influence the Party advocated the *vía pacífica* to Communism, returned representatives and senators to Congress, and had a hand in drafting the new Constitution of 1925. The Comintern made every effort to force the Party to drop this line in favour

---

[a] P. Serviat, *40 aniversario de la fundación del Partido Comunista* (Havana, 1965), pp. 103–21.

[b] *SSSR i Latinskaya Amerika*, p.70. But Mella's own account (*Lucha de Clases* (Havana), 16 Aug. 1925) makes no mention of swimming out to the ship.

[c] Serviat, p. 114. One member of this group was Yunger Semjovich, alias Fabio Grobart, who was generally reputed in the following years to be one of the Comintern's chief links with the Cuban Party and the organizer of its clandestine apparatus. After some years of residence in the Soviet bloc, Grobart returned to Cuba in 1961 and continued to play a role in Fidel Castro's regime—a remarkable instance of the continuity of Moscow's influence in the Cuban revolutionary movement for more than forty years.

[d] According to R. J. Alexander, *Communism in Latin America* (New Brunswick, 1957), p. 271. Eudocio Ravines claims that the Central Committee of the Cuban Communist Party disapproved of his hunger strike and expelled him from the Party (*La gran estafa* (Santiago, 1957), biographical note on Mella).

[e] Victor Alba, *Esquema histórico del Comunismo en Iberoamérica* (Mexico, 1954), p. 97. Alba also suggests that the Comintern may have been privy to the murder of Mella, who had aroused the jealousy of Codovila and Vitorio Vidale (alias Sormenti and Carlos Contreras). Slightly different versions of the circumstances surrounding Mella's death are given by other writers (e.g. Alberto Baeza Flores, *Las cadenas vienen de lejos* (Mexico, 1960), pp. 81–5), and the full truth will probably never be known.

[f] *El Movimiento . . .*, Preface.

of one of Bolshevik militancy. Directives to this effect were sent to the Party in 1926 (43) and delegates were dispatched from the South American Secretariat to enforce compliance. At the Party's 7th Congress in January 1927, the Comintern line prevailed, at the cost of a serious rift between the Hidalgo wing and the pro-Comintern group headed by the more pliant Elías Lafertte.[10] Dissensions within the Chilean Party remained grave enough to make it necessary for the Comintern spokesman at the Buenos Aires Congress to define as the primary task of the Party in that country to 'reorganize the centre and establish firm links with the provinces'.[a] Nor was the Chilean Communists' task made any easier by Moscow's misjudgement of the political situation in their country.[11]

Failure of ultra-Left tactics

The intransigent ultra-Leftism of the 'third period' continued to determine Comintern tactics until the switch to Popular Front tactics as defined at the 7th Comintern Congress at Moscow in 1935. (10). Attempts to follow the extremist line in Latin America brought the Communists little success. They led, within a few months of the Buenos Aires Congress, to the Mexican Government taking stern measures against the Mexican Communist Party and breaking off diplomatic relations with the Soviet Union. A year and a half later the Argentine Government decided to suppress Yuzhamtorg, which provided useful cover for Communist activity in the River Plate area. On two occasions, however, it seemed possible that direct revolutionary action might pay off, though the degree to which the Comintern shaped and guided these endeavours is not easy to ascertain. The first occurred in September 1931, when a serious mutiny broke out in the Chilean fleet. Communist agitators had a hand in this, though it seems probable that the basic causes were the grievances resulting from hardship occasioned by the world economic crisis.[12] The Chilean Communists also failed the following year to turn to revolutionary account the proclamation by a group of radical-minded officers of a short-lived 'Socialist Republic'.

The 1932 rising in El Salvador

The other arena of revolutionary activity was El Salvador, where the Communists had been making rapid headway in organizing the Indian peasantry and infiltrating the rank and file of the army. By the beginning of 1932 they felt strong enough to attempt a general rising against the dictatorship of General Maximiliano Hernández Martínez. The rising was suppressed with the greatest ferocity and resulted in the destruction of the Party apparatus and the execution of its leaders. The extent of Comintern involvement in this venture is hard to assess. There is some evidence that Comintern influence in its planning was exercised through the International Red Aid, and through the United States Communist Party which had been entrusted by the Comintern

[a] *El Movimiento . . .*, p. 106.

with special responsibility for Latin America.[a] At the 1929 Buenos Aires Congress, a Salvadoran delegate had made a strong plea for the Comintern to give his country firmer guidance,[b] and it seems possible that the 2nd Congress of the Latin American Communist Parties, of which details have never been disclosed as to its time or place, may have been largely concerned with events in El Salvador.[c]

The 1935 rising in Brazil

The Comintern's main target for revolutionary action in Latin America was Brazil. There the Communists had at first made only slow headway against the influence of the anarcho-syndicalists entrenched in the labour movement. But in the late 1920s they won over to their cause a political-military figure of considerable charismatic appeal. Luiz Carlos Prestes had risen to fame some years before in the rebellion of *tenientes*, or junior officers, when he had led an insurgent column on a legendary trek through the hinterland of Brazil, proclaiming his determination to overthrow the government and introduce a more just social order. Forced into exile, he had been approached by emissaries of the Brazilian Communist Party and the South American Secretariat, had been converted to Marxism, and was invited in 1931 to the Soviet Union. There he had joined the Comintern and been given a seat on the Executive Committee in 1935. In April of that year he returned clandestinely to Brazil to take over the leadership of an armed rising. This was to be effected by means of the National Liberation Alliance, a radical opposition movement which the Communists proceeded to infiltrate and which proclaimed Prestes as its President. Though he was formally not even a member of the Brazilian Communist Party, Prestes was selected by the Comintern to be its leader and the Party was instructed to receive him as such (**53**). A number of Latin American Communist leaders had been invited to Moscow to attend the 7th Comintern Congress, which was scheduled to be held at the end of 1934. By the time it was decided to postpone the Congress, the Latin American delegates were already on their way and advantage was taken of their presence in Moscow to work out the strategy for Brazil.[d] According to the Peruvian Communist Eudocio

[a] 'Instructions for the Salvadoran Party during 1931 and 1932, before the disastrous Communist uprising in January of the latter year, came from the New York headquarters of the Communist Party of the United States' (Alexander, p. 37). Alexander also states (p. 367) that 'contact between the Salvadoran Communists and the Comintern was close, being maintained particularly through the International Red Aid. Agustín P. Martí, one of the chief Salvadoran Communist leaders, was the representative of the Caribbean Bureau of the International Red Aid in El Salvador.'

[b] *El Movimiento . . .*, p. 174.

[c] A number of Latin American Communist leaders are known to have met in Montevideo in October 1931, ostensibly under the auspices of *Confederación Sindical Latino-Americana*, and then to have travelled on to Moscow to attend a Profintern Conference. They included the Chilean Communist leader Lafertte, the Brazilian Arnaldo da Silva, two Peruvians, the Comintern representative Guralsky (under the name of Juan de Dios) who had taken over the running of the South American Secretariat from Codovila (E. Lafertte, *Vida de un comunista* (Santiago, 1961), pp. 234–40).

[d] It seems likely that the 3rd Latin American Congress, which 'recognised that Brazil is moving towards a deep revolutionary crisis' (**49**), held at least its most important sessions in Moscow, and not in Montevideo as officially stated.

Ravines, who attended the discussions with the Russian leaders,[a] the decisions then taken represented a compromise between the views of Dimitrov, the chief proponent of the new Popular Front line, and the policy of violent tactics still favoured by Manuilsky. The Popular Front approach would, in short, be used in Brazil to achieve the seizure of power by violent means, rather than by the 'non-violent' methods usually associated with this phase of Communist policy.

The 7th Comintern Congress

When the 7th Congress met in the summer of 1935, Dimitrov was able to report that the Brazilian Communists had laid a 'correct foundation' through the establishment of the National Liberation Alliance, and urged them to go on to form a people's liberation army for the coming struggle (**52**). Wang Ming, the rapporteur on Latin American affairs, spoke in similar terms (**51**).[b] In Brazil itself, the patent Communist affiliations of the Alliance provided the authorities with the pretext they needed for banning it, but they were unable to put a stop to the clandestine military preparations (**49**). The Comintern organizers themselves appear to have had difficulty in restraining some of the more militant revolutionaries who wanted to set up soviets and proclaim the immediate establishment of soviet power instead of broadly based peasant leagues and Popular Front committees (**50**). In the last week of November, Prestes issued a proclamation calling on 'all the forces of the Revolution' to be 'ready to fight for popular liberties' (**54**). The revolt broke out, first in Natal and Recife, and then in Rio. Despite some initial successes, it was suppressed, and Prestes, together with the chief Comintern emissaries, the German Communist ex-deputy Arthur Ewert ('Harry Berger'), Rodolfo Ghioldi, and many others were arrested (**55**). The failure of the rising was a grave setback to Comintern designs in Latin America, and also led to a break with Uruguay, the only Latin American republic to maintain diplomatic links with Moscow.[c]

Popular Front tactics in Chile and Cuba

Popular Front tactics along the lines of the *vía pacífica* yielded better results.

---

[a] Ravines (*La gran estafa* (Santiago, 1957), pp. 255–7) states that those attending the closed sessions on Brazil were Dimitrov, Manuilsky, Kuusinen, Guralsky (head of the South American Secretariat), Motilev (expert in 'Front' organizations), Miroshevsky (Soviet Latin American expert and historian), Prestes and da Silva (for the Brazilian CP), Rodolfo Ghioldi (Secretary of the Argentine CP and S. American Secretariat expert on Brazil).

[b] Wang Ming, a Chinese Communist whose real name was Ch'en Shao-yü, represented the Chinese CP at Comintern headquarters between 1933 and 1937, when he returned to take up a succession of posts in the Party and Government. He returned to Moscow in the mid-1950s. Little was then heard of him until the Chinese border dispute of early 1969, when he contributed an anti-Mao article to a Canadian newspaper which was given considerable publicity by Tass. When reporting on Latin American developments at the 7th Comintern Congress, Brazilian sources allege that he was indiscreet enough to declare that 'this Alliance was created on the secret but direct initiative of the Brazilian Communist Party, according to the confidential instructions received from the Soviet Legation in Montevideo' (*Relatorio*, p. 7).

[c] See above, p. 9.

The Comintern sent a team headed by Ravines to implement this policy in Chile. He himself later left the Communist ranks, but the Chilean Communist Party succeeded in improving its public image and forming an alliance with the respected Radical Party, whose candidate was elected to the presidency in 1938. Although this represented a considerable tactical success for the Chilean Communists and the new Comintern line, it is not easy to see what practical advantage Moscow reaped from it. The Chilean Popular Front, unlike its European counterparts, was not anti-Fascist—it actually participated in an electoral alliance with the former dictator Carlos Ibáñez and the small local Nazi Party—nor did the Popular Front Government, which only declared war on the Axis on the eve of the allied victory, offer the Soviet Union any help in the Second World War.

The other Latin American country where, after a slow start, the Communists implemented the Popular Front *vía pacífica* line with some success was Cuba. In May 1933 Martínez Villena, the Secretary-General of the Cuban Communist Party, was sent back to Havana from Moscow, where he had been working at Comintern headquarters, but failed to lay down a line of unambiguous opposition to Machado's dictatorial regime or to secure for the Party the leadership of the popular forces which forced the dictator to flee the country in the following August. The Communists, still committed to the militancy of the 'third period', preferred to turn their energies against the short-lived leftist regime of Dr Ramón Grau San Martín which followed, inciting the workers to take over the sugar-mills and to set up workers' 'soviets' in a number of them. The Comintern, dissatisfied with the Party for not turning the situation to better account, sent an emissary to Cuba at the beginning of 1934 to carry out a thorough purge,[a] and Blas Roca took over as Secretary-General of the Party. At about the same time the rightist Government of Carlos Mendieta and Fulgencio Batista was set up. When the Cuban Communist Party attempted to implement the new Popular Front line of rallying a broad opposition of the Left, old rivalries prevented an alliance with Grau and his following, the *Auténticos*. Once again the Party shifted its ground and achieved a rapprochement with Batista, who legalized their Party in September 1938, encouraged their influence in the labour movement, and finally—in 1943—gave them representation in the cabinet—thus allowing them the distinction of being the first Communist Party of Latin America to be so represented.

War, Cold War, and Peaceful Coexistence

The German invasion of the Soviet Union in June 1941 cleared the way for a new phase in Soviet-Latin American relations. Many Latin Americans sympathized with the Allies and welcomed the Soviet Union as a valuable reinforcement to their cause. Those who feared Russian instigation of revolution in their own countries had their fears to some extent allayed by Moscow's formal dissolution of the Comintern and by the Latin American Communists' sudden

---

[a] A. Suárez, *Cuba: Castroism and Communism, 1959–66* (London, 1967), p. 5.

discovery that the British and Yankee capitalists whom they had so long denounced were their allies in the war against the Fascist powers. As the course of the war turned against the latter, it became increasingly clear that the Soviet Union would emerge as one of the great powers likely to dominate the postwar world. Between 1943 and 1945 the major Latin American republics (with the exception of Argentina), together with a number of the lesser ones, including some ruled by right-wing dictatorships as in the Dominican Republic and Nicaragua, decided to establish or re-establish relations with Moscow. These relations were however blighted by the harsh climate of the cold war which Stalin himself accused them of intensifying by backing Washington's 'aggressive policies' at the United Nations (**56**). By the time he died in 1953 only three Latin American republics—Mexico, Uruguay, and Argentina—still retained diplomatic links with Moscow. Better prospects for an extension of Soviet influence had already been opened up in the late 1950s by Bulganin's and Khrushchev's formulation of the policy of 'peaceful coexistence' (**57, 58**), when Castro's rise to power in Cuba at the beginning of 1959 introduced unexpected new opportunities, but also new complexities, into the Latin American scene.

Cultural contacts

Though Latin America still remained marginal to Soviet interests in other parts of the world, its historical, social, and economic problems began to receive closer attention in the Soviet Union during the 1950s, and in 1961 a Latin American Institute was set up to promote research into these fields (**59**). The great figures of Latin America's past were reassessed in a more favourable light, contemptuous and ill-informed descriptions of the Latin American countries and their inhabitants appeared less frequently in the Soviet press,[a] and many more works dealing with aspects of Latin American history began to be published.[b] At the same time a campaign was launched to project a more favourable image of the Soviet Union tarnished by the events of 1956 in Hungary (but soon enhanced again by the prestige of her Sputnik achievements), and to create goodwill and influence public opinion in Latin America through the standard media of propaganda and public relations. The establishment of the Committee for Cultural Relations with Foreign Countries in 1957 was followed, two years later, by the founding of a Society for Friendship and Cultural Co-operation with Latin American Countries. 'Friendship Societies' were set up in the Latin American countries, tours by Russian musicians, artists, ballet dancers, and scholars were arranged, and prominent Latin Americans were invited to the Soviet Union. The volume of broadcasting

[a] For examples of the offensive and contemptuous tone of articles written during the cold-war period see docs. 81, 114, and 130.

[b] Between 1946 and 1948 some three works on Latin American history were published annually in the USSR. In 1956 8 titles were published, in 1957 12, and in 1958 15 (M. S. Alperovich, 'Izucheniye istorii Latinskoy Ameriki v Sovietskom soyuze', in *Latinskaya Amerika v proshlom i nastoashchem*, p. 454).

directed to Latin America was steadily increased[a] and young Latin Americans were invited in growing numbers to study in the Soviet Union.[b]

Front organizations

The climate of 'peaceful coexistence' favoured the development of 'front organizations', particularly in those countries where the local Communist Party was small, illegal, or discredited. The most useful of such bodies, in the Latin American context, have been the World Council of Peace, the International Association of Democratic Lawyers, the International Organization of Journalists, the World Federation of Democratic Youth, and the World Federation of Trade Unions (WFTU). Under the ostensibly professional, cultural, or humanitarian façade of these organizations, Soviet political objectives could be quietly pursued. Thus, for instance, at the time of the 1962 Cuban missile crisis, whilst ignoring the installation of the Soviet rockets which had precipitated the crisis, the World Council of Peace could denounce the United States for its 'aggressive acts'. The International Association of Democratic Lawyers campaigned for the release of imprisoned Communist leaders, whilst the Federation of Democratic Youth and the International Union of Students sponsored congresses which served to intensify and co-ordinate the anti-Yankee sentiments of Latin American student organizations. The least effective of the front organizations proved perhaps to be the WFTU, which aimed to further Communist influence in the labour field; the Regional Bureau (*Confederación de Trabajadores de América Latina—CTAL*) set up to this end in Latin America in 1938 made some headway but lost influence from 1947 onwards and had to be wound up. Subsequent labour organizations founded with the same purpose did not succeed in establishing themselves.

Economic relations

The Soviet Union never succeeded in developing a significant trade with Latin America during the 'cold war' period, but made a fresh bid to do so in the more benign atmosphere of 'peaceful coexistence'. Trade agreements were concluded with Argentina in August 1953 (**76**), with Uruguay three years later, and with Brazil at the end of 1959 (**87**). The benefits to be derived from trade with the Soviet Union have been extolled, with varying degrees of sophistication, by Soviet statesmen and diplomats and by local Communist spokesmen (**119, 131**). Access is promised to a potentially vast new market for Latin America's products in return for the capital goods needed for its own development (**63, 64**). Nor need the Latin Americans deplete their short supply of foreign currency, since the

---

[a] By 1965 Soviet broadcast programmes in Spanish, Portuguese, and Quechua had reached a weekly output of about 100 hours.

[b] In 1961 some 2,500 foreign students were believed to be studying in the USSR, nearly one-eighth of them Latin Americans. By 1964 the total had risen to nearly 20,000, with a more than proportionate increase in the Latin American contingent. The bulk of the latter was made up of Cubans, the number of other Latin Americans amounting to something over 400. By 1967 there were 200 Chileans alone studying at the Patrice Lumumba University in Moscow with scholarships awarded by the Chilean-Soviet Cultural Institute (**101**).

Soviet Union preferred bilateral payment arrangements. If they accepted loans from the Soviet Union, they would pay interest rates of between 3–4 per cent, which compared favourably with those generally offered by the West. From the mid-1960s, moreover, the terms offered by the Soviet Union allowed the Latin Americans to make part of their payment for Soviet capital equipment in the form of exports of their own manufactured goods—a concession to the aspirations expressed by the Latin American countries at the 1965 UN Conference on Trade and Development to the effect that they should cease to be considered as mere suppliers of commodities.[a] Furthermore, trade with the Soviet Union could be regarded as a gesture of independence from United States economic hegemony and might improve a government's bargaining position *vis-à-vis* Washington. A by-product of the development of commercial relations which was of benefit to the Soviet Union, though scarcely to the Governments of her Latin American trading partners, was that it sometimes provided a means for her to finance the local Communist Parties through the granting of commissions on deals negotiated with the help of Party members.[b]

Obstacles to Soviet trade

But trade with the Soviet Union proved also to have its difficulties and drawbacks for the Latin American countries. If they carried the commercial flirtation with Moscow too far, they risked frightening off foreign investment and damaging their all-important economic connections with the United States. Where their need was for more sophisticated capital equipment, the Soviet Union could not always supply it. In markets where the Russians were able to compete (e.g. agricultural machinery) European and United States manufacturers were generally firmly entrenched, and Latin American customers had reason to fear that if they obtained such goods elsewhere the supply of spares and after-sales services might not be so reliable. The tendency was, in any case, for the Soviet Union to export more raw materials than capital goods to Latin American countries. The latter could not feel assured that, on purely economic grounds, their basic commodities were really needed by the Soviet Union. She might take them to suit temporary requirements or even—as she was prepared to take Cuba's sugar—on a long-term basis if the political advantages were deemed sufficiently great. Nor could the Latin American exporters be sure that such surplus sugar or coffee would not be resold at cut prices on the world market. For these reasons, the volume of trade between the Soviet Union and Latin America fluctuated a good deal from year to year and showed great

[a] The 1966 trade agreement with Brazil envisaged a Soviet credit of $100 m. and entitled Brazil to pay up to 25 per cent in manufactured or semi-manufactured goods. Under the 1967 trade agreement with Chile, the latter could supply up to 30 per cent of the total in manufactured and semi-manufactured goods.

[b] At the end of 1968 Manuel Mora Valverde, the Costa Rican CP leader, was instrumental in negotiating the first sale of a large consignment of Costa Rican coffee to the Soviet Union. In a statement to the party newspaper *Libertad* (7 Dec. 1968), he declared that any commission received by him would be credited to the Bloc of Workers, Peasants, and Intellectuals, the cover organization for the banned Costa Rican CP.

instability in its commodity composition. One year a country might export a sizeable quantity of its chief commodity only to see this drop to next to nothing in the following. In the first half of the 1960s the Soviet share of the region's total trade (apart from Cuba) never reached 1 per cent of the total, and was confined to Argentina, Brazil, Uruguay, and to a lesser extent Chile, Mexico, and Colombia. It lagged far behind the Soviet Union's trade with the other parts of the underdeveloped world.[a]

Soviet aid policy

In the mid-1950s the Soviet Union also began to launch an economic aid offensive, on the lines of the aid programme sponsored by the Western powers, which reached its peak between 1958 and 1961. Here too Latin America (with the exception of Cuba) found a place, albeit a modest one.[b] The country which appears to have been selected as the most promising recipient, after Cuba, was Bolivia. In 1958 that country had arraigned the Soviet Union in the United Nations for 'economic aggression' by maliciously releasing quantities of tin from her stock-pile for the purpose of ruining Bolivia's markets and destroying her mining industry (91). It was partly to make good this unfavourable impression, and perhaps also in the hope of reorientating a revolution which had been frustrated by Western influence, that Chairman Khrushchev, taking advantage of his visit to the UN General Assembly, and following up his personal meeting with Castro a fortnight before,[c] informed the head of the Bolivian delegation that his Government was prepared to extend aid to Bolivia which would permit that country to achieve the long cherished aspiration of building its own tin smelter and so freeing itself from dependence on the foreign imperialists who monopolized the processing of Bolivia's chief product (93). A Soviet mission was sent to Bolivia a couple of months later for detailed negotiations (94). On the eve of its arrival in La Paz, it was announced that the Bolivian Government had received an advantageous new offer for the rehabilitation of the Bolivian mining industry on the part of the United States, Germany, and the Inter-American Development Bank. Nothing came of the

[a]   *Soviet trade with Asia, Africa, and Latin America,* 1955–62*
(m. rubles)

	1955	1958	1962
Asia	122	459	636
Africa	40	189	265
L. America	58	58	96

* Except Cuba.

Source: *Mirovaya ekonomika i mezhdunarodnye otnosheniya*, no. 3, 1964, p. 87, quoted in M. Pierpont Gehlen, *The Politics of Coexistence* (1967), p. 195.

[b] In the period 1954–65, only 5·4 per cent of the total aid offered to developing countries by the Soviet bloc (half of it from the USSR) went to Latin America, as compared with 18·1 per cent to Africa, 40·5 per cent to Asia, and 36 per cent to the Middle East.

[c] See p. 46.

Soviet offer of a tin smelter, and subsequent overtures for the exchange of diplomatic missions between Bolivia and the Soviet Union were not taken up.[a]

Inter-Party relations: the role of Brazil

Inter-Party relations, which had been interrupted by the Second World War and the formal dissolution of the Comintern in May 1943, were resumed at the end of the war, the Foreign Relations Department of the Central Committee of the CPSU taking the place of the former Comintern headquarters apparatus in Moscow. By far the strongest Communist Party in Latin America was that of Brazil. In Prestes, who had publicly declared in 1946 that in the event of a war between Brazil and USSR the Brazilian Communists would side with the Soviet people (**79**), the Party had a leader who enjoyed the Russians' full confidence. The situation in Brazil, according to the over-optimistic reports submitted by the Party leaders, seemed ripe for revolution, for which the 1935 fiasco could be seen as a dress rehearsal, much as the unsuccessful rising of 1905 in Russia had been a dress rehearsal for the October Revolution. The Brazilian Communist Party was thus assigned an 'overlord' role *vis-à-vis* the other Latin American Parties, as the Mexican and United States Communist Parties had been given a similar role with regard to Central America and the Caribbean by the Comintern in the 1920s.[b] At the same time, the CPSU took care to exercise the most rigid control over the policy and activities of the Brazilian Party.[13] After the latter had been outlawed and relations with the Soviet Union broken off in 1947, the Party declined in numbers and influence until its fortunes revived under the João Goulart regime, only to be still more drastically repressed under Humberto Castelo Branco in 1964.

The Sino-Soviet dispute

In the meantime, another factor was beginning to make itself felt in the Latin American Communist movement. From the mid-1950s the Chinese leaders were beginning to show an increasing interest in the revolutionary potentialities of Latin America.[c] Delegations of left-wing Latin Americans began to receive invitations to visit China, where it was impressed on them that conditions in their countries resembled those in pre-revolutionary China and that their path to social and economic transformation would be the same. It was argued that the Soviet Union had become an industrialized and neo-bourgeois state, and

---

[a] In January 1968 President René Barrientos was reported as saying that the USSR had been invited to open trade relations by buying Bolivia's tin, provided that Bolivia's sovereignty was respected (Interpress report from La Paz, 28 Jan. 1968). The following May the President was stated to have put out feelers for obtaining Soviet aid in return for opening relations (*Le Monde*, 7 May 1968). On 17 June he was reported to have stated that Moscow had turned down the Bolivian requests for a loan (Radio La Cruz del Sur, 20 June 1968). In February 1969 he declared that the exchange of diplomatic missions depended on the readiness of the Soviet Union to help Boliva develop her oil industry.

[b] Osvaldo Peralva, *O retrato* (Belo Horizonte, 1960), p. 199.

[c] For useful surveys of the development of Chinese interest in Latin America see Victor Alba, 'The Chinese in Latin America', *China Quarterly*, Jan.-March, 1961, and Ernst Halperin, 'Peking and the Latin American Communists', ibid., Jan.-March, 1967.

that the Bolsheviks' seizure of power, since it was based on an urban proletariat, offered no valid precedent to a largely rural area like Latin America. The Chinese experience, in short, was held up as the model for Latin America, and the Maoist technique of guerrilla warfare as the only correct form of revolutionary struggle. The threat to Moscow's leadership of the Latin American Communist Parties implicit in the Chinese thesis was all the stronger in that it appeared to have much in common with the new creed of 'Fidelismo' which was beginning to have a strong appeal to the radical Left, especially the young. Furthermore, the challenge came at a time when de-Stalinization was loosening Moscow's authority over party leaders who were themselves vulnerable to the charges of having exploited the personality cult. Veterans like Codovila of Argentina, Prestes of Brazil, and Mora Valverde of Costa Rica had dominated their respective Parties for three decades. Though all reaffirmed their loyalty to the Soviet line at the 1960 Moscow Conference, they could no longer ignore the gravity of the Sino-Soviet divergence, nor the serious implications it was likely to have for their own parties.

In the course of the early 1960s the pro-Chinese dissidents split off to form splinter groups in Chile, Uruguay, Argentina, and some other countries, and proved strong enough to establish rival Communist Parties of their own in Brazil (1962), Peru (1964), Colombia (1965), and Bolivia (1965). The majority of the Central Committees of the old parties, however, remained loyal to Moscow, though in some cases (e.g. in Peru) the issue remained in doubt for some time, and in others (e.g. in Venezuela) 'anti-Soviet elements' continued to challenge the pro-Moscow leadership for several years. The CPSU found it expedient to reinforce the loyalty of Party leaders not only by frequently summoning them to Moscow but by intensifying the practice of sending delegates to Party conferences in the countries concerned (**120**). The Paraguayan Communist Party suffered a schism led by the veteran Communist Oscar Creydt (**132**–4), and Moscow had considerable difficulty in rebuilding a reliable Central Committee. But in general the pro-Chinese factions remained minuscule groups with no serious hope of winning over a majority of the Communist movement and still less of overthrowing the Governments of their countries. Their existence, and that of the pro-Cuban extremists, nevertheless posed a problem for Moscow and for the orthodox parties. The Soviet line professed in theory to see no fundamental contradiction between violent and non-violent tactics. Communist militants were supposed to switch freely from one tactic to the other as the situation warranted, violent action being inevitable whenever a reactionary dictatorship or pseudo-democratic regime (terms which could be invoked to describe almost any Latin American Government) rendered progress by non-violent means impossible. The Cuban thesis, whilst admitting the theoretical possibility that Communists might come to power by the *vía pacífica*, declared that this had never happened, and was never likely to happen. Since, in Castro's phrase, 'the duty of the revolutionary is to make a revolution', there was in practice no alternative to the *vía armada* which, in Latin America, meant guerrilla warfare. Nor should such action be postponed until conditions were deemed to be ripe; the revolutionaries—as 'Che' Guevara argued in his famous book—could themselves create such conditions by starting an armed revolt.[a] The Cubans were to prove themselves more consistent practitioners of these theories than the pro-Chinese groups who too often stood on the side-lines when the violence they advocated erupted. Thus the Peking-orientated Communists of Peru were no readier than their Moscow-orientated rivals to back the initiative of the Cuban-inspired extremists who launched an abortive guerrilla rising in 1965. Nor, in Bolivia, did the pro-Chinese Communist groups offer any more help than did the leadership of the official Party, which was staunchly pro-Moscow (**95**), when Guevara himself made his ill-fated bid to put his theories to the test in 1967.

Guerrilla action in Venezuela

Venezuela promised for a time to be a country where the pro-Soviet Communists and advocates of guerrilla action might make common cause. Though the Government was headed by a lapsed Communist, President Rómulo Betancourt, and had no relations with Moscow, the latter was not averse to exploring the possibilities of resuming relations, and with this end in view the Soviet Ambassador in Mexico paid a visit to Caracas in 1961. He was given to understand that a renewal of relations would not be considered so long as the Communists pursued the campaign of guerrilla action and urban terrorism which they had launched against the Government in conjunction with the pro-Cuban *Movimiento de la Izquierda Revolucionaria* (MIR). It seems probable that the Ambassador also took the opportunity of consulting Venezuelan Communist leaders who were holding the Party's 3rd Congress in Caracas at the time. Since armed actions were steadily stepped up with the aim of making it impossible to hold the general elections at the end of 1963, it must be assumed either that the Soviet Union agreed with these tactics or that they failed to impose a contrary line on the Venezuelan Communist Party, whose most experienced leaders were at the time in prison. After the failure of the terrorist campaign to prevent the holding of the 1963 elections the guerrilla campaign seemed to have spent its force, and by mid-1966 the pro-Soviet leaders, who, though challenged by the extremists, remained in control of the Party (**147**), were quietly de-emphasizing it. Castro, however, continued to urge all-out militancy and gave open backing to Douglas Bravo, suspended from the Party for persisting in the course of guerrilla warfare, and in March 1967 he publicly branded the pro-Soviet leadership of the Party as 'a group of theorizing charlatans' who had never been in earnest in promoting armed struggle.

Attempts to co-ordinate revolutionary strategy

In Colombia, Guatemala, Peru, and other countries the Cubans also tended to support extremist groups in preference to the orthodox Communist Parties. The resulting confusion in the revolutionary movement, coupled with the setback to Communist hopes after the defeat of their candidate in the Chilean presidential elections and the overthrow by the military of President Goulart's leftist regime in Brazil, called for fresh measures of co-ordination. In the hope

[a] *Guerrilla Warfare* (New York, 1961), pp. 15 ff.

of achieving this, the Latin American Communist Parties sent delegates to a conference held, apparently in Havana, in November 1964. It is not known whether this conference was the result of Cuban or Soviet initiative, or whether it was attended by Soviet representatives. Its outcome was a compromise between the Cuban and Soviet standpoints. The conference deplored the growing Sino-Soviet rift, urged conciliation between Moscow and Peking and unity within the Latin American Parties, and an intensified hemispheric campaign in support of Cuba. In return, Castro is believed to have pledged that he would cease supporting non-Communist extremist groups. The published communiqué called for a continental campaign of solidarity in support of the Venezuelan people's struggle for liberation, and praised the freedom-fighters in Venezuela, Colombia, Guatemala, Haiti, Paraguay, and Honduras. After the conference, delegates were sent to Moscow and also to Peking where they were coldly received and their pleas for a reconciliation with Moscow were rebuffed.[a]

The Tricontinental Conference

At the beginning of 1966 a fresh attempt was made to co-ordinate tactics for Latin America within the larger framework of Communist strategy towards the Third World. The Soviet Union welcomed the holding of the Tricontinental Conference in Havana as a step towards expanding the Afro-Asian People's Solidarity Organization (AAPSO), where Chinese influence was strong, into an Afro-Asian Latin American Solidarity Organization (AALAPSO), in which the Russians could count on the support of a score of Latin American revolutionary parties. They would have preferred the new organization to be established at Cairo, but soon found themselves obliged to defer to the demands of Castro that Havana should be the site of the AALAPSO secretariat, and also of the Committee to Aid Liberation and the separate Latin American Solidarity Organization (OLAS). Although, on the eve of the Conference, Castro had publicly rebuked China for failing to honour her economic commitments to Cuba and for inadmissible attempts to distribute propaganda, the extremist line taken by the Chinese delegation in vituperation of the United States and urging the opening of 'revolutionary second fronts' was in fact more to his liking than the Soviet delegation's relatively moderate line. S. R. Rashidov, leader of the Soviet delegation, reaffirmed 'fraternal solidarity with the armed struggle waged by the patriots of Venezuela, Peru, Colombia and Guatemala for freedom against the puppets of imperialism' (60). The Soviet declarations, if they did not go far enough to satisfy the more militant Latin American revolutionaries, certainly aroused the alarm and indignation of the Latin American Governments. The latter protested to the Soviet Government, both through the Organization of American States (OAS) and the United Nations, and (in the case of Uruguay, Brazil, Argentina, and Chile) through diplomatic channels. The disclaimers and assurances given in reply by the Soviet Government (143) were received with some scepticism and served to underline the dilemma with which the Soviet Union was increasingly faced in

[a] *World Marxist Review*, Sept. 1968, p. 10.

trying to reconcile her interests in developing closer diplomatic economic and cultural relations with the Latin American Governments with her commitment as the vanguard of the world revolutionary movement aiming at the overthrow of those same Governments. It is in the context of this basic dilemma that we must trace the course of Soviet policy towards the individual countries of Latin America since the end of the Second World War.

Postwar Soviet Relations with Individual Countries

Uruguay

Diplomatic relations between Uruguay and the Soviet Union were renewed by an exchange of notes in January 1943.[a] The course of relations has subsequently fluctuated greatly, deteriorating at recurrent suspicions of Soviet instigation of subversion and labour unrest (as in October 1953) and improving at the prospect of increased trade. The latter has shown still more violent fluctuations, rising in 1958—a year in which a strong Soviet delegation visited Uruguay (**135**) —from an annual average of less than $2 million to over $15 million, and temporarily carrying the Soviet Union to second place (after the United Kingdom) as the chief customer for Uruguay's wool crop. Amongst the recurrent causes of disquiet on the part of the Uruguayan authorities has been the size of Soviet trade and diplomatic missions (**136**),[b] whose activities they have sought to control by restricting their numbers and freedom of movement. In April 1961 the Uruguayan Government reacted sharply to a clumsy Soviet démarche aimed at forcing Uruguay into criticism of the United States in the UN General Assembly for alleged instigation of the abortive Bay of Pigs invasion attempt against Cuba. By the end of 1965, the Uruguayan Government was again considering a rupture of relations, which the Acting Soviet Foreign Minister V. V. Kuznetsov sought to avert by giving assurances to the Uruguayan Ambassador in Moscow of Soviet non-interference in Uruguayan affairs and hints of very favourable terms for the supply of Soviet oil products. Uruguayan misgivings were however deepened the following month by the presence of a strong Soviet delegation, headed by S. R. Rashidov, at the Tricontinental Conference in Havana.[c] In reply to the diplomatic representations which this occasioned (**142**), the Soviet Government hastened to assure the Uruguayan and other Latin American Governments that Rashidov's statements were those of an individual and not of the Soviet Government (**143**), that the Conference had no political significance since it was concerned only with social and economic matters, and that the Soviet policy of non-interference in other nations' affairs remained unchanged. Nevertheless, a statement (**61**) made a month later by Leonid Brezhnev on the 'courageous

[a] USSR, *Soviet Foreign Policy during the Patriotic War: Documents and Materials*, trans. Andrew Rothstein (London, 1946–8), i, 197–8.

[b] In 1958 the Soviet Legation was reported as having a staff of 25 diplomats and 60 clerical employees, as compared with 21 and 45 respectively employed at the US Embassy, and 11 and 32 in the British Embassy (*El País*, 29 June 1958).

[c] See above, p. 28.

liberation struggle of the peoples of Latin America' and the CPSU's 'internationalist duty' to do its utmost to support it was scarcely calculated to increase the credibility of these assurances.

A more effective move on the part of Moscow to allay Uruguayan distrust was the offer of a $20 million credit for increasing commercial exchanges, and the prospect of assistance for the ambitious Salto Grande Dam project. But fresh difficulties soon arose to prevent this offer being taken up. In August 1966 the Uruguayan Communist Party held its 19th Congress at which Rodney Arismendi, its Secretary-General, forecast an intensification of labour unrest. The CPSU sent a fraternal delegation to the Congress headed by V. S. Tolstikov, First Secretary of the Leningrad Provincial Committee who, though asserting his Government's wish for closer economic and cultural relations with Uruguay and circumspect in his endorsement of the resolutions of the Tricontinental Conference, affirmed full support of the Uruguayan Communist Party and its line. At the beginning of October, as the predicted labour unrest increased, the National Council protested to the Soviet chargé d'affaires that members of his staff had been actively instigating this unrest, and four officials were expelled, whilst action was also taken against a number of representatives of Soviet trading organizations (137). These moves led to further talk of an imminent rupture of relations, but the Soviet Union evidently valued her diplomatic foothold in Montevideo too highly to go to this extreme. Instead, an exchange of notes took place on 21 February 1967 reopening the question of the Russian offer of credit and setting up a mixed commission to study measures for the general development of trade between the two countries. The Soviet Union repeated her offer of credit on several further occasions, a special trade mission being sent to Uruguay in December 1967 with a view to pursuing the matter, but by March 1968 the offer had been made no less than six times without any final conclusion being reached by the Uruguayan authorities.

The Uruguayan CP and the CPSU

In the meantime, the Soviet Union set great store by the Uruguayan Communist Party as a reliable instrument for promoting her line of peaceful coexistence and non-violent tactics for the accession to power in Latin America. The veteran Communist Eugenio Gómez, who had perhaps become too much of an Uruguayan elder statesman, had been replaced in 1955 as Secretary-General of the Party by Rodney Arismendi, in whom Moscow came to have great confidence as the Latin American Communist leader most able to avoid prejudicing official relations between Uruguay and the Soviet Union by keeping the Communists within the spectrum of 'respectable' political parties whilst preserving a suitably revolutionary stance through cultivating good relations with Castro and perhaps even influencing him to adhere to the Moscow line.[a] The reliance placed on Arismendi and the Uruguayan Communist Party was

[a] Arismendi had paid a number of visits to Cuba, and was with Castro during the latter's visit to the Soviet Union in 1963. Special marks of Moscow's favour to him were the tributes published in *Pravda* to mark his 50th birthday, and the award to him of an honorary doctorate by the University of Moscow. The citation mentioned his book *Problemas de una revolución continental* (Montevideo, [1962]), which was later issued in Russian translation.

shown by the sending of strong CPSU delegations to Uruguayan Communist Party Congresses (**138–9**), and the warm reception given to Arismendi by Brezhnev and other Soviet leaders when he conferred with them in Moscow in March 1967 (**140**). The Uruguayan Communists later demonstrated their loyalty to the Moscow line by strongly supporting the Soviet invasion of Czechoslovakia in 1968 (**141**).

Mexico

Relations between Mexico and the Soviet Union were resumed in 1943 and developed more smoothly than in the inter-war period, despite the continuing low level of trade between the two countries and the friction occasionally caused by suspected Soviet meddling in Mexico's internal affairs. A serious incident of this sort occurred in 1959, when two Russian diplomats, Nikolay V. Aksenov and Nikolay M. Remisov, were expelled for alleged encouragement of a Communist-fomented railway strike.[a] In the same year A. I. Mikoyan visited Mexico to open an impressive Exhibition of Soviet Science and Culture and used the occasion to refer, in exaggerated and tendentious terms, to the close affinities which he claimed to see between the Mexican and Russian Revolutions, and to the mutual antagonism of the two countries to 'Yankee imperialism' (**127**). These remarks were coolly received, one leading newspaper observing that 'the Russian official who is visiting us may continue to enjoy Mexican hospitality and to say whatever he likes; but without trying to involve us in useless conflicts and misunderstandings with those who are now our good neighbours and friends' (**126**). Official pronouncements on Mexican-Soviet relations have been pitched in a lower key.[b] Mexico's ruling Party, the *Partido Revolucionario Institucional* (PRI), has continued to remain firmly in the saddle, and though oscillating between Left and Right according to the political sympathies of the President in office, has shown no prospect, as Moscow had originally hoped, of letting itself be steered towards a second, Marxist, revolution. Soviet policy was therefore to maintain correct relations with the government in power whilst retaining discreet contact with the Mexican Communist Party which sometimes opposed and sometimes supported it. Nor were the Mexican Communists always as obedient as might be wished to the Moscow line; alone of the orthodox Latin American parties, they openly expressed criticism of the Soviet invasion of Czechoslovakia (**129**). As extra strings to their bow, the Russians had thought it prudent to cultivate close relations with the influential ex-President Lázaro Cárdenas, who had sponsored a new left-wing movement which sent its own representatives to the Tricontinental Conference held in Havana in 1966. Moscow had also, over a number of years, fostered a special relationship with the influential fellow-travelling labour leader Vicente Lombardo Toledano, whose own following,

[a] Communiqué issued by the Mexican Ministry of Foreign Affairs, 1 Apr. 1959.

[b] Though the joint communiqué of 30 May 1968 (**128**) affirmed Soviet support for the concept of a nuclear-free Latin America and 'respect for Mexico as a non-nuclear zone', the Soviet Union declined to meet Mexican wishes that she should sign Protocol II of the Treaty of Tlatelolco which would have precluded her from sending nuclear arms to Cuba or other Latin American states.

the *Partido Popular* (later named the *Partido Popular Socialista* or PPS) emerged as both rival and counterpart to the Communist Party.[a]

Argentina

The Soviet attitude towards Argentina after the Second World War showed a remarkable degree of opportunism. At first, Moscow was strongly opposed to any suggestion of cultivating friendly relations with that country. It had not been forgotten that it was the Argentine Government which had taken the initiative in moving the Soviet Union's expulsion from the League of Nations in 1939 for attacking Finland (**39**). The Russian press had frequently denounced Argentina for her pro-Axis sympathies during the war and had castigated the 'Fascist Farrell-Perón regime' and criticized the Western Allies for recognizing it (**65, 67**). Nor had Moscow been placated by Argentina's last-minute declaration of war against the Axis. Molotov had sought to deny Argentina an invitation to the San Francisco Conference (**66**) and only agreed to her admission to the United Nations after the Western Allies had agreed to make a corresponding concession in favour of the Lublin Government of Poland.[b] A few months later Moscow suddenly reversed her policy. Perón won the presidential elections in February 1946 and was installed as President on 4 June. Two days later it was announced that Argentina and the Soviet Union had decided to establish diplomatic relations (**68**). The Soviet press explained away this volte face as the result of the mounting pressure of Argentine public opinion, which had forced the Argentine Government to take this 'sound initiative' (**69**).[14]

Argentine-Soviet trade

The pattern of trade between the two countries fluctuated widely from year to year, and was characterized by the heavy imbalance of Argentina's exports over her imports from the Soviet Union. Following the signing of a trade and payments agreement in 1953 (**76**), trade rose in 1954 to over $71 million, but then fell off, in spite of a vigorous Soviet trade-promotion campaign in 1958, and the offer to Argentina of a credit of $100 million with which to develop her oil industry (**77–8**), and did not surpass this figure until 1965. The following year it rose still further as a result of an Argentine grain-for-Soviet-oil deal. The level of trade declined again after General Juan Carlos Onganía's seizure

[a] The Russians appear to have subsequently changed their view about the utility of supporting the PPS as a second string to the Mexican CP and to have favoured a merger between the two. In September and October 1964 Shlyapnikov, Vice-President of the Committee of Youth Organizations in the Soviet Union, visited Mexico and is believed to have urged this course on the PPS leaders without success. The 1964 Yearbook of the Great Soviet Encyclopaedia (p. 312) declared that Lombardo Toledano's party 'considers itself Marxist but follows an opportunist line'. This caused great offence amongst PPS leaders, who protested sharply to the Soviet Embassy. Their representations must have had some effect, for the offending passages were removed from subsequent editions of the Year Book, which restored Lombardo Toledano to his former status as 'the eminent trade unionist and social worker'.

[b] See John A. Houston, *Latin America and the United Nations* (New York, 1956), pp. 28 ff.

of power, despite a more flexible economic policy on the part of Moscow, which included an offer to enter into a consortium with British interests for the construction of the ambitious El Chocón hydro-electric dam project in northern Patagonia.

Diplomatic relations

Diplomatic relations came under strain on a number of occasions without ever reaching the point of rupture. The first crisis arose as the result of Soviet attempts to exert political influence over the large communities of Russians and other Slavs resident in Argentina and the River Plate countries,[15] and later through Moscow's attempt to repatriate members of the Russian communities to the Soviet Union.[a] Other causes of discord were the rapid growth in size of the Soviet Embassy in Buenos Aires (subsequently limited to ten diplomatic and twenty non-diplomatic staff), and the expulsion of certain of its members on charges of espionage and encouragement of subversion;[b] a series of anti-Soviet incidents which took place in Buenos Aires in the course of 1961 (71–2); and the alarm aroused by the presence of Soviet fishing vessels in Argentine coastal waters, which occasioned a number of incidents, the most serious of which was that of the *Michurinsk* in 1967 (74). The inauguration of Arturo Illia's administration in 1963 had raised hopes of improved relations in Moscow (73), and the establishment of General Onganía's strongly anti-Communist regime in 1966, which was particularly outspoken in condemnation of Soviet action against Czechoslovakia two years later (75), was the subject of critical comment in the Soviet press.

Brazil

Diplomatic relations were established between Brazil and the Soviet Union in April 1945,[c] missions were exchanged the following year and withdrawn again the year after. From the outset, the course of Soviet-Brazilian relations was troubled. By the beginning of 1946 the Soviet press was denouncing the growth of Fascist trends in Brazil and complaining that 'the anti-Soviet campaign in Brazil is spreading and producing new gems of lies every day'.[d] In March of the same year indignation and alarm were aroused in Brazil by a public declaration by the Secretary of the Brazilian Communist Party that, in the event of a war between the Soviet Union and Brazil, the party would side

[a] In a press interview of 13 July 1956 President Pedro Aramburu put the number of repatriated Russian immigrants at about 3,000 for that year, and expressed special concern for those amongst them who had Argentine citizenship. He stated that his Government had started an inquiry to ascertain whether all were returning voluntarily, and announced that the scheme would be suspended if it were found that any compulsion had been used. The repatriation continued during the rest of 1956 and throughout 1957, though on a reduced scale.

[b] In April 1959 a group of five Russian diplomats was expelled. They included the Counsellor Nikolay Belo'us, who was later appointed Soviet Ambassador in Bogotá (see p. 38, note f).

[c] For the exchange of Notes see *Pravda*, 4 Apr. 1945.

[d] *New Times*, 1 Dec. 1946, pp. 29–30.

with the former **(79)**.[a] Before the end of the year, Moscow was protesting that 'slanderous fabrications' against the Soviet Union were reaching intolerable proportions **(80)**, and countered with a campaign of abuse culminating in attacks on the person of the President of the Republic and on the Brazilian armed forces **(81)**. Other causes of friction also arose between the two countries including incidents centring round the staff of the Brazilian Embassy in Moscow and hostile demonstrations organized by local Communist Parties against Brazilian diplomatic missions in a number of other capitals. The Brazilian Government's banning of the Communist Party, which had been making alarming headway, and Brazil's participation in the 1947 Rio Pact of Mutual Assistance, were probably also contributory causes. In October 1947 the Brazilian Ambassador in Moscow was accordingly instructed to notify the Soviet authorities that his Government had decided to break off relations between the two countries **(82)**. The rupture lasted for fourteen years.

Trade relations

Trade links survived the break in political relations. President Juscelino Kubitschek's policy of rapid industrial expansion had placed a great strain on his country's economy and foreign exchange reserves and increased the urgency of finding fresh markets for its products. It was in the hope of alleviating these difficulties that a Soviet-Brazilian trade agreement was signed at the end of 1959 **(87)**. The ensuing expansion of trade between the two countries, though still modest, proved useful and led to the conclusion of a more ambitious trade agreement in 1963 **(89)**. Nor did Marshal Castelo Branco's anti-Communist coup of April 1964 lead to any serious break in economic relations. After negotiations in the following year, in which a Soviet offer to finance the construction of an ambitious dam and hydro-electric scheme in Paraná was considered but finally turned down by the Brazilians, a protocol was signed in August 1966 whereby the Soviet Union offered to extend a $100 million credit and made the important concession of agreeing to take a quarter of her imports from Brazil in the form of manufactured or semi-manufactured goods **(90)**. No marked increase has, however, occurred in the annual volume of Soviet-Brazilian trade, which continues to consist mainly of the exchange of Soviet petroleum for Brazil's coffee, cotton, and other traditional agricultural products.

Diplomatic relations renewed

The resumption and further development of political relations with Brazil, after the rupture of 1947, remained an objective of Soviet policy. The victory of Jânio Quadros in the presidential elections at the beginning of 1961 seemed to augur well for this and was welcomed in Moscow **(88)**.[b] A personal message from

[a] That this was no passing indiscretion by Prestes, but the considered policy of the Party was made clear by the issuing of a manifesto, over the signature of Prestes and other Party leaders, in March 1949, reaffirming that, in the event of an 'imperialist war', they would fight against 'the oppressors of Brazil' (*A Classe operaria* (São Paulo), 16 Mar. 1949).

[b] *Izvestiya*, 8 Feb. 1961.

Khrushchev and Brezhnev, couched in unusually warm terms and with appreciative references to the independent line now beginning to be followed in Brazil's foreign policy, was sent to the new President (**83**). By the time Quadros's reply (**84**) appeared in the Soviet press, its author had ceased to be President of Brazil. Negotiations for the resumption of diplomatic relations nevertheless continued with his successor, João Goulart, and were successfully concluded the following November. Reviewing the course of relations, both in the political and economic field, some fifteen months later, Khrushchev found cause for satisfaction and for an optimistic assessment of future prospects (**85**). Though the installation of Marshal Castelo Branco's regime in the following year dashed these hopes and gave rise to some Soviet complaints of fresh anti-Soviet actions (**86**), diplomatic relations between the two countries continued to develop on a correct, if no longer such a cordial footing. The tenor of Soviet reporting on Brazil remained generally critical.[a]

Chile

Chile established relations with the Soviet Union in November 1944.[b] Since President González Videla's Radical administration had taken three Communists into the Government at the end of 1946, it seemed likely that these relations would develop favourably. But owing to the growing tensions of the cold war, the President decided to drop the Communist ministers from the Government in April 1947, and later to ban their Party. He also severed relations with several Soviet bloc countries on the ground that they had been subverting the local Slav minorities and stirring up labour trouble. Though these charges were directed primarily against the Yugoslavs rather than the Russians, relations with the latter were exacerbated by a machine-gun attack on the Russian Embassy in Santiago, and the Soviet refusal to give an exit permit to the Russian daughter-in-law of the Chilean Ambassador in Moscow. Relations between the two countries were accordingly severed in October 1947 (**96**). The bitterness aroused on both sides by these developments was reflected in the sharp exchanges between the Chilean and Soviet representatives in the Security Council (**97–8**), where Chile had taken the initiative in arraigning the Soviet Union for instigating the Communist take-over in Czechoslovakia.

Renewal and development of diplomatic relations
By the time of the presidential election of 1964, the Communists, legal once more, had entered into an electoral alliance with the Socialists and seemed to be within reach of gaining power. The Party was large and well organized and

---

[a] V. Kobysh, the *Izvestiya* correspondent, was expelled from Brazil. (For an account of this incident, see ibid., 10 July 1966.)

[b] Feelers for the establishment of diplomatic relations had been put out by Chilean and Soviet representatives in Europe as long ago as 1925 (*Dokumenti*, viii, nos. 337 (p. 575) and and 360 (p. 644)). According to the historian of the Chilean CP, H. Ramírez Necochea (*Orígen y formación del Partido Comunista de Chile* (Santiago, 1965), p. 246), the Chilean Government had been led to make these démarches by the founder of the CP, L. E. Recabarren, but 'the pressure of reactionary forces prevented them from meeting with success'.

included influential figures such as the celebrated poet Pablo Neruda. Victory, however, went to the Christian Democrats, whose successful candidate took some of the wind out of his left-wing opponents' sails by restoring relations with the Soviet Union as a means of improving the country's trading position and demonstrating the independent line it proposed to take in foreign policy. Though Eduardo Frei's Government protested, as did that of other Latin American countries, at Soviet participation in the Tricontinental Conference at Havana, to whose machinations it attributed the subsequent labour troubles in the Chilean copper-mines (**100**), and despite the very close relations known to exist between the CPSU and the Chilean Communist Party (**99**) which opposed his Government, a trade agreement was concluded between Chile and the Soviet Union in January 1967 and relations continued to develop steadily in the economic, cultural, and political spheres during Frei's administration (**101**).

Cuba (pre-Castro)

Cuba was the first Latin American country to establish diplomatic relations with the Soviet Union during the Second World War (October 1942). This may be partly explained by the strong influence enjoyed by the Communists in the administration of Fulgencio Batista, whose presidential campaign they had backed two years before. In 1943 they were rewarded by a seat in his cabinet and they also controlled the officially-recognized Cuban *Confederación de Trabajadores de Cuba*. Soon after the end of the war, however, relations came under the strain of the cold war. Protests were exchanged, some of them on trivial pretexts, as when the Soviet Legation took offence at the inclusion of a grotesque mask of Stalin in Havana's traditional carnival procession (**110**). More serious grounds for protest, in the Cuban view, were the statements made by Communist leaders in a number of countries that their first loyalty would be to the Soviet Union in the event of another war.[a] A critical article published by the Cuban Vice-President of the Republic in the Cuban press provoked a violent counter-attack in *Pravda* which was reproduced and disseminated inside Cuba by the Soviet Embassy. This led in turn to a protest motion in the Cuban Senate, from which the three Communist senators abstained and presented a counter-motion criticizing the Vice-President's actions 'which affect our foreign relations and our international policy'. The unconditional support which the Soviet Union could count on from the Cuban Communists in any dispute with the Cuban Government may be gauged from the public utterances of their leaders at this time (**111–12**).

Batista regained power in 1952 by a coup d'état but failed to renew the alliance with the Communists, who had been losing ground, particularly in the labour movement, since he had left office in 1944. The Russians appear to have reached the conclusion that Batista was now irrevocably committed to Washington and that they had more to lose than gain by retaining their links with his regime. An incident (similar to that which was to occur in Venezuela three months later) in which two Russian diplomatic couriers carrying bags presumed to contain propaganda material were refused entry into Cuba

[a] See pp. 33–4.

furnished them with a suitable occasion for breaking off relations (**113**). Batista was denounced in the Soviet press as a Yankee puppet, and Cuba depicted as an American colony (**114**). Despite the severance of diplomatic relations, the Soviet Union continued to trade with Cuba.[a]

Colombia

Colombia had recognized the Soviet Union in 1935, but took no steps to exchange diplomatic missions until 1943. Relations failed to develop to any considerable extent and were brought to an end following the murder, in April 1948, in the streets of Bogotá, of the popular Liberal leader Jorge Eliécer Gaitán and the ensuing widespread rioting. Communist responsibility for these events has been alleged but never proved, and seems unlikely.[b] Following reports that foreign conspirators, including two Russians, had been involved, the Soviet Legation issued a démenti (**102**), and later a sharp protest over the indignities to which certain Soviet diplomats had allegedly been subjected (**103**). The Colombian Government, after issuing and then withdrawing an announcement stating that relations with the Soviet Union had been broken off, informed the Soviet chargé d'affaires on 3 May of their wish that, since his mission had ceased to serve any useful function, it should be withdrawn. Whether or not this amounted to a formal rupture of relations, Colombia and the Soviet Union thereafter remained without diplomatic links for almost twenty years.

The development of relations with Colombia, culminating in the reactivization of diplomatic links at the beginning of 1968, posed delicate problems. To strengthen an 'oligarchy' economically was denounced by Castro as a betrayal of the revolutionary cause (**106**), but approved by the Colombian Communist Party as helping to weaken the grip of the 'Yankee monopolies' (**107**). Many Colombians held reservations as to the Russians' real intentions. Though the Soviet Union seemed eager to promote trade and might appear as a vast potential market for Colombia's coffee (**104**), there seemed little reason to believe that the Soviet leaders would see advantage in encouraging any modification in the Russians' traditional tea-drinking habits, and fears were even expressed that any coffee acquired from Colombia would simply be resold on the world market, to the detriment of Colombia's regular trade channels. Nevertheless, some trade developed between the two countries during 1966, and a trade-and-payments agreement was signed in Moscow in the following July. The chief political obstacle lay in what remained of *la violencia* —the endemic rural banditry to which the Colombian Communist Party had

[a] Sales of Cuban sugar to the USSR were as follows ($US): 1953, 763,025; 1954, 808,463; 1955, 36,409,907; 1956, 14,981,000; 1957, 41,981,000; 1958, 14,072,388 (Dirección General de Estadísticas, *10 años de balances comerciales, 1949–58* (1960)).

[b] It seems probable that Communist and other extremist agitators (including Fidel Castro, then a radical Cuban youth leader) had gathered in Bogotá to prepare some action designed to discredit or protest against the 9th Inter-American Conference which had been convened at Bogotá at the time to lay the foundation of the new OAS. The USSR was also sharply critical of the Conference, which 'represents a far-reaching attempt to convert the "Inter-American System" into a political and military bloc under the aegis of the United States' (*New Times*, 12 May 1948, p. 16).

attempted to give a more specifically political orientation. Though it concentrated its activity in the towns, the Party had established its influence over certain rural enclaves,[a] where the Government's writ did not run, and controlled some guerrilla units of its own.

The Government of Lleras Restrepo had repeatedly declared that it would only re-establish diplomatic relations with the Soviet Union if the latter refrained from interference in Colombia's internal affairs.[b] The Communist Party was on record as pledged to support guerrilla action, and indignantly denied allegations that it had gone back on its pledge in order to facilitate the resumption of relations between Colombia and the Soviet Union.[c] Though conclusive evidence is lacking, it seems likely that soon after these relations had been re-established at the beginning of 1968, the Party nevertheless decided, at Moscow's behest, to de-emphasize its guerrilla activities and to convert such detachments as still remained loyal (for some militants were expected to pass over to the guerrilla bands not under Communist control) into more passive 'self-defence detachments'. In a statement welcoming the resumption of relations with the Soviet Union, the Party reaffirmed its resolve to continue the struggle for structural changes in Colombia, without specifying which form the struggle would take (**109**). Moscow's attitude towards the Colombian Government varied according to the prospects of establishing relations with it.[d] With regard to its attitude towards the guerrillas, a Soviet spokesman had attempted to evade the dilemma by asserting that, whilst sympathizing with every 'national-liberation movement', the Soviet Union regarded it as each country's internal affair and would not intervene to support it (**105**). After the resumption of relations these assurances were redoubled[e] but were received with some scepticism when it became known that the newly appointed Ambassador to Colombia had himself previously been declared *persona non grata* by the Argentine Government for taking a hand in subversive activities.[f]

---

[a] First over the reputedly 'independent republics' of Sumapaz and Viotá, and later over Marquetalia and a few other districts. The Communists formed local 'self-defence units' which were then transformed into the more offensive *Bloque Gerrillero del Sur*, later styled the *Fuerzas Armadas Revolucionarias Colombianas* (FARC); those of pro-Chinese orientation were controlled by the CP of Colombia Marxist-Leninist, and were known as the *Ejército Popular de Liberación* (EPL), and the pro-Cuban guerrillas as the *Ejército de Liberación Nacional* (ELN).

[b] This was made clear in the President's State of the Union Message of 20 July 1967 and re-emphasized in his speech after the resumption of relations (**108**).

[c] In an article published in *Pravda* (27 Apr. 1966), Gilberto Vieira, Secretary-General of the Colombian CP, praised the 'patriotic character of the guerrilla struggle' in Colombia. Later in the year he indignantly denied 'poisonous' allegations that the Party had ceased to support the guerrillas in order to smooth the way for the conclusion of a Colombian-Soviet trade agreement (*Voz proletaria*, 15 Dec. 1966).

[d] While a Soviet trade mission was in Bogotá in March 1967 hoping to negotiate a trade agreement, Soviet press criticism of the Colombian Government for its recent moves against the local Communists was muted but again stepped up once the mission had left (see *Pravda*, 31 Mar. 1967 and *Izvestiya*, 30 Mar. 1967 for the sharpest attacks).

[e] Statement of Ambassador Belo'us to *El Tiempo*, 28 Mar. 1968.

[f] Nikolay Belo'us had previously served as Counsellor in the Soviet Embassy in Buenos Aires. He and three other Soviet officials were asked by Arturo Frondizi's Government to leave the country in April 1959 (*El Siglo* (Buenos Aires), 22 Mar. 1968).

Bolivia

Bolivia established relations with the Soviet Union in 1945. Though some radical leaders of the mine workers and intelligentsia pressed for effective links with Moscow, and the Revolution of 1952 was of partly Marxist inspiration, the *Movimiento Nacional Revolucionario* Government party looked to Washington for economic support and declined to exchange diplomatic missions with the Soviet Union. In 1957 the Russians began to release large quantities of cheaply priced tin, thereby forcing Bolivia to cut back sharply on her production, and leading, in September 1958, to the collapse of tin prices on the world market.[a] In a statement at the General Assembly the following month, the Bolivian delegate designated this Russian dumping as 'economic aggression' designed to cause unemployment and social chaos in his country which Moscow hoped to turn to her political account **(91)**. The Soviet Union indignantly repudiated this accusation and offered to build a tin smelter for Bolivia in token of their good will **(92–3)**.[b]

Venezuela

Venezuela had somewhat reluctantly established relations with the Soviet Union shortly before the end of the war in order to smooth her way to full participation in the San Francisco Conference. Relations were slow to develop, first on account of the 1945 coup which brought to power President Betancourt, whom the Russians distrusted as a lapsed Communist, and secondly, through the ousting of his Government by a further military coup of November 1948. Moscow delayed recognition of the new junta until March of the following year, and signified her distaste for it by keeping only a chargé d'affaires at Caracas. In June 1952 an incident occurred in which two Russians, alleged to be members of the Soviet Embassy but suspected by the Venezuelans of being subversive agents, were refused admission to the country despite the personal intervention of the Soviet chargé d'affaires **(144)**. Mutual protests over this incident prompted each country to declare the severance of relations with the other **(145–6)**. Prospects for a restoration of diplomatic links seemed brighter after the fall of the Pérez Jiménez dictatorship in 1958, and the visits paid to Moscow by the Venezuelan Minister for Mines and Petroleum, and that paid to Caracas by the Soviet Ambassador accredited to Mexico marked a further improvement of relations in 1961. But the Venezuelan Government was alarmed at the threat posed to her traditional markets in the West by increasing exports of Soviet oil to that area. Though the Soviet Union is reported to have given her informal assurances on this matter, and also to have expressed approval of the Organization of Petroleum Exporting Countries (OPEC),

---

[a] According to a page-advertisement placed by the Bolivian Government in the *New York Times* on 2 October 1958, under the heading of 'Bolivia—victim of Soviet Aggression', this Soviet dumping had forced Bolivia to make a $17½ million cut in her own production and was facing her with the choice of either closing the mines altogether or continuing to run them at a loss.

[b] See above, p. 24.

recently formed on Venezuelan initiative,[a] no move was made to restore formal relations. The Christian Democrats in Betancourt's administration were strongly opposed to such a course, and the Government, harassed by mounting Communist-sponsored guerrilla and urban terrorist action, is believed to have made it clear that no Soviet mission would be welcome in the country so long as this state of affairs continued. With the Communists' switch to *vía pacífica* tactics in 1966,[b] the Government seemed more disposed to a renewal of at least commercial relations with the Soviet Union, but 1968 drew to an end without Caracas following Bogotá's lead in this direction.

Guatemala

After a long period of dictatorial rule, Guatemala embarked in 1944 on a decade of constitutional democracy and reform, first under Juan José Arévalo and then under Jácobo Arbenz. Voices were soon raised that their regimes were being infiltrated by Communists and were coming under increasing Soviet influence. Relations had been established with the Soviet Union by Arévalo's Government in April 1945; a Guatemalan Legation opened in Moscow but closed again after a few months. The Soviet Union opened no diplomatic mission in Guatemala, but appears to have kept in touch with the Guatemalan regime through the Soviet Embassy in Mexico City.[c] In early 1953 the Arbenz Government thought it advisable to deny charges of its increasing pro-Soviet trend in a note to the Secretary-General of the United Nations (**121**). Though welcoming its radical and anti-United States stance, Moscow appears to have been discreet in its attitude towards the Arbenz Government and sceptical as to its chances of survival in view of the important American economic interests involved in the country (**122**).

Overthrow of Arbenz

At the beginning of 1954 events began to move towards a crisis. At the 10th Inter-American Conference held at Caracas in March of that year, a resolution was passed, with the Guatemalan situation clearly in mind, affirming the resolve of member states not to permit the establishment in the western hemisphere of any branch of 'international Communism' (**123**). This resolution was opposed by the Guatemalan delegation on the grounds that it was merely designed to provide legal justification for intervention by the United States or her puppets against any Government whose progressive nature might threaten her economic interests (**124**). The arrival at Puerto Barrios of the Swedish s.s. *Alfhem* in May

---

[a] R. J. Alexander, *The Venezuelan Democratic Revolution* (New Brunswick, 1964), p. 142.

[b] See above, p. 27.

[c] According to the testimony of US Ambassador Peurifoy to a US House of Representatives' Select Committee (*Communist Aggression in Guatemala* (Washington, 1954), p. 118), 'the Soviet Union itself did not plant its own diplomatic mission in Guatemala, as this would have been too obvious a link between the Guatemalan Communists . . . and the great Soviet fatherland. . . . The Soviet did not show its hand openly, but operated through satellite missions, commercial travellers, and its own travelling officials, such as the commercial attaché of the Embassy in Mexico City.'

with a consignment of some 2,000 tons of arms from Eastern Europe brought matters to a head by appearing to justify the charges that Guatemala was becoming a spearhead for the spread of 'international Communism'. Before these arms could be put to use by the Guatemalan Government, exiles under the command of Colonel Carlos Castillo Armas, who, after an abortive coup in 1950, had been preparing an invasion from bases in Nicaragua and Honduras, crossed the Guatemalan frontier. Ten days later, after some minor clashes and the army's withdrawal of support from Arbenz following his refusal to agree to demands for the dismissal of Communist officers, the Government fell.

Dispute referred to the Security Council

The main battlefield was to be not in Guatemala but in the UN Security Council, which met on 20 June to consider the dispute in response to an urgent request by the Guatemalan Government. Brazil and Colombia, with the support of the United States, argued that the dispute should not be handled by the United Nations but by the OAS, which had already been seized of the matter. The Soviet Union backed Guatemala's plea that it was a matter for the United Nations (125) and used its veto to prevent the Colombian-Brazilian resolution from being carried, but at a meeting of the Council five days later was unable to secure adoption of an agenda which would have enabled the Security Council to proceed further in the matter. In the meantime, the Inter-American Peace Committee of the OAS had set up a Fact-Finding Committee which was preparing to proceed to Guatemala when Arbenz was forced from office and replaced by a three-man junta. The Security Council was then informed by the new Minister for Foreign Affairs that, since peace and order had been restored in his country, there was no reason why the Guatemalan question should remain on the Council's agenda. The Soviet Union had failed both to secure the survival of a Central American Government to which it had given at least strong moral support, and to establish the principle that such disputes should be referred primarily to the United Nations, where it could have a say in settling them, instead of to a regional organization in which United States influence was manifestly paramount.

The Dominican Republic

The Soviet Union was soon to return to the same charge in the Security Council over another Latin American issue—that of the Dominican Republic. The principle of whether the OAS or the United Nations should be primarily responsible for handling disputes in this area had assumed increased importance since the United States had already used its influence in the OAS to secure the passing of the Declaration of San José (157) and seemed resolved to take further steps to enforce collective action against the Castro regime and the Soviet position in Cuba. A favourable opportunity for restating the Soviet case occurred in August 1960, when the OAS adopted a resolution condemning the interference of the Trujillo dictatorship in the internal affairs of Venezuela. An additional reason prompting the Soviet action in the Security Council was probably the wish to quash rumours that Moscow was considering a favourable response to the overtures which the Dominican dictator, General Rafael Leonidas Trujillo, had recently been making for the establishment of diplomatic relations.[a] In raising the question in the Security Council (**115–16**), the Soviet representative was thus careful not to dissent from the disapprobation of the Trujillo regime expressed by the Latin American and United States Governments, but to repeat the Soviet arguments that the handling of disputes of this nature, particularly where the enforcement of sanctions was involved, was a matter for the United Nations and not for the OAS. This view did not however prevail, and when, in 1965 a fresh crisis blew up in the Dominican Republic and a popular rising precipitated the landing of American marines and the operations of an ostensibly OAS peace force, the Soviet representative could do no more than denounce these actions in the Security Council and repeat the arguments—again to no avail—that the dispute should be taken out of the hands of the OAS and be handled by the Security Council (**117–18**).

Cuba under Fidel Castro

If the Soviet Union found little scope for action in the United Nations, and none in the OAS, for furthering its policies with regard to Latin America, it had secured a valuable foothold within the western hemisphere itself. In the early 1960s, Cuba moved from the orbit of the United States into that of the Soviet Union. The development was the more unexpected in that the course steered by the revolutionary regime in power in Havana had been set not by the Cuban Communist Party[b] but by a revolutionary *caudillo* whose relations with it in the past had been cool. On 26 July 1953 an attack had been launched by small anti-Batista groups of armed men against the Moncada barracks at Santiago de Cuba, in a desperate attempt to shake his regime. Its members were not Communists who had been persecuted and finally outlawed following the rupture of Cuban-Soviet relations,[c] but the followers of a little-known youth leader called Fidel Castro, and the venture was denounced by the clandestine Communist press as 'adventurist putschism'. Nor did the Communists see any reason to modify their disapproval of violent tactics when, three and a half

---

[a] 'In the middle of the summer Enrique de Marchena, who had represented his country at the UN at the time of the snubbing of Eisenhower in 1958, was sent on a mission to the USSR to see what could be done. He carried with him no precise plan. Rather, he was to test the Russian reaction. He got as far as Cairo but failed to obtain a visa to enter Russia. Early in November Johnny Abbes [who was head of Trujillo's Military Intelligence Service] made a trip to Czechoslovakia and entered into negotiations with Russian and Polish representatives for diplomatic relations and an agreement of some kind. These efforts were likewise unproductive, but only because of Russian disinterest' (R. D. Crassweller, *Trujillo* (New York, 1966), p. 425). On 1 September 1960 the Dominican radio announced that General Arturo Espaillat might be appointed Ambassador to the USSR.

[b] The Cuban Communists had changed the name of their party from *Unión Revolucionaria Comunista* to *Partido Socialista Popular* (PSP) in the Second World War. After Castro's advent to power it was linked in July 1961 with the other two parties supporting him in the *Organizaciones Revolucionarias Integradas* (ORI), which in February 1963 became the *Partido Unido de la Revolución Socialista* (PURS). This was in turn renamed the *Partido Comunista Cubana* in October 1966.

[c] See above, p. 37.

years later, Castro resumed his struggle against the Batista regime from his guerrilla base in the Sierra Maestra. It was only in the summer of 1958, when it began to seem possible that the guerrillas might after all be able to cause Batista's downfall, that the Party sent a member of its Central Committee, Carlos Rafael Rodríguez, to confer with Castro in the Sierra. The terms of the agreement reached between Castro and the Communists have not been made public. Though the Party gave permission to individual members to join the guerrillas and supported Castro's 26 July Movement in some anti-Batista actions in the towns, its total contribution to Fidel Castro's victory remained slight.[a]

Moscow's cautious welcome

There is no evidence that the Soviet Union had any contact with Castro during the Sierra Maestra period, apart from any reports which individual Communists such as Rodríguez may have passed to Moscow, nor did the Soviet leaders show any particular interest in his movement or foresee the extraordinary prospects which his victory was later to open for them.[b] A few days after his entry into Havana and the establishment of a Provisional Government, Marshal Voroshilov addressed a letter to its President, Dr Manuel Urrutia, announcing Soviet recognition of the new Cuban Government (148). The letter, which was cautiously worded and contained a curious reference to the principle of peaceful coexistence, made no mention of any proposed resumption of diplomatic relations and seems to have been intended as a means of keeping a foot in the door whilst Moscow took stock of the new situation.[c] The CPSU was probably first officially seized of the new situation at its 21st Congress, at the end of January 1959, when a Cuban Communist spokesman gave an account of the events which had just led to the fall of Batista, greatly exaggerating the role played by the Cuban Communists,[d] and allegedly even by the Socialist camp as a whole, and appealing for 'further help' from the world Communist movement (149). The Soviet leaders showed themselves in no hurry to respond to this appeal. They possibly had misgivings that Castro's regime would develop along purely nationalist lines and would at best follow a third-world policy of non-alignment. The Soviet Union too was moving at this time towards the limited rapprochement with the United States which was to express itself in the 'spirit of Camp David', and had

[a] See Suárez, pp. 26–9 and P. R. J. Furtak, *Kuba und der Weltkomunismus* (Cologne, 1967), pp. 64–9.

[b] Even as late as October 1958 the Russians appear to have had little expectation of Castro's victory. In an interview granted to a Brazilian journalist on 3 October, Khrushchev referred in the same breath to 'the tragic fate of Guatemala and the heroic but unequal struggle of the Cuban people' (*Mezhdunarodnaya zhizn*, no. 11, 1958).

[c] It was subsequently claimed in the note published on 8 May 1960 on the revival of diplomatic relations between Havana and Moscow (152) that 'these relations were in effect resumed by virtue of the recognition extended to the Government of the Republic of Cuba in January 1959 by the USSR'.

[d] Blas Roca was later forced to give a more accurate picture and to admit that the PSP 'made a late and feeble entry into the war' (speech to the 8th Congress of the Uruguayan CP, quoted by Suárez, p. 159).

no wish to choose that moment for a provocative intervention in the Caribbean. The Russians thus confined themselves, throughout 1959, to taking a number of cautious soundings in Cuba.[16]

The first formal contacts between the Cuban and Soviet Governments did not take place until February, 1960—more than one year after Castro's advent to power—when Vice-Premier Mikoyan arrived to open a Soviet Exhibition in Havana. Mikoyan had gone to Mexico on a similar mission,[a] and on 3 November of the previous year, *Revolución*, the organ of Castro's 26 July Movement, had suggested that advantage should be taken of his presence in the neighbouring country to invite him to Cuba.[b]

Soviet-Cuban trade and diplomatic relations

The most important outcome of Mikoyan's visit was the conclusion, on 13 February, of a trade agreement for the purchase by the Soviet Union of nearly 5 million tons of Cuban sugar over the next five years, together with the offer of $100 million credit for economic aid (150). Twenty per cent of the payments for Cuba's sugar were to be in foreign currency, the remaining 80 per cent in Soviet goods, including 6 million barrels of oil annually. On ratification of the treaty, it was announced that the Soviet Union would increase its purchase of Cuban sugar to 1 million tons in 1960. In addition, the Soviet Union later promised to take from Cuba the 700,000 tons left on her hands through Washington's decision to cut Cuba's sugar quota. These agreements had the effect of initiating the drastic reorientation of Cuba's trade from the United States to the Soviet Union and of forging close links to that country through the provision of an assured market for the basic export on which the whole Cuban economy depended. Whether the supply to Cuba of Russian arms was also discussed at this stage is not known; Mikoyan certainly took pains to deny it (151).

The joint communiqué issued at the time of Mikoyan's visit also fore-shadowed the resumption of diplomatic relations between Cuba and the Soviet Union (152). The formal announcement of the resumption followed on 8 May.[c] Shortly afterwards a deputation headed by Captain Núñez Jiménez left for Moscow and handed an invitation to Khrushchev from Castro to visit Cuba.

[a] See above, p. 31.

[b] Suárez (p. 81) attributes Castro's momentous decision to turn to the USSR largely to his overmastering desire to acquire from some other sources the arms which the United States were now denying him: 'On the same day, and in the same issue of *Revolución*—showing, to my mind, the relation between the two questions—the British were threatened with the loss of the Latin American market, and even of their investments there, if they persisted in refusing to supply jet planes to Cuba so as not to antagonize the United States.'

[c] The first Cuban Ambassador appointed to Moscow was Faure Chomón, a former leader of the 13 March Revolutionary Directorate, an old rival of the PSP but now associated with it and with the 26 July Movement as the officially organized backing of the Castro regime. The Soviet Government chose as its Ambassador to Havana Sergey Mikhailovich Kudryavtsev, an official who had made his career in the Soviet Intelligence Service. As First Secretary at the Soviet Embassy in Ottawa, he had played a leading part in the spy-ring transmitting atomic information to Moscow (Rl Commission to Investigate the Facts relating to the circumstances surrounding the communication . . . of secret and confidential information to agents of foreign powers, *Report* (Ottawa, 1946), p. 85).

Khrushchev received the Cubans warmly, accepted the invitation to visit their country, and in reply to a question, declared that the Soviet Government had no wish to set up a military base in Cuba, as that was against its policy, and that, in any case, 'they had only to press a button in any part of the Soviet Union for rockets from that country to fall on any other part of the planet' **(153)**. A few weeks later, in a speech of 9 July, Khrushchev reverted to this theme and declared that 'in case of need, Soviet artillerymen can support the Cuban people with their rocket fire' **(154)**. Although prefaced with the phrase 'figuratively speaking', Khrushchev's threat made a considerable stir, eliciting a warm welcome from Castro (who added his gloss that the rockets offered were real, not 'figurative'),[a] and a sharp reaction from President Eisenhower, who asserted that the United States would not 'permit the establishment of a regime dominated by international Communism in the Western hemisphere'.[b] Soon after this exchange, a military delegation headed by Raúl Castro, Minister of the Cuban Armed Forces, arrived in Moscow for negotiations. No details were released of the resulting agreement, but a joint communiqué was issued re-affirming, without specifically restating Khrushchev's rocket threat, that the Soviet Union 'would use everything to prevent United States armed interven-tion against the Republic of Cuba' **(155)**. A similar assurance was contained in Khrushchev's message of greeting on the 26 July anniversary celebrations **(156)**. On reviewing the march-past of the unarmed militia on that occasion, Castro announced that fresh supplies of arms for them had already reached Cuba.[c]

The Soviet admonitions may have been addressed not only to the United States but to any Latin American countries contemplating taking individual or collective action against Cuba. The OAS, meeting in Costa Rica at the end of August, reacted by issuing the Declaration of San José denouncing the threat of intervention by an extra-continental power and Sino-Soviet designs to gain a foothold in the hemisphere **(157)**. This in turn elicited from Castro his Declaration of Havana welcoming 'the aid spontaneously offered to Cuba by the Soviet Union' and 'its offer to support Cuba with the aid of rockets' **(158)**. This, and other statements by Cuban leaders, showed an evident eagerness to hold the Soviet Union to a specific undertaking to come to Cuba's aid in the event of attack, whereas the Soviet statements suggest a wish to water down the threat contained in Khrushchev's 9 July speech and to leave the nature of Soviet support less clearly defined.[d] This was brought out in an interview granted to a Cuban journalist by Khrushchev on 22 October, in which the Soviet leader took care to shift the emphasis of his remarks to an assurance of the Soviet Union's desire for peace **(160)**.

---

[a] *Hoy*, 12 July 1960.

[b] *AFP, 1960*, p. 476.

[c] From Czechoslovakia (statement of 18 Sept. by Guevara, quoted by Suárez, p. 93).

[d] The controversial reference to rockets in Khrushchev's 9 July speech was later regarded as an embarrassment in the USSR and was omitted from the version of his speech given in the official collection of documents on Cuban-Soviet relations, *Narody SSSR i Kuby naveki vmeste* (Moscow, 1963).

Closer links with the USSR and China

In the meantime, Fidel Castro and Khrushchev had met during their attendance at the United Nations sessions in New York. Some degree of personal rapport seems to have been established between them, though hardly to the fulsome degree indicated in the official accounts (**159**). What transpired in their private interview is not known. Castro may well have given signs of wishing to move faster and further along the path of radical reforms at home and membership of the Socialist bloc abroad than Khrushchev deemed wise.[a] The rift between Peking and Moscow was widening and offered Castro new scope for manoeuvring. Diplomatic relations between Havana and Peking were established in September, and at the end of the following month 'Che' Guevara signed an agreement in Peking whereby the Chinese undertook to buy 1 million tons of Cuban sugar in 1961 and offered a $60 million credit for the purchase of Chinese goods and technical assistance.[b] Though, at the same time, the delegates of the PSP attending the Congress of 81 Communist Parties in Moscow were showing themselves loyal supporters of the Soviet line, Moscow must have been alive to the danger that Castro's Revolution would be attracted into the Chinese orbit. This consideration doubtless prompted the Russians to improve the terms of the new Soviet-Cuban agreement which was announced in a joint communiqué of 19 December 1960. This pledged the Russians to purchase 2,700,000 tons of sugar in 1961 at 4 cents a pound, and offered other important measures of economic aid (**161**). The Cubans, for their part, expressed support for 'peaceful coexistence' and other Soviet policies.

Rupture with the US

The joint communiqué did not, however, reflect any real identity of view between Havana and Moscow. After the inauguration of J. F. Kennedy as President of the United States in November, Khrushchev was anxious to revive 'the spirit of Camp David'. But Castro, either genuinely fearing an invasion by the United States (for reports were already rife that preparations for a CIA-sponsored attack by Cuban exiles were far advanced), or as a means of keeping up the revolutionary fervour of his followers, announced that invasion was imminent and precipitated the rupture of relations with the United States. In his speech of 2 January 1961 he averred that the imperialists would take as their pretext the alleged setting-up of Soviet rocket bases in the island (**163**). Speaking at a reception in Moscow on the same day, Khrushchev made a declaration in almost identical terms (**162**). This simultaneous disclaimer of any intention to take the step which the Russians were in fact to take a year and a half later, with such momentous consequences, suggests that even at this early stage in the Cuban-Soviet rapprochement the two leaders may at least have had the possibility in mind.

[a] Suárez, pp. 112–19.
[b] *Hoy*, 4 Dec. 1960.

The Bay of Pigs invasion fiasco

On 17 April 1961 the long expected CIA-sponsored landing of Cuban exiles took place at the Bay of Pigs. Though his armed forces were to prove capable of crushing them within a matter of hours, Castro took the precaution, on the eve of the invasion, of reinforcing his claim on Russian support by proclaiming the 'Socialist' nature of the Cuban Revolution, and thus, by implication, Cuba's full adherence to the Soviet bloc (**164**). The speedy collapse of the invasion attempt and Washington's consequent loss of face allowed Moscow to extract the maximum propaganda advantage from her pledges of support for Cuba without the necessity of implementing them (**165**). Khrushchev did not, however, reaffirm his specific threat to retaliate with rockets, and he once again disclaimed any intention of setting up military bases inside Cuba (**166**). It is also significant that in none of these statements did the Russians endorse Castro's assertion of the 'Socialist' nature of his Revolution.[a] Nor, when President Osvaldo Dorticós visited Moscow the following June in the hope of securing Soviet endorsement for Castro's claim that Cuba should now be considered a fully fledged member of the Soviet bloc, did the joint communiqué issued on that occasion go beyond the statement that 'Cuba has achieved its revolution independently and has freely chosen the road of socialist development' (**167**).

Moscow's caution was understandable. There was no precedent in Communist experience for a national leader, albeit one with great popular appeal, radical leanings, and manifest anti-United States sentiments, yet lacking any certain grounding in Marxism or record of militancy in an orthodox Communist Party, asserting his country's membership of the Soviet bloc. Cuba was situated only ninety miles from the United States, and could not easily be defended by the Soviet armed forces without risk of nuclear war. Nor could Castro himself, with the ambitions and unpredictability of a *caudillo*, be relied upon not to embroil his Soviet sponsors in some unwise revolutionary adventure in Latin America. Probably Castro himself realized that he would need to take two further steps if his membership of the Socialist camp was to be made more acceptable to Moscow. He would need to de-emphasize the personalist nature of his regime by forming a new Communist Party, in which the old PSP would merge its separate identity and which, though nominally directed by its Central Committee, he could in reality control. He would also need to produce the Marxist-Leninist credentials required of a Communist leader.

Formation of a new Cuban CP

In his speech of July 1961 Castro accordingly announced the formation of a

---

[a] The PSP, too, was hesitant in admitting the claim. The Party organ *Hoy*, in its issue of 18 April, contained only a passing reference to 'our patriotic, democratic and Socialist Revolution', and ten more days passed before a more specific, but still guarded, commentary on the subject was published. This indicates that it was not Moscow and the Cuban Communists, but Fidel Castro himself, who was setting the pace for Cuba's advance towards complete identification with the Communist world.

new political party, to be known as the *Organizaciones Revolucionarias Integradas* (ORI), and in a television appearance on 1 December 1961 he revealed details about his alleged Marxist background and made his profession of faith: 'I am a Marxist-Leninist, and I shall be a Marxist-Leninist until the last day of my life!' (168). But Castro was soon to show that his interpretation of Marxism-Leninism might not always coincide with Moscow's. In an interview with *Pravda* and *Izvestiya* correspondents, he paid tribute to the concept of peaceful coexistence but laid repeated stress on Cuba's determination to go on supporting the struggle of the oppressed peoples against 'imperialism'.[a] This creed was stated in still more explicit terms on 4 February 1962 in the Second Declaration of Havana,[b] which made no mention of peaceful co-existence or other Moscow-approved formulas, but presented guerrilla militancy as the panacea for the ills of the third world. Whatever reservations they may have entertained privately with regard to the tactics advocated by Castro, neither Moscow nor the Cuban Communists thought it opportune to voice their dissent;[c] but the warmest welcome for the Second Declaration of Havana came, significantly, from Peking.[d]

Disgrace of old-guard 'sectarianists'

Castro's decision to merge the PSP with his own followers entailed the risk that the new revolutionary Party might fall under the control of the 'old-guard' Communists and generate enough strength of its own to challenge his own authority. To nip this danger in the bud and serve notice on the PSP that he still remained the master, he next moved against Aníbal Escalante, who had been systematically appointing former PSP members to key posts with precisely this aim in view. In March 1962 Castro denounced him for 'sectarianism' and exiled him to the Soviet bloc. Moscow decided to endorse this action. Castro was now referred to as 'Comrade', and Cuba's place in the Soviet bloc was confirmed by listing that country, together with all the other 'Socialist' states, in the traditional May Day slogans. Within two years from the formal establishment of diplomatic relations, Cuba had become linked to the Soviet Union by a variety of powerful economic, political, and cultural ties (170). The extent to which she had also become militarily involved with the Soviet Union was soon to be dramatically demonstrated.

Request for Soviet arms announced

Ever since the summer of 1960 Soviet statesmen had been declaring, in varying tones of menace, that the Soviet Union was prepared to use rockets in the

---

[a] *Pravda*, 29 Jan. 1962.

[b] This was proclaimed by Castro in January 1962 and called on all oppressed races and classes to follow Cuba's example and fight for their liberation.

[c] Blas Roca, with the agility which had led him previously to salute Batista as a 'noble-hearted man of the people' and 'bastion of democracy' (*Hoy*, 5 Feb. 1941 & 1 July 1944) and to censure Castro's anti-Batista actions as 'putschism', now hailed Castro as 'the best and most effective Marxist-Leninist of our country' (ibid., 22 Apr. 1962).

[d] New China News Agency, 12 Feb. 1962 (*Survey of the Chinese Mainland Press* 2680, 16 Feb. 1962).

defence of Cuba. They had, however, emphatically denied—and continued to deny even after the presence of rockets in Cuba had been established beyond any doubt—that they had any intention of setting up rocket bases inside Cuba **(162, 169)**. Exactly when a definite decision to set up such bases was taken is difficult to say; most probably in June 1962, when a high Soviet official— S. R. Rashidov, a candidate member of the CPSU Presidium and later the chief Soviet delegate to the Tricontinental Conference—is known to have been in Cuba, and when two Cuban delegations, one headed by Raúl Castro and composed of army officers, the other headed by Guevara and Emilio Aragonés, visited Moscow. A communiqué issued at the conclusion of the visit by the latter delegation admitted for the first time that Cuba had asked for 'aid in the form of armaments and the appropriate technical specialists' **(171)**. No mention, however, was made of rockets.

The installation of rocket bases

On whose initiative, and for what purpose, was the decision taken to instal the rockets? The statements on the subject by the chief protagonists are ambivalent and at times contradictory. In the account of the crisis which Khrushchev later gave to the Supreme Soviet **(179)**, he claimed that he acted in response to a Cuban request and solely in order to help defend Cuba from threatened attack by the United States; this specific statement was later modified into the general assertion that the two Governments had 'reached agreement' over installing the rockets.[a] Castro's version of the affair is different. In his speech of 2 January 1963 he denied that Cuba had made any request and affirmed that their introduction had been decided by mutual agreement. On other occasions he bluntly attributed the initiative to the Russians.[17] Each side, no doubt, made their own calculations of advantage and risk before agreeing to take the fateful decision. There seems little doubt that the Russians' real objective was less their alleged anxiety to protect Cuba than to alter the whole balance of global strategy to their advantage by one bold stroke.[b]

The 1962 missile crisis

The missile crisis of October 1962, which led to a direct confrontation between the United States and the Soviet Union, will be examined here only for its impact on Cuban-Soviet relations.[c] On 11 September—some three days after

[a] 'The Soviet Government and the Government of Cuba reached agreement on the delivery of missiles to Cuba' (*Pravda*, 14 July 1963).

[b] An exhaustive analysis of Soviet calculations is given in A. L. Horelick and Myron Rush, *Strategic Power and Soviet Foreign Policy* (Chicago UP, 1965, pp. 141–56).

[c] The messages exchanged between President Kennedy and Chairman Khrushchev and other relevant documents have been widely published and may be conveniently consulted in the State Department's *American Foreign Policy: Current Documents for 1962* and in D. L. Larson, ed., *The Cuban Crisis of 1962; selected documents and chronology* (Boston, 1963). The complete text of Khrushchev's crucial letter of 26 October to President Kennedy has never been published in full, but extracts will be found in Robert Kennedy's *Thirteen Days* (New York, 1968). A valuable day-by-day account of the confrontation is given in Elie Abel's *The Missile Crisis* (New York, 1966).

the first rockets are believed to have been unloaded in Cuba, the Soviet Union issued a statement asserting that these shipments were purely an 'internal affair' and that the Soviet Union had, in any event, 'no need' for rocket bases outside her own territory (**172**). On 22 October President Kennedy announced that ballistic missiles had been installed in Cuba and that a naval blockade of all shipments of offensive arms would be imposed until they were withdrawn (**173**). The Soviet Union replied by issuing a statement justifying its action and tabling a resolution in the Security Council accusing the Americans of endangering the peace.[a] On 26 October U Thant, in an attempt at mediation, sent a letter to Castro urging that work on the launching sites should be suspended.[b] On the same day a high Soviet official in the United States approached the United States Government with an assurance that the missiles would be withdrawn if Washington undertook not to invade Cuba. President Kennedy also received a personal message from Khrushchev, highly emotional in tone, which held out some hope that the Russians might be prepared to back down rather than risk the unleashing of a new world war. The following day (27 October), however, saw a hardening of attitude both in Havana and in Moscow. Castro rejected U Thant's request, reaffirmed Cuba's right to possess whatever arms she deemed necessary, and threatened to shoot down any combat plane infringing Cuban air-space; one U2 plane was indeed shot down, and others fired on.[c] On the same day, Khrushchev sent a second letter to President Kennedy raising the terms for a settlement of the crisis by demanding that American missiles be withdrawn from Turkey in exchange for the withdrawal of Soviet missiles from Cuba. The hardening of the Soviet attitude may have stemmed not only from a desire to save as much face as possible before backing down but in part at least from Castro's violent reaction to his protector's evident readiness to withdraw. President Kennedy chose to ignore Khrushchev's second, sharper letter and signified his agreement to the proposals contained in Khrushchev's first letter. A further exchange of letters between the two statesmen marked the end of the acute stage of the confrontation and its settlement over Castro's head.

Post-crisis relations

Khrushchev's decision to pull the missiles out of Cuba left Castro humiliated and resentful. Though he was later to admit that he had agreed to the missile bases being established in Cuba and had been opposed to their dismantling,[d] he limited his comments in his 1 November speech to referring in general

---

[a] Security Council doc. S/5187, 23 Oct. 1962.

[b] UN Press Release SG/1359, 27 Oct. 1962 (Larson, pp. 152–3).

[c] The Cubans, and not the Russians, were responsible for shooting down the U2. See Castro's speech of 1 May 1964 (*Hoy*, 2 May 1964), and Raúl Castro's boast: 'When different persons from different places were asking us not to obstruct the negotiations we gave the order to fire against every aeroplane' (speech of 23 May 1966, quoted in *Verde Olivo*, 28 May 1966). See also Suárez, pp. 170–1.

[d] 'We agreed to the setting up of strategic thermo-nuclear missiles in our territory; furthermore, not only did we agree that they should be brought here but we were opposed to their being removed!' (speech of 13 Mar. 1965; *Bohemia*, 19 Mar. 1965).

terms to the existence of 'some differences' between the two countries which he was confident could be settled by friendly discussion, and he reaffirmed that 'nothing should come between the Soviet Union and Cuba' (174). Khrushchev, for his part, lost no time in trying to repair the damage. On 2 November Mikoyan arrived in Havana 'for a friendly exchange of views with our close friend, Premier Fidel Castro' (176). On the same day President Kennedy informed the nation that the Soviet bases were being dismantled and that the progress of the Soviet withdrawal would be carefully followed (175). Three weeks later he announced that Khrushchev had undertaken also to remove the IL-28 bombers stationed in Cuba (178). Castro had likewise fought to keep these weapons in Cuba, but had been forced to announce that he would concur in their withdrawal if the Soviet Union insisted (177).

Mikoyan's visit, which lasted for more than three weeks, was only the first stage in the difficult task of repairing Cuban-Soviet relations. In the commercial field exchanges had also fallen below expectations, and a Cuban delegation led by C. R. Rodríguez returned to Havana in December with little to show. On 8 February 1963, however, a new economic agreement for the current year was announced. Cuba received a further credit from the Soviet Union and the Russians were reported to have also agreed to raise the price paid for Cuban sugar and to have permitted the Cubans to forego a million tons of the quota due to them so that the Cubans could gain foreign currency by selling it on the world market.[a] It is possible that the economic agreement was accompanied by some political understandings, such as an undertaking on the Cuban side to press on with the construction of an integrated Communist Party on orthodox lines, and on the Soviet side the recognition of Cuba as a fully fledged 'Socialist' state.[b]

Support for Cuba reaffirmed

In January 1963 the Soviet Deputy Foreign Minister V. V. Kuznetzov paid a short visit to Havana. Nothing is known of the subject of his discussions with Castro, but the official communiqué issued at the time pledged Soviet support for the 'Five Points' which Castro had put forward as a means of snatching some advantage from the solution of the missile crisis.[c] Assurances were also given in a number of official statements, though couched in general terms, of Soviet readiness to come to the defence of Cuba in the event of any attack against her. The most specific of these pledges was that given by the Soviet Defence Minister, Marshal Malinovsky, in February (180).

The sharpening dispute between Peking and Moscow acted as a spur to the Russians to repair their relations with Castro. Khrushchev's discomfiture over the missile crisis presented the Chinese with too good an opportunity to miss, and their denunciation of 'capitulationism'—from which they took good care

[a] *New York Times*, 2 June 1963; *Hoy*, 27 Dec. 1963.
[b] Suárez, p. 180.
[c] These were that the US should lift its 'economic blockade', cease supporting counter-revolutionary activities, halt 'pirate raids', stop violating Cuban air space and territorial waters, and withdraw from the Guantánamo naval base.

to exempt the Cubans—grew more and more outspoken.[a] Castro, whilst proclaiming Cuba's intention of remaining strictly on the sidelines, was quick to exploit the room which the dispute gave him for manoeuvring (181). Though it was clear that Peking could never take the place of Moscow as a source of effective military and economic supply, a few gestures in that direction might well cause Moscow to raise the terms offered to him.

Castro's first visit to Moscow

When, on 28 April, in response to a cordial invitation from Khrushchev, Castro arrived in Moscow for a five-weeks visit, he was given a hero's welcome and made the object of the most flattering attention. The joint communiqué issued over the signature of Khrushchev and himself towards the end of his stay declared that discussions had been conducted in an atmosphere of 'warmth and complete mutual understanding' and had revealed a complete identity of views between the participants (182).

On returning to Cuba, Castro gave an enthusiastic account of his visit to the Soviet Union and expressed his admiration for its people and for its leader, whom he described as 'an extraordinarily human person' and 'of most luminous intelligence'.[b] Each side had reason to feel satisfied. Castro's personal prestige had been enhanced and his country recognized as a full member of the Soviet bloc, increased economic (and possibly military) aid had been promised, and the militant creed of his Declarations of Havana endorsed. Khrushchev could feel confident that the damage to Cuban-Soviet relations had been made good and that Castro would not follow a line at variance with his policy of 'peaceful coexistence'. But the Cubans soon showed that they were still far from accepting all Soviet positions. In his annual 26 July speech Castro reverted to his militant call for Revolution throughout Latin America, and declared that those who followed Cuba's example 'will have the firm support of the Soviet Union and the whole Socialist camp'.[c] Soon afterwards there followed the publication *in extenso* of the famous letter of 14 June from the Central Committee of the Chinese Communist Party to the CPSU[d] as well as the latter's reply, showing that Cuba still wished to maintain as neutral a stance as possible in the Sino-Soviet dispute. Cuba's refusal to sign the Nuclear Test-Ban Treaty was a further demonstration of independence (183).

Castro's second visit

In January 1964 Castro again visited the Soviet Union. The reasons for this

---

[a] 'In the Cuban events, the Cuban people and their leaders were determined to fight to the death to defend the sovereignty of their fatherland; they displayed great heroism and high principle. They did not commit the error of adventurism, nor did they commit the error of capitulationism. But during the Cuban events certain people first committed the error of adventurism, and then committed the error of capitulationism, wanting the Cuban people to accept humiliating terms which would have meant the sacrifice of the sovereignty of their country' (*Peking Review*, 15 Mar. 1963, quoting *Red Flag* of 4 Mar. 1963).

[b] TV interview, 4 June 1963.

[c] *Hoy*, 27 July 1963.

[d] *Peking Review*, 21 June 1963, published in *Cuba socialista*, Aug. 1963.

second visit are not altogether clear; the impact on the international situation of such grave events as the death of President Kennedy and the outbreak of serious anti-American riots in Panama, and also concern about Cuba's economic situation may well have been factors. The joint communiqué issued at the end of the visit reaffirmed the common policies and attitudes which had been formulated last May and spelled out Cuba's closer identification with the Soviet line and even indicated a certain readiness—despite the inevitable denunciation of United States' actions, especially in Panama—to reach a détente with Washington (**184**). The most important result of the visit was probably in the economic field. The decision already indicated in the previous joint communiqué that Cuba should concentrate on increasing sugar production rather than proceed with grandiose plans for industrialization was now underwritten by a new long-term agreement for Soviet purchases of Cuban sugar at stable prices (**185**).

The fall of Khrushchev

The period of relatively good Soviet-Cuban relations and an apparent readiness on the Cuban side to find a *modus vivendi* with the United States lasted, with fluctuations, until the fall of Khrushchev in October 1964. This event took place only a few hours before the arrival of President Dorticós on an official visit to Moscow, but no substantial change in policy or attitude was reflected in the joint communiqué issued at the end of his visit beyond a sharper tone in the denunciations of United States 'imperialism' (**186**). Some weeks later leaders of the Latin American Communist Parties met, apparently in Havana, and drew up a number of resolutions reaffirming the unity of the Cuban and other Communist Parties in support of the Soviet line and implicitly condemning the Chinese position.[a] The resolutions also denoted a success for Cuba in that they stressed the need to rally support for her and approved the tactics of armed struggle in Venezuela, Colombia, Guatemala, Paraguay, and Haiti.[b] That Cuba had no intention, however, of letting other parties dictate the line she was to follow was made clear in Castro's speeches of 2 January and 13 March 1965 (**187, 189**).[c] In the latter speech Castro criticized the Chinese (without alluding to them by name) for 'smuggling in the apple of discord' and making propaganda in Cuba. To remain neutral in the Sino-Soviet dispute was growing more and more difficult, and the dispatch of a delegation headed by his brother Raúl to attend the Consultative Meeting of Communist Parties in Moscow at the beginning of March seemed to indicate that, if he had to choose between the contenders, Castro would opt for the Russians. Nevertheless, his speech of 13 March also revealed Castro's dissatisfaction with the scale of the

---

[a] 'With diabolic aims and in order to further their anti-Marxist plans by exploiting the sympathies which Revolutionary Cuba enjoys amongst Communists from various countries, the Soviet revisionists had organized this meeting in Havana' (*Zeri i popullit* (Albania), 16 Feb. 1965. See also p. 28).
[b] Text in *Revolución*, 19 Jan. 1965; see also comment in *World Marxist Review*, Mar. 1965.
[c] Castro's warning seems to have been aimed at the Chinese rather than the Russians, who published the full text of his speech in *Pravda*, 16 Mar. 1965.

military assistance which the Communist powers were giving to Vietnam and —by implication—might one day be required to give to Cuba.

New 'transitory' differences with Moscow

When, six weeks later, the American marines landed to forestall a threatened Communist take-over in Santo Domingo, the Soviet Union could do nothing beyond denouncing the United States in the Security Council. Whatever alarm Castro may have felt privately at this Soviet passivity in an area so vital to his own security, he confined himself to qualifying as 'transitory' such differences as might arise between members of the Socialist camp **(190)**. 'Che' Guevara, whose impatience with what he deemed to be Soviet lukewarmness in the revolutionary cause had made it advisable for him to leave Cuba for a tour of Africa,[a] where new revolutionary openings could be investigated in compensation for those now denied to Cuba in Latin America, gave freer expression to some of his misgivings about Soviet policy **(188)**. Cuba was now finding herself more and more exposed to the pressures of the Sino-Soviet dispute, and on 18 September Castro had to protest strongly to the Chinese chargé d'affaires against the dissemination of Chinese propaganda amongst officials and members of the armed forces.[b]

The new Cuban CP

At the beginning of October it was announced that a Central Committee had been set up for the *Partido Unido de la Revolución Socialista* (PURS) and that the latter would in future be known as the Cuban Communist Party. This step towards what promised to be the strengthening of collective leadership and the institutionalizing of the Cuban Revolution along orthodox lines may have been the fruit of patient Soviet diplomacy and was at once welcomed by Moscow **(191)**. In his speech announcing the changes, Castro stressed that each Party had the right to interpret Marxism-Leninism in its own way—a theme which he was to develop more fully in later speeches **(189)**. Later in the same month the Soviet Foreign Minister Gromyko paid a four-day visit to Cuba. No announcement was made as to the subject of his discussions with Castro, but these may well have included the line to be followed at the Tricontinental Conference scheduled to meet in Havana in the following January.[c] The Russians seem to have been taken aback by the sharp reaction of the Latin American Governments to the endorsement given by the Soviet delegate to the militant resolutions sponsored by the Conference, and their ingenuous disclaimers served less to allay alarm than to irritate the Cubans.

[a] Guevara returned to Cuba in mid-March 1965 but—perhaps out of deference to the Soviet Union—was given no further role in Cuban public life. In his speech of 3 October Castro read out his famous letter declaring that Guevara had left to continue his revolutionary calling elsewhere. Nothing more was heard of his movements until it became known in the spring of 1967 that he was leading an incipient guerrilla movement in Bolivia, where he was killed the following October.

[b] 'Statement of 5 February 1966 by Fidel Castro', *Cuba socialista*, Mar. 1966.

[c] See above, p. 28.

Criticism of Soviet Latin American policy

It was now becoming clear that the more the Russians succeeded in developing their economic and political links with other Latin American countries, the greater would be the strain imposed upon their 'special relationship' with Cuba, and the more difficult to reconcile Castro's insistence on 'instant revolution' with Moscow's more cautious long-term objectives. Castro took particular exception to the friendly relations which Moscow had been at pains to cultivate with President Frei's Christian Democrat administration in Chile, and to the Soviet overtures to the 'oligarchic' Government in Bogotá which had been taking firm action against the Colombian guerrillas (**193**). But Moscow showed little disposition to be influenced by Cuban views. In January 1967 the Soviet Union extended important credits to Chile[a] and reaffirmed her conviction that trade could benefit both the Soviet and Latin American economies 'no matter what obstacles were placed in the way'. The Soviet press, however, continued to voice support for Cuba and revolutionary action in Latin America.[b] That Cuban and Soviet objectives nevertheless remained difficult to reconcile was suggested by the cool reception given to the Soviet Prime Minister when he unexpectedly visited Havana in June 1967, after attending the United Nations and conferring with President Johnson at Glassboro (**194**).[c] No official communiqué was issued as to the scope of the talks, but the composition of the teams taking part in them suggests that they were concerned with military and economic questions as well as with the line which the Cubans intended to follow at the forthcoming OLAS Conference.

The OLAS Conference

The OLAS Conference of 31 July–10 August 1967 (to which Moscow sent observers) presented the Soviet Union with something of the same dilemma which they had encountered over the Tricontinental Conference—how to endorse revolutionary action in Latin America without sacrificing their relations with the Governments in power. The Conference reaffirmed the Cuban thesis that the surest path to revolution was that of armed struggle, and in closed session and in the teeth of opposition from representatives of the orthodox Latin American Communist Parties, passed a resolution criticizing the Socialist powers for supporting the 'oligarchies'. Though this resolution was withheld from publication, Castro repeated the same strictures in his closing speech to the Conference (**192**). He also savagely attacked the pro-Moscow Venezuelan Communist Party for abandoning violent in favour of non-violent tactics. Though Moscow did not react directly to these criticisms, disapproval was obliquely expressed through the reproduction in the Soviet

[a] See above, p. 36.

[b] On 20 May 1967 Tass reported the beginning of a Week of Solidarity with the Latin American peoples, and the Soviet press proceeded to publish numerous articles in support of Cuba and guerrilla movements in Venezuela and Colombia.

[c] Though Kosygin was given a warmer send-off, suggesting that at least some improvement in Soviet-Cuban relations had resulted from his visit, Tass described the talks as 'a frank exchange of opinions'—a euphemism normally indicating disagreement.

press of articles written by Latin American Communist leaders critical of the Cuban line.[a] At the same time, efforts were made to minimize the differences with Havana by renewed declarations of Soviet support for Cuba in the face of an alleged intensification of United States pressure against her. But the real state of Cuban-Soviet relations was revealed by Castro's decision to send to the fiftieth anniversary celebrations in Moscow only a low-powered delegation which took little part in them and returned before they were over. Castro also declined (January 1968) to send a delegation to Budapest for the Consultative Meeting of Communist Parties called to consider the convening of a world conference of Communist Parties.

The shortage of oil supplies

The political differences between Moscow and Havana were not eased by the latter's mounting economic difficulties and the obvious handle which the latter offered for the exercise of Soviet pressure. At the beginning of January 1968 Castro announced that strict petrol rationing would have to be introduced. He declared that the Soviet Union, on whom Cuba wholly depended for her oil supplies, had made a 'considerable effort' to meet Cuba's growing needs, but her ability to keep pace with them was limited.[b]

Disgrace of the 'microfaction'

Speculation that Moscow would, and indeed should, exploit this situation as a means of making Castro toe the line was soon to be forthcoming from an unexpected quarter.[c] At the end of January it was announced that a 'microfaction' led by Aníbal Escalante and composed of members of the former Communist Party (PSP) had been arrested for activities against the Revolutionary Government for which they had attempted to enlist Soviet support. Details of these alleged intrigues, together with the names of the Soviet officials concerned, were given in a long statement to the Central Committee of the Cuban Communist Party by Raúl Castro, who took care, however, to qualify his strictures by a reference to the 'exemplary conduct' of most Soviet officials towards the Revolutionary Government (**195**). Fidel Castro also addressed the Central Committee on the subject at even greater length, but his speech was not published—so he later affirmed—since that would have raised 'questions of a diplomatic nature' (**197**). The fate of the 'microfaction'—Escalante and over thirty others received individual sentences of up to fifteen years imprisonment—

---

[a] An important article of this nature by the General Secretary of the Chilean CP, Luis Corvalán, was reproduced in *Pravda* on the eve of the opening of the OLAS Conference. On 25 October a still more outspoken article by the veteran Argentine Communist Rodolfo Ghioldi was published. Two days later *Pravda* published yet another article by Corvalán commending Soviet efforts to develop relations with Chile and other Latin American countries.

[b] *Granma*, 3 Jan. 1968.

[c] The Russians seem to have anticipated that they might be accused of trying to exert pressure in this way. A detailed report in *Pravda* of 29 December 1967 listing the number of shipments made to Cuba and asserting that 'the Soviet Union accurately honours signed contracts' was presumably published to disarm criticism in advance of Castro's statement.

led other 'old Communists' to declare hastily that their admiration for the Soviet Union would always be subordinate to Cuban national interests (**196**).[a]

Continuation of strained relations

If the castigation of the 'microfaction' and their Soviet sympathizers was intended as a warning to the Russians against any intervention in Cuba's internal affairs, Moscow refused to rise to the bait.[b] Some weeks later, however, the opportunity was taken to restate the Soviet position in an authoritative article by Professor Volsky, the Director of the Latin American Institute in Moscow. Volsky reminded his readers that whilst 'Cuba itself chose Socialism', this choice had been made possible thanks to the existence and the help of the Soviet Union (**62**), and as far as the revolutionary prospects in other parts of Latin America were concerned, the local Communist Parties were rightly making every effort to combine all forms of struggle rather than concentrate on any one of them (i.e. Cuban guerrilla tactics). As for economic relations between the two countries, Castro made a point, in a speech of 13 March 1968, of reminding his listeners of the bitter experience 'of having to depend to a considerable degree on things which come from outside and how that can become a weapon and at least create a temptation to use it against our country' (**197**). Havana's announcement, ten days later, that the 1968 trade protocol between Cuba and the Soviet Union had at last been signed after an unusually long delay 'because a mid-term trade treaty was being negotiated . . . and the two sides had not reached common viewpoints' (**198**) revealed that he had solid grounds for misgivings.[c] It was thus scarcely surprising that his Government should have reached an agreement the following month with Rumania on terms 'very favourable' to Cuba for the supply of oil-drilling equipment which would step up the exploitation of Cuba's own oil resources and thus lessen her independence on the Soviet Union in that vital sector of her economy.

The invasion of Czechoslovakia

The Soviet invasion of Czechoslovakia in August 1968 forced Castro, like other political leaders throughout the world, to define his attitude towards the

[a] This statement by Carlos Rafael Rodríguez is in interesting contrast to the fulsome expression of devotion to the Soviet Union previously voiced by other 'old Communists' (**111–12**).

[b] Soviet comment on the 'microfaction' affair seems to have been limited to a brief Tass report published in *Pravda* of 30 January which refrained from mentioning that the crimes imputed to the 'old Communists' had been their dissatisfaction with Castro's failure to follow the Moscow line and their attempts to induce the Soviet Union to bring him to heel.

[c] The protocol came within the framework of the 1965–70 Cuban-Soviet trade agreement. The Cubans are believed to have sought an extension of the protocol to cover the remaining three years of the treaty period, but to have met with Soviet unwillingness to underwrite their freedom of economic manoeuvre to this extent. The statement issued by Moscow on the signature of the protocol glossed over these differences and implied instead Soviet generosity in extending to Cuba a credit of $328 million 'to pay for expenditure involved in the import of commodities from the USSR'. This may have been intended as an oblique reminder of the extent of Cuban indebtedness to the Soviet Union, now estimated at between $1–2 billion.

realities of Soviet power. Up to the invasion, the Cuban press had reported fully and fairly objectively on the course of Soviet-Czechoslovak relations, and some choices of phrase had even indicated a certain sympathy for Prague. Castro's frequent assertions that every Party had the right to choose its own revolutionary path and to interpret Marxism-Leninism according to its own lights might also have been thought to predispose Cuba in favour of the Czechoslovak case. But in a radio and television broadcast of 23 August Castro declared his support for the Soviet action. It was, he asserted, a 'bitter necessity', since Czechoslovakia was 'moving toward a counterrevolutionary position' (199). National sovereignty, he admitted, had been violated, but the necessity of preserving the Revolution overrode purely legal considerations. The invasion of Czechoslovakia was probably also seen by Castro as a not unwelcome development since it threw into relief the defects of the 'revisionist' brand of East European communism in contrast to the militant Cuban brand, and lessened the prospect of any rapprochement between the Soviet Union and the United States which might endanger the existence of his own Revolution. Castro's qualified support for the Soviet action in Czechoslovakia came at a time when his country's economy, heavily dependent on Soviet goodwill, was facing increasing difficulties.[a] It marked a new stage of gradual improvement in Cuban-Soviet relations which found expression in the warm reference to the Soviet Union made by Castro in his Anniversary Speech of 2 January and by the satisfactory outcome of current Soviet-Cuban trade discussions early in 1969.

The Soviet balance-sheet at the close of 1968

By the end of 1968 the Soviet Union could look back upon half a century of relations with Latin America—relations tenuous enough at first and marked throughout with interruptions and setbacks. On the scale of global priorities, the area still ranked modestly, for the shadow of the United States' political, economic and military might lay heavily over it. But Latin America's very proximity to the West's centre of power might be seen as the measure of its interest for the Soviet Union. Even a limited extension of the latter's influence in this sensitive area—the proverbial 'backyard' of the United States—might have telling effects. A stroke of fortune, rather than design, had led to the flouting of Washington's power and the emergence of a state which proclaimed itself to be Communist, and was certainly revolutionary and anti-American, within 100 miles of the United States' borders. For more than ten years, despite economic pressure and indirect efforts to dislodge him, Fidel Castro had maintained himself in power. So much was to the gain of the Communist

---

[a] According to Orlando Castro Hidalgo, an officer of the Cuban Intelligence Service who defected to the United States early in 1969, Fidel Castro had signed a secret agreement with the USSR in the previous year undertaking to mute his criticisms of the Soviet Union and the pro-Moscow Latin American Communist Parties in return for a Soviet pledge to maintain a high level of economic support, including increased deliveries of oil, and to provide an additional 5,000 technicians to stiffen Cuba's lagging economy (*Christian Science Monitor*, 16 July 1969).

camp. But this advantage was to some extent offset by the fact that Moscow's Cuban ally was costly to support, unpredictable, fiercely nationalistic, averse to guidance from Moscow, and determined not only to run his country according to his own interpretation of Communism, but to foment convulsions on the mainland of Latin America where and how he fancied, regardless of the interests of his Soviet ally. The latter now maintained diplomatic relations with six other countries—Mexico, Brazil, Uruguay, Chile, Argentina, and Colombiaᵃ—and trade relations with a number of others. The Russian invasion of Czechoslovakia had shocked the Latin American Governments into a realization of the hollowness of Moscow's lip-service to the principle of non-interference in the affairs of other states to which they attached such cardinal importance. Yet, significantly, none of the countries which had relations with Moscow was prompted to break them off, as they had (with one exception) broken them off with a patently subversive Cuba. How serious, in fact, was the Soviet Union now to be taken as a purveyor of revolution in the Western hemisphere? The statements of her spokesmen on this score had always been contradictory, and her policies now appeared increasingly pragmatic and ambivalent. Their true direction would only become apparent in the years ahead.

ᵃ Negotiations with Peru were also at an advanced stage but diplomatic relations were not formally established until 2 February 1969.

6

Supplementary Notes

[1](p. 2) Marx was commissioned to write his article for the *New American Cyclopaedia* (1859). He based his assessment of Bolívar's character and achievement on the memoirs of Ducoudray-Holstein, a Frenchman who had fought in the French revolutionary wars and served briefly as chief of staff to Bolívar before throwing up his post and returning to Europe where he sought to justify his conduct by denigrating the Liberator. Nor, despite the remonstrances of the editor of the Cyclopaedia who objected to the partisan treatment given to the subject, did Marx show any disposition to modify his hostile view of Bolívar: 'As regards the "Partisan style"', he wrote to Engels on 14 February 1858, 'I have certainly somewhat gone beyond the usual tone of an encyclopaedia. But it would have been asking too much to present this most cowardly, brutal and wretched canaille as a Napoleon' (*Marx-Engels Werke* (Berlin), xxix. 280). Soviet historians seem at first to have neglected, or to have been ignorant of, Marx's essay, but from the late 1930s the official encyclopaedias began to draw heavily upon it for their brief references to Bolívar and the wars of independence. However, in the 1959 and subsequent editions of the *Small Soviet Encyclopaedia* the references to Marx's essay are dropped. The authors of an article in *Voprosy istorii* (Nov. 1956, p. 53) had already declared that 'one cannot consider as correct the negative evaluation of personality and activity of Bolívar made in this article. Marx did not have at his disposal a number of most important data.'

[2](p. 3) Roy states in his *Memoirs* (p. 194) that Borodin 'had come to the New World as the first emissary of the newly founded Communist International. . . . He had lived in the United States as Michael Gruzenburg, with which name he was born in a Hebrew priestly family. He further confided that Lenin knew him by that name.' Borodin's mission was to smuggle a quantity of crown jewels, sewn into the lining of two leather suitcases, into the United States. 'The proceeds were to be used firstly to relieve the distress of the stranded trade delegation, and the remainder to finance the Communist Movement in the New World.' The cases went astray, but after many adventures, were recovered and returned intact to Moscow. When he arrived in Mexico, Borodin was penniless, but was assisted by Roy out of subsidies advanced to him by the Germans for anti-Allied work. Charlie Phillips, an American Communist living at the time in Mexico City, states (interview with 'Manuel Gómez', *Survey*, no. 53, October 1964, p. 33) that Borodin 'said he had come to Mexico with credentials from the Soviet Government as Ambassador to Mexico, and he did have, I understand, such credentials, though I never asked to see them. But he wanted to have President Carranza sounded out. He was to present these credentials only if there was an indication that they would be accepted, and that the Soviet Government would be recognised by Carranza. He could not get a favourable response to that. Carranza was very anti-American, but he was pro-German, and he had no intention of rocking the boat to the extent that everyone—all of the great powers—would be against him. Borodin had another mission, even if he became Ambassador to Mexico, and that was to finance and operate the organisation of what we would now call Communist movements in Latin America, with Mexico as the Centre. . . . He was very ignorant about Latin America.'

[3](p. 3) 'With Borodin's consent, I planned his meeting President Carranza. He readily accepted an invitation to a dinner party, on which occasion a friend of mine who had recently come to Mexico would have the privilege of being presented to him. The President of the Chamber of Deputies, don Manuel, the Rector of the University, Maestro Caso, and the Foreign Minister, were the other guests.

'Borodin rose to the occasion and made a very good impression on the President

60

and other distinguished guests who were surprised to meet a highly cultured man calling himself a Bolshevik. He announced that the new regime in Russia fully sympathised with the struggle of the Latin American peoples against imperialism and was eager to help it in every possible manner. With that purpose, a Latin American Bureau of the Communist International should be established in Mexico, provided that His Excellency the President of the Republic consented. I was to be in charge of the proposed Centre to organise resistance to American Imperialism.

'Carranza saw the prospect of his dream of a Latin American League being realised in a different form. He would not miss the opportunity and requested Borodin to transmit his good wishes to the head of the new regime in Russia. For Carranza to say so might not have been more than a gesture of courtesy. But made in the presence of his Foreign Minister and the head of the Legislative branch of the State it could also be taken for a *de facto* recognition of the new regime in Russia. In subsequent talks, the latter two dignitaries hinted that it was meant to be so.

'Borodin felt that he had scored a diplomatic victory which would raise his prestige in Moscow. Regarding the President's gesture of courtesy at the dinner party as the green signal, the Foreign Minister granted the facility for Borodin to contact the West European Bureau of the Comintern in Holland. The good offices of the Mexican Government enabled him also to get in touch directly with Moscow via Scandinavia. ... He reported his diplomatic achievement as well as the failure to carry out the original mission, but also mentioned that all possible attempts were being made to recover the loss, and that in the meantime most urgent requirements had been met out of unexpected local resources.

'Whilst writing his reports, which I transmitted through the Mexican Foreign Office, Borodin relapsed into his habitual secretiveness. ... He never showed me the reports nor discussed them with me' (Roy, *Memoirs*, pp. 20–2). Borodin left Mexico after a few months and returned to Moscow, where the Comintern sent him to play a leading role in the Chinese Revolution.

[4](p. 4) There was undoubtedly a good deal of popular enthusiasm at that time in Mexico for the Communist Revolution in Russia, coupled with total ignorance as to its nature. This is well illustrated by an experience related by Roy in his *Memoirs* (p. 154) where he describes meeting a military commander in N.W. Mexico and asking his permission to organize a branch of the Socialist Party in that area. The Mexican readily gave his permission and surprised him by exclaiming: 'We are all Bolsheviks'. He then went on to explain: 'I don't know what is Socialism; but I am a Bolshevik, like all patriotic Mexicans. ... The Yankees do not like the Bolsheviks; they are our enemies; therefore the Bolsheviks must be our friends, and we must be their friends. We are all Bolsheviks.'

[5](p. 5) Pestkovsky did not drop his Latin American activities after his return to Moscow. In 1928, under the pen-name of Andrey Volsky, he published the first Soviet monograph on Latin American history: *Istoriya meksikanskikh revolyutsy* (see J. Gregory Oswald, *The Soviet Image of Latin America* (Austin, Texas UP for Conference on Latin American History, 1970)). He also worked under Piatnitsky in the important Organization Department of the Comintern. According to Eudocio Ravines (*La gran estafa* (Santiago, 1957), entry under Pestkovsky in the Appendix) he continued to concern himself with Latin American affairs under the assumed names of Ortega and Banderas; a delegate of the latter name figures in the records of the 6th Comintern Congress as criticizing the theses presented by Jules Humbert-Droz, head of the ECCI's Latin American Section (*Inprecorr*, no. 72, 1928, p. 1307). Ravines states that he was ultimately accused of being a counter-revolutionary and enemy of the people and disappeared in one of Stalin's purges.

[6](p. 7) On 23 May 1940, just under three months before the assassination of Trotsky, an unsuccessful *attentat* was carried out by a group of armed men who broke into Trotsky's residence. The raid is believed to have been organized by Siqueiros. 'The year before he had returned from Spain, where he had commanded several brigades during the Civil War. . . . The Communist party had censured him recently for misdemeanours in handling of party funds. He was hurt and eager to regain favour. . . . He called on men who had fought under him in Spain, and on Mexican miners' (Isaac Deutscher, *The Prophet Outcast: Trotsky (1929–40* (London, 1963), pp. 485–6).

[7](p. 7) President Portes Gil recalls that 'Mme Kollontay was replaced by Dr Makar, who was very far from possessing the qualities of diplomatic ability and tact which characterized his predecessor. On the contrary, Dr Makar, with whom I had dealings on several occasions, was a man without much culture, with little knowledge of our conditions, and of limited intellectual abilities. He undoubtedly bore the chief responsibility for Mexico's rupture of friendly relations with Soviet Russia in January 1930. . . . The Soviet Legation in Mexico was a centre for political and propaganda unrest. Meetings of a political nature, which many of our nationals were invited to attend, were frequently held there. These persons were trained in agitation activities and then sent out from it for purely political ends to the different states of our country. . . . The so-called Mexican Communists of those days used to receive from them instructions and money they needed in order to attack the Mexican Government' (*Quince años de política mexicana* (1941), pp. 373–81).

[8](p. 9) Richard Krebs, alias Jan Valtin, who worked for a number of years as a courier for the Comintern, states that 'the money intended for Latin America was generally sent through the Soviet commercial agency, Yuzhamtorg, to Buenos Aires' (J. Valtin, *Sans patrie ni frontières* (New York, Editions de la Maison Française, 1941), pp. 254–7). Special couriers were sometimes sent, as he himself was sent to Montevideo for a meeting of the Profintern-sponsored *Confederación Sindical Latino-Americana* in 1929, with large sums of money sewn into the lining of specially prepared suitcases (such as those previously carried by Borodin) which were then handed over to representatives of the South American Secretariat.

[9](p. 11) For nearly a decade, first as head of the Latin Secretariat and then of the Latin American Secretariat, the chief Comintern official concerned with Latin America was Jules Humbert-Droz, a former Swiss Protestant minister and friend of Lenin during the latter's exile. Other Comintern officials concerned with Latin American affairs were the Swiss 'Stirner', the Bulgarian Minieff ('Stefanov'), and the Russian Vasiliyev. As an associate of Bukharin, Humbert-Droz later incurred the suspicion of Stalin, who censured him at an ECCI meeting on 19 December 1928 for his allegedly Rightest attitude to the German question. He was forced by Manuilsky to make self-criticism (published in *Inprecorr*, 6 Nov. 1930, p. 1043) and at the end of 1931 gave up his Comintern post and returned to Switzerland, where he continued to work for the Communist Party until expelled from it in 1943 (D. Drachkovitch and R. Lazitch, *The Comintern; Historical High-Lights* (Stamford UP, Hoover Inst., 1966), pp. 226–31). He was succeeded as head of the Latin American Secretariat by A. Guralsky.

[10](p. 17) Even Lafertte, who came to be the leading figure in the Party, did not always take kindly to the guiding hand of the Comintern, to judge from the guarded references contained in his memoirs: 'The Communist International was an office which did a lot of good to the Communist Parties, specially to those which were new fledgelings, like the Chilean. . . . The International gave us the experience of the whole world labour movement. Our relations with it were limited to the interchange

of experience. To imagine that anyone in Moscow ever attempted to settle the internal problems of Chile is simply absurd. . . . The South American Secretariat helped us positively with advice and information. At the Congress which was held in 1926 it sent us an important letter (**43**) criticizing our Party regarding its organization which was based on meetings, its leaders, and its parliamentary representatives. . . . The Congress had an enormous importance on account of the fundamental change applied to the organic systems. The system of meetings was done away with, and cell activity was adopted. . . . Miguel Contreras, from the Secretariat of the Communist International in Buenos Aires, attended this Congress, discussed matters with us, got to know our problems, and when he was properly informed, he gave his opinion. But this was very far from being what many people believe or say they believe; an inspector. No; the Communist International did not send inspectors, but comrades, friends. Nevertheless, I think there were some who did more harm than good on account of their overbearing character, or because they enforced the line in a dogmatic way, thus bringing a negative influence to bear on the militants of weak parties' (E. Lafertte, *Vida de un comunista* (Santiago, 1961), pp. 186–7).

[11](p. 17) Lafertte (pp. 210–14) relates that a Chilean Communist named Donoso had visited Moscow—presumably in 1928—to report to the Comintern on the situation in Chile. 'He explained what errors had been committed, the effects of the repression and the attempts made by the Ibáñez dictatorship to dismantle piece by piece the whole labour organization which had been built up through years of struggle.' But to his great surprise, Donoso noted that the comrades of the International attached no credence to his words. They did not seem to be impressed by the disastrous picture he had painted and which basically represented the plight of the Chilean labour movement. 'The information which we have received from Chile', they told him, 'is totally different.' Lafertte goes on to blame the then Secretary of the Party, Iriarte, for having misled the Comintern by sending unjustifiably rosy accounts of the situation in Chile.

[12](p. 17) This is the conclusion reached by Boris Goldenberg (*Der Ostblock und die Entwicklungsländer* (Hanover), no. 26, Dec. 1966, pp. 377–97) on the basis of the available evidence. General Bravo, who played a prominent part in the political events of the times, writes that 'the members of the armed forces were very badly paid as it was. A further reduction of their rations would practically condemn them to starvation'. But he goes on to assert that 'the root of the mutiny must be sought for in the cells which had been formed on the warship *Almirante Latorre* whilst it was in England for repairs. This should not surprise us, for—as we know—similar cells appeared on ships of the British navy and started an uprising that more or less coincided with the Chilean fleet mutiny' (Leonidas Bravo Ríos, *Lo que supo un auditor de guerra* (Santiago, 1955), pp. 29–30). Lafertte relates (*Vida de un comunista*, pp. 229–40) that the Communist Party organization in Coquimbo knew in advance that the mutiny would break out, and informed him to this effect, but he affirms that 'we helped the mutiny, and those who had taken part in it after it had been suppressed, as far as we were able; but we had nothing to do with starting it'. After its failure, Lafertte travelled to Montevideo to confer with the South American Secretariat, and then on to Moscow. Whilst he was still there, the Communists made an armed assault on a barracks at Copiapó, with considerable loss of life. Lafertte disclaimed any knowledge of or responsibility for this action and maintained that it was a 'police provocation'. The truth seems to be that the Chilean Communists were at the time still so divided into factions and local branches acting independently that no effective control was exercised by the Central Committee or the Comintern. The latter later pronounced that 'the revolutionary events of 1931 and 1932 found the Chilean

Communist Party insufficiently prepared' (*Kommunisticheski international pered VII Vsemirnym Kongressom: materialy* (Moscow, 1935)).

[13](p. 25) Osvaldo Peralva, the Brazilian Communist who was sent to the Party School in Moscow in 1953 and learned in detail how this control was exercised, discovered that the effective leader of the party was 'Silva Lobos', a Russian whose real name was Andrey Mikhailovich Sivolobov. 'There was not a single document of importance in the Brazilian Communist Party which had not been submitted for the prior approval of Sivolobov and received his imprimatur before being issued.' Sivolobov would secure the dismissal of Brazilian Communist officials to whom he took a dislike and overruled decisions of which he disapproved, e.g. the Communists' intention to support an official project for land reform, in case it might win the sympathy of the peasantry for the 'bourgeois Government' and rob the Communists of a valued watchword. Sivolobov's domination proved the more unfortunate for the Party because of his ignorance of the real conditions in the country. One blatant illustration of this ignorance was his advocacy of the formation of an 'Autonomous Negro Republic' within Brazil (Peralva, *O retrato*, pp. 26 ff.). Another was his assessment of the Social Democrat Party (PSD) led by President Kubitschek and supported by conservative landowners as a 'workers' party' (ibid., p. 34). The relevant passages were reproduced in *O Globo* in order to show up the extent of Russian ignorance of Brazilian politics. The appearance in 1966 of Sivolobov's *Economic Problems of the Alliance of the Working Class and the Peasantry in Latin America* suggests, however, that he continued to be regarded as a leading Soviet specialist on Latin America.

[14](p. 32) The initiative had, in fact, come chiefly from Moscow. As a first step towards the establishment of diplomatic relations, a Soviet commercial mission arrived in Buenos Aires in April 1946, headed by Konstantin Vasiliyevich Shevelev, subsequently appointed commercial attaché at the Soviet Embassy. Shevelev also made contact with the Argentine CP, whose organ *La Hora* abruptly ceased criticizing the Perón regime and turned its guns against the Anglo-Saxon powers. Except for Catholic papers like *El Pueblo*, the Argentine press as a whole welcomed the establishment of diplomatic relations, though *La Prensa* (8 June 1946) criticized Soviet attempts to show that the initiative came from Argentina, and expressed the hope that some form of apology had been received for the treatment meted out to Argentina's last diplomatic representative after the Revolution.

[15](p. 33) At the end of the Second World War, at least 300,000 settlers of Russian origin were living in Argentina, as well as large communities of Poles and Yugoslavs. Following the setting up of the Slav Committee in Moscow in mid-1942, attempts were made to reawaken the Slav consciousness of these groups. A Co-ordinating Committee was established in Montevideo with a view to welding together their varied organizations and imposing a unified political line. A Soviet official, Valentin Vasiliyevich Ryabov, played a leading role in this work, first as Soviet Consul in Montevideo and, after the establishment of diplomatic relations between the USSR and Argentina, as member of the Soviet mission in Buenos Aires. In November a Slav Congress was held in Buenos Aires, as a result of which there was formed the *Unión Eslava* which, under the presidency of the Russian Pavel Shostakovsky, succeeded in bringing most of the Slavs in South America under its control. The Stalin–Tito rift in 1948 proved a grave setback for the *Unión Eslava*. Though the Soviet Embassy in Buenos Aires forbade a discussion of the dispute in the Union and attempted to impose the Moscow line, rival factions came to blows at the 3rd Slav Congress held in Buenos Aires in 1949 (**70**). In April of that year the Argentine authorities issued a decree dissolving the Union and its affiliated organization. It was later revived and in 1955 organized a further Congress which endorsed the Moscow-

sponsored World Peace Appeal and called for further measures to unify the Slav communities in the Western hemisphere. These communities do not, however, appear to have figured as a major factor in Soviet policies in Latin America.

[16](p. 44) These soundings appear to have been made both through their regular channels with the PSP, and direct with those elements in the 26 July Movement which they considered reliable. The *Washington Post* of 22 Aug. 1959 reported that Vadim Kochergin, a Soviet intelligence officer, had visited Cuba in May 1959, ostensibly on a trade union mission, but actually in order to give the Cuban Communists guidance on how best to penetrate the Castro Government. Shortly afterwards, in June, according to Daniel James (*Cuba: the First Soviet Satellite in the Americas* (New York, 1961), pp. 235–8) the first contacts were established in Mexico City between Soviet intelligence officers and Ramiro Valdés, Castro's chief intelligence officer. What is certain is that there arrived in Havana at the beginning of October, ostensibly as an accredited Tass correspondent, the Soviet official Aleksandr Alekseyev, who subsequently joined the staff of the Soviet Legation and was later promoted over the heads of his colleagues to be Soviet Ambassador to Cuba. According to S. Cazalis, a well-informed and independent commentator writing for the Communist newspaper *Hoy* under the pseudonym of Siquitrilla, Alekseyev was the bearer of a personal message to Fidel Castro from Khrushchev, which he delivered after the trial and sentencing of H. Matos, the anti-Communist former comrade-in-arms of Castro, had shown that the latter was now firmly committed to the pro-Communist line (S. Cazalis, *Cuba Ahora* (Caracas, 1967), p. 50). Khrushchev's message was allegedly to reassure Castro that he had no need to use the PSP as intermediaries but could deal directly and personally with Moscow, and reportedly ran as follows: 'The Soviet Government wishes to express to you that it does not consider any party as an intermediary between itself and you. Comrade Khrushchev puts all his support behind you, whom he considers to be the authentic leader of the Revolution.' Confirmation of this story is lacking, but it would certainly help to explain Castro's confidence in moving against Aníbal Escalante, one of the foremost leaders of the PSP, on the grounds of 'factionalism', and Moscow's speedy endorsement of this step.

[17](p. 49) 'Moscow offered them to us. . . . They explained that in accepting them we would be reinforcing the Socialist camp the world over, and because we had received important aid from the Socialist camp we estimated that we could not decline. That is why we accepted them. It was not in order to assure our own defence, but first of all to reinforce Socialism on the international scale. Such is the truth, even if other explanations are furnished elsewhere' (interview given by Castro to Claude Julien of *Le Monde* (*Le Monde*, 22 Mar. 1963)). To another correspondent he stated that the proposal to instal rockets, 'which surprised us at first and gave us pause', stemmed from the Russians: 'We thought of a proclamation, an alliance, conventional military aid. . . . They reasoned that if conventional military assistance was the extent of their assistance, the United States might not hesitate to instigate an invasion, in which case Russia would retaliate and this would inevitably touch off a world war. . . . Under these circumstances, how could we Cubans refuse to share the risks taken to save us?' (Jean Daniel, 'Unofficial envoy; an historic report from two capitals', *New Republic*, 14 Dec. 1963). A full discussion of these various versions will also be found in A. Suárez, *Cuba: Castroism or Communism, 1959–66* (London, 1967) pp. 161–2.

Documents and Extracts

I. ANTECEDENTS

1. Tsarist Russia's interest in Latin America: paper prepared by Professor Volsky for a Conference on Latin American History, 1967:[1] excerpt (*p. 2*)

Economic and political relations of the Soviet Union with the countries of Latin America are on the increase. Annually expanding cultural and scientific relations serve to stimulate the growing interest of the Soviet people in Latin America's rich historical background, its distinctive culture, and the present day problems of that part of the world. Russian interest in Latin America extends over a long period of time. I should like to emphasize, therefore, that this interest in Latin America and the life of its people is not a passing fancy and did not develop overnight. This interest has its own history. Permit me to recount a few facts.

The first word of the New World in Russia dates back to 1530, and is recorded in the manuscript of the learned monk, Maxim Grek, who came to Moscow at the invitation of the Russian Tsar Basil III. In one of his commentaries, Maxim Grek makes special mention of Cuba, and this is the first geographical reference to the New World known in the Russian language. In the latter part of the eighteenth century, during the years 1782–4, Feodor Karzhavin, the Russian writer and translator, visited Cuba. All available evidence indicates that he was the first Russian to have spent some time in Latin America. One of the first Latin Americans to visit Russia, during 1786–7, was the distinguished leader of the liberation movement of the peoples of Latin America, Francisco Miranda, who sought support of European governments.

The study of Latin America by Russian researchers begins in the first quarter of the nineteenth century. From 1821 to 1828, an expedition to Brazil was undertaken by the Russian scholar, academician G. I. Langsdorf. The expedition produced a major study of the indigenous population of the Amazon River basin.

The struggle for liberation by the peoples of the colonies of Spain and Portugal gained great sympathy in the progressive circles of Russia.

Trade relations evolved between Russia and Latin America in the 1830's and 1840's, and cultural relations were established in the last half of the century. At that time, diplomatic relations between Brazil, Argentina, Mexico, Uruguay and Russia were also established.

The growth of scientific interest in the study of problems of that part of the

[1] V. Volsky (Director of the Latin American Institute, Moscow), 'Izucheniye Latiniskoy Ameriki v SSSR', in J. Gregory Oswald, ed., *The Soviet Image of Latin America* (Austin, Texas UP for Conference on Latin American History, 1970).

world and research on the life, customs, and culture of its peoples expanded apace with the broadening ties between Latin America and Russia. In the second half of the nineteenth century and in the beginning of the twentieth century, many Russian scholars visited Latin America to study its natural phenomena, climate, fauna, and flora. Among them was the founder of Russian climatology, Alexander Voeikov, the geographer and ethnographer, Veniukov, and the botanist, Al'bov. A clear indication of the interest of Russian researchers in the countries of Latin America was the complex expedition of 1915, comprising five young Russian scholars joined to study different scientific aspects of this region of the world. Their purpose was to study the natural life of South America, the material and spiritual culture of the Indians, and to compile ethnographic and zoological collections.

Direct ties and contacts between scientific institutions of Russia and the countries of Latin America were established before World War I. In 1910, for example, the Physiological Institute of Moscow University sent its scientific works to Caracas, Montevideo, Havana, the Museum of Natural History in Valparaíso, and others. The Naturalist Society of St Petersburg exchanged publications with the National Museum of Sao Paulo and with the scientific societies of Montevideo and Santiago. The National Library of Rio de Janeiro exchanged books with the public libraries of St Petersburg, Odessa, and the library of Moscow University.

The bases for research on Latin America, and ties between institutions and individual scholars were thereby established in Russia. Established in our country, at the same time, were the foundations for the systematic study of this part of the world and for the development of Latin American studies as an independent branch of science.

2. Karl Marx on Simón Bolívar:[1] excerpts (*p. 2*)

... The Colombian congress opened its sittings in January 1821, at Cucuta, published, August 30, a new constitution, and after Bolivar had again pretended to resign, renewed his powers. Having signed the new constitution, he obtained leave to undertake the campaign of Quito (1822), to which province the Spaniards had retired after their ejection by a general rising of the people from the isthmus of Panama. This campaign, ending in the incorporation of Quito, Pasto, and Guayaquil into Colombia, was nominally led by Bolivar and General Sucre, but the few successes of the corps were entirely owed to British officers, such as Col. Sands. During the campaigns of 1823–4, against the Spaniards, he no longer thought it necessary to keep up the appearance of generalship, but leaving the whole military task to General Sucre, limited himself to triumphal entries, manifestos, and the proclamation of constitutions. Through his Colombian bodyguard, he swayed the votes of the congress of Lima which, February 10, 1823, transferred to him the dictatorship, while he secured his re-election as President of Colombia by a new tender of resignation. His position had meanwhile been strengthened, what with the formal recognition of the new state on the part of England, and what with Sucre's

[1] *New American Cyclopaedia*, ed. Ripley and Dana (New York, 1859), iii. 445–6.

conquest of the provinces of Upper Peru, which the latter united into an independent republic, under the name of Bolivia. Here, where Sucre's bayonets were supreme, Bolivar gave full scope to his propensities for arbitrary power, by introducing the 'Bolivian code', an imitation of the Code Napoléon. It was his plan to transplant that code from Bolivia to Peru, and from Peru to Colombia—to keep the former states in check by Colombian troops, and the latter by the foreign legion and Peruvian soldiers. By force, mingled with intrigue, he succeeded indeed, for some weeks at least, in fastening his code upon Peru. The President and Liberator of Colombia, the protector and dictator of Peru, and the godfather of Bolivia, he had now reached the climax of his renown. . . .

In the year 1827,[1] from which the decline of his power dates, he contrived to assemble a congress at Panama, with the ostensible object of establishing a new democratic international code. Plenipotentiaries came from Colombia, Brazil, La Plata, Bolivia, Mexico, Guatemala, etc. What he really aimed at was the erection of the whole of South America into one federative republic, with himself as its dictator. . . .

Under the pressure of his bayonets, popular assemblies at Caracas, Cartagena, and Bogota, to which latter place he had repaired, anew invested him with dictatorial power. An attempt to assassinate him in his sleeping room at Bogota, which he only escaped by leaping in the dark from the balcony of the window, and lying concealed under a bridge, allowed him for some time to introduce a sort of military terrorism. He did not however lay hands on Santander, although he had participated in the conspiracy, while he put to death General Padilla, whose guilt was not proved at all, but who, as a man of colour, was not able to resist. Violent factions disturbing the republic in 1829, in a new appeal to the citizens, Bolivar invited them to frankly express their wishes as to the modifications to be introduced into the constitution. An assembly of notables at Caracas answered by denouncing his ambition, laying bare the weakness of his administration, declaring the separation of Venezuela from Colombia, and placing Paez at the head of the Republic. The Senate of Colombia stood by Bolivar, but other insurrections broke out at different points.

Having resigned for the fifth time, in January 1830, he again accepted the Presidency and left Bogota to wage war on Paez in the name of the Colombian congress.[2] Towards the end of March, 1830, he advanced at the head of 8,000 men, took Caracuta, which had revolted, and then turned upon the province of Maracaibo, where Paez awaited him with 12,000 men in a strong position. As soon as he became aware that Paez meant serious fighting, his courage collapsed. For a moment he even thought to subject himself to Paez, and declare against the congress; but the influence of his partisans at the congress vanished, and he was forced to tender his resignation, and notice being given

---

[1] The Congress of Panama was convened in 1826. Only the plenipotentiaries of Mexico, Colombia, Peru, and Guatemala (which then included Central America) attended the congress, with observers from Britain and the Netherlands.

[2] Bolívar did not leave Bogotá until 8 May 1830. His alleged campaign against Páez has no factual foundation.

to him that he must now stand by it, and that an annual pension would be granted to him on the condition of his departure for foreign countries. He accordingly sent his resignation to the congress, April 27, 1830. But hoping to regain power by the influence of his partisans, and a reaction setting in against Joaquim Mosquera, the new President of Colombia, he effected his retreat from Bogota in a very slow manner, and continued, under a variety of pretexts, to prolong his sojourn at San Pedro until the end of 1830, when he suddenly died.

The following portrait is given him by Ducoudray-Holstein:[1] 'Simon Bolivar is 5 ft 4 inches in height, his visage is long, his cheeks hollow, his complexion livid brown; his eyes are of middle size, and sunk deep in his head, which is covered thinly with hair. His moustaches give him a dark and wild aspect, particularly when he is in a passion. His whole body is thin and meagre. He had the appearance of a man 65 years old. In walking, his arms are in continual motion. He cannot walk long but becomes soon fatigued. He likes his hammock, where he sits and lolls. He gives way to sudden gusts of resentment, and becomes in a moment a madman, throws himself into his hammock, and utters curses and imprecations upon all around him. He loves to indulge in sarcasms upon absent people, reads only light French literature, is a bold rider, and passionately fond of waltzing. He is fond of hearing himself talk and giving toasts. In adversity, and destitute of aid from without, he is perfectly free from passion and violence of temper. He then becomes mild, patient, docile, and even submissive. In a great measure he conceals his faults under the politeness of a man educated in the so-called beau monde, possesses an almost Asiatic talent for dissimulation, and understands mankind better than the mass of his countrymen.'

3. Lenin's view of the neo-colonial status of Argentina:[2] excerpt (*p. 2*)

The division into two powerful groups of countries—possessors of colonies and colonies—is not the only feature typical of this period. There is also a variety of forms of dependent countries which formally are politically independent, but which are in fact caught up in the net of financial and diplomatic dependence. We have already referred to one of the forms—the semi-colony. An example of another is provided by Argentina.

'South America, especially Argentina,' writes Schultz Gaevernitz in his work on British Imperialism,[3] 'is so dependent financially on London that it may almost be described as a British commercial colony.' Schilder,[4] on the basis of a report of the Austro-Hungarian consul at Buenos Aires, estimates the total

---

[1] A French soldier of fortune who, after serving for a time under Bolívar, broke with him and later published memoirs strongly critical of the Liberator.

[2] 'Imperialism; the highest stage of Capitalism', *Collected Works* (Moscow, Inst. of Marxism-Leninism, 1962), xxvii. 383.

[3] *Britishcher Imperialismus und englischer Freihandel zu Beginn des 20 Jahrhunderts* (Leipzig, 1906), p. 318.

[4] Sigmund Schilder, author of *Die auswärtigen Kapitalsanlagen vor und nach dem Weltkrieg* (Berlin, 1918) and other economic studies.

of British capital invested in Argentina in 1909 at 8·75 billion francs. It is not difficult to imagine with what firm bonds British finance capital (and its faithful 'friend' diplomacy) is linked with the Argentine bourgeoisie and with the leading circles of its whole economic and political life.

II. THE COMINTERN PERIOD

1 Latin America

4. Soviet Relations with Argentina and other South American countries in 1927: official account[1] (*p. 8*)

At the beginning of 1927 there were indications that Argentina and Bolivia would be prepared to establish normal relations with the USSR. However, the rupture of Anglo-Soviet relations caused those countries, in which the part played by Great Britain is very great, to hold back. To the same influence must be attributed the spreading of malicious fictions at the door of the USSR regarding her alleged intervention in the internal affairs of the South American republics, specially Bolivia. In that country, in connection with a rising by part of the Indian population,[2] slander against the USSR was launched by members of the Government, specially by the Minister of Foreign Affairs.

This campaign against the USSR was roundly refuted by Comrade Kraevsky, the Soviet commercial representative in Uruguay.

---

[1] *Dok. Vnesh. Pol.*, x. 595 (reproduced from *SSR—God raboty pravitelstva* (Moscow, 1928)).
[2] In August 1927, against landowners in the Chayanta district.

5. Latin America's place in Comintern thinking: Bukharin's opening speech to the 6th Comintern Congress, 17 July 1928:[1] excerpt (*p. 11*)

Comrades, during the years since the Fifth Congress, our movement has grown in breadth and depth. The word Communism, the organisational principles of the Communist movement, Lenin's clear and distinct words, have, for the first time penetrated vast territories, new continents, new peoples, and new sections of the working class. South America is for the first time widely entering the orbit of influence of the Communist International. . . .

The South American parties are well represented at our Congress. Of course, this shows that our movement has extended to the South American countries. These countries are now particularly important for us as they play a very important although peculiar role in world politics. We have already pointed out the growing aggressiveness of North American capitalism in South America; we have also pointed already to the war of liberation Nicaragua is waging against the imperialist invasion of the United States.[2] We are all perfectly aware of the greatest importance of Mexican resistance, and we also know that such resistance and a powerful popular movement against North American imperialism is now developing in several countries of South America. We know perfectly well that this problem is intertwined with certain internal problems in the respective countries, particularly with the agrarian problem and the struggle against Fascism. On the question of tactics in the South American countries, there are various currents among us. I cannot deal now with all the controversial points. I would like however to emphasize the point that from the viewpoint of struggle against war and against imperialism and in general, from the viewpoint of the development of powerful national revolutions and power-ful agrarian revolutions—which will most likely reveal the tendency to become transformed into social revolutions—the whole gamut of South American problems is assuming increasing significance from day to day.

6. 'Izvestiya' on commercial relations with South American states, August 1928[3] (*p. 8*)

After spending some days in Moscow, Comrade B. I. Kraevsky, managing director of Yuzhamtorg[4] and the commercial representative of the USSR in Uruguay, is now returning to South America.

In an interview with a representative of the Soviet press, Comrade B. I. Kraevsky declared that as a result of numerous discussions with Soviet economic organizations a significant development of commercial operations could be noted this year with the South American states.

Special interest had been aroused by the South American sheep imported here for the first time, and by the recognition that they were fully suited for breeding in the USSR.

[1] *Inprecorr*, viii (25 July 1929), p. 706 and xl (13 Aug. 1929), p. 871.
[2] A force of Marines had been sent to Nicaragua in 1927 to support the conservative regime of President Adolfo Díaz.
[3] *Izvestiya*, 2 Aug. 1928 (*Dok. Vnesh. Pol.*, xi/271, pp. 460–3).
[4] Soviet trading agency for S. America.

Referring to commercial relations with individual countries, Comrade Kraevsky stressed that with Argentina, Chile, and Uruguay there had recently been established very good trade relations which gave grounds for hoping for a still closer rapprochement with those countries.

With regard to Brazil, there had so far been only occasional purchases, mainly of raw hides. The development of further purchases in other branches, e.g. coffee, cacao, rubber, etc., was hampered by the fact that commercial relations with that country had not been restored.

Although business circles in Brazil are showing greater interest in trade relations with the USSR, it must be stated that the attempts made by some groups who are hostile to us to place every sort of obstacle in the way of trade between the USSR and Brazil are meeting with some success, and this is undoubtedly harmful to both countries.

But in general the development of trade between the USSR and the South American countries is making good headway. Thus, for example, for the first year of commercial relations with South America (1925/6) Yuzhamtorg's turnover amounted to $4·5 million. In 1926/7 the total rose to $14·5 million, and for the first half of 1927/8 our turnover with South America is already $12·5 million.

Comrade Kraevsky observed that in the past year important success had been achieved in the field of financing our import operations. Without this source of credit, we should have been unable to develop our operations as intensively as is now the case. Thanks to the credits which we have received and are latterly still receiving we have been able to switch our purchases of a whole series of goods from European markets direct to South America. The future tempo of the development of trade operations with South America will doubtless largely depend on the credit facilities which we can obtain in the near future.

With regard to our exports to South America, Comrade Kraevsky pointed out that in this field prospects are good. South America imports 90 per cent of its supplies from outside the area and offers full scope as a very rich market for our goods. Nevertheless, the development of our exports to South America is mainly hampered by the fact that our economic organizations cannot yet adjust themselves to satisfying the requirements of the South American market. This applies to the quality of goods, their assortment and packing, which plays an important part since they have to cross the Equator and pass through the tropics and so need special packing.

At the present time, Narkomtorg[1] is taking a number of measures to promote our trade operations with South America, which open up good prospects for the sale of our petroleum products, salt, anthracite, cement, veneers, fish products, etc.

Comrade Kraevsky observed that recently thanks to loading ships with mixed cargoes a considerable lowering of freight charges had been made possible. This had naturally given a strong filip to our exports to South America.

[1] The People's Commissariat for Trade.

Replying to a question as to how political relations between the USSR and the South American countries were developing, Comrade Kraevsky replied that the USSR's political relations with Argentina and Chile were improving in proportion as trade relations between them developed. Banking and commercial circles in those countries saw clearly that the absence of normal diplomatic relations seriously hindered the further successful development of trade with the USSR. Hence the increased pressure from the general public in South America on their Governments for the speedy establishment of diplomatic relations with the USSR.

'I have no doubt', said Comrade Kraevsky, 'that, with the rise to power of the party of Irigoyen (the new President of Argentina) relations between the USSR and Argentina will before long take on a more normal character.'

Asked for an explanation as to why the Argentine Government was still tolerating the presence of the former Tsarist Ambassador Stein,[1] Comrade Kraevsky replied that in this affair the policy of the Argentine Government was not altogether clear. On the one hand it had declared that Stein was not recognized as an 'official representative of Russia' and this was in line with parliamentary requirements. On the other hand, the Argentine Government had permitted, and was still permitting, Stein to issue all sorts of illegal documents to the Russians living in South America, though these documents are not recognized by the Soviet Government, nor by those countries with which we are in normal diplomatic relations. In this way Stein has been brazenly deceiving citizens to whom he issues these documents for cash, and the impression is consequently widespread that the Argentine Government, with full knowledge that Stein is acting on his own authority and issuing invalid documents, nevertheless allows this scandal to continue.

With regard to Chile, the interest which is being shown there for the development of commercial relations with the USSR is evidence that the ground is quite ready for the establishment of diplomatic relations in the very near future.

With the Uruguayan Government, with which we have established diplomatic relations, our mutual relations continue to develop normally and satisfactorily in the interest of both countries.

In reply to a question as to whether the South American countries are well informed about the USSR, Comrade Kraevsky declared that those republics have hitherto been drawing their information about the Soviet Union mainly from those European sources which have been spreading the most loathsome slander about the USSR. Only recently, in connection with the establishment of direct trade relations between the South American countries and the USSR, has more or less objective information become available about the USSR. The Soviet commercial representative in Uruguay publishes a newspaper in Spanish which throws light on our economic and cultural achievements over the last decade, specially following the civil war. This journal is highly esteemed in business circles.

---

[1] Yevgeni Fedorovich Stein.

7. Revolutionary prospects and tasks in Latin America:
6th Comintern Congress Theses on the revolutionary element in colonial and semi-colonial countries, December 1928:[1] excerpts (*p. 12*)

6. The growing economic and military expansion of North American imperialism in the countries of Latin America is transforming this continent into one of the most important junction points of the antagonism of the whole imperialist colonial system. The influence of Great Britain, which before the war was the decisive influence in these countries, and which reduced many of them to the position of semi-colonies, since the war is being replaced by a still more close dependence on their part on the United States. By means of its increased export of capital, North American imperialism is conquering the commanding positions in the economy of these countries, is subordinating their governments to its own financial control and, at the same time, inciting one against the other. This aggressive policy of American imperialism is more and more taking on a character of undisguised violence, passing over into armed intervention (Nicaragua). The national-emancipatory struggle against American imperialism which has begun in Latin America is taking place for the most part under the leadership of the petty bourgeoisie. The national bourgeoisie, which represents a thin stratum of the population (with the exception of Argentine, Brazil, and Chile) and which is connected, on the one hand, with the big landowners and, on the other hand, with American capital, is in the camp of the counter-revolution.

The Mexican Revolution, which began as a revolutionary peasant struggle for land against the landowners and the church, at the same time to a considerable degree assumed the character of a mass struggle against American and British imperialism, and led to the formation of a government of the petty bourgeoisie, which endeavoured to keep itself in power by means of concessions to the big landowners and to North American imperialism.

The peasant risings, strikes of workers, etc. in Ecuador directed against the Government of the landlords of the maritime provinces, and of the Guayaquil bankers and commercial bourgeoisie, ended in a military coup d'etat and the establishment of a military dictatorship in 1925. The series of military revolutions in Chile, the guerrilla war in Nicaragua against North American imperialism, the series of risings in South Brazil, the uprising of the agricultural labourers in Patagonia in Argentina, the revolt of the Indians in Bolivia, Peru, Ecuador, and Colombia, the mutinies and spontaneous general strikes and mass demonstrations in Venezuela and Colombia, the mass anti-imperialist movement in Cuba and throughout the whole of Central America, Colombia, etc.—all these events of the last few years bear witness to the widening and deepening of the revolutionary process, and in particular, to the ever-growing popular indignation in the Latin American countries against world imperialism. . . .

[1] *Inprecorr*, viii/88, 12 Dec. 1928, pp. 1660–1 & 1675.

The immediate tasks of the Communists

40. In Latin America the Communists must everywhere actively participate in the revolutionary mass movements directed against the landlord regime and against imperialism, even where these movements are still under the leadership of the petty bourgeoisie. In so doing, however, the Communists may not under any circumstances politically subordinate themselves to their temporary ally. Whilst struggling for the hegemony, during the revolutionary movements, the Communist Parties must strive in the first place for the political and organisational independence of their Parties, securing its [*sic*] transformation into the leading party of the proletariat. In their agitation, the Communists must specially emphasise the following slogans:

1. Expropriation without compensation and the handing over of a part of the big plantations and latifundia to the collective cultivation of the agricultural workers, and the distribution of the other portion between the peasants, tenant farmers, and colonists.

2. Confiscation of foreign enterprises (mines, industrial enterprises, banks, etc.) and of the big enterprises of the national bourgeoisie and big landlords.

3. The repudiation of State debts, and the liquidation of any kind of control over the country on the part of imperialism.

4. The introduction of the 8-hour working-day and the stamping out of semi-slave-like conditions of labour.

5. The arming of the workers and peasants and the conversion of the army into a workers and peasants militia.

6. The establishment of the Soviet power of the workers, peasants and soldiers, in place of the class rule of the big landlords and of the church. The central place in Communist agitation must be occupied by the slogan of a workers' and peasants' government, in contradiction to the so-called 'revolutionary' governments of the military dictatorships of the petty bourgeoisie.

The fundamental pre-requisite for the success of the whole revolutionary movement in these countries lies in the ideological and organisational strengthening of the Communist Parties and in their connection with the toiling masses and with the mass organisations. The Communist Parties must unceasingly strive for the organisation of the industrial workers into class trade unions, especially the workers in big enterprises owned by imperialism, for the raising of the level of their political and class-consciousness and for the eradication of reformist, anarcho-syndicalist and corporate ideology. At the same time it is necessary to organise the peasants, tenant farmers and cultivators into peasant unions.

It is necessary to assist the extension of sections of the League against Imperialism, in which Communist fractions must carry on work. Very important is the closest possible mutual cooperation between all the revolutionary mass organisations of workers and peasants, and primarily of the Communist Parties, in the countries of Latin America and their connection with the corresponding international organisations and also with the revolutionary proletariat in the United States.

8. The role of the South American Secretariat: statement by 'Comrade Luis' (Jules Humbert-Droz), ECCI delegate at the 1st Latin American CP Congress, Buenos Aires, June 1929:[1] excerpts (*p. 10*)

The South American Secretariat is an intermediary organ of which the Communist International avails itself as a means of maintaining relations with the Latin American Parties. The very fact of its creation is evidence of the Communist International's effective concern for co-ordinating revolutionary work in Latin America, and is first and foremost a step taken to help the political conformation of our Parties. If there is some truth in the criticism voiced against the Communist International by some comrades for rather belatedly turning its attention to the Latin American countries, I think the criticism is exaggerated. It is clear that the Communist International could not 'discover' the whole world all at once, and in so far as Communist work in some countries is recent, it may be said that it has been developed by stages. . . . We are now beginning to penetrate into Latin America.

Amongst those Latin American countries, some seem to me to be specially important, e.g. those in the Caribbean area, and we ought to devote special attention to them. It is true that our South American Secretariat is a very long way off from that centre, for which reason we have decided to form a sub-secretariat in Mexico, to serve as an extension of the work which the South American Secretariat carries out. If the creation of this sub-secretariat has been delayed, that was due to the inadequacy of relations between the Mexican Party and the Communist International. Two or three months ago we took the measures necessary to ensure this coordination.

9. 'Izvestiya' on commercial relations with Latin American countries, July 1929[2] (*p. 8*)

The current year, Comrade Kraevsky stated, has shown very clearly the great interest which the South American market represents for us not only as a source for the import of raw materials but also as a base for the sale of exports from the Soviet Union.

During Yuzhamtorg's four years of activity, the volume of our trade with the countries of South America has steadily increased. In 1925/6 our imports from South America amounted to 10,710,000 Argentine pesos, and our exports to 71,400 pesos. In 1927/8 our imports rose to 43,495,395 pesos and exports to 1,648,504. In the first half of 1928/9 our imports already amount to 26,935,987 pesos, and our exports to 3,779,000 pesos.

Until last year, our operations with South America developed chiefly along the lines of imports; from the beginning of last year there has been a strong increase in our exports, which are three times as high as last year's figures. In South America we mainly purchase hides, quebracho extract, wool, live sheep, iodine, etc; last year we also bought nitrate. There are however a wide range of

[1] *El Movimiento . . .*, pp. 366–7.
[2] *Izvestiya*, 24 July 1929 (*Dok. Vnesh. Pol.*, xii/233, pp. 413–14).

goods such as coffee, cacao, Brazilian resin, all of which we have up to now been buying in Europe or North America at excessive rates.

Thanks to the mixed freights which Yuzhamtorg has arranged to ship from the South American to Soviet ports, and vice versa, we have secured, and are still securing, considerable reductions in the costs incurred in transporting imports and exports. At present the cost of transhipping a ton of cargo from South America to Soviet ports varies between 25–28 shillings instead of the previous 60–70 shillings, and the transport of a ton of cargo from Soviet to South American ports averages 17 shillings as against a previous average of 45–50 shillings when transhipment was necessary.

The reduction of freight charges has made it possible to place in the South American market Soviet goods such as petroleum products, salt, anthracite, wood products, veneers; foodstuffs (fish products, lentils, green peas); manufactured goods (small lamps, cigarettes, matches, etc). In the first half of 1928/9 purchases from individual countries were as follows: from Argentina, 50 per cent of the total, from Uruguay 39 per cent, from Brazil 4·5 per cent, from Paraguay 3 per cent, and from Chile 3·5 per cent. In the same period, sales to Argentina amounted to 83 per cent of our total, and to Uruguay about 17 per cent.

Until April of the current year we had no transactions with Bolivia. In April we concluded an agreement for the first time with the Bolivian Government for the supply of matches over a ten-year period. This contract was concluded in spite of the strong opposition of eleven countries participating in the trade. Our contract with the Bolivian Government dealt a mighty blow at the Swedish match syndicate which had a twenty-five years monopoly for the supply of matches, and owned a factory there which it was obliged to close for the time being.

The strong pressure brought to bear on the South Americans by European banks with the aim of stopping the financing of our import and export operations proved fruitless; on the contrary, we managed to achieve a considerable increase in the financing of our import operations. In the current year all our import purchases were financed within the space of 4–7 months, in which time, as in the previous year, until a financial blockade was organized against us, we had recourse to open credit only in respect of 20 per cent of our purchases whilst 80 per cent allowed us credit to a Soviet port. This shows that the sober businessmen of South America do not let themselves be misled into all sorts of political adventures against the Soviet Union.

The organizers of anti-Soviet propaganda have striven not only to hinder our credit operations with the banks, but also to complicate our relations with the South American Governments, specially with the Argentine Government. The bureau of permanent propaganda against the Soviet Union in Geneva fabricated in October 1928 a series of provocative documents attempting to prove to the South American Governments, that of Argentina in particular, that Yuzhamtorg was a propaganda organization, using its commercial activity as a camouflage. The organization of every sort of provocation against Yuzhamtorg is led by the British Ambassador in Argentina together with the former Ambassador Stein. This whole campaign concocted by the enemies of the Soviet

Union was reshaped when there was a change of Presidents (October 1928). Knowing that the new President, Irigoyen, was well disposed towards the Soviet Union, this campaign, as pointed out above, sought by all possible means to prevent the recognition of the Soviet Union by the Argentine Government. Nevertheless, all this did not prevent us from establishing the best relations with the present Government of President Hipólito Irigoyen.

Official organs, specially in Argentina, now realize that the continued rapid growth of economic relations with the Soviet Union is bound up with the establishment of diplomatic relations.

10. Popular Front tactics: 7th Comintern Congress resolution on fascism, working-class unity, and the tasks of the Comintern, 1935[1]: excerpt (*p. 17*)

In the colonial and semi-colonial countries, the most important task facing the communists consists in working to establish an anti-imperialist people's front. For this purpose it is necessary to draw the widest masses into the national liberation movement against growing imperialist exploitation, against cruel enslavement, for the driving out of the imperialists, for the independence of the country; to take an active part in the mass anti-imperialist movements headed by the national reformists and to strive to bring about joint action with the national-revolutionary and national-reformist organizations on the basis of a definite anti-imperialist platform.

11. Resolution on Manuilsky's report at the 7th Comintern Congress, 1935:[2] excerpt

To help with all their might and by all means to strengthen the USSR and to fight against the enemies of the USSR, both under peace conditions and in the circumstances of war directed against the USSR, the interests of strengthening the USSR, of increasing its power, of ensuring its victory in all spheres and in every sector of the struggle, coincide fully and inseparably with the interests of the toilers of the whole world in their struggle against the exploiters, with the interests of the colonial and oppressed peoples fighting against imperialism; they are the conditions for, and they contribute to, the triumphs of the world proletarian evolution, the victory of socialism throughout the world. Assistance to the USSR, its defence, and cooperation in bringing about its victory over all its enemies must therefore determine the actions of every revolutionary organisation of the proletariat, of every genuine revolutionary, of every Socialist, Communist, non-party worker, toiling peasant, of every honest intellectual and democrat, of each and every one who desires the overthrow of exploitation, Fascism, and imperialist oppression, deliverance from imperialist war, who desires that there should exist brotherhood and peace among nations, that socialism should triumph throughout the world.

[1] Jane Degras, ed., *The Communist International, 1919–43: Documents*, iii. 367.
[2] *Inprecorr*, no. 44, 1935, pp. 1146–7.

2 *Mexico*

12. Parliamentary and revolutionary tactics: directives from the Comintern to the Mexican CP, 21 August 1923[1] (*p. 3*)

We received your communication with reference to the Second National Congress of your Party, and the verbal report of your delegates to the Session of the Communist Youth International.

The resolutions adopted at your Congress indicate that the process of securing ideological clarity within the Party is progressing favorably. But we deem it our duty to go into some detail with reference to certain concrete problems on which we do not find that a clear attitude has been adopted on your part.

The Question of Parliamentarism

The break with the policy of anti-parliamentarism, and the decision to participate in the elections, is a decisive step forward, not only for the development of your Party, but for the development of the whole Mexican labor movement. But this very fact makes it necessary that the Communist Party should examine and prepare with the greatest care everything that is undertaken in connection with this question. The parliamentary struggle must not tax the strength of the Party to such an extent that the work of organization and education among the wide masses suffers, or that the activity of the fractions within the trade unions is hampered. The daily struggle of the workers against the employing class, and the struggle of the peasants against the landlords, must be the basis of our revolutionary activity from first to last, and must be the point on which the organization and guidance of the revolutionary class struggle must focus. We want to remind you of the decisions of the Second Congress of the Communist International on the question of parliamentarism, and we expect you strictly to adhere to them. It is important, above all, that you make concrete plans for parliamentary activity. Discussion on the attitude to be taken by your future representatives in the Chamber of Deputies and on local government bodies on the various questions on the agenda of the next session, or on the proposals the party will make, must be opened immediately in your meetings and in your Party press, and must be conducted from an exclusively revolutionary point of view. The parliamentary struggle of the communists is not one of reforms, but a struggle against the bourgeois system of society, a struggle to unmask bourgeois democracy, the entire spirit of which is to deceive the workers and peasants. The communists do not intend to 'capture the Chamber of Deputies';

[1] US House of Representatives, Cttee on un-American Activities, *The Communist Conspiracy: Strategy and Tactics of World Communism*, pt. 1: *Communism outside the United States* (Washington, 1956), pp. 242–51.

bourgeois parliaments do not allow themselves to be captured. The aim of the working class, on the contrary, is to smash parliament and to substitute proletarian organs of power (Factory Councils, Councils of Peasants and Soldiers, etc.).

But it would make the struggle of the bourgeoisie against the communists much easier if the latter did not send class enemies of the bourgeoisie to the parliamentary institutions. Of course, the Communist Party must not content itself with a purely opposition policy. The representatives in the district organizations, especially, must do everything possible to help the poor sections of the population. They must make practical proposals for the protection of workers, housing, free education, etc. They must show that the bourgeois government sabotages every earnest attempt at fundamental change, and refuses to carry it through; they must 'develop the keenest revolutionary propaganda on this basis without fearing to come in conflict with the State power.' (Thesis of the Third Congress).

The Party must not undervalue the dangers of opportunism that confront its representatives in the chamber of Deputies. These dangers are extraordinarily great, owing to the existing anarcho-idealistic mentality of your Party comrades and because of your inexperience in parliamentary struggles. Your representatives may be unconsciously dragged in the wake of the so-called socialist parties, labor parties, or agrarian parties. This danger will be especially great if the Party is already participating in the elections for provincial governments. Of course, the results of elections indicate our strength and influence over the masses, but we must on no account sacrifice our communist principles and the revolutionary class struggle in order to obtain a victory at the polls. Therefore, the choice of comrades who are to represent the Party in the national or provincial parliaments must be made very carefully. Before a comrade can be considered as a candidate, he must have behind him at least a year of activity within the Party itself or within a revolutionary trade union organization, and, in his attitude in general and his participation in the struggles of the labor movement in particular, he must have demonstrated his loyalty and discipline toward the proletarian revolution. The members of the Mexican Chamber of Deputies draw extraordinarily large salaries; the communist representatives must relinquish a considerable part of their pay to the Central Committee of the Party, even to the extent of retaining for themselves only as much as a good worker can earn. A comrade who cannot agree to this decision unhesitatingly must not even be considered as a candidate of a revolutionary labor party. The entire parliamentary activity must be under the guidance of the Party, which must have unlimited right of control over the representatives. Against comrades who either consciously or unconsciously sabotage the decisions and instructions of the Party, or whose general demeanor shows that they dare not venture to raise the demands of the Communists in the face of the bourgeois or socialist parties, the Party Executive must immediately take energetic proceedings, and, if necessary, must expel them from the Party. It will be easily understood that the parliamentary struggle in the rural districts will not assume the same form as in the industrial cities. Among the peasants the struggle must center above all on the control of the 'Municipios' and the

'Comites Ejecutivos Particulares.' Besides the decisions of the national agrarian program of the Party, you must work out detailed instructions for the activity of the sections depending upon the local conditions prevailing in the various regions concerned. One of your most important problems concerns your activities with reference to the agrarian question, and your influence among the wide masses of peasants who live in poverty and misery. In a country where 75% of the population consists of poor peasants, the working class can carry through a proletarian revolution successfully only by allying itself with these peasants and recognizing their interests as its own class interests. At this very moment the peasants are being threatened by the Government. Obregon, with the tacit support of all the left bourgeois and petty-bourgeois parties, is trying to deprive the peasants of their arms. The slogan of the Government: 'Our national forces guarantee land to the peasants,' is nothing but the beginnings of petty-bourgeois democratic betrayal. To counteract this, the communists must proclaim that 'The only guarantee the peasants have for the security of their land is the weapons they hold in their own hands.' Therefore, fight against bourgeois militarism and demand that the peasants be armed and that communal peasant corps be formed.

In the cities the Party will fight for seats in the Ayuntamientos, for representatives in the 'Juntas de Conciliación y Arbitraje,' and for the control of the Labor Department by organized workers. On the question of the regulation of Article 123,[1] the Party must work out concrete proposals. This is a question on which you must force the laborites to follow suit. You must call upon Morones[2] and company to advocate our revolutionary proposals on the subject of labor legislation. Under no circumstances must the Party resort to compromise in this matter. We repeat that the entrance of your Party into the arena of the parliamentary struggle signifies a triumph of revolutionary class policy over the anarcho-petty-bourgeois ideology and tactics of the syndicalists; but bound up with this victory is the danger to which all the so-called revolutionary parties of Mexico have hitherto succumbed, i.e. of 'reforming' a party, which is struggling for the class interests of the poor peasants, into a Party of 'superior' proletarians and petty-bourgeois intellectuals, seeking for careers; a Party pursuing a policy of continual compromise with bourgeois democracy at the expense of the workers and peasants. The Communist Party must therefore exercise continual self-criticisms of the work and tactics of every worker in the Party. But, at the same time, every comrade, as soon as the Party has decided on a definite tactic and has resorted to action, must observe the strictest discipline, and as long as the need for action lasts, must renounce adverse criticism. A Party can fight only when it is united. The Communist Party will gain decisive political importance when it is able, within the frame-work of the nation, to work out a united class policy of the workers and peasants, and to organize a united struggle for the realization of this policy. The Party must be conscious of the historic role of the working class, which consists in supplanting the bourgeois social system by that of the proletariat, i.e., a communist system.

[1] Art. 123 of the Mexican Constitution affirms the rights of the workers to organize in trade unions, to strike, to social benefits, etc.
[2] Boss of the official Mexican labour organizations.

The proletariat forms the overwhelming majority of the population and only when the Communist Party understands how to fight and pursue a policy on behalf of the daily needs and the class interests of this majority, will it become the leading party of the proletariat and of the proletarian revolution.

The Communist Party of Mexico and the Oppressed Countries of Central America

In conclusion, we want to say a few words about the significance of the nationalist and revolutionary struggle for freedom in the Central American countries. The capitalist development of North America and the backward economic and social development of the countries of Latin America determine the political attitude of the United States towards the countries of the South. The drying up of the purchasing power of Europe is forcing American products into the South American markets. In the American capitalist press one notices a stronger imperialist tendency towards the South than ever before. What has been done in the West Indies and in Central America, can be tried in Mexico and South America as well. In Cuba, Haiti, San Domingo; in Guatemala, Costa Rica, Honduras and Panama, the American 'system,' the most ruthless exploitation of the proletariat, reigns supreme. Revolutionary workers are persecuted and thrown into prison. Such organizations as oppose Gompers[1] are disrupted, betrayed and violently crushed by the agents of the local and American governments. The peasants, who are held under conditions of Medieval slavery, are stripped to the bone and controlled by cudgel and whip. The workers' press is suppressed, the frontiers are controlled, the censorship is severe, for the world must not discover how American capitalism is murdering the Negroes and Indians of those countries. The America which advocated Wilson's Fourteen Points has been violating for years the national freedom of the West Indian and Central American Republic. The most primitive rights of existence of these people are being trampled underfoot. The United States hopes 'in time' to parcel out Mexico into single 'independent' territories. It is already openly advocating the annexation of fruitful Lower California to the United States as a territory. In Yucatan and in the State of Chiapas, the Americans are fanning the flames of the separatist movements. But times are changing. Even in these backward areas, the proletariat is awakening, is organizing, and is beginning to understand its class condition. In Cuba the revolutionary trade union movement is again raising its head after the defeat it suffered in 1921 at the hands of reaction. In Guatemala a Communist Party of Central America has been founded; in Mexico the revolutionary labor movement has such strong roots that neither the claws of American capital nor of any other capital can tear it to pieces. But the conception is still lacking of the fight for freedom for all the oppressed masses in the West Indies, in Central America and in South America, against the imperialism of the oil magnates and industrial barons of Wall Street. The workers and peasants of Mexico and

[1] Samuel Gompers, President of the American Federation of Labour.

Central America especially must stand close together. The aim of the common struggle must be to create a League of Central American Workers' and Peasants' Republics. It is the duty of the Communist Party of Mexico to announce this slogan with all revolutionary fervor to the oppressed masses of Central America. The Mexican Party must treat exhaustively the question which we have roughly sketched here. In conjunction with the Communist Party of Central America and the communist group in Cuba, a programme of work and action must be prepared. But the communists must be conscious of the fact that this is not only a most difficult and dangerous matter but one of grave responsibility. The American capitalists will not look on in silence. They will mobilize all their bourgeois hangmen, their hirelings, spies and agents, to stifle your voices. The best of you will be thrown into prison or murdered treacherously. But your fight is the fight of the dawn against the night; it is the fight of the near future, which belongs to the proletariat.

In the most important industrial countries of Europe, the working class is being confronted with a decisive struggle. The European revolution may at any moment develop into a reality. The American bourgeoisie will not sit quietly by while the mastery of capitalism in Europe is smashed by the fist of the working class. Hundreds of transports will cross the Atlantic Ocean, loaded with the cannon fodder of counter-revolution, with thousands of tons of munitions and weapons, with barrels of plague and cholera bombs, in order to put an end to the world revolution. The United States will swing the lash of starvation over the countries where the European revolution is victorious. But the European revolution shall triumph.

We expect the workers of all American countries to contribute to this victory. We expect you to fight against the efforts of the counter-revolution to recruit the white and colored fascisti and unemployed of America; to fight against the attempt to set the machinery in motion for the defeat of the European revolution; we expect you to control the railways and ships in order to prevent them from coming to the assistance of European reaction.

Agitation on these lines must be organized by you immediately. The workers of America must be prepared when the workers of Europe rush into battle.

The Russian Revolution is the heroic prelude to the World Revolution. The victory of the working class in the most important countries of Europe assures the victory of the proletariat in all countries. But the destruction of the last stronghold of capitalist imperialism, the overthrow of the North American bourgeoisie, is the task of the workers and peasants of all the American countries.

The Communist International, the World Party of the revolutionary proletariat, is convinced that the workers and peasants of Mexico will fight shoulder to shoulder with the international working class until the victory of the world revolution is achieved.

FOR THE EXECUTIVE OF THE COMMUNIST INTERNATIONAL

13. Mexico, as a base for the extension of Soviet influence: report by Chicherin to the 3rd session of the CPSU Central Executive Committee, 4 March 1925:[1] excerpt (*p. 4*)

... We have succeeded in re-establishing diplomatic relations, which give us a political base in the new continent, with the neighbor of the United States, Mexico. The Mexican Government is based on the Right trade unions and the radical small bourgeoisie. The Soviet Republic is extraordinarily popular in Mexico. Our plenipotentiary representative, Pestkovsky, met in Mexico the most enthusiastic reception, receiving constantly from all sides expressions of the most friendly, even enthusiastic attitude toward the Soviet Republic. Mexico gives us, thus, a very convenient political base in America for the development of our further ties.

14. Mexican Federation of Labour resolution on Soviet intervention in labour disputes adopted at its 7th annual convention, 6th March 1926:[2] excerpt (*p. 5*)

... 3. That a courteous invitation be extended by the Central Committee to the diplomatic representative of Russia accredited to Mexico so that his office may abstain from lending moral and economic support to the so-called radical group, enemies of the Mexican Federation of Labor and of the government.

15. Communication to Pestkovsky from the Central Committee of the Mexican Federation of Labour by direction of its 7th Congress, March 1926:[3] excerpt (*p. 5*)

'To the Minister of Russia in Mexico City.'

... There was also considered by the Convention the report referring to the fact that in the diplomatic mission in your charge moral and economic support is lent to so-called Communist radical groups, the enemies of the Mexican Federation of Labor and of our government.

This Central Committee was ordered by the Convention to inform you in your character as representative of Russia in Mexico that the Mexican labor movement represented by this confederation maintains the principle that the workers of each country must be organized in accordance with their opinions and necessities and that no nation has the right to impose nor to lay down for another the doctrine which must control its activities.

16. Speech by Aleksandra Kollontay, Soviet Minister in Mexico, on presenting her credentials, 24 December 1926:[4] excerpts (*p. 5*)

... It is now two years since the Republic of Mexico and the Soviet Union renewed their friendly and official relations, and it is with great satisfaction and sincere pleasure that the working people of the [Soviet] Union take note that,

---

[1] *FRUS, 1927*, i. 362–3.   [2] ibid., i. 363.   [3] ibid., i. 363.
[4] *Dok. Vnesh. Pol.*, ix. 603.

during all that time, there has arisen no serious incident to trouble the sincere, fraternal, and friendly relations existing between the two nations.

But in the relations between our two countries there has hitherto lacked one essential factor—the development of direct trade between the Republic of Mexico and the USSR. One of the most urgent tasks of my mission in Mexico is that of finding means to promote commercial activity between the United States of Mexico and the Soviet Union. The people of Soviet Russia now stand in increasing need of a great number of Mexican products and would be very happy if they succeed in establishing direct commercial contact between the Republic of Mexico and the Union, without needing to have recourse to intermediary countries. . . .

17. Mme Kollontay's interview with President Calles: letter to Maksim Litvinov, 30 January 1927:[1] excerpt (*p. 5*)

As I have already reported to you by telegraph, I had my first working interview with Calles on 21 January. I judged it opportune to call and speak with him in connection with the disagreeable stir caused by Kellogg's pseudo-revelations about our propaganda.[2] As you will see from the information bulletin sent to you, Kellogg had only the flimsiest and most unconvincing material to go on, without the backing of a single serious fact or document.

My interview with Calles was very friendly. He thanked me for my efforts to build up our relations on a basis of sincerity and said that he valued the establishment of stable and friendly links with the USSR. He referred to the special nature and character of Mexico's 'revolutionary Government' which claims to represent working-class elements and not the great capitalists, and again emphasized that we had many points of contact in the struggle against the imperialist tendencies of the capitalist states.

We touched upon our mutual relations with Labour, which, as you know, forms the basis and backing of the Calles Government, and in this connection expressed our mutual hope that closer contact and better information would remove many occasions for estrangement and even for hostility on each side.

Finally, although *en passant*, we spoke about a trade treaty and the desirability of beginning negotiations which, of course, would need to continue for some time.

18. Instructions to oppose the Government of President Calles: statement by Manuel Díaz Ramírez, delegate to the 6th Comintern Congress, 20 August 1928[3] (*p. 4*)

In 1923 we had the directive which came to us in a letter from the Executive

[1] *Dok. Vnesh. Pol.*, x (1965), no. 21, p. 34.

[2] Secretary of State Kellogg informed the Senate Foreign Relations Committee in January 1927 that 'the Bolshevik leaders have had very definite ideas with respect to the role which Mexico and Latin America are to play in their program of world revolution. . . . Latin America and Mexico are conceived as a base for activity against the United States' (Robert H. Ferrell, *The American Secretaries of State and their Diplomacy*, xi (New York, 1963), p. 33).

[3] *Inprecorr*, 8 Nov. 1928, p. 1465.

Committee of the Communist International to the Mexican Proletariat. In one of the paragraphs it reads as follows:

Calles will be obliged to yield to imperialism. It is evident he represents for the masses of workers and peasants the struggle against the bourgeoisie and the clericals, and consequently will be supported by them. It is the task of the Communist Party to destroy the illusions of the masses in the government of Calles. The policy of the Calles government will open the eyes of the Mexican proletariat and the workers and peasants of Mexico will understand that there are only two policies; either the dictatorship of the proletariat under the slogan of all power to the workers and peasants, or the dictatorship of the bourgeoisie.

19. Statement by the ECCI delegate at the 1st Latin American Communist Congress, Buenos Aires, 3 June 1929:[1] excerpts (*p. 6*)

Up to now, our Parties have concentrated their efforts too exclusively on purely military organization, without attempting the corresponding political organization, in order to implant amongst the masses the will to struggle for workers and peasants' power. The example of the recent civil war in Mexico is typical in this respect. Our comrades of the Peasant League in the region of Vera Cruz, armed and organized in peasant battalions, were the first to penetrate into Vera Cruz to rout the counter-revolutionary troops. They fought valiantly, but they fought as troops loyal to the Government of Portes Gil and to Tejeda, the Governor of the province. They did not set up soviets in the region which they dominated. They did not, arms in hand, summon a workers' and peasants' congress for the state of Vera Cruz in order to press the fundamental demands of the workers and peasants of Mexico in this struggle, but they worked as auxiliary troops for the Government, without any objective or aim other than those pursued by the Government; to overcome the rebels and restore Portes Gil's power.

They ought to have struggled against the revolts of reactionary generals—as they did—yes; but at the same time, to have struggled for the fundamental demands of the Mexican masses, and to organize them in political and military form, around a political programme for the development of the revolutionary movement.

... The Mexican Revolution has reached a point which demands the greatest activity from our Party. The Government of Portes Gil, using the most brutal methods of repression against our Party, can do nothing else but fight against our revolutionary syndicates and also the Peasant League, if the latter retains and develops its loyalty to its revolutionary programme.

Our Party will have to defend its legality by mobilizing the masses over which it has influence; it is by mass action that its defence can be effective. Taking the measures necessary to safeguard itself, it must not adapt itself to go underground without first struggling, by means of mass action, to impose its legality. But this mass action should be carried out with the perspective of Mexico's revolutionary development, according to the general directives we

[1] *El Movimiento . . .*, pp. 92–3 & 105.

have fixed in our instructions to the Mexican Party and in general theses. The Party must consolidate its organizations and its ideology which is still strongly influenced by the 'Agrarian League'; a clear and unequivocal correction of past errors, independent action on the part of the Party, increasing political action, and a firmer, more systematic leadership corresponding to a more iron discipline. Galván[1] must be faced with the necessity of choosing between the Party and Tejeda. It is not a question of Galván; it is a question of the ideology of the Party, of its independent action, of its need to lead the revolutionary struggle against the government. If Galván does not get off the fence he can block the Party action more than anyone else. He must choose. Work now at the base of the Peasant League and the syndicates to strengthen ties with the masses and not to make our influence depend on bosses who may or may not be reliable. *Caudillismo* must be rooted out from our ranks.

20. ECCI manifesto urging resistance to the 'Fascist' Government, July 1929:[2] excerpts (*p. 7*)

The assassination of our two heroic comrades Rodriguez and Gomez,[3] who fell under the fire of the executioner, and the most shameful and cynical terror launched against the Mexican workers and peasants, together with the dissolution of the Communist Party, the prohibition of the workers' and peasants' revolutionary press, and the arrest of the best militants active in the consisting [consistent] struggle against imperialism completely unmasked the self-styled 'revolutionary' Government of Portes Gil, Calles, & Company, showing the whole world that the Mexican Government has become an openly fascist Government and an agent of North American imperialism. . . .

In developing its fascist policy as agent of North American imperialism, the Mexican Government is driving the workers from all the positions that they had conquered during the past years. The strike movements of the Mexican workers against foreign employers are persecuted. With the aid of the social-fascist Morones, the Mexican Government is working to break up the organizations of the revolutionary workers.

Furthermore, the few gains made by the peasants during the revolution have been destroyed. The big landed proprietors and capitalist agriculturists are taking back what little land they were forced to give over to the peasants. After the 'freethinkers' Calles and Gil—at the order of Yankee imperialism—got down on their knees before the Pope in order to guarantee 'social peace' in the districts of American silver exploitation, which were recently the scene of civil war, we find the Mexican clergy managing somehow to get back its former positions and regain the landed property that was taken from it by armed force. Already government troops are disarming the peasants and dissolving the guerrilla battalions, or transforming them into fascist organs of struggle.

[1] Ursulo Galván, a Mexican peasant leader and member of the Presidium of the Peasant International. Subsequently expelled from it for refusing to obey the directive to turn against the Government.

[2] Degras, *The Communist International*, iii. 71–3.

[3] José Guadelupe Rodríguez and Salvador Gómez, Communist peasant leaders who were shot in Durango on 13 May 1929.

Deprived of their arms, the peasants will find it impossible to defend their gains and their rights.

The petty-bourgeois elements, the intellectuals, the 'liberal' landed proprietors, and the elements of the young national bourgeoisie which has become degenerate and extortionist—these groups which form the social basis of the Portes Gil Government, have cowed [cowered] before the rising wave of the revolutionary movement of the workers and peasants, and under the pressure of North American imperialism have betrayed the cause of the national independence of Mexico; they have betrayed the interests of the workers and peasants of Mexico for the benefit of exploiting Yankee imperialism—they have betrayed the common cause of the peoples of Latin America, and have passed into the camp of the most rabid enemies of the working masses of Mexico. Yankee imperialism has gained another 'victory' in its campaign of expansion.

This 'victory' is piling up new explosive material in the world and constitutes a new step ahead by the United States on the road of preparation for imperialist war.

The lesson of these events is that there is but a single force left in Mexico which can and will consistently and energetically lead the struggle against imperialism; this is the Communist Party of Mexico.

The Mexican masses have grown more class conscious through experience and do not hide their sympathy for the communist party. During the past years the Communist Party of Mexico has gained very great political influence, and is being transformed more and more into a rallying-point and centre for political leadership of the movement of the workers, while it organizes around the Mexican proletariat the peasants, the poor Indians, and the anti-imperialist movement of Mexico in the struggle for the conquest of land and for national independence.

The unrest, discontent, and combative spirit of broad masses of Mexican workers and peasants is rising from day to day. The working masses of Mexico are reacting with increasing force against the treachery of the self-styled 'anti-imperialist revolutionists' and the reaction which they have launched. The workers and peasants of Mexico are faced with the question: either meet the fascist battalions of Portes Gil under the banner of the Workers' and Peasants' Government—or allow themselves to be crushed and subjected to the worst conditions of slavery and oppression under the yoke of Yankee imperialism.

There is no possible hesitation before this alternative. . . .

Mexican workers! Rally around your Communist Party! Build up your revolutionary trade unions!

Mexican peasants! Do not give back your arms to your exploiters who will use them to crush you! Rally around the proletariat, organize yourselves in your Peasant League, cleansing it of all traitors, prepare to carry on a great struggle under the valiant leadership of the Communist Party, to get the land from the big proprietors! Down with imperialism and its accomplices. Long live national independence!

Comrades, workers and peasants of Latin America!

Protest with vigour against the threat coming from the fascist Government of

8

Mexico, which, if it is not warded off, will affect the entire anti-imperialist workers' and peasants' communist movement of Latin America.

Comrades, workers and peasants of all countries!

Your duty is to take a vigorous stand against Mexican fascism! Not a single communist party, not a single workers' organization, not a single truly anti-imperialist organization must fail to raise its voice of protest against the fascist Government of Mexico.

21. Mexican protest to the Soviet Government: note from the Mexican Ambassador in Moscow to Maksim Litvinov, 20 July 1929:[1] excerpt (*p. 7*)

... Being aware, as we are, of the political structure of the Soviet Union and of the connection between its Government and the Communist Party, and also the relations between the said Party and the Communist International, we think that, should unjustified attacks continue to be made by theoreticians not familiar with the economic, political, and social lines along which Mexico is developing, the result will be a serious deterioration in the cordial relations which exist, and which we hope will continue to exist, between the people and Government of Mexico and the people and Government of the Soviet Union.

... [The Mexican Government] would be gratified if the Commissariat over which you preside would take steps, in whatever form you may deem reasonable and expedient, for a visit to Mexico on a reciprocal basis of a commission of Soviet representatives for the purpose of acquainting itself with the real conditions of the country.

22. Rejection of the protest: note from Litvinov to the Mexican Ambassador, Silva Hercog, 26 October 1929[2] (*p. 7*)

In your note of 20 July, Mr Ambassador, you expressed surprise, in the name of your Government, with regard to certain articles and commentaries appearing in the Soviet press, and also with regard to the manifesto of the Communist International on events in the internal life of Mexico. Pointing out what, in your opinion, you considered, Mr Ambassador, to be the inaccurate and unjustified views put forward in the said articles and manifesto, you expressed the fear that an incorrect reporting of Mexican events would be detrimental to the friendly relations between the peoples of the USSR and the United States of Mexico, and you put forward in this connection a proposal that the Soviet Government should send an official mission to Mexico so that it might form a correct assessment of events on the spot.

This note was the subject of a lengthy interview which you, Mr Ambassador, had with the Deputy Commissar for Foreign Affairs, Mr Karakhan, in the course of which he gave you the most exhaustive explanations, indeed assurances, regarding the immutability of the friendly relations between our

[1] *Dok. Vnesh. Pol.*, xii (1929), no. 329, p. 574.
[2] Ibid., pp. 572–4.

Governments. In a personal conversation with myself, you nevertheless expressed the wish to receive a written answer to your note.

To meet your wishes I can do no more than repeat what Mr Karakhan has already told you verbally, namely that the Soviet Government, like any other Government, cannot hold itself responsible for the contents of articles, observations, and statements in the organs of the press. The responsibility in such cases lies with the authors of the articles, and in some cases, with the editorial management of the newspaper. The Soviet Government, for its part, is not disposed to consider the anti-Soviet articles and remarks in Mexican organs of the press as expressing the viewpoints and feelings of the Mexican Government.

The mention in your note of the manifesto of the Communist International cannot but occasion serious surprise. You are naturally not unaware, Mr Ambassador, that the Communist International is a completely autonomous international organization, independent of any government or state, and is directed by the representatives of the Communist Parties of almost every country in the world. The activity of that organization has nothing to do with the Soviet Government, nor can it in any circumstances serve as the object of diplomatic correspondence with the National Commissariat for Foreign Affairs.

Whilst fully appreciating the motives prompting your proposal for the dispatch of an official mission to Mexico, I venture to question the expediency of such a step, which might be wrongly interpreted as interference in the internal affairs of the United States of Mexico. Convinced of the great sympathy felt by the peoples of the Soviet Union for the Mexican people, and of the immense interest for the life of that people on the part of the Soviet public, the Soviet Government has no intention of placing any obstacles in the way of Soviet study by journalists and representatives of social organizations who might wish on their own initiative to visit and study Mexico.

In conclusion, permit me, Mr Ambassador once again to assure you, and through your intermediary the Mexican Government, of the absolute immutability of the friendly relations which have long existed, and still persist, between our Governments, and to express my firm conviction that these relations will not be affected by any articles whatsoever in the Soviet and Mexican press. . . .

The rupture of diplomatic relations

23. Soviet press comment on the rupture of relations, January 1930:[1] excerpts (*p. 8*)

Mexico has severed relations with Russia, and has recalled her Minister from Moscow. England once did the same thing, but after two years it was found necessary to restore relations. This rupture of relations proved a material loss to England.

[1] *Rabochaya gazeta*, 28 Jan. 1930.

In the international world, the Mexican Republic does not carry much weight, and if five years ago we openly welcomed the establishment of relations with that country, the chief reason was that until that time Mexico had been carrying on the fight against foreign imperialism, against the oil-kings of the United States and the local landowners and feudal aristocracy.

The present decision of the Mexican Government interests us in another way, namely in its relation to American politics. It is all very well for the American Minister for Foreign Affairs to state that 'America did not give Mexico any advice, and was in fact ignorant of Mexico's intentions'; the working masses of the [Soviet] Union know the value of such assurances. We must remember, now on the very day of the seizure of the Chinese Eastern Railway by the Chinese Generals, that the United States Government stated that it was the outcome of unexpected events. In reality, it was the United States that egged China on to such an adventure.

At the present moment, it is beyond doubt that America is the guiding hand in Mexico. The part now played by American imperialism in the affairs of Mexico means the betrayal of the small bourgeois bloc in Mexico into the hands of the foreign capitalists, the landowners, and the feudal aristocracy.

In these circumstances it is obvious that Mexico loses her independence with regard to international affairs and that the Mexican bourgeois and landowners, in order to please the American capitalists, are directing their internal policy against the proletarian masses and against the Mexican Communist Party.

If these were the aims of the American capitalists when they pressed Mexico to break relations with the Soviet Union, under the excuse of the famous 'propaganda'—what does it mean? It means that America, passing through a serious economic crisis and threatened by the revolutionary movement of the proletariat, is taking upon herself the duties of world policeman, and the role of leader of the united capitalists' attack on the USSR.

But the capitulation of the Mexican petty bourgeoisie does not mean the abandoning of further revolutionary demonstrations on the part of the working masses. It merely means that our proletarian Government, which has only just straightened out the conflict over the Eastern Chinese Railway, cannot for one moment relax its vigilance, but must increase it.

24. Statement by Litvinov on the rupture of relations, 1 February 1930[1] (*p. 8*)

The recall of the Mexican chargé d'affaires from Moscow, which was preceded by a statement thereon by the Mexican Deputy Minister for Foreign Affairs, M. Estrada, is not in the least in accordance with anything that has happened in the actual course of relations between the two States. The relations between the two countries and Governments have throughout left nothing to be desired. I am convinced that the Mexican people and their former Government valued very highly the sympathy of the peoples of the Union with Mexico's struggle against its subjection to the interests of the imperialist Powers, and with its

[1] Degras, *The Communist International*, iii. 437–8.

desire to strengthen its independence. In their turn, the Mexican ambassadors in Moscow constantly assured us of the deep sympathy of the Mexican people for our Union, and this was far from being an empty diplomatic phrase. It is self-evident that no conflicts, whether of a political or economic character, arose or could arise between the Soviet Union and far-off Mexico. Nor were there any indications of dissatisfaction from one side or the other. The suggestion that the departure of the Mexican ambassador, M. Herzog [Silva Hercog], from Moscow some weeks back was of a political character is wholly false. In taking leave of me, M. Herzog explained his departure partly on personal grounds, and partly by the instructions from his Government to examine certain questions in central Europe. No protests were made by M. Herzog, or by his predecessors, or by the Mexican Government to our representatives in Mexico.

With these friendly relations existing between ourselves and Mexico, the Mexican Government's well-known telegram to us in connexion with the Soviet-Chinese conflict was in itself a clear indication that external influences were exerting greater pressure on Mexico.

The Mexican chargé d'affaires was unable to give me any other official explanation of the rupture of relations than a reference, clearly dragged in by the hair, to alleged 'communist intrigues' conducted in various countries against Mexico 'on the orders of Moscow'. He adduced no concrete facts, for no such facts were at the disposal of his Government, which might justify, if only in the eyes of the Mexican people themselves, not merely a rupture, but even any kind of deterioration in relations with the Soviet Union. The Mexican Government did not, of course, dare to accuse us of interference in internal Mexican affairs, for this would have been a monstrous lie, but merely referred to some intrigues in third countries, allegedly dictated by Moscow. The affair is too ridiculous to spend much time upon it, but since no other causes for the rupture of relations exist or have been adduced by the Mexican Government, it can only be assumed that the Mexican Government in the given case, acted under the pressure of external forces, and that there no longer exist in Mexico those prerequisites which at one time made possible the establishment of normal and even completely friendly relations with the Soviet Union. We can therefore only express our sympathy with the Mexican people in this affair.

25. Statement by President Pascual Ortiz Rubio at the opening of Congress on events leading up to the rupture of relations, 1 September 1930:[1] excerpt (*p. 7*)

At the end of last year, a delicate situation arose between China and the USSR, which gave rise to fears in other countries that hostilities might break out, the grave results of which might imperil the peace of the nations. With this in mind, and acting in concert with the opinion and action of other powers, the Government of Mexico, as a signatory to the Treaty for the Renunciation of

[1] Mexico, Secretaría de Relaciones Exteriores, *Un siglo de relaciones internacionales de México* (1935), pp. 419–21.

War, to which both the countries engaged in the dispute also adhered, addressed messages to the ministries of Foreign Affairs both in Nanking and Moscow, informing them in the most cordial and friendly manner possible of its most sincere desire, in the conflict which was developing, that a solution should be found in conformity with the observance of that commitment, and in particular of Article 11 of the treaty, for a peaceful settlement, both in the interests of the welfare of the two countries and of the general benefit of the world; reminding them, at the same time, of the friendship maintained with the two countries and their Governments and expressing the hope that this could be one of the factors which might be taken into account in an agreement being reached between the two powers in dispute. At the same time, the Government of Mexico informed the Governments of the Central American republics of the steps it had taken in this affair.

The Chinese Government replied to the Mexican Government's message with an explanation of the situation and an assurance that, apart from adopting protective measures in defence of its territorial sovereignty, China would readily adhere to Article 11 of the said treaty, which provides for the settlement of international differences by peaceful means, and that it was prepared at any time, within reasonable bounds, to negotiate a settlement with the Soviet Government, and also that it was resolved not to act in any way contrary to the spirit of the treaty to which it continued adhering. At the same time, the Chinese Government handed to our Minister in Tokyo an appeal to the signatories of the Pact against War explaining its situation *vis-à-vis* the Soviet Government.

The Government of the USSR, far from responding to this markedly friendly and disinterested initiative, replied verbally to the Mexican Government, through its representative in this capital, that it was unwilling to accept any démarche invoking the said Pact, but the official representing the Secretariat for Foreign Affairs notified the afore-mentioned Soviet representative that the Mexican Government was within its rights, as a signatory of the said treaty and acting in good faith, to use its best offices, as far as morally possible, in order to avoid conflicts likely to endanger the peace of the nations. Without directly answering our appeal, the Soviet Government, by means of its official press, sharply attacked the Governments of all those powers which had reminded it of its commitment, and made passing references to Mexico in markedly impertinent terms. On this account the Mexican Government protested to the Soviet representative in our country and to the Government in Moscow, through our Minister in that capital, pointing out and rejecting the unseemliness of this attack.

At the same time, there took place in several countries a number of demonstrations of a Communist nature, directed and promoted from Moscow, in front of the buildings of our diplomatic missions and consular offices. This situation, together with the evidence in the possession of the Mexican Government regarding the propaganda carried out in Mexico in political and private centres, and other equally pernicious and aggressive activities, by official elements and by irresponsible persons from the Soviet Government, determined our own Government to suspend all official contact with the Government of the USSR, whilst at the same time informing the nation that the recent Mexican revolutionary Governments had agreed to maintain friendly relations with Soviet Russia, according to their international norm of respecting all foreign sovereignties, so that Mexican sovereignty might likewise be respected by all nations, and as manifest evidence of their liberal and lofty outlook; for knowing the risks which it would have to incur and the unjustified criticism which has sometimes been levelled against it on account of its friendship for the Soviet regime, it wished to show that mark of sympathy for a people which has traditionally suffered in the cause of liberty. Unfortunately, this lofty conduct was not properly appreciated by Russia who, by sometimes raising difficulties for our nationals or by carrying on political propaganda in Mexico amongst our nationals and foreigners, and sometimes by committing acts of rude insolence and feigned misunderstanding of our démarches, or by organizing in different countries demonstrations against the Mexican Government and against our institutions and ideals, ended by creating a situation which it was neither possible nor seemly to go on enduring with the calm with which, for our part, we had been putting up with them; furthermore, as the most elementary common sense teaches, the Mexican Government has every right, in the name of its laws and its principles, not to permit alien elements to meddle in our political activities which, according to the Constitution and the usage of all nations, are exclusively reserved to its own nationals; nor should the said aliens take our territory as the theatre for their machinations and intrigues against Mexicans; for which reasons, making use of this inalienable right, the Government did not permit them to go on living in our midst and is prepared to act energetically to make them respect the country and its laws to take action against all who seek to use the nation as a cloak for the shady manoeuvres of harmful and undesirable aliens.

In consequence of this declaration, the Mexican Government ordered the closing of its Legation in Moscow and at the same time communicated this measure to the Soviet Minister who, a few days later, closed his Legation and left our country.

Whilst deploring that these grave errors [on the Soviet side] should have forced us to adopt an energetic conduct of defence and protest, the Mexican Government declares that it will continue to extend its best wishes and most cordial sympathies to the people of Russia, as a factor of importance and lofty destinies in the life of mankind.

3 *Uruguay*

26. Note from the Uruguayan Under-Secretary, J. C. Cedeiro Alonso, to the Soviet Minister in Montevideo, Aleksandr Minkin, announcing the suspension of diplomatic relations, 27 December 1935[1] (*p. 9*)

I have the honour to inform you that the Government of this Republic has decided to declare suspended the diplomatic relations which have hitherto existed between Uruguay and the Union of Soviet Socialist Republics.

The reasons which have forced the Government of Uruguay to adopt this attitude are fully set out in the decree which is reproduced below. . . .

'Montevideo, December 27th, 1935.

'In view of the statement submitted to the Ministry for Foreign Affairs by the Brazilian Embassy concerning the course of the recent disturbances of public order in its country, which were put down by the public authorities with the help of the loyal forces and by the means authorised by the Constitution; whereas that statement affirms that the insurrection was of a definitely Communist character and was inspired by the ideas put forward at the seventh Congress of the Third International, which met at Moscow in the middle of the present year; whereas it is asserted that the early stages of the movement took place in accordance with the methods recommended by the above-mentioned Congress; whereas it is also formally stated that the Soviet Government instigated and supported the communist elements in Brazil through the Soviet Legation accredited to our Government, to such extent that the Brazilian Chancellor, Dr Macedo Soares, took occasion to state, at a meeting of the Government in the Cattete Palace, that Brazil was faced with a genuine foreign aggression; whereas, when the first intimation of the revolutionary movement in Brazil was received through the Embassy at Rio, and when its nature and scope and its possible ramifications in our country were realised, the Executive informed the Brazilian Government of its desire to co-operate in a friendly manner in ascertaining the facts and of our determination to take the necessary steps for that purpose; whereas the Brazilian nation, to which we are bound by ties of close neighbourhood and traditional friendship, proposes to undertake a drastic campaign against revolutionary Communism, and appeals for our co-operation and that of the whole of America, the foundations of whose social, political and international structure are threatened by violence; whereas the Brazilian Government's solemn affirmations are corroborated by our own information, which may be summarised as follows.

'1. According to the documentary material in the possession of the Ministry for Foreign Affairs, all the speakers at the above-mentioned Moscow Congress advocated the adoption of new offensive tactics, in accordance with which

---

[1] *LNOJ*, 17th yr., no. 2, Feb. 1936, ann. 1586, pp. 233–5.

international Communism was to ally itself with all advanced parties, even if they were not Communist, forming a united front with the idea of achieving by stages the ultimate objective of full revolutionary Communism. They therefore said that an alliance could be formed with any advanced Government, even if it were supported by parties which were not specifically Communist. It would therefore be conjectured that Communism would form an alliance, as has occurred in Brazil, with the party known as the "National Alliance of Freedom", the leader of which is Luis Carlos Prestes. Prestes was the leader of the suppressed revolution, and mobilised on its behalf all the elements under his influence, so justifying the name of "The Knight of Hope", which was given to him amidst applause, at the Moscow Congress, by the delegate Van Mine [Wang Ming], Rapporteur on questions relating to South America.

'2. According to the information supplied by the Brazilian Embassy and that obtained by our own Government, the Soviet Legation at Montevideo has issued bearer cheques for large sums for purposes which cannot be ascertained, although there is strong reason to believe that they were used on the lines of the statement attributed in this connection by the Brazilian Government to the above-mentioned member of the Moscow Congress, Van Mine.

'3. According to reliable information, the Communist Congress of the Third International opened and closed with cheers for the Moscow Government and its supreme head, Stalin. Its spirit may be summed up in the words with which the delegate Van Mine concluded his report on South America: "We have programmes and an objective for the struggle, universal Socialism; we have strategy and tactics for the world revolution; we also have the fortress of the revolutionary struggle, the Union of Soviet Socialist Republics; we have a single world party, the Communist International; and we have a single and supreme chief, the great Stalin". (The house rose and applauded.) No distinction can be drawn between the Third International of the Moscow Congress and the Soviet Government. In the Soviet Union, there is no other lawful party than that which holds the ideology professed by the Government. In that singular democracy, the only effective votes are those of the Communist proletariat; non-Communist ideology is forbidden, and its votes disqualified. Accordingly, any Government must emanate from the sole existing party, which it must obey on pain of being turned out. Thus, party and Government are inseparable. The party is split up into two entities which differ only in form and in the division of labour, the one being given the name of party for purposes of propaganda at home and abroad, and the other specialising in executive action.

'And whereas the international privileges enjoyed by foreign diplomatic representatives prevent the authorities from gaining possession of certain material evidence which can normally be obtained by ordinary acts of judicial investigation that could be performed in premises not exempt from the national jurisdiction; whereas there is sufficient justification for suppressing one of the causes of unrest which disturb a friendly country, that country being convinced that the Soviet Legation at Montevideo is a centre of the Communist activity which has just been responsible for such bloodshed in that country; in accordance with the statements made by the Ministry for Foreign Affairs to the Brazilian Foreign Office in its letter of November 26th, after the outbreak of the revolution, and confirmed in its letter of December 14th; whereas we feel called upon, not only as an act of international solidarity, but in order to safeguard internal tranquillity, to put an end to the activities of the Soviet Legation in our territory until the unrest caused in our local situation has disappeared; having regard to the powers conferred on the Executive by Article 158, paragraph 17, of the Constitution: the President of the Republic in Council decrees as follows:

'*Article* 1.

'Diplomatic relations between Uruguay and the Union of Soviet Socialist Republics are hereby suspended. The Minister Plenipotentiary, M. Alexander Minkin, shall be informed that he will be granted the customary facilities for his departure and other steps connected therewith.

'*Article* 2.

'The acting Chargé d'Affaires of Uruguay at Moscow shall be instructed to leave the territory of the Union of Soviet Socialist Republics after complying with the proper formalities.

'*Article* 3.

'The present decree shall be communicated. . . .

(*Signed*) TERRA, José ESPALTER, Augusto César BADO, Alfredo BALDOMIR, Martin R. ECHEGOYEN, Zoilo SALDIAS, César G. GUTIERREZ, César CHARLONE, Eduardo Blanco ACEVEDO, Jorge HERRÁN,'

It only remains for me to inform you that the Chief of the Protocol has special instructions, when handing you your passports, to facilitate your departure from the territory of the Republic.

27. Note from the Soviet Minister, Aleksandr Minkin, to the Uruguayan Minister for Foreign Affairs, José Espalter, denying the Uruguayan charges and protesting at the suspension of relations, 28 December 1935[1] (*p. 9*)

... I have the honour to acknowledge receipt of your note of the 27th instant, informing me of your Government's decision to suspend diplomatic relations between Uruguay and the Union of Soviet Socialist Republics.

I cannot but express my astonishment at being unable to find in your note, which relates to such a grave step as the breaking-off of diplomatic relations between two countries whose friendly relations have always pursued a completely normal course and have served as a basis for the establishment of regular commercial relations, a single fact justifying your conclusions.

As you are doubtless aware, my Government has duly stated with the necessary explicitness that there is no connection between the Soviet Govern-

[1] *LNOJ*, 17th yr., no. 2, Feb. 1936, ann. 1586, pp. 235–6.

ment and the Communist International and that my Government is not responsible for the activities of the Communist International.

It is therefore not really pertinent or expedient for me to discuss the very lengthy part of your note consisting of an extract from a speech stated to have been delivered at the Congress of the Communist International.

You endeavour to base your argument on the connection between my Government and the Communist International and the bond between them and refer to the character of the elections in the Union of Soviet Socialist Republics, a nation which you venture to describe as a 'singular democracy'; moreover, you arbitrarily assert that only the 'Communist proletariat' takes part in those elections.

This assertion is categorically refuted by my country's Constitution and its baselessness is obvious in view of the fact that more than 100 million electors took part in the last elections in the Union of Soviet Socialist Republics.

Leaving on one side, therefore, your references to the decisions and deliberations of the seventh Congress of the Communist International, which have nothing whatever to do with the problem of diplomatic relations between our two countries, I will now turn to the charge contained in your note to the effect that the legation of the Union of Soviet Socialist Republics in Uruguay 'instigated and supported the Communist elements in a neighbouring State' and that 'according to the information supplied by the Embassy of a friendly country and that obtained by our own Government, the Soviet legation at Montevideo has issued bearer cheques for large sums for purposes which cannot be ascertained'.

These unproved charges are apparently based on the statement made on its faith and honour by the Brazilian Government and on the conjectures made in regard to the speeches delivered at the Congress of the Communist International. Your note contains no definite confirmation of any of the charges, which is only natural, since no proof exists nor can exist because the allegations are false.

The legation of which I am in charge has never assisted directly or indirectly the Communist Party or any other political party in South American countries and has never remitted funds to any country—including Brazil—either by means of cheques or by any other method.

I therefore categorically refute the above-mentioned charge, which I am obliged to describe as a pure fiction.

In your note, you state that your Government is breaking off relations for the purpose of safeguarding 'internal tranquillity'.

In this case again, the assertion that diplomatic relations with the Union of Soviet Socialist Republics constitute a threat to public order in Uruguay is not backed up by any evidence.

I formally assert that the legation of the Union of Soviet Socialist Republics in Uruguay has at all times performed solely and exclusively, and in the strictest possible manner, the functions provided for and allowed by the rules of Public International Law, and that this legation has never had anything to do with the internal affairs of Uruguay and has never intervened in party strife either in this country or in any other American country.

Without prejudice to the attitude which my Government may subsequently adopt, I wish to enter a strong protest against the false charges made against the Soviet Government and the legation of which I am in charge and to refute them categorically.

28. Note from the Uruguayan Minister for Foreign Affairs to the Soviet Minister rejecting the Soviet note, 28 December 1935[1] (*p. 9*)

I have taken cognisance of your note of to-day's date and desire to inform you that I do not consider it proper to discuss the reasons for the suspension of diplomatic relations with the Union of Soviet Socialist Republics, since you are no longer accredited to our Government as diplomatic representative.

Moreover, in view of the unsuitable terms employed by your Excellency, I am obliged to inform you that I cannot keep your note which I am therefore returning and which I was surprised to see had been published this afternoon.

29. Further protest by the Soviet Minister to the Uruguayan Foreign Minister, 30 December 1935[2] (*p. 9*)

I have the honour to acknowledge receipt of your note dated the 28th instant, with which you have returned my note of the same date after taking cognisance of its terms.

As you will have inferred from the clear and unequivocal terms of my note, its chief object was to place on record my protest against the charges made against my Government and its legation in Uruguay, and categorically to refute the facts on which those charges were based.

In particular, my note was designed to clear up by means of documentary evidence the specific charge that this legation had sent large sums of money to Brazil in the form of bearer cheques; this should not be difficult, since, even if they are paid in another country, cheques must be returned to the banking establishment on which they were drawn.

I sincerely regret therefore that you should consider that the reasons which induced the Uruguayan Government to suspend diplomatic relations with the Union of Soviet Socialist Republics cannot be properly discussed; without, however, entering upon a discussion, I consider it only right that I should be informed of the specific acts of which the legation of the Union of Soviet Socialist Republics is accused, or, at all events, of those over which your Government has or may have control and on which its decision has been expressly based.

I accordingly take the liberty of insisting that I be informed of the details—including the date, amount, number and establishment on which they were drawn—of the cheques which it is asserted were issued by the legation of the Union of Soviet Socialist Republics and which according to your note of the 27th instant, 'there is strong reason to believe' were used by this legation for

---

[1] *LNOJ*, 17th yr., no. 2, Feb. 1936, ann. 1586, p. 236.
[2] Ibid., pp. 236–7.

the purpose of rendering financial assistance to the Brazilian revolutionaries.

I greatly regret that the publication of my note regarding the suspension of diplomatic relations between your country and the Union of Soviet Socialist Republics should have surprised you, but this attitude was adopted in the first place by the Ministry for Foreign Affairs, which published your note of the 27th instant. I consider the Ministry's attitude, like my own, to have been quite correct and appropriate to the case.

With reference to your statement that it is not proper to discuss with me the reasons for the decision to suspend diplomatic relations between our two countries, I desire to inform you, before concluding the present note, that, in my opinion, a diplomatic representative in my position has in every case the right, in accordance with the rules of Public International Law, to act as I have done.

30. Soviet press comment on the suspension of relations: article by
D. Zaslavsky, 'The Office-Boys of the Brazilian Reactionaries',
30 December 1935[1] (*p. 9*)

Uruguay lies off the main track of international diplomacy, and its leaders have hitherto been able to appear on the scene without attracting too much attention to themselves or their country. In fact, nobody has noticed them. They are wholesalers in trade and peddlers in politics. Like other American small landowning ruling classes, they are essentially representatives of the large English and United States firms. They always have their doubts about who should be in power. That is why they always start trembling whenever a President is overthrown, or popular unrest breaks out, in a neighbouring state, even when it is also one of small landowners and only local importance.

In South America truly momentous events are on foot. In Brazil the broad popular movement for freedom still goes on. We understand that the Brazilian reaction wishes to conceal in every possible way the mass character of the struggle which the broad popular masses are leading against it. To this end it is making use of the shoddy old means of provocative lies against the USSR. The old hack-work legend of 'the hand of Moscow' is trotted out. But Brazil has no relations whatsoever with the USSR. In Rio de Janeiro, however, they recall that such relations do exist between Uruguay and the USSR. The appropriate directives are sent to Montevideo. And the rulers of Uruguay, those self-important buffoons, petty office-boys of the Brazilian reactionaries, willingly exert themselves and hasten to carry out their orders and play the role of saviours of 'internal peace' of the South American countries.

There is no need to waste time unmasking this absurd and pitiful fabrication. It is more to the point to turn to the conduct of the Uruguayan Government itself. When the revolutionary events took place in Brazil, the little tradesmen in Montevideo began to tremble. When the revolutionary movement was suppressed, the little tradesmen grew saucy. They resolved to take a diplomatic step which could not fail to draw on them the attention of the entire world. They 'severed' relations with the USSR.

[1] *Pravda*, 30 Dec. 1935.

The rulers of Uruguay responsible for this comic-opera gesture accompanied it with a note, the whole tone of which might earn it a worthy place in our *Krokodil*. It was doubtless composed by the most learned and intelligent minister of the Uruguayan Government, who could well have occupied an honourable post as Inspector at some provincial school in Tsarist Russia.

The note was written according to the old White Guard prescriptions dating back to the time of the united imperialist hordes' attack on the Soviet Union. First and foremost it complains of the greetings to Comrade Stalin of the 7th Comintern Congress, which nearly caused the downfall of Brazil by passing a Resolution on the United Front. That is really the height of absurdity. The Uruguayan rulers heard at the time the speeches made at the Comintern Congress, they watched with distress the delegates to the Congress being welcomed by leading people in the Soviet Union—yet they never complained. For half a year they held their peace and never stammered out a word, then all of a sudden they flew into a rage, not only on their own account, but on behalf of everybody, and resolved to save the whole world by their exertions.

And another thing which these provincial shysters from Montevideo write is about some cheques sent by someone or other to somebody else, but who received those cheques and for which purpose is not known. All this small-town twaddle is written in a document which is strongly reminiscent of Ivan Nikiforovich Dovgochun's libel against Ivan Ivanovich Pererepenko,[1] but it is not called libel in the old legal sense of the term but a diplomatic note. This is the small-town twaddle concocted according to anti-Soviet and Fascist recipes which our diplomatic representatives have to deal with.

Until recently we had no diplomatic relations with Brazil's office-boys in Montevideo. But neither for them, nor for their heirs of the same brood, will it again be easy to 'recognise' us. They have only to ask the Uruguayan diplomats in Mexico. As is well known, the Mexican Government at one time 'severed' relations with the USSR. And when they later came to themselves and wanted to re-establish these relations, they were told that this would only be possible on condition they admitted that their 'accusations' against the Soviet Union had been groundless, and the rupture itself without any justification.

International diplomacy, in which the Soviet Government takes part, is not —however many somersaults the acrobats may make—just a circus arena where they go on cracking their whip at Moscow with impunity. The Uruguayan Government may, or may not, recognize the Soviet Union; that is something to be decided according to their own intellectual lights. But they are obliged to respect the rules of elementary decency. Uruguay is a member of the League of Nations. Clause 12 of the Charter of the League lays upon all its members the obligation not to have recourse to the severance of relations without preliminary discussions either in the form of arbitration or in the Council. This the Uruguayan Government has not done. Hurling an aggressive challenge at the Soviet Union, it has disregarded its obligations as a member of the League of Nations. It thought it could get away with disregarding these obligations.

---

[1] Two Ukrainian squires who fell out over a fancied slight in the 'Tale of How Ivan Ivanovich Quarrelled with Ivan Nikiforovich' in Gogol's *Mirgorod*.

There exist however norms of conduct for all states, whatever their size and type of government.

31. The winding up of the Soviet trading agency Yuzhamtorg, 1 January 1936[1] (*p. 9*)

On the proposal of the People's Commissar for Foreign Trade, Comrade A. P. Rosengoltz, the Soviet economic organizations which hold the majority of the shares of the Uruguayan Company Yuzhamtorg (through which all foreign trade transactions between Uruguay and the USSR are carried out) have resolved to call a special meeting of shareholders with a view to the liquidation of Yuzhamtorg.

Trade between the USSR and Uruguay during recent years is illustrated by the following figures:

(000 *rubles*)

	Uruguayan imports from USSR	*Uruguayan exports to USSR*	*Balance of trade in favour of Uruguay*
1934	1,267	2,092	+825
1935*	513	1,475	+962

* 11 months

Our imports from Uruguay consist basically of wool and hides. As can be seen from the above figures, the balance of trade between the USSR and Uruguay is strongly in favour of Uruguay. For the first eleven months of 1935, our imports from Uruguay are nearly three times as great as our exports to Uruguay.

The nature of our exports to Uruguay—mainly petroleum products, timber, and manufactured goods exports—is such that they can easily be switched to other markets. In addition, Uruguay has never played a part of any consequence as a market for Soviet exports. On the other hand, Uruguay is keenly interested in Soviet purchases as she has a very favourable balance of trade with the USSR which buys from her goods which constitute her main exports.

Soviet arraignment of Uruguay at the League of Nations

32. Statement by Litvinov to the League Council, January 1936:[2] excerpts (*p. 9*)

I would like to begin by assuring you, Mr President, that the Soviet Government would not deliberately take up the time of the Council of the League of Nations with the question of the rupture of diplomatic relations between Uruguay and the Union of Soviet Socialist Republics if this affected only the interests of these two countries, more especially since the interests of the Soviet Union remain practically untouched by this rupture. You will have little

[1] *Pravda*, 1 Jan. 1936.   [2] *LNOJ*, 17th yr., Feb. 1936, pp. 90–5.

difficulty in realising that the 170 million population of our Union is not likely to feel very acutely the absence of relations with remote Uruguay. . . .

. . . Diplomatic relations between Uruguay and the Union of Soviet Socialist Republics were theoretically established by an exchange of notes on August 22nd, 1926, on the initiative of the Uruguayan Government. The Soviet Government eliciting the fact that the Uruguayan Government was in no great hurry to exchange diplomatic missions, reconciled itself to a state of affairs in which relations were maintained through the agency of the representatives of both States in other countries. When, however, in the summer of 1933, the Uruguayan Government spontaneously expressed the desire to exchange missions, the Soviet Government agreed to this, and, in March 1934, a Uruguayan mission arrived in Moscow, a Soviet mission arriving in Montevideo two months later.

Throughout the existence of these missions, neither controversies, conflicts, nor serious misunderstandings between the two States arose. The only subject of discussion between the Uruguayan mission in Moscow and the People's Commissariat for Foreign Affairs concerned exclusively the matter of finding suitable quarters for the mission. Discussions between the Soviet Minister in Montevideo and the Uruguayan Foreign Office were limited to three points. The first concerned one Simon Radovitsky, an anarchist, imprisoned in Uruguay on a charge of terrorist attempts. The Uruguayan Government, for reasons of internal politics, desired to deport Radovitsky to the Soviet Union, on the plea that he was born in Russia. As, however, Radovitsky is not a Soviet citizen, the Soviet Government refused to admit him to the country. Somewhat surprisingly, this apparently insignificant matter caused an altogether disproportionate reaction on the part of the Uruguayan Government. The President of the Republic himself took a personal interest in it, repeatedly endeavouring to obtain the consent of the Soviet Minister to the deportation of Radovitsky, actually taking his refusal as a personal offence, and making no attempt to conceal his resentment.

Next, our Minister had to make a protest in October last to the Uruguayan Foreign Minister against an attack on the Soviet Union by a reactionary Uruguayan newspaper in the course of a campaign against local Communists and anti-Fascists, and against the application to Italy of sanctions. In a telegram of October 26th, 1935, the Soviet Minister, M. Minkin, cabled to me as follows:

'In reply to my oral protest, the Uruguayan Foreign Minister asserted that he was unable to influence the Press, but assured me that the Government did not share the views expressed in the article. During further conversation, the Minister remarked that the President still nourished resentment on account of Radovitsky, regarding the refusal to admit the latter to the Soviet Union as showing a lack of good feeling towards himself. The question of Radovitsky, added the Foreign Minister, is becoming here a political issue.'

Finally, in a telegram of December 10th, 1935, from M. Minkin, I read as follows:

'The Uruguayan Foreign Minister tells me that the President of the Republic would consider himself compensated for our refusal to admit Radovitsky if we would buy two hundred tons or so of Uruguayan cheese. I would recommend, for the improvement of relations with President Terra, the purchase of a small consignment of cheese.'

But the Soviet Government, despite the recommendations of our Minister, did not see its way to purchasing Uruguayan cheese. In this connection, M. Minkin cabled to us on December 19th:

'The secretary of the President informs me that our refusal to grant his request regarding cheese is interpreted as a fresh display of lack of consideration towards himself and may weaken his arguments in favour of the maintenance of relations between Uruguay and the Union of Soviet Socialist Republics.'

I have related all this so that you may see for yourselves that the only grievance advanced by the Uruguayan Government, both in Moscow and in Montevideo, consisted in our refusal to admit Radovitsky and to purchase Uruguayan cheese. There has not been a single complaint of incorrect conduct on the part of the Soviet mission in Montevideo, or of its interference in internal affairs in Uruguay or any other South-American Republic. Indeed, as I have just had the honour to read to you, on October 26th, 1935, the Uruguayan Minister for Foreign Affairs assured our Minister that his Government did not share the views accusing the Soviet Government advanced by certain Uruguayan newspapers.

All this made still more surprising the note received by the Soviet Minister at Montevideo declaring that the Uruguayan Government had resolved to break off diplomatic relations with the Soviet Union. . . .

. . . Uruguay, in taking upon itself to break off relations with the Soviet Union, without submitting the conflict to arbitration, or to the enquiry by the Council, has thereby infringed the Covenant of the League. This fact must be acknowledged, whatever the nature of the conflict, for the article I have just quoted admits of no exceptions. If Article 12 mentions also resort to war, it does not follow that ruptures which do not lead to war are excluded from the effect of that article. It is exactly because a rupture of relations may sometimes result in war that Article 12 tries to exclude sudden ruptures from international practice, prescribing some preliminary procedure which may avert the rupture as well as its possible consequences.

The guilt of the Uruguayan Government is the greater in that the reason given in its note for a rupture had not formerly been advanced either in any preliminary negotiations whatsoever, in correspondence with, or representations to, the Soviet Government. Any grievances touched upon by the Uruguayan Government in diplomatic conversations, regarding, as I have already stated, the admission of Radovitsky, or the non-purchase of cheese (if this latter can really be regarded as a grievance), were certainly not mentioned in the note of the Uruguayan Government. We would, moreover, seek in vain, even in the note itself, for any serious cause for a rupture. The note is extremely verbose, and touches upon some controversial points, which have, however, nothing whatsoever to do with the matter before the Council of the League. I am prepared, in the right place and at the right moment, to discuss any point even of merely academic interest, but at the present moment I will confine

9

myself to the question before the Council—the infringement by Uruguay of the Covenant of the League—and will not enter into the fruitless discussion of problems which can never be settled by the Council of the League.

Two facts may be regarded as incontrovertible: first, the Uruguayan Government has broken off diplomatic relations with the Soviet Union; second, the reason advanced by the Uruguayan Government for a rupture was not submitted either to arbitration or to enquiry by the Council of the League, as stipulated in Article 12 of the Covenant. Even if the Uruguayan Government had had a real grievance, this would not by any means do away with the infringement of the Covenant, or justify its action.

... The accusations against the Soviet Government and its mission in Montevideo, mentioned in the Uruguayan note, are entirely unfounded. As a matter of fact, there is not a single precise accusation, not one definite fact laid to the charge of the Soviet Government, or of the Soviet mission in Montevideo, in the Uruguayan note. In this note, the Uruguayan Government does not actually assert anything, merely expressing assumptions, and even these mainly not its own. For instance, the note contains the words: 'It is definitely asserted' (by whom and when it is not said) that 'the Soviet Government instigated and supported the Communist elements in Brazil through the agency of the Soviet mission to our Government'. I declare categorically that this assertion, by whomsoever it was made, is absolutely untrue. Neither the Soviet Government, the Soviet mission in Montevideo, nor any other agents of the Soviet Government instigated and supported Communist elements, whether in Uruguay or in any neighbouring State, for the Soviet Government is consistently true to its policy of non-interference in the internal affairs of other States. I challenge the Uruguayan Government to produce evidence, if it has any, to the contrary. And I declare in advance that no such evidence can be forthcoming. ...

Another reference to the Soviet mission in Montevideo is to be found in the note to the effect that, 'according to the information supplied by the Brazilian Embassy and that obtained by our own Government, the Soviet Legation in Montevideo has issued bearer cheques for large sums for purposes which cannot be ascertained'. And so the Soviet mission labours under the accusation of having transmitted unknown large sums at an unknown date to unknown persons, and, their purpose and destination being undiscovered, it is to be assumed that they were expended on the financing of revolts in Brazil! It seems to me that a legal training is not necessary for the comprehension of the utter irresponsibility and baselessness of such accusations. If the cheques were transmitted in Montevideo, surely it ought not to be hard to find out through the Uruguayan banks, on which these cheques were drawn, the exact numbers, amounts, dates and so on! The Uruguayan Government did not even take the trouble to obtain and check such details, obviously because investigation would not only have shown the utter absurdity of the statements, but would have convinced the Uruguayan Government that the Soviet mission in Montevideo, during the two years of its existence received altogether for its own requirements—for equipment, the purchase of motor-cars, salaries—about 55,000 American dollars, of which sum it did not transmit any money anywhere outside Uruguay. In any case, we feel entitled to insist that the Uruguayan Government produce proofs to the Council of the League regarding the only concrete fact advanced in its note.

If, however, there are no definite accusations in the Uruguayan note, there is a long discussion of the point that, seeing that not long ago there was a revolt in Brazil, and that there is a Soviet Mission in Uruguay, there must be some connection between these two phenomena. Even if it were a question of a country in which perfect internal peace usually prevailed, in which there was always perfect harmony among the various sections of the population, and this peace and harmony were suddenly interrupted two years after the arrival in a neighbouring country of a Soviet mission, there would be no grounds for making this mission responsible for what occurred in that country. But I would ask you, gentlemen, to bear in mind that the country in question is Brazil, whose whole history is nothing but an uninterrupted chain of internal disorders, risings, mutinies, revolutions, conspiracies, upheavals, and *coups d'État* for the violent substitution of one set of rulers by others. . . .

. . . The history of Uruguay is as far from presenting a picture of internal tranquillity as that of Brazil. . . .

. . . Risings and revolts in Brazil and Uruguay seem to be of quite frequent occurrence and obviously originate in profound internal causes. This being the case, what are the grounds for seeking to lay the blame of the last rising in Brazil to the door of the Soviet mission in Montevideo? Does, really, the history of the Brazilians or the Uruguayans lead us to believe that they can be in need of guidance from outsiders in the art of risings, or have they not shown themselves as past-masters of that art? . . .

33. Statement by Alberto Guani, representative of Uruguay, to the League Council, January 1936:[1] excerpts (*p. 9*)

. . . The Soviet complaint against us asserts that Uruguay, referring to representations said to have been made by the authorities of a third State, has decided to break off diplomatic relations with the Union of Soviet Socialist Republics, and that the third State in question is our friend and neighbour Brazil, which has recently witnessed on its own soil the sanguinary Communist insurrection of November.

The events that preceded that insurrection were as follows: The seventh Congress of the Communist Third International had just been held in Moscow, from July 25th to August 25th, 1935. Several meetings had been devoted to the question of the organisation of revolts and revolutionary movements in the various Latin-American Republics. On August 7th, Comrade Van Min [Wang Ming] presented a report on that subject. At its meeting on August 20th, the Congress, on Van Min's report, incorporated the Communist Parties of Peru, Colombia, Venezuela, Costa Rica and Puerto Rico in the Third International. During the same meeting, the Congress referred to its Bureau the question of the admission of Panama, Ecuador and Haiti. At the same Congress Van Min remarked that it was probably one of the last occasions on which he

---

[1] *LNOJ*, 17th yr., no. 2, Feb. 1936, pp. 95–8.

would have to address the Congress on Brazilian affairs, as the valuable collaboration of Comrade Carlos Prestes, who had just become a member of the Executive Council of the Komintern, was available. That collaboration would enable him to continue in Brazil, with full authority, the work he had already begun on behalf of the Third International.

The Rio de Janeiro paper *Correo da Manha* of December 11th, a copy of which I have before me, in reproducing Van Min's statements with regard to Communist activities in Brazil, attributes to him a remark to the effect that the National Liberating Alliance (the party of Prestes in Brazil) was established under the secret direction of the Communist Party in Montevideo in accordance with confidential instructions received from the Soviet Legation in Montevideo. Van Min concluded his observations with the following utterance: 'I hope and desire that the work undertaken by our good comrades in Brazil will be successful. That will be a proud moment and a great triumph for the Moscow Government and the Third International.'

I beg to draw attention to this significant point. In the list of countries, which is in alphabetical order, the instigator of the last revolt in Brazil, Carlos Prestes, is No. 4, whilst Stalin is No. 35. I invite attention to this circumstance in order to show the close connection which exists between the Komintern and the Soviet Government in the matter of the bolshevisation of Latin America. It was therefore one of Stalin's colleagues in the Direction of the Komintern who was charged with the organisation of the sanguinary Communist rising in Brazil.

The usual attempt will no doubt be made to delimit the responsibilities. But we all know, from the Moscow official Press itself, the authority—the dictatorial authority we might say—which M. Stalin exercises in the Soviet Government. The report of the Komintern Congress also shows the dominant rôle played in the Komintern by this personage, who is closely and directly associated with the most important decisions of the internal and external policy of the Soviets.

In presence of the definite origins of the sanguinary tragedy which has just been played out in Brazilian territory, in presence of the sorrows of a country desolated by an inexplicable civil war, the distinguished Brazilian Minister for Foreign Affairs, M. Macedo Soares, said at a Government Council meeting: 'We are faced with nothing less than foreign aggression'. What were we to do, we who were giving hospitality to the Soviets in our own territory, when, taking advantage of their official prerogatives, they spread the fires of revolution amid a friendly people, awaiting only a suitable moment to extend the conflagration to our own country?

The increase in the Soviet agitation in South America to which I have alluded, the recent revolution in Brazil, the warnings given by the Government of that friendly country and its formal denunciations in view of the strict Brazilian surveillance of the Communist affiliations, the funds required for these criminal undertakings which could only reach Brazil across the Uruguayan frontiers, and, finally, the exceptional fact that Montevideo was the only American capital in which the cover of diplomatic immunities could be utilised in support of such operations, since Uruguay was the only country in Latin

America where the Soviets had a recognised official representative—all these concurrent considerations, definite as they were and speaking for themselves, and backed, moreover, by internal and external testimony alike, have fully convinced my Government that it was a matter of national and international necessity for us to put an immediate stop to a situation which placed Uruguay before the dilemma of temporising with the Soviet Legation in Montevideo or proving without delay to our neighbours and friends in America that we were at one with them in the defence of a peace and order which were being menaced.

My Government could not hesitate an instant as to the line it was called upon to take. We could not do otherwise than make use of our elementary right of self-defence, by withdrawing the prerogatives and putting a stop to the official activities of the Soviet Legation in Montevideo, pending the establishment of a less alarming atmosphere. . . .

Uruguay, which, in 1933, entered into effective diplomatic relations with the Union of Soviet Socialist Republics, to-day feels compelled, for the reasons stated, to revert to the position before that date. In so doing, she asserts that, while the relations in question have been interrupted, there is no conflict in the matter and that she has made no complaint against the Moscow Government.

The motives which gave rise to the internal decision by which the Uruguayan Government interrupted those relations come within the category of questions which are the exclusive concern of States. . . .

34. Further exchanges between Litvinov and Guani, January 1936:[1] excerpts (*p. 9*)

M. LITVINOFF . . . I note with satisfaction that the representative of Uruguay, has not denied any of the facts which I advanced this morning, and he has not brought forward any evidence in support of the accusation contained in the Uruguayan note concerning the Soviet mission in Montevideo. He has preferred to hide behind a smoke-screen and expatiate about the Komintern, the Third International and the identity of the former organisation with the Soviet Government. Those arguments can be read any day in any German paper or in other reactionary papers of other countries. There is nothing new in what the representative of Uruguay has told us on that point.

It would appear, moreover, that all these elements existed when Uruguay asked us to send a diplomatic mission to Montevideo and when Uruguay, in the person of M. Guani, supported the invitation to the Soviet Union to join the League. Our Government has not changed its policy since that time, and that furnishes no proof as to why Uruguay has considered it necessary to break off its relations with the Soviet Union, seeing that the Komintern existed formerly, and no change has taken place in the situation. . . .

. . . If the Council would care to study the character of the last Brazilian revolt, I should be quite willing to help it, in an academic manner, in order to convince my colleagues that the revolt had no Communist character. Indeed, I can give quotations from certain Latin-American papers concurring with that view.

An Argentine paper said: 'To suggest that the movement in Brazil bore a Communist character would raise it above the level of South-American revolutions the object of which is, in general to substitute one dictatorship for another.'

I quote also from a Chilean paper: 'It was a popular movement provoked by the excesses of the regime. The leaders of the movement did not try to introduce Soviet proletarian or Communist ideas, which, as everybody knows, is the aim of Communism. It merely tried to introduce a national Government, a strong Government, capable of doing away with the excesses of the oligarchy, with speculation, and with political and social corruption.'

They were bourgeois papers, not Communist papers, which testified in these terms to the character of the last Brazilian revolt. Moreover, the responsibility for the movement has been officially accepted by the 'National Liberating Alliance', in which are represented many bourgeois parties, and the fact that M. Prestes, a Communist, took part in the revolt does not make the whole revolt Communistic. The same M. Prestes had taken part in many Brazilian revolts before he became a Communist; on one occasion, he even took part in revolts together with his friend, M. Vargas, the President of Brazil, who, moreover, did not object very strongly to M. Prestes' revolutionary activities; it was only when Prestes worked against him that the latter felt obliged to explain M. Prestes' action by influence from outside. Why was Prestes able formerly to work without assistance from outside, and why was it only in the recent incidents that he was obliged to have assistance from Moscow? The Uruguayan representative fails to explain that.

M. Guani wishes us to believe that the revolt took place in Brazil because a certain Chinese Communist, Van Min [Wang Ming], made a speech in Moscow, in which he expressed sympathies with the movements of liberation in all countries, Brazil included. M. Guani wishes to convince us of the instrumentality of speeches made ten or twenty thousand kilometres away from the place of the revolution. He nevertheless knows quite well that such an argument is unconvincing, for he referred unwittingly to an inaccurate account of a speech by the same Chinese Communist at Moscow in which reference was made to the activities of the Soviet mission at Montivideo. It was later declared openly in a Moscow paper, the *Pravda*, on January 15th that the statement made was false, and Van Min then rectified the matter and stated that he had made no reference whatever to the Soviet mission at Montevideo in his original speech. I am sorry that M. Guani should have been misled on this point. I think it is a fact that the forged speech did appear in certain Latin-American papers, although M. Guani probably did not know that it had already been exposed as a forgery. I was right when I told you this morning that if evidence were produced in this connection, that evidence would prove to be a forgery.

Whatever may be the sympathies of Chinese, French, British or Soviet Communists with the revolutionary movement, whatever may be the comradeship between Stalin and Prestes, this has no bearing on the matter under discussion. Until it is proved that the Soviet Government, the Komintern or any other organisation has used the Soviet mission at Montevideo as an agency for giving instructions or assistance to the Brazilian Communist movement, so long as the Soviet mission does not come into question, the acts of the Communists of China, Japan, England or elsewhere can have no bearing on the matter. . . .

M. GUANI . . . The Soviet representative would like the Council to open a public investigation, with all the available evidence, into only one part of the facts which gave rise to my Government's decisions—namely, the part concerning the secret investigations made by our police in the Montevideo banks. Those investigations were carried out confidentially mainly in view of the diplomatic privileges enjoyed by the head of the Soviet mission in Uruguay, privileges which we were anxious to respect to the end.

I regret I cannot follow M. Litvinoff in these suggestions. The reason for our presence here is not to hold a sort of judicial enquiry to which the Soviet representative and I would be the parties. If I agreed to anything like that, I should be going directly counter to the legal standpoint adopted by my Government in this matter and which I described to you this morning. I have already pointed out to the Council that an internal political decision by my Government such as that brought before you by the People's Commissary for Foreign Affairs of the Soviet Union is purely a matter of its internal jurisdiction. I could not lay on the Council table the secret report of our police or the confidential information given us by the Montevideo banks or the correspondence exchanged between our Foreign Minister and his colleagues in the different American chancelleries. All such information forms part of the purely internal records of the case. I can give my colleagues on the Council a formal assurance that the nature of this information is sufficiently disquieting and serious to have served as an element, coupled with all the considerations and facts I mentioned this morning, in the decision of December 28th, concerning which the Soviet Union has brought its charge at Geneva.

M. LITVINOFF—I cannot follow the arguments of the representative of Uruguay. If the matter relates only to the domestic affairs of Uruguay, why is the Council wasting its time in examining the question now? Since the Uruguayan Government has decided to come and discuss the question here, to make statements, to open a discussion and to reach a decision, it must surely give all possible help to the Council to throw some light upon the facts and to reach a decision.

M. Guani cannot expect the Council to say 'We believe M. Guani, and we do not believe M. Litvinoff'. The Council's decision must be founded on facts, and to appreciate facts proofs must be forthcoming.

It is true that banks have no right to disclose the secrets of their clients, to say how much money they receive, or what they do with it. But I am ready to ask M. Minkin to write to the banks authorising them to reveal their secrets, to say how much he received during his stay in Montevideo, to whom he paid his money, on what date and under what conditions. It seems to me, therefore, that the whole question of police secrets and bank secrets no longer exists.

What I wish is a decision based on a full knowledge of the facts. To all that the representative of Uruguay has said on the other questions, I have replied.

What is of importance to me is to prove the futility of the accusations made against the Soviet representative in Montevideo, who has been reproached with having abused his privileges. That is a serious accusation, and, in order to make it, proof is necessary. Once again, I repeat that the question of police and bank secrets cannot be raised before the Council, since I am prepared to authorise the banks to supply all possible proof, to indicate the numbers of the cheques, etc. We are prepared to send a letter to that effect. We are ready to throw all possible light on the actions of the Soviet mission in Montevideo. I personally am not at all in a hurry. This discussion can be adjourned if it is so desired, in order to await the reply from the banks. All I want is a demonstration of the truth and all the truth.

No one has the right to calumniate a private person. No one has the right either to calumniate a State. When that is done, the nation is justified in refuting the accusations made against its honour and to demand proof of the calumnies contained in diplomatic and public documents. Any State must be held responsible for its statements with regard to another State.

M. GUANI—I must insist on the position taken by my Government in this matter. We hold that the rupture of diplomatic relations with the Soviets in the present case, and in view of the circumstances which preceded it, is a case of self-defence for Uruguay. It is a question within the sphere of our country's municipal law. Consequently, a question of that kind cannot properly be submitted to an international court of law, even the Council. We consider that the powers of which we have availed ourselves are powers which definitely belong to us. That is the position to which we intend to adhere.

35. Resolution of the League Council, 24 January 1936[1] (*p. 9*)

Whereas the representative of Uruguay refuses to give the proofs demanded by the Government of the Union of Soviet Socialist Republics, alleging that the question is one of internal law;

Whereas the representative of the USSR has stated that he is satisfied by Uruguay's refusal to prove the charges brought against the Soviet Legation in Montevideo and that he is prepared to leave the question to the judgment of international public opinion, a course which the representative of Uruguay also accepts for his country:

Whereas the Council is dealing with the question under Article 11, paragraph 2, of the Covenant and, its mission being essentially one of conciliation, any resolution it may take must be adopted unanimously;

The Council:

Expresses the hope that the interruption of diplomatic relations between Uruguay and the USSR will be temporary, and that the two countries will take a favourable opportunity of resuming those relations;

Invites the two parties to refrain from any act which might be harmful to the interests of peace and to the resumption of their diplomatic relations in the future.

[1] *LNOJ*, 17th yr., Feb. 1936, p. 138.

36. Soviet press comment on the League debate, January 1936[1] (*p. 9*)
Geneva, 24 January (TASS). In Geneva circles, today's resolution by the Council in regard to Uruguay's rupture of relations with the USSR is considered to be a very important international political success for the USSR. In particular, they draw attention to the following points:

1. The resolution indirectly, but very clearly, condemns the action of the Uruguayan Government since it recommends that relations between the two countries should be restored.

2. The resolution indirectly recognizes that Uruguay had no grounds for breaking off diplomatic relations with the USSR, or at least no such grounds as the League of Nations would recognize.

3. The resolution puts it on record that the representative of the Soviet Union asked that evidence should be produced, and offered for his part to supply any evidence that might be required. But the representative of Uruguay refused to produce the necessary evidence. All understood that he did not produce it because he had no evidence. All understood that his claim that it was a purely domestic affair did not hold water, since the representative of Uruguay recognized the competence of the League, by appearing before the Council to give evidence.

4. With regard to the infringement of Article 12 of the League's Charter, the sense of that article is so clear that any elucidation of the meaning would only weaken its sense. The more so, since for such elucidation to be binding, it would need to be adopted unanimously, including by the representative of Uruguay, who however stubbornly denied that there was any infringement of Article 12 on the part of Uruguay. Moreover, in this connection he would be able to count on the support of his Latin American friends.

They also stress here that the League of Nations debate on this affair has specially disappointed those anti-Soviet elements who were hoping that nearly all the capitalist governments represented in the Council would exploit the occasion to drag in the Comintern and propaganda. In fact, not a single member of the Council decided to support the Uruguayan thesis in this question, not even the Argentine delegate. The latter particularly refused to play the Uruguayan game when he announced at the session yesterday evening that Argentina had not yet restored diplomatic relations with the USSR only because she had not received any explanation about an incident involving an Argentine diplomatic colleague at the time of the October Revolution. The Argentine delegate thereby indicated that the misgivings inspired, according to the delegate of Uruguay, by the alleged 'danger' represented by the Soviet missions in Latin America made no impression on the Argentine delegate. There are some who even see in this attitude of the Argentine delegate an invitation to the USSR to liquidate the 1918 incident and renew diplomatic relations.

----

[1] *Pravda*, 25 Jan. 1936.

4 Argentina

Diplomatic relations

37. Protest by Maksim Litvinov regarding facilities extended to the former representative of the Tsarist Government and offer by the Soviet Government to enter into diplomatic relations, 3 April 1923[1] (*p. 8*)

A passport issued by the Russian mission in Buenos Aires bearing the signature of 'Ambassador Stein' has been presented to the Russian authorities. The Soviet Government has appointed no one to be its representative in Argentina and declares that it accepts no responsibility for the activities or liabilities of the officials of deposed Russian Governments, and regards these activities and liabilities as illegal and inoperative. The Soviet Government requests the Government of Argentina to prevent the said Stein from continuing to exercise his functions in the name of the Russian Government, and also to publish an appropriate statement for the guidance of interested persons, e.g. émigrés desirous of repatriation, who might in misunderstanding apply to Stein.

The Russian Government requests you to take the appropriate steps to restore diplomatic relations between our two countries, for which the Russian Government is always ready.

38. Statement by the Argentine representative at the League of Nations, Ruiz Guiñazú, giving Argentina's reason for rejecting Soviet overtures, January 1936:[2] excerpt (*p. 8*)

The Argentine Government has never recognised the Government of the Soviets and consequently has had no diplomatic relations with it. Let me add that it was never possible for such relations to be established because at the beginning of the Soviet regime there occurred an unprecedented attack on our Legation at St Petersburg and because the Soviet Government had not given the explanations requested, in conformity with the rules of international law, although it was shown that the offence had been committed by Soviet officials. That is why the Argentine Republic has no diplomatic relations with the Soviet Union.

39. Argentina proposes the expulsion of the USSR from the League: telegram from the Minister for Foreign Affairs, José María Cantilo, to the Secretary-General, 4 December 1939[3] (*p. 32*)

Now that the Fourth Committee is in session, the Argentine Government

---

[1] Telegram to the Argentine Minister, *Dok. Vnesh. Pol.*, vi (1962), no. 137, pp. 240–1.
[2] *LNOJ*, 17th yr., Feb. 1936, p. 103.
[3] Ibid., 20th yr., Nov.–Dec. 1939, ann. 1756/iv, p. 511.

considers that before it deals with the administrative and budgetary questions coming within its province, a formal protest should be made against the aggression of which the Soviet Union has been guilty against Finland in violation not only of the principles of the League of Nations, but also of the most elementary dictates of justice and humanity. This violation, which is all the more odious in view of the enormous difference in material forces, justifies the immediate expulsion of the Soviet Union from the League. The creation of fronts inside countries for the purpose of facilitating the spread of Communism constitutes a danger to which nations that place respect for human life, conscience and liberty above all else cannot remain indifferent.

Soviet intervention in the Argentine CP factional struggles

40. Letter from the Comintern Secretariat to the Argentine CP, November 1926[1] (*p. 13*)

The group expelled from the Communist Party of Argentina, having failed in its attempt to split the revolutionary vanguard of that country by forming a so-called Workers' Communist Party, is still carrying on its anti-Communist propaganda abroad, not only through its newspaper entitled *La Chispa*, but also by means of circular letters addressed to the revolutionary organizations. Through these pamphlets calumnies are spread against the leaders of the Communist Party of Argentina, with the aim of thereby discrediting the revolutionary action of our party and starting intrigues against it. The anti-Communist character of these so-called 'Communist workers' has already been denounced in the Open Letter we recently sent to the Argentine Communist Party approving the activity of its Central Committee. We will confine ourselves to pointing out that the activity of this group has fully justified our decision and has proved that the sole mission of these elements is that of fighting against the revolutionary organization of Argentina's working masses. The alleged vows of friendship towards Soviet Russia and the Comintern professed by this group are no more than the mask which serves to veil their counter-revolutionary purpose. It is impossible to be a friend of the Soviet Revolution and the Comintern whilst fighting by every means, including murder, against the Communist Parties which form the firm bases not only of the first proletarian revolution, but also the means of supporting the development of a world revolution. The Comintern already knows these tactics, which have been employed by all the traitors to the Communist cause, to pretend in words to be a friend of the international Communist movement, but in fact to seek to disrupt the Communist Parties in their own countries. We therefore warn the revolutionary organizations in America to be on their guard against these alleged 'Worker Communists' and we call on them to denounce those elements, as the Comintern has done, as enemies of Communism and agents of the employers.

[1] *La Correspondencia Sudamericana*, 30 Nov. 1926 (*El Movimiento . . .*, pp. 376–7).

41. Establishment of the Soviet trading organization Yuzhamtorg, 1927[1] (*p. 8*)

New York, 29 December (TASS). It is reported from Buenos Aires that President Alvear of Argentina has approved the law establishing 'Yuzhamtorg' as a limited company with a capital of $1½ million (2,738,000 rubles). Kraevsky has been appointed president of the new company. According to Yuzhamtorg's charter, its purpose is to develop commercial relations between the USSR and South America. The management of Yuzhamtorg is planning to establish branches in different commercial centres in a number of South American states.

42. Raid on the headquarters of Yuzhamtorg, July 1931[2] (*p. 8*)

New York, 1 August 1931 (TASS). It has been announced from Buenos Aires that the police have raided Yuzhamtorg.

In the course of the raid the police arrested 160 employees and confiscated books, codes, and correspondence.

The *New York Times* writes that the raid was undertaken as the result of complaints by Argentine industrialists who accused Yuzhamtorg of dumping and of applying 'dishonest competitive methods'.

The correspondent of Associated Press links the raid to the campaign which Uriburu, the President of the Republic, is waging against the Communists. . . .

The interrogation of the arrested employees and the examination of the documents confiscated in the raid has begun. From various reports from semi-official sources published in the newspapers, Yuzhamtorg is accused of conducting 'economic warfare against Argentine importers by means of widespread dumping of non-Russian goods'. The Argentine press has accused Yuzhamtorg of selling wood products and petroleum at under cost price in Argentina. The newspapers write that Yuzhamtorg activity was 'working to the detriment of Argentine industry' and was 'promoting Communism'.

The press is publishing wild fabrications regarding the links between Yuzhamtorg and Communist activity in the countries of Latin America.

The international proletariat and the workers of the USSR have received the announcement of the Argentine police's bandit raid against Yuzhamtorg with feelings of the greatest indignation and outrage. This raid can only be compared to Joynston Hicks' gangster-attack on Arcos. We know that behind the back of the Brazilian [*sic*] attackers stand the powerful imperialist states which control the policy of Argentina and other countries of Latin America.

The insolent accusation that the Soviet Union is guilty of dumping and of 'promoting Communism' is only a pretext.

The raid on Yuzhamtorg is a clear anti-Soviet demonstration. The industrial and political growth of the USSR and the strengthening of her international position have stirred up the capitalists' hatred of the USSR. The raid once more underlines the threat of intervention against the Soviet Union.

The Soviet Union will know how to protect herself against those who rush to attack her.

[1] *Isvestiya*, 1 Jan. 1928 (*Dok. Vnesh. Pol.*, xi, p. 11).   [2] *Pravda*, 4 Aug. 1931.

5 *Chile*

43. Directive from the South American Secretariat of the Comintern for the bolshevization of the Chilean CP, November 1926[1] (*pp. 17, 63*)
The Chilean Communist Party is now about to engage in preparatory discussions for the next Congress.[2] These discussions should take as their basis the objective analysis of the present situation of the country and the political and organizational tasks of the Party. The South American Secretariat of the Communist International desires to offer its assistance to the Chilean comrades with a view to contributing towards a proper preparation for the Congress and to the latter directing its discussions towards the correct political line in view of the interesting prospects opened up by the present situation of Chile. With this end in view we propose to analyse very briefly the situation of the country and make fraternal criticism of the faults and weaknesses noted in the sister party so that this criticism and the concrete conclusions drawn from it may serve the purpose of educating the militants and contribute, through a discussion of this open letter in the cells and base organizations of the Party, to the next Congress being a means of raising the Chilean Communist Party's ideological level.

The political situation
Three fundamental aspects stand out in Chile's political situation. In the first place, the weakness of the bourgeoisie which is divided under the influence of competing imperialisms and obliged to seek one of two ways out of the present situation: either to look for support to the working masses and follow a demagogic policy or else to seek in Fascism the means to maintain and consolidate their power. Recent events indicate that, in face of the well defined attitude of the Communists, the Chilean bourgeoisie is leaning towards Fascism. But Fascism is but a proof of the weakness of the bourgeois class, as it shows up the inadequacy of bourgeois democracy in the defence of its own political and economic privileges and clearly demonstrates that it is thinking of having recourse to Fascism as the only means of securing them.

In the second place, the general economic crisis and unemployment. This crisis manifests itself specially in the nitrate industry, but it has enormous repercussions throughout the whole life of the country. This crisis is a call to the working masses to play a most important role in the present economic situation. The nitrate industry provides, through its export duties, half the resources of the Chilean budget. The crisis of the nitrate industry thus has strong repercussions on the state and on the political situation, weakening still

[1] *Justicia* (Santiago, organ of the Chilean CP), 30 Nov. 1926.
[2] The Congress opened on 1 January 1927.

further the political situation of the Chilean bourgeoisie, at the same time as it aggravates the economic situation of the working masses.

In the third place, there is the question of imperialism. English imperialism holds the first place through its domination of the most important industries. Certain economic positions are retained by German capital. Yankee imperialism is beginning to struggle to some practical effect against the hitherto predominant influence of English imperialism, as is shown by its development in the nitrate industry and the question of loans.

The question of Tacna and Arica[1] is a clear proof that the political influence of Yankee imperialism is becoming decisive.

These three questions are basic to Chile's present political position. And in them the working class has a most important role to play. The consequence of these three basic aspects of Chile's present political situation is to cause a terrible aggravation of their living conditions. The only salvation for the labouring masses is to have a great Communist Party, a mighty mass party, which, following a clear political line, knows how to lead the working class in its struggle against the threat of Fascism, against the prospect of misery created by the economic crisis and imperialist slavery.

The forces and organization of the Chilean Communist Party

Do we have in Chile a Communist Party which is equal to the present situation? Let us briefly analyse the situation of the Party, its forces, and the state of its organization.

There are two important facts on the credit side of the Communist Party: (1) its influence over the labouring masses. The electoral successes of the Party show that its influence is very important. The recent electoral victory in the North is an eloquent proof of this influence. (2) The preponderant role played by the Party in the trade union movement through its close connection with it. In this order of things, the influence of the Party is almost exclusive.

But the political influence of the Party cannot be turned to proper account because of its organizational state. The lack of organization is characterized by three main questions:

1. The Party is not organized on the basis of factory cells, the basis for every Communist Party.

2. Too few new members are being enrolled.

3. The Party's proletarian basis is absolutely inadequate.

These three failings are most important, since they could lead either to the Party being transformed into an exclusively electoral party, or else turn it into a sect. In either case, the Party would be unable to fulfil the tasks demanded by the present situation of Chile.

The organizational failings have been aggravated by others such as the lack of organic liaison between the organizations themselves, and between the

---

[1] Tacna and Arica had been seized by Chile in the War of the Pacific (1879–83). United States attempts at mediation (1922–6) produced no immediate solution but led in 1929 to an agreement between Chile and Peru by which the former retained Arica and the latter Tacna.

organizations and the Central Committee; and bad distribution of work. Amongst the youth in general there has been demonstrated in practice a total lack of central leadership. In the sport movement the same lack can be noted. In work amongst women there can be seen the same lack of effective party work, and likewise the lack of any central leadership. These facts denote the absolute inadequacy of the work in these different activities.

The deficiencies can be partly attributed to lack of cadres of politically able militants; but it is no less certain that the party cadres are resistant to this sort of activity, since Party cadres can only be formed through good organization and through good practical work. These are the two conditions which determine the formation of cadres of militants capable of Communist work. And it can be said that it is rather the lack of practical work that hinders the formation of Party cadres, and not that the lack of this practical work is due to the lack of cadres of politically capable militants.

The absence of work of political training in the Party has resulted in petty quarrels, which ought to be cleared up and solved through an objective discussion of political questions such as those to be found in certain sections (e.g. Santiago, Valparaiso, Valdivia, etc.), degenerating into personal struggles. This threat of a certain personalism stems from the lack of political training in the Party.

With regard to questions of organization, mention should be made of the abnormal relations between the Party and the trade unions, the confusion between the work of the party and of the trade union organizations. The same confusion exists in respect of the press. This state of affairs found expression—and was at the same time one of its causes—in the lack of Communist trade union fractions. The danger of this situation can be grave, since it may lead the Party to be transformed into a Labour Party, or cause the Party to forfeit its role as general staff of the proletarian movement.

Lack of systematic work to organize the peasants can also be noted.

But the most abnormal situation, from the organizational point of view, was the position of the parliamentary fraction in the Party. In the first place, we must stress the way—completely unusual for a Communist Party—by which Party candidates were elected, an electoral contest taking place inside the sections, after which votes were cast for the candidates. In the second place, the practice of certain sections and certain Communist representatives who sent a part. of their parliamentary emoluments to the sections where they had been elected, denying the Central Committee, despite Party statutes, the right to dispose of these quotas for the needs of the Party as a whole.

In the third place, the lack of discipline of the parliamentary fraction, when some parliamentarians did not apply the resolutions of the Central Committee, either when voting in the Chamber or in their extra-parliamentary work.

In the fourth place, the inadequacy of effective control apparatus by the Central Committee over the activities of the parliamentary fraction.

These organizational deficiencies led to absolutely inadmissible situations, intolerable in a Communist Party, in which the parliamentary fraction was trying to transform itself objectively into a second directing centre within the

Party, and in which the parliamentary fraction passed itself off in front of the masses as the only representatives of Communism.

These trends aggravated the danger of the Party turning into an exclusively electoral organization and were survivals of forms of reformist organization.

The South American Secretariat of the Communist International notes with satisfaction that recently the National Executive Committee has been working to rectify these errors of organization; by starting the work of organizing factory cells where objective conditions permit; normalizing and organizing Party work in the trade unions through the creation of the Central Trade Union Commission, and of Communist fractions, and by organizing a good distribtion of the Party's political work and that of the Chilean Workers' Federation in the central organ, *Justicia*; by creating the Bulletin of the National Executive Committee as a means of liaison and guidance for the sections of the Party; by intervening in the conflicts which existed in some sections and determining their solution to the benefit of Party unity; by sending members of the National Executive Committee to the sections and thus reinforcing the latters' links with the National Executive Committee and giving them political help and guidance; by struggling energetically for the maintenance of discipline in the parliamentary fraction and by defending Communist principles in the question of parliamentary quotas; by taking the first steps to organize work amongst women, pioneers, and youth.

The South American Secretariat also notes that the National Executive Committee of the Chilean Communist Party has improved its relations with the upper echelons of the Comintern.

But the South American Secretariat considers that in addition to these measures, the situation in Chile requires that other organizational tasks be undertaken. The growing threat of Fascism and of military dictatorship requires from the Chilean Communist Party as one of the necessary tasks, that, side by side with its legal apparatus, the Party should organize an illegal apparatus capable, under any circumstances, of guaranteeing the prosecution of Communist action.

The internal political situation of the Party

Before examining the different political tendencies and errors which manifested themselves in the Party, we must make it clear that the root of the same lay in the inadequate theoretical training of the Party and the meagre political life of its component groups.

Restricting ourselves to an examination of Party activity in the period between December 1925 and the present date, we can note that, despite the errors committed, the line followed by the National Executive Committee was in general correct. The National Executive Committee struggled against Right and Left deviations and for the unity and discipline of the Party. As indications of the correct political position of the Committee we can cite the campaigns carried out against war and on behalf of the freedom of Sacco and Vanzetti;[1]

---

[1] Found guilty of a murder in Massachusetts and executed in 1927 after a trial which aroused much public interest and which dragged on for over seven years.

certain initiatives of the single trade union front, such as the formation of the Guild Union; the campaigns against the social laws; the energetic electoral campaigns in the North; the position which the Party took up regarding the incidents in October when there appeared the first threats of a Fascist dictatorship (in this respect it may be noted that the Party's attitudes towards Col. Ibáñez's moves compelled the Fascist elements, who were carrying out a confusionist policy with the aim of attracting or at least neutralizing the working masses, to disclose their intentions openly and reveal their hatred of the proletarian classes); the position of the Party with regard to URSACH,[1] denouncing its leaders' flirtation with Fascism and tending to wrench the working masses of that party away from the influence of their leaders.

We must now formulate our most important observations regarding the political line of the National Executive Committee. They are as follows:

1. An insufficiently clear concept of the need to create a mass party, with a serious proletarian basis, aggravated by the confusion reigning as to the role of the Party and the work of the Communists in trade union organizations.

2. The absence of any concrete political work, resulting from a lack of understanding tactical questions relating to propaganda and the conquest and organization of the masses on the basis of the struggle for their immediate demands. We can mention, for example, the lack of any programme of immediate demands.

3. The lack of any clear notion about, and the commission of certain partial errors in respect of tactics of the single front. As a practical example we may mention the position adopted by the Party regarding a popular front proposal put forward in parliament by the Wage-Earners.[2]

4. The National Executive Committee, whilst defending a position which was in general correct against some parliamentarians on the Tacna and Arica question, failed to draw the full conclusions from their attitude and to explain before the Party masses the true line on this issue, since it was only in recent months that they took up a clear and definite position on the question.

We must state that in general these partial errors of the National Executive Committee have an objectively radical tendency, that is to say, one of Communism's infantile maladies, but evidently arise as a reaction against the Rightist tendencies of many members of the Party—a reaction which, through lack of political education, assumed erroneous forms.

With respect to the internal situation of the Party, in addition to the lack of active political life of the organizations in general, and to a certain personalism in some sections, there existed a Leftist tendency, one of Communism's infantile maladies, which was specially notable in that it was clearly manifested in the anti-Party struggle of the Santiago section. The members of this section committed a grave error in leaving the Party when they published a newspaper and a circular against the National Executive Committee and ranged themselves in open opposition to the Party, being carried away by their mistaken radical

---

[1] *Unión Republicana Social de Asalariados de Chile*—the Republican Social Union of Chilean Wage-Earners, with which the Communists had formed an electoral alliance.
[2] The URSACH: see n. 5.

tendencies and subordinating the Party's interest to that of some of the section's former leaders.

The South American Secretariat notes that, thanks to the efforts of the National Executive Committee, these militants have returned to the Party and recognized the errors they committed. The Party's work of political education should lead to the disappearance of these mistaken radical tendencies and avoid the repetition of such grave faults of discipline.

Much more pronounced, clear, and dangerous is the Rightist tendency. The South American Secretariat of the Communist International must state that it is not a question here of partial errors but of a certain conception as manifested in theoretical questions and tactical and practical conclusions.

The position of the newspaper *Justicia* under the political guidance of Comrade Hidalgo[1] in the Tacna and Arica question was not only non-revolutionary and non-class; it brought the Party into a reformist position conducive to the strengthening of the state apparatus and the bourgeoisie.

This lack of a class position in the question of the bourgeois state represented a very marked reformist and democratic bourgeois tendency which leads to reformist practice, which was also manifest in the interventions of various Communist representatives in parliament.

Comrade Quevedo,[2] for example, in a speech made on the 25 May about the bourgeoisie's brutal attack against the workers' right of assembly, not only did not say a single word about the bourgeois state as a coercive apparatus of the bourgeoisie against the proletariat, but he even declared he was defending the constitutional position 'for the dignity of the nation', and was 'only defending the constitutional position' against 'the abuse of the authorities', which is tantamount to assuming a position identical with that of any common bourgeois democrat.

The same Comrade Quevedo, making a politically useful intervention on recognizing Russia, framed all his arguments from the viewpoint of the bourgeoisie's economic interest, insisting on the recognition of Russia 'in the present circumstances, when our principal industry is in danger', and even making erroneous allusions with respect to the dictatorship of the proletariat in Russia which meant abandoning the standpoint of the interests of the proletariat and going over to that of the national bourgeoisie.

Another illustration of this open break with the interests of the proletariat is the intervention of Comrade Hidalgo in the Senate on the question of protectionism for the national industry, in the session of 12 June. Comrade Hidalgo declared: 'the Government ought to give decisive help to its industries', and pledged his 'help and support' for everything conducive to the protection of the national interests, since he considered the application of this economic principle to be 'the only way to save the country in the critical situation in which it finds itself'. Comrade Hidalgo did not take into account that the only protectionist policy which a Communist ought to defend is the protectionist policy of a proletarian state for its own socialist industry.

[1] Manuel Hidalgo Plaza, senator for Tarrapacá and Antofagasta.
[2] Abraham Quevedo, deputy for Valdivia.

The protectionism of a bourgeois state for its capitalist industry means the aggravation of the exploitation of the working masses. And in the concrete case of Chile's industry, the request for protectionist measures is a demand from the most conservative, backward part of the Chilean bourgeoisie anxious to 'preserve' decentralized industry, its old technical methods of exploitation, at the cost of the working masses. The defence of this principle therefore means support for the most reactionary part of the bourgeoisie and the most complete lack of understanding for proletarian interests.

On the agrarian question, Comrade Quevedo, in an article in *Justicia* (1 May) wrote: 'We do not care whether they [the landowners] are expropriated with compensation, as in Mexico, or without it, as in Russia.' This is a fundamental error on the principal point of the Communist International's agrarian programme, and a complete confusion between Mexico's petty-bourgeois agrarian reform and the social revolution carried out by the Russian workers and peasants.

These erroneous conceptions must naturally influence almost all the practical work of the parliamentary fraction, above all when completely erroneous conceptions are held in the parliamentary fraction regarding the tasks of the Communist representatives in the bourgeois parliaments. For example, in Comrade Sepúlveda Leal's[1] speech of 26 May in parliament we find the following explanation of the tasks of a Communist delegate: 'We are here in the Chamber so that, by dint of criticism, we may perfect the capitalist regime and thereby contribute to this democratic republic perfecting its methods of administration and government.' We believe that this erroneous conception needs no further commentary on our part.

The virtually electoral character of the Party's organization and the abnormal position of the parliamentary fraction, from the viewpoint of organization which we have referred to, aggravate this situation and make objectively still more dangerous this Rightist tendency of the majority of the parliamentary fraction, above all when they made certain attempts to defend these opportunist tendencies against the political line of the National Executive Committee, with a view to weakening the latter's authority.

However, it would not be right in the present situation of the Party to deduce from these facts that recourse must be had to strict disciplinary measures to the point of excluding the comrades who have such concepts. In the present situation of the Party, the best way to avoid the dangers of this Rightist tendency is not that of applying mechanical disciplinary measures in political questions, but of struggling energetically against these conceptions and of clearing them up politically in front of all the Party and making these errors a means for the Party's political education.

With regard to the parliamentary fraction, the National Executive Committee must organize and apply a strict control mechanism over their activity, at the same time giving the comrades of the parliamentary fraction the greatest opportunity to hold previous discussions with the National Executive Committee on the political issues which require their intervention. The application

[1] Ramón Sepúlveda Leal, Deputy for Valparaiso.

of the resolutions taken by the National Executive Committee will need to be defended with all necessary disciplinary measures, specially with regard to the parliamentary fraction, since that is the most advanced position held by the Party in bourgeois territory.

We must hope that the Party, with the development of its political capacity, will surmount the legacies of its social-democratic past and will help all sincere comrades to rectify their errors and be guided by the Leninist line, but at the same time that it will energetically oppose all those who want to persist in these errors and un-Communist conceptions which would carry the Party along the social-democratic road and prevent it advancing along the path of bolshevization.

Perspectives and tasks of the Chilean Communist Party

Basing itself on the analysis of the country's political and economic situation, and the Party's political and organizational position, the Congress must resolve the tasks which the Party needs to perform in the days ahead.

The aggravation of the economic situation of the country (despite certain possible improvements in some branches of industry) and the increase of imperialist penetration are the most obvious perspectives entailing as their consequences a greater differentiation within the bourgeois forces and the sharpening of the class struggle between proletariat and bourgeoisie.

The precautions taken by the Party against a Fascist military dictatorship during the events of last October have been completely justified by the development of events. This danger of a Fascist military dictatorship is growing more and more evident.

In connection with these perspectives, the Party must discuss previously in its base organizations and then in the Congress the political tasks which the latter ought to adopt for the days ahead.

The South American Secretariat deems it useful to indicate those which, in its view, are the most important, stressing before it starts to enumerate them the need for the Chilean Communist Party to devote special attention to the nitrate and coal regions, since they are the centres of greatest proletarian concentration, the most industrialized and of greatest importance in the political and economic life of the country, and offer the most favourable perspective for the Communist movement.

Let us now pass on to enumerate the most important tasks, in the view of the South American Secretariat of the Comintern:

a) In the political domain
1. The struggle against imperialism. Theoretical explanation in the Party organs of the modern system of imperialist servitude, what it represents for the proletariat, the peasants, and the middle classes. Propaganda in favour of the single front for the struggle against imperialism.

2. *Campaign on the economic crisis and unemployment*, and against bourgeois attempts to overcome them at the expense of the working classes. This campaign must be carried out on the basis of the Party's programme of immediate

demands, linked with the latter's general watch-words and propaganda for the workers' and peasants' government.

3. The struggle against the danger of a military Fascist dictatorship. According to events, this campaign may be brought to the forefront of the Party's political action. Clear explanation of the dangers to the workers of this dictatorship and campaign for the single anti-Fascist front must form the political content of this campaign.

4. Struggle against the capitalist offensive which is presented beneath the form of the social laws, and attempts by the bourgeois class to divide and corrupt certain categories of the proletariat in order to bind them to the interests of the bourgeoisie.

5. Energetic campaign for the unity of the trade union movement. Propaganda for national and international trade union unity and for the programme and tactics of the Red International of Labour Unions.

6. Campaign against the reformist parties and anarchist groups, specially against the recently organized Party of the Wage-Earners with the object of politically opposing the reformist leaders and conquering for Communist influence the sincere workers who are under the influence of those leaders.

7. Systematic propaganda amongst the peasants, based on the latters' programme of immediate demands and the agrarian programme of the Communist Party, and tending to unite the workers of city and countryside in the struggle against the capitalists and big landowners.

b) In the Party's internal political domain

1. Reinforcement of the political life of the Party's organizations.

2. Permanent and systematic work of the Party's political education and the training of its cadres.

3. Political struggle against deviations of the Left and, above all, of the Right. Full explanation amongst the Party masses of all the political errors of the comrades responsible for them as a means of politically educating the Party.

4. Devote special attention to the work of the Communist Youth organizations. Systematic political and organizational help for the Communist Youth.

5. Improvement and normalization of the Party press and preparation of the necessary work for the publication of a special central organ for the exclusive use of the Party.

c) In the trade union domain

1. Normalization of relations between Party and trade unions. The present confusion between Party and trade unions does not permit the Party to perform its role of leading organ of the proletarian movement and is a hindrance to the Party's propaganda and political work. This situation involves the danger of subordinating the Party's action to the organizations of party-less masses. For the trade unions, this confusion represents a hindrance to the liberty of its propaganda and action within the politically less mature masses, which it ought to organize on the basis of the struggle for its trade union interests. The confusion between Party and trade unions may hinder the latter from carrying out their mission of bringing together the great labouring masses.

2. As a fundamental concrete task in this domain, the Party must create

Communist trade union fractions, which must be led by the Communist sections' trade union commissions and be under the direction of the National Executive Committee's trade union commission.

3. Separation of the work of Party and trade unions in the press, devoting one part of those organs to form a Party organ, and the other to form that of the Chilean Workers' Federation, or creating wherever possible special organs for the Chilean Workers' Federation and the Party.

4. Systematic work in the trade unions with a view to trade union unification —in the first place, by unifying the trade unions of the same branch of industry. In the trade unions which do not belong to the Federation, the tasks of the Communists should be those of forming groups of trade union unity and propaganda for the principles of the Red International of Trade Unions.

5. In the campaign on the economic crisis and unemployment, the tasks of the Communists in the trade unions are those of struggle to get the trade unions to fight for their immediate demands (wages, length of working day, help for the unemployed, etc), organizing help for the unemployed and forming organizations for the same.

6. Energetic work inside the Guild Unions to convert them into true organizations of the single proletarian front.

7. To struggle in the trade union movement for the national grouping of trade unions by industries and the creation of national directing centres for the same.

8. Propaganda in the trade unions for sending a South American workers' delegation to the USSR.

9. Work to achieve closer relations between the Chilean Workers' Federation and the Red International of Labour Unions.

d) Tasks of peasant organization

1. Communists working in the trade unions must struggle to get the rural workers and poor peasants, who are now organizing in unions according to various trades, to form their own special organizations.

2. To reinforce the activity of the League of Tenant Farmers on the basis of a programme of immediate demands and to struggle to link that organization with the other peasant organizations.

3. The general aim of the Party in this domain should be to work to prepare for a Congress of peasant organizations in order to create a broad national peasant organization affiliated to the International Peasant Council in Moscow.

e) In the domain of Party organization

1. To continue systematic organization of Party cells and organize the cells' political work.

2. Organization of systematic educational courses for the political training of militants.

3. Organization of a recruitment week with the aim of creating a broad proletarian basis for the Party.

4. Broadening the Central Committee by up to nine members, allowing the different regions to be represented on it; the north (nitrate), the south (coal), and the centre (Valparaiso). Organizing the work of the Central Committee

with the effective participation of all its members. A better distribution of work within the Central Committee, by applying the system of commissions.

5. Reinforce liaison between centre and sections.

6. Create section committees in all places where important sections exist.

7. Normalization of the situation of the parliamentary fraction within the Party. Creation of the parliamentary committee. Strict application of party statutes in the question of quotas. Modify the form of electing the candidates by getting them proposed by the section committees and definitely nominated by the Central Committee.

8. Devote special attention to youth. Creation of youth sections in the Party wherever possible. Organization of Youth Congress for the definitive formation of the Federation of the Communist Youth, affiliated to the Youth International. The Party to help Youth in organizing a Workers' Sporting Federation (section of the Red International of Sport).

9. Creation of a Central Commission for Women and the systematic organization of work amongst women in all grades of Party organization.

10. Organization of sympathizers, on the basis of concrete work and with a view to a permanent collaboration with the Party.

11. Strengthening of the Central Committee's bulletin as a means for achieving closer links between centre and sections, facilitating the centre's directing work, and contributing to the political education of the Party.

12. Strengthening the editorship of the Party's press organs, and active participation of all responsible Party comrades in the same, by periodically sending in articles. The central organ *Justicia* should be specially strengthened; it should be more closely linked with the Central Committee and transformed into an organ for the political education of the Party.

13. Creation of a network of worker-correspondents for all Party organs.

14. Regular liaison with the South American Secretariat for the dispatch of reports to the latter and, through its intermediary, for the establishment of regular liaison with the Comintern. Preparation for the sending of a Chilean Communist Party delegation to the next Comintern Congress.

Appeal to all affiliates

With these concrete remarks, the South American Secretariat of the Communist International concludes the most important observations prompted by the present state of the country and of the Communist movement. It hopes therewith to offer once again its fraternal help to the Chilean comrades in pursuit of their work of bolshevizing the Party by taking to heart the experiences of the international Communist movement, particularly of the Russian Communist Party which, under Leninist leadership, succeeded in leading the toiling masses along the path of their definitive liberation.

In this sense the militants of the Chilean Communist Party should understand that the criticisms formulated in this open letter pursue no other purpose than the Leninist education of our sister party, which is all the more necessary in that the Chilean Communist Party is the party with the most influence amongst the masses out of all the South American Communist Parties, and that the political situation of this country offers favourable perspectives for the Communist movement which, if they are to be turned to full advantage, require a Communist Party more and more capable of fulfilling its role as vanguard and leader of the exploited masses. Only through the path of bolshevization can the Chilean Communist Party efficiently fulfil this mission. All its militants must lend their best efforts to speed the process of bolshevizing the Party. Every militant should make the self-criticism of his own errors, of the prejudices he has inherited from social democracy, and avoid the faults of Communism's infantile malady. Every Communist militant must remember that there was no judge more zealous in condemning their own errors than the Russian Bolsheviks themselves, which permitted them not only to put right possible errors but to find the right way along the path of class struggle. That is why, by tirelessly struggling against deviations of Right and Left, recognizing their own errors and analysing their faults and learning from them politically, the Russian Bolsheviks have succeeded in forming an iron party with a discipline which cannot be shaken and a Leninist orientation with cadres of capable leaders, and a party which is the unchallenged vanguard not only of the Russian proletariat but of the whole international proletariat.

The Chilean Communists must follow their example. To begin with, it is necessary for this open letter from the South American Secretariat of the Communist International to be carefully studied in the Party's base organizations, and then by the delegates in Congress, with the profound desire to work effectively for the bolshevization of the Party.

The South American Secretariat of the Communist International appeals in this sense to all members of the Party. The watchword must be that the Chilean Communist Party's next Congress is to be a bolshevization Congress, or a Leninist Congress, to pay to the chief of the international proletariat our unforgettable master Nicholas [sic] Lenin, our homage of practical work for the bolshevization of the Chilean Communist Party.

And as the Congress will be meeting on the anniversary of the death of the leader of the Chilean workers, Comrade Recabarren, let the militants and Congress pay him practical homage by getting hundreds of new proletarian militants to join the ranks of the Chilean Party. With the conquest of new proletarian forces for Communist action in Chile, the problems which our Party has to face may be more easily resolved.

The Communist International hopes that the next Congress will mark the progress of the bolshevization of the Chilean Communist Party. It is as a contribution to this that the South American Section of the Comintern sends this open letter and appeals to all militants of the Chilean Communist Party to use it for starting an intensive preparatory work for the Congress, with the watchword that the latter should be a bolshevization Congress.

For the bolshevization of the Party, for Leninism, for work—comrades—to make the next Congress open a new stage for the Chilean Communist Party!

The South American Secretariat of the Communist International, in the name of the Communist International and of the South American Communist Parties, in the confidence that all militants of the Chilean Communist Party will prepare for this task, ends by saluting the beginning of this new stage with expressions of solidarity and encouragement in the work of bolshevization which has to be undertaken.

Long live the bolshevization of the Chilean Communist Party! Long live the Chilean Communist Party!

6 *Colombia*

The strike in the banana plantations, 1928

44. Open letter to the Revolutionary Socialist Party from the Comintern on the reasons for its failure, February 1929:[1] excerpts (*p. 13*)

We have received your report on the great strike in the banana plantations. . . . Your letter proves to us that the experiences which the Colombian proletariat and its class Party have just had through the strike in the banana plantations, though hard and painful and costing such great sacrifices, has nevertheless helped to educate and orientate the Party towards a policy which is more correct and capable of preparing class battles with better prospects of success. . . . The fierce and heroic struggle of the plantation workers demonstrated the extraordinary revolutionary aggressiveness and spirit of sacrifice and struggle of the Colombian workers. If there have been no signs as yet of the solidarity of the rest of the proletariat of the country, and if the disintegration of the army has not been spontaneously produced, the cause must be sought in the fact that there do not yet exist in Colombia a strongly organized and disciplined Communist Party and mass labour unions, and that preparations for the struggle and the organizing of solidarity and of disintegration in the army were insufficient or non-existent before the outbreak of the strike, and that such acts are not improvised in a matter of days.

45. Debate at the 1st Latin American CP Congress, Buenos Aires, June 1929:[2] excerpts (*p. 13*)

Comrade Luis[3] (representing the ECCI), . . . This leads us to consider the

---

[1] *Documentos políticos* (Bogotá), May-June 1960.
[2] *El Movimiento* . . ., pp. 96–7, 108–12, 121, 127–8, 177, & 198.
[3] Jules Humbert-Droz, head of the Latin American Section of the Comintern, Moscow.

essential links between strikes, mass demonstrations in general, and the revolutionary movement. Our Colombian comrades have expressed in this respect absolutely erroneous ideas which we must oppose, or else they will lead to clearly counter-revolutionary positions. Amongst the Party leaders some hold that a strike is one thing, and revolution another which has nothing in common with it. Not every strike, of course, can develop into a revolution; that depends on the breadth of the movement, the state of mind of the masses, and their objective revolutionary situation, and it would be a mistake to want to expand every strike into insurrection; but it would also be absolutely wrong and dangerous to consider that revolution—*our* revolution, and not that of the Liberal generals—would break out without vast strike movements and great mass demonstrations. To imagine, as do some Colombian comrades, that a strike is harmful for the revolution because it distracts the efforts of the workers from the essential revolutionary objective is to misunderstand Marxism and Leninism.

We have the concrete example of the banana zone strike and the attitude of the CCCC[1] in Colombia. Here was a strike unanimously supported by the 32,000 workers of the United Fruit Company, and enjoying the sympathy of the peasant and petty bourgeois masses of the region. It was triggered off by immediate demands, but then assumed a clear political character, not only in Colombia, on account of the dispatch of troops, but also in the international field for the importance of the conflict and its anti-imperialist character. The army which had been dispatched fraternized with the strikers, disintegrated, offered the workers its arms; the generals were forced to swear on the red flag that they would not betray the workers. A solidarity movement was organized in Magdalena province, which commands the essential lines of communication between the capital and Barranquilla. The Central Committee sent out its orders for solidarity action through the whole country—a correct and necessary decision; it gave the belated order to develop the movement, a correct order but issued too late. And what did the CCCC do—the Party's military committee? It hindered the solidarity action, issued counter-orders throughout all the country, since this banana-zone strike was not a part of the revolutionary plan prepared in accordance with the Liberal generals. The revolution had to develop in accord with the strategy of these great soldiers. The banana-zone strike, which had all the character of an insurrection, developed in a way which could make of it the centre of Colombia's revolutionary movement, and the starting point of the Colombian Revolution. It is the wrong conception of a 'Revolution' unconnected with strikes over immediate demands, the Liberal petty-bourgeois conception of the coup d'état, of the little conspiratorial groups, which contributed broadly to the defeat of the strike and prevented it from growing into a real revolutionary movement. We must draw the lesson from this experience to avoid a repetition of such mistakes.

Prieto:[2] The situation is very complicated. It has been analysed in a letter sent by the Communist International, which we did not receive, and the con-

---

[1] *Comité Central Celular Comunista.*

[2] Moisés Prieto, later a leader of the left-wing Liberals, a state governor and cabinet minister.

tents of which we have only learned through its publication in the South American Secretariat's review.[1] The difficulties and persecutions of which our Party has been the victim, the neglect in which it has been left by the Communist International, and its lack of help during the crisis of the struggle, confer no right on Comrade Luis or on the Communist International to subject us to the merciless criticism which the former directed against us in this Congress, and in the above-mentioned letter. I blame the Communist International which, by its neglect of our Party, has been the cause of our having so many difficulties in our action. . . .

Referring to the question of the Comintern's Open Letter, I should point out that the Communist International advises our Party to do exactly what our Party, in our report sent to Moscow, said ought to be done. We stress, and the Communist International now stresses to us, that we ought to organize the masses. But this is not the problem; the problem is *how* to organize them, how to find ways of doing so.

We were sent a representative of the Red International of Labour Unions (RILU), but he had no credentials to act politically; . . .

Let me refer, comrades, to our alliance with the Liberal forces. The Open Letter of the Communist International also deals with this question. I refer to the criticisms directed against us regarding the single front with the Liberal forces. The comrade delegate from RILU in Colombia ought to explain all this, as he was the one who proposed and took the leading part in it.

Mahecha:[2] . . . The balance-sheet of the banana zone strike was cruel; 1,004 men, women and children killed; 3,068 wounded, more than 500 imprisoned, and hundreds of comrades sentenced to many years imprisonment. . . . This tragic balance-sheet was due to the Bogotá comrades' lack of decision. They gave us no solidarity for the strike or order to make the Revolution. No matter whether the blame lies with the CCCC or with the Executive Committee; the fact is that we were left in the lurch. The South American Secretariat of the Communist International ought to intervene in the affairs of our Party to make a little order.

Austine:[3] Comrade Prieto has declared that the Communist International has neglected the Colombian movement and the Party. Nothing could be further from the truth! The Colombian comrades must know that when there arrives in a country a RILU delegate, if he is a member of the Communist International, this delegate is informed of the political problems of the world Communist movement and can therefore help the Party in its work, according to the line approved in the congresses of the Communist International. It seems childish to make an artificial distinction based on credentials. This question has to be cleared up so that comrades may be quite sure that when a RILU delegate, a member of the Communist International, resides in and works in a country, this resolution has been taken in accord with the Comintern. . . .

To be able to judge the activities and the conduct of the Colombian Section of the Communist International, we must know the social composition of the

[1] *Correspondencia sudamericana*, nos. 12, 13, 14 (2nd ser.), May 1929.
[2] Raúl Mahecha, a labour leader of anarcho-syndicalist antecedents.
[3] Rabaté, a Frenchman, later sent as Profintern delegate to Spain.

Revolutionary Socialist Party of that country. Though calling itself Revolutionary Socialist, it is a Party which has nothing in common with a Communist Party. It is a Party which has considerable influence over the masses, but goes on practising the methods traditional to parties which are based on *caudillismo*. There are leaders with perfect hierarchies, whilst the base does no more than carry out orders from above, without previous discussion of the problems. The Party is really composed of those leaders, organized after the fashion of a general staff, whilst the mass can be considered outside the Party, since—I repeat—it discusses nothing but only carries out the resolutions. This general staff is composed of 50 per cent peasants (with some smallholders), 20 per cent intellectuals or petty bourgeois, 10 per cent workers, and the rest difficult to classify. The Revolutionary Socialist Party is formed of old Liberal militants disgusted with the inactivity of the Liberal Party and adversaries of conservatism, who have formed a party which cannot be considered a Bolshevist party. The very social composition of the Party, in which the proletariat does not figure preponderantly, explains the political errors committed by the Party, which lacks the knowledge of Marxism which it needs.

I have the impression, and have had it since I came to Colombia, that the adhesion of the *Partido Socialista Revolucionario* to the Communist International is not motivated by the tendency to modify its ideology and to shape its tactics according to Comintern dictates, but that it is a Party which wants to shelter behind the prestige of the Communist International, to see itself backed by the world Communist movement in order to take over power, and then not follow the path traced for it by the Third International. That this impression is well based is borne out by the following fact. Whilst delegates of the Colombian Party were in Moscow to convey its adhesion to the Communist International, a plenary assembly was held in Colombia where important decisions were taken without finding out in advance what Moscow thought about them. It seems to me that the tactic was to confront the Communist International with *faits accomplis* so as to avoid being obliged, if the Communist International recognized the Party, to carry out the line which the Comintern might trace. In reality, their assembly did nothing but entrust the leadership to a single man: Tomás Uribe Márquez. . . . In addition to this personal leadership, known as the CCCC, there existed an Executive Committee, or Committee of Honour, composed of writers and Liberal parliamentarians. This was explained away as a means of preparing the revolutionary movement by misleading the bourgeoisie with the Executive Committee, whilst the leadership was really vested in the CCCC. But they did not only mislead the bourgeoisie; they also misled the Communist International which came to believe in the existence of such an Executive Committee, whereas it existed only in name. . . .

Prieto: . . . Comrade Luis has declared that the Communist International has only recently 'discovered' Latin America, but I must add that it still does not know it. Its criticisms of the Latin American movement are of a dialectical richness which we all admire, but it lacks a real knowledge of the psychology of, for example, the masses which make up and should continue to make up, the revolutionary movement. . . .

Comrade Luis. When Comrade Prieto says that we do not know the situation in Colombia well, he does not take into account that the reports at the disposal of the Communist International have been received by us from the delegates themselves to our international organization, and that they were most contradictory. In Moscow, the following happened. One delegate spoke in fantastic terms of the armed movement which was about to break out immediately, and of Colombia's subjective and objective revolutionary conditions. Then another arrived and gave us a report that was quite the reverse of the first. Later there came a third comrade, who gave us particulars which were again different from the previous ones. With these contradictory reports no comrade could think that the Communist International could do more than it has done for the movement, for these not very serious reports which we received did not allow us to give proper consideration to the situation in Colombia. . . . So Comrade Prieto has no right to criticize the Communist International for allegedly 'disinteresting' itself about Colombia.

7 Peru

Comintern guidelines for the development of the revolutionary struggle

46. Memorandum drawn up by the Comintern Secretariat (undated, but probably 1927)[1] (*p. 15*)

Comrade Raymondo,[2] fraternal delegate of the Peruvian trade unions to the Congress of the Red International Labour Unions, addressed a number of questions to the Secretariat of the Communist International as to whether it would be opportune to found a Communist Party, and what would be the tasks of the Peruvian working class. To these questions the Latin Secretariat of the Communist International has replied as follows:

1. *Concerning the situation of Peruvian working class and peasants and their ties with the international proletariat.*

The Peruvian working classes and peasant masses live in conditions identical to those of the working and peasant masses in the majority of the Latin American countries.

Penetration and exploitation by Yankee imperialism make the country a

[1] Martínez de la Torre, *Apuntes* . . ., ii, pp. 393–6.
[2] Julio Portocarrero, a founder member of the Peruvian CP.

semi-colony, where semi-feudal conditions still prevail in agriculture, where the working class is exploited, and where Yankee imperialism has found in the Government of the country an instrument for the oppression of the working masses so as to be able to exploit them more.

The revolutionary struggle of the workers and peasant masses against Yankee imperialism and against exploitation by the great rural landowners of capitalism for land and better working and living conditions, the revolutionary struggles of the peasants against the oppression of their race, against their exploitation and plunder, the struggle of the masses against the Government of oppression, is the same struggle of all Latin American workers against Yankee imperialism and its agents and against the great landowners and the national bourgeoisie. This struggle of the Latin American workers is equally a part of the vast revolutionary front of the colonial and semi-colonial peoples against the imperialism of the capitalist metropolises, a part of the struggle of the working class and the poor peasants of the whole world against their exploiters and against the capitalist system.

2. *Why has the Peruvian proletariat not yet formed a Communist Party like the workers of the other Latin American countries?*

Up to the present, the formation of a Communist Party in Peru, and the linking of the Peruvian proletarian movement with the international revolutionary movement, and in particular with the revolutionary movement of the other Latin American republics, has had to contend with the influence acquired over the revolutionary workers in the period of the People's University[1] by Haya de la Torre's group, now organized in the APRA, whose general orientation and international activity have virtually isolated the Peruvian movement from the international revolutionary movement.

3. *Why has APRA been an obstacle for the formation of a Communist Party in Peru?*

APRA denies the need for Peruvian workers to form their class Party and to link this party of the Peruvian proletariat with the international proletarian movement. APRA wishes to be itself 'a great anti-imperialist Latin American party which is fighting for the freedom of the people'. In this great Latin American party—a sort of Latin American Kuomintang—the people are exhorted to organize without distinction of class. According to APRA, the workers should not create their own party in order to defend their class interests. Petty-bourgeois elements—the intelligentsia—ought to have the leadership and hegemony of the workers' and peasants' revolutionary movement. For the APRA leaders, the Mexican Government, which capitulates more and more to Yankee imperialism, disarms the peasants and represses workers' strikes, or Senator Borah, one of the most typical representatives of Yankee imperialism, is of more use in the anti-imperialist struggle than the workers and peasants (letter of Haya de la Torre to Comrade Lozovsky). For this reason, their leaders prefer to seek contacts and understandings with

[1] An offshoot of the University Reform Movement which started in Córdoba, Argentina, in 1918 and spread to Peru, where Haya de la Torre took the lead in founding a People's University for educational work amongst the urban poor and built up APRA as his political following.

representatives of the allegedly anti-imperialist bourgeoisie, rather than seek a close alliance and collaboration with the revolutionary workers and peasants of the whole world, with the oppressed peoples of all the colonies.

This also explains why the APRA leaders make themselves the tools of a narrowly nationalistic policy and ally themselves to the campaign of the worst imperialists against the 'inferior races'. Haya de la Torre has just joined the anti-Chinese Committee in Mexico, and given public approval to its campaign against the immigration of Chinese into Latin America, at a time when all the revolutionaries and anti-imperialists of the whole world are on the contrary supporting the heroic struggle of the Chinese workers against imperialism. To support at this time an anti-Chinese committee is virtually to support the campaign of the imperialists against the Chinese revolution and betray the interests of the international anti-imperialist struggle.

This general orientation of APRA, which limits its horizon to Latin America, which undervalues the role of the working and peasant masses and over-values the role of bourgeois intellectuals and politicians, has found expression in the split provoked by APRA within the Latin American anti-imperialist movement itself. APRA signed with reservations the anti-imperialist resolution of the Brussels Congress of the International League against Colonial Oppression. Since then, it has withdrawn and placed itself outside the International League, which is the only large, anti-imperialist revolutionary organization of all the oppressed peoples. Instead of merging with the Anti-Imperialist League of America, which has an influence and organization throughout the American continent, the APRA leaders have maintained and deepened the division of the anti-imperialist forces of Latin America—a division which can only benefit Yankee imperialism. APRA has influence only in Peru. In the other countries of Latin America, the anti-imperialist movement is organized in the Anti-Imperialist League of the American Continent, section of the International League against Colonial Oppression. By refusing to adhere to the latter, and by refusing to unify the anti-imperialist American movement, APRA is isolating the Peruvian revolutionary movement and performing a service to Yankee imperialism by dividing the Latin American revolutionary anti-imperialist movement, and preventing the co-ordination of this movement with the international revolutionary movement against imperialism.

4. *Can APRA replace the Communist Party for the Peruvian proletariat?*

APRA is not a class organization. It wants to be a political party grouping together different classes (workers, peasants, petty bourgeoisie) against Yankee imperialism. But the Peruvian workers and peasants, whilst, like the petty bourgeoisie, they have the will to struggle against imperialism, also have interests of their own—class interests—which are not the same as those of the petty bourgeoisie of the cities and of the intellectuals who direct APRA.

The workers struggle against imperialism and the reactionary Government, but they are also struggling against their masters, against the capitalism which exploits them for higher wages, better working conditions, for the eight-hour day, etc. They are quite aware that APRA cannot lead this struggle on their behalf, since they have organized workers' syndicates which are class organizations of the proletariat. The agricultural workers struggle against the terrible conditions of slavery under which they have to labour, and lead the class struggle against the great *latifundistas* and in favour of the fight for the land. The landless peasants wage a fight for land against the landowners and should form associations of poor peasants. But the class struggle cannot only be led by professional syndicates; it should be led in general and carried over into the political field by a class party, the Communist Party, grouping together the most class-conscious worker élite. If the Peruvian workers have realized the need to create class syndicates in order to struggle against their exploiters, they will also realize the need to create a Communist Party to lead the class struggle without faltering, and to extend it to the whole political life. The petty bourgeoisie cannot realize these aspirations of peasants and workers. The example of the Mexican Government, the Kuomintang in China, and the 1925 revolutionary Government in Ecuador,[1] prove that when the petty bourgeoisie seizes power, thanks to the action of the workers and peasant masses, it puts a break on the revolutionary movement, vacillates between the revolutionary pressure of the masses and the pressure of the bourgeoisie and imperialism, and ends up by turning its blows against the peasants and workers, disarming them, and trying to find a compromise with imperialism.

If, instead of creating a class party, the Peruvian working class puts its trust in APRA for heading the struggle, it will suffer the same experiences to its own cost and will then realize that APRA cannot defend its interest and that the Communist International was right to say that it should form a Communist Party.

5. *On linking the Peruvian workers with the international revolutionary movement.*

The revolutionary struggle of Peruvian workers and peasants cannot be successfully developed unless it is first co-ordinated with the struggle of the workers and peasants of Latin America and of the whole world.

The dispatch of a fraternal delegate from the Peruvian syndicates to the Profintern, and his participation in the setting up of a Latin American Labour Secretariat, is a first step in this direction.

The workers of Peru should create their own Communist Party, affiliated to the Communist International, and organize a national labour organization which they should get to adhere to the Latin American Labour Secretariat and the Profintern. They should strive to have APRA merge with the Anti-Imperialist League in order to link their anti-imperialist movement with the Latin American mass movement against imperialism and with the International League against Colonial Oppression.

6. *Is the Communist International prepared to receive delegates from APRA for discussions regarding the disagreements mentioned above?*

The Executive of the Communist International, which condemns the petty-bourgeois ideology and the anti-Communist action of APRA, does not consider it useful to invite a delegation from APRA. But out of consideration for the Peruvian revolutionary workers, misled as to the role of APRA, the Secretariat of the Communist International will always be prepared to hold

---

[1] The revolutionary coup carried out by army officers, most of them from the Sierra, to end a decade of domination by Guayaquil banking interests.

discussions with a delegation about Peruvian revolutionary problems, should the APRA leadership, under the pressure of the Peruvian working class, decide to send a delegation to discuss the above-mentioned disagreements with the Executive of the Communist International.

7. *On the formation of a Communist Party.*

In Peru there exist isolated Communists who are in agreement with the programme and tactics of the Communist International. These elements must take the initiative in building up a Peruvian Communist Party. The Secretariat of the Communist International is ready to help them in this task.

47. Moscow's view of APRA: statement by A. Lozovsky to the 4th RILU Congress, Moscow, 7 April 1928:[1] extracts (*pp. 11, 14*)

There is a Peruvian comrade, Haya de la Torre, who has created an organization called APRA. This comrade has the idea that, in order to struggle against American imperialism, an alliance can be made with anyone. And at the beginning of 1927, a comrade who came from abroad told me that Haya de la Torre had expressed the idea that if war were to break out between North America and Japan, it would be necessary for the people of Latin America to support Japan against North America, since Japan is very far away whereas North America is the nearer enemy. It is therefore possible to reach an agreement with Japan in order to get rid of North America, American imperialism and so on.

I wrote him a letter in which I explained that this conception has nothing in common with revolutionary tactics and our very important experience of world war. There were Socialists and trade unionists who made accommodations with a foreign imperialism on the pretext of liberating their country, and they finished up by themselves—and not imperialism—becoming victims of these accommodations. I afterwards received a reply from him dated the beginning of May 1927—a very interesting reply—in which he explains that the problem of the struggle against American imperialism is a very important problem, and that it is necessary to draw together all the forces of every country into the struggle. What forces, he asks, can we have? I told him that in the struggle against American imperialism it is also and above all else necessary to make a common front with the workers of North America. First and foremost, then, our organization in Latin America, then the common front with the proletariat of North America, to oppose American imperialism. To this he answered me that the North American proletariat is imbued with imperialist prejudices, that it is for the most part imperialist, and not to be relied on. 'We can', he writes, 'find allied forces in North America, but in other classes, not in the working class. We must ally ourselves with whatever force can help us against the United States. Senator Borah, for instance, is most useful to us, more useful to us than a great number of workers. That Borah happens to be a bourgeois Liberal, so much the worse! All the same, he is useful to us.'

I don't know what Senator Borah is doing against American imperialism. I

[1] Martínez de la Torre, *Apuntes . . .*, ii. 279–81 (quoting RILU *Bulletin* (Paris), yr., 11, no. 79, 17 Aug. 1928)

really have not the least idea. At any rate, no one in the International knows anything about his anti-imperialist activity. Now you can see what this point of view amounts to! In my opinion, it is the most dangerous point of view for the working class. What, in fact, is Senator Borah doing in the United States? It is imperialism in different guise, and that is all. Should he replace Coolidge tomorrow, we should witness the same murdering of Nicaragua, Panama, and any other country of Latin America and the whole world. Comrade Haya de la Torre is a good element, and a very honest man; but he is a comrade who thinks it possible to make a united front with Senator Borah; but Borah will never make a united front with him. You are quite aware of that. But he is a comrade who hopes to make use of Senator Borah against American imperialism—this can lead the movement along the path of adventures. This may cost us dear. If the comrades want to see it, I have the full text of Comrade Haya de la Torre's letter and could circulate it.

This internal discussion has touched on one of the problems of revolutionary tactics. There are comrades who say that anybody should be made use of. Yes, on condition that they are not themselves made use of, but in order to use them, one must first of all be strong. Without this, there will be manoeuvring, but no policy. When, for instance, in our great October Revolution, the great strategist of the proletarian Revolution, Lenin, manoeuvred, he used to say: We must manoeuvre, we must retreat, this or that force must be made use of. But he did not say that anyone whatsoever could be made use of. Above all, it is necessary that we should not be made use of by others. We need to be very strongly organized, we need to be strong from the ideological point of view, to have a party hard as steel, and a working class so united that not one of its members could be torn away from us by the manoeuvres of its enemies.

Comrades, there are manoeuvres, but not 'accommodations'. I know that in the Latin American countries the term 'politics' has become compromised. Above all, amongst the anarchists. They say that politics and parliamentary jockeying are more or less the same thing. No, politics and parliamentary jockeying are not the same thing. Lenin always teaches us that politics is the science of handling millions of workers and peasants. When the great masses begin to move, politics consists of making millions of workers and peasants manoeuvre. There is consequently a danger that should some war or other break out, a war involving North America, a certain number of politicians will begin to make these little accommodations in the hope that Latin America may gain something through, for example, the victory of Japan.

Latin America will gain nothing, absolutely nothing. It would only exchange one yoke for another. Our tactics ought to consist in this; to work for the defeat of all imperialism, for the defeat of our own bourgeoisie. These are the tactics. It is not to make an accommodation with the most ferocious enemies of the workers' movement, of the working class.

48. Letter from ECCI Political Secretariat conveying instructions for the formation of the Peruvian CP, end 1929 or early 1930[1] (*p. 15*)

Even before the Peruvian Communist Party has been formed, whilst you are still only laying its foundations within the working class, Leguía[2] and the imperialism which he serves have declared war on Communism and begun to persecute your groups on the ridiculous pretext of a plot crudely forged by their police agents.

This war on Communism, and this repression against your group, prompt us to write to you on a number of urgent questions relative to the formation of the Peruvian Communist Party, its links with the working and peasant masses, and its immediate tasks, whilst reserving a more profound examination of the economic, political, and social situation of Peru for a further letter.

The Formation of the Communist Party

From the reports which we possess about Peru, we judge the situation to have become favourable for the foundation and operation of a Communist Party in your country.

The economic and social structure of the country is, in its general lines, like that of the greater part of the other Latin American countries. Imperialism—Yankee imperialism, first and foremost—colonizes the country and makes use, for the exploitation of the toiling masses of workers and peasants, of the great landowners and the national bourgeoisie, who are also interested in the exploitation and enslavement of the working people. The growing exploitation of the riches of the soil and sub-soil by the imperialist enterprises has promoted the development of the proletariat and its concentration in the great plantations, mines, oilfields, etc. The working class has grown in size; the development and concentration of industrial enterprises will make the proletariat increasingly class-conscious, and make it a more and more important and active factor in the struggle against imperialism, feudalism, and the capitalist system in general. The increasing intensification of methods for exploiting the workers' labour in the mechanized enterprises will drive them to struggle and revolt. To the concentration and growth of the numerical strength of the proletariat there is thus added the prospect of a fuller and more vigorous struggle against the exploiters. The workers' unions, following the process of the proletariat's formation and concentration, are being organized, developed, and directed towards mass revolutionary action and are abandoning both the reformist corporativism and the verbalistic radicalism of the anarchists. The work of concentrating and unifying the workers' organization in a Peruvian General Federation of Labour proceeds step by step with the same process throughout the whole of the South American continent. The semi-servile situation of the broad toiling masses, oppressed and driven from their lands by the imperialists, confronts the country with the immediate prospect of insurrectional struggles against feudalism and imperialism. These ambitions make it necessary to found a Communist Party as the party of the Peruvian proletarian class.

[1] Martínez de la Torre, *Apuntes . . .*, ii. 496–508.   [2] President of Peru 1919–30.

In the course of the last year, you have begun a certain work of ideological clarification. Through contact with the experience of the revolutionary movement in China and Mexico, and starting from your own experiences in Peru, you have been waging an ideological fight against APRA and against its influence over the workers of Peru. Against the confused ideology of APRA and its false and dangerous idea of a political organization grouping together different social classes beneath the hegemony of the petty bourgeoisie, you have championed with ever greater clarity the idea of the formation of a class party of the proletariat, you have realized and made others realize the role of the different classes in the revolutionary movement, the necessity for the hegemony of the working class, for its political and organizational independence with respect to the allies which it should draw into the revolutionary movement.

This campaign of ideological clarification has removed a large part of the obstacles which were impeding the formation of a Communist Party in Peru. It has shown, on the contrary, the absolute urgency of its creation. You have taken yet another step. By liquidating the weak APRA organizations in Peru and abroad, parallel with the ideological campaign directed against it, you have created a Communist group, proletarian for the most part, and thus laid the foundations for a real class party of the proletariat.

All this proves that the hour has arrived for your group to confront the organization of the Communist Party in the national order, attracting the best workers into its ranks, and recruiting from amongst the working masses, first and foremost from the industrial and agricultural workers, the militants of which will constitute the Communist Party of Peru.

From conversations with your representatives during the Buenos Aires Congress,[1] we were nevertheless able to note that some uncertainty reigns amongst you as to whether it is now opportune to proceed to the enlargement of your group and the creation of the Communist Party of Peru.

Some comrades are hesitating to open the doors of the Communist group and permit the admission of a great number of workers for fear it may lose its political orientation. Others believe that the very name of 'Communist' is incapable of attracting the working mass since the bourgeoisie has managed to discredit it and make a bogey of it. Finally, persecution by police and Government and the prospect of illegality or semi-legality for the Party are making many comrades hesitate and are causing them to seek, in the setting up of another party—a Socialist Party—a way out of these difficulties. We think that the persecutions at present launched against you—the Communist plot by means of which the governmental clique in the service of imperialism is striving to terrorize the working masses and the Communists themselves—tend to strengthen these tendencies amongst you to put off the foundation of a Communist Party and thus find a way out of your difficulties through creating a 'Socialist' Party.

We believe that such a course would be a serious error which would have unfortunate consequences for the future development of your action.

As we have shown, the objective situation favours the foundation of the

The 1st Latin American Communist Congress, held in Buenos Aires in June 1929.

Party. Leguía and his Yankee masters have realized it as well as ourselves, and are striving to nip the Communist Party in the bud and smother it by means of police repression and so alienate the masses from it. The Communist group must not retreat before Leguía's offensive; it must not excuse itself by abandoning Communism in the face of the proletariat and creating a 'Socialist' Party which would mask and conceal Communism from the eyes of the masses.

Governmental repression must, on the contrary, be made the point of departure for a great campaign of agitation amongst the working masses in favour of the Communist Party. Show up the stupidity of the police myths about the Communist plot, but also tell the workers: 'Leguía invents such stupidities because he wants to destroy the Communist Party, because he wants to alienate the workers from it, since the Communist Party wants to organize the struggle against imperialist exploitation, against the dictatorship of the great landowners, against the slavery of the native masses, in favour of the workers' and peasants' government of Peru, and for an anti-imperialist Federation of workers' and peasants' soviets in Latin America. It is because the Communist Party defends the working class and the peasant masses that it threatens the privileges of those who live on the work of the workers and peasants that the exploiters and oppressors of the working people fear it, want to crush it, and strive to discredit it in the eyes of the masses.' In this way you must turn the Communist plot into a means of agitation on behalf of the Communist Party and a means of extending its organization with the masses and firmly linked to them.

You need have no fear of expanding your basic Communist group by organizing the workers, even those of the latter who have as yet no Communist training. You need only be cautious of the non-proletarian elements, petty-bourgeois intellectuals and others, whom you must remove from your Party unless they have given proof of their devotion to the proletariat, particularly in times of repression and class struggle. The Party must thus be implanted in the heart of the masses, rooted in textile factories and the other industrial enterprises of the cities where there is already some basis thanks to the work of the trade union organization. But above all it must be rooted in the mines, in the oilfields, in the great plantations—and even in the feudal latifundia of the sierra amongst natives who are still subject to medieval servitude. Once thus deeply rooted amongst the most exploited masses, the Communist Party will not be able to be destroyed by the repression of police and *patrón*; in its struggle for existence, in its battles as the head of the proletariat against the exploiters, there must be forged an ideology and organization worthy of a true proletarian party, and through its example it will draw into revolutionary alliance the peasant masses and those important strata of the petty bourgeoisie which can play a revolutionary part provided they are drawn into the struggle by the working classes.

In connection with this need to create and develop the Communist Party, we would like to add to the arguments already put forward in Buenos Aires our opinion concerning your plan to form a Socialist Party.

Your delegates to the Buenos Aires Congress communicated to us your intention of organizing a 'Socialist' Party in Peru—a mass party, able to exist legally, and controlled by Communist groups for which it would be the legal instrument within the heart of the workers' and peasants' masses. The arguments adduced in support of this plan stress the difficulty of organizing a Communist Party in Peru on account of Leguía's police dictatorship, the scanty sympathy of the masses for Communism, the need not to remain a small closed, illegal, group, but to organize the revolutionary masses in a great political party led by Communists, etc.

The idea that a Communist Party should not remain a restricted and closed circle, a sect of Communists who are ideologically very advanced but without influence over the masses, is absolutely correct.

The Communist Party should tend ceaselessly to link itself closely with the revolutionary working and peasant masses and intervene as a political factor in Peruvian life, mobilizing and drawing this mass movement behind its leadership. The development of the organization and the political education of the Communist Party can only be achieved by struggling, fighting, and toiling with the mass of workers and peasants, studying the experiences gained in the light of our revolutionary theory, correcting errors and weaknesses, and thus accumulating experience and greater political capacity.

Your plans are different, according to the statements made in Buenos Aires by one of your representatives. In your plan, or at least in the thinking of some of you, it would be a matter of creating a Socialist Party, with a broader basis than the Communist Party, that is to say, by accepting intellectuals and petty-bourgeois revolutionary elements who would not be acceptable in the Communist Party, and with a narrower political programme—a 'minimum' programme of immediate demands—to be publicized amongst the workers, whilst concealing the revolutionary 'maximum' programme.

We do not know the extent to which you all support this idea, but in the form in which one of your comrades has expressed it we must combat it as most dangerous to the very future of your movement. To create a 'Socialist' Party possessing a broader basis than the Communist Party and open not only to the workers but also to certain strata of the petty bourgeoisie which you yourselves deem unacceptable to the Communist Party on account of their non-proletarian ideology, is really tantamount to reverting to *Aprismo* in a roundabout way beneath a different label—reverting to a multi-class party, to confused revolutionary ideology, to a Kuomintang more dangerous than APRA because it is better organized, more centralized, more disciplined, and since it has all the character of a political party, it would inevitably clash with the Communist Party and you would then be faced with carrying through a heavy task, struggling fiercely to win over the workers, who are today under your influence, from the influence of the petty bourgeoisie which you wish to keep your Communist Party clear of and which with the certain favour of the Government, would assume serious influence in the Socialist Party. The example of the Socialist Party of Ecuador, formed by a clandestine Communist group which controlled it and which now sees itself compelled to expel its deputies and purge its ranks to avoid degenerating into an opportunist party in the services of the Government, must make you understand the danger of such a party duality, above all when the Communist group is still weak and the possibilities of development of a mass Socialist Party are great. The Communist group will find difficulty in controlling it, and will be burdened by the action of the police who will strive demagogically to convert it into a party of governmental collaboration.

The idea of giving this party a minimum programme whilst concealing the revolutionary programme represents another danger which, added to the first, reveals the true character which such a party would at once acquire.

The idea of endowing this party with a minimum programme distinct from the maximum programme is anti-Leninist, anti-Marxist. A Communist Party cannot act in this way. The Communist Party starts out from the immediate demands of the masses in order to draw them into the class struggle, into the mass action which strives to develop and lead on to a higher revolutionary level. It does not separate immediate demands from the final revolutionary objective; it considers them as a means of mobilizing the masses, getting them moving, drawing them on to revolutionary action. It considers the linking of immediate demands with the final objective, from the point of view of its historical development, through the movement born of day-to-day demands, in order to guide the masses towards the seizure of power.

To separate immediate aims from the final objective, as the minimum programme does, is a reformist point of view which sees in the reform an objective in itself and not a means of drawing the proletariat towards the sole objective of its class action—the seizure of power by the working class. It must also be realized that no serious 'reform' can be attained by the working class without a struggle to gain it, and that no reform won after a great struggle can be preserved by the workers without an incessant struggle against the exploiters.

This reformist character which lies at the 'broader' social basis of the Socialist Party and the minimum programme can be recognized in the very name of the party you wish to found. The name of 'Socialist Party' is linked to a whole history of betrayal of proletarian interests, to the history of the Second International which, from Noske to Zoergiebel,[1] is that of the assassination of the best forces of the revolutionary proletariat in order to save imperialism. In Peru itself, the name of 'Socialist Party' is discredited by the experience already made, and has nothing about it to attract the working class. It could only attract those petty-bourgeois elements frightened by the name of 'Communism' which the workers' movement ought to combat and not organize together with the forces of the workers.

It is an illusion to believe that a 'Socialist' Party possessing a social basis and political action which is clearly Communist and only differing from a Communist Party in name might enjoy greater legal possibilities and escape police repression through this subterfuge. A Socialist Party could have no legal existence in Peru, where every revolutionary manifestation is ruthlessly suppressed by the dictatorship, except by converting itself into a reformist party respectful of legality without any clear ideology, without a firm political line, manipulated secretly by the agents of Leguía in order to betray the workers' interests, and only serving at best the interests of the petty bourgeoisie and only

---

[1] Gustav Noske and Karl Zörgiebel, German Social Democrat leaders active in suppressing revolutionary risings after the First World War.

winning over the worker and peasant masses in order to convert itself finally into the principal enemy of the Communist Party, by placing the masses at the service of imperialist policy.

The only way to attain the formation of a mass Communist Party in Peru is to develop your Communist group into a true Communist Party, drawing into it the best revolutionary working and rural labouring elements, even though they may not yet be Communists with a sound Marxist education; it is enough that they should be orientated towards mass revolutionary action and working-class struggle and organization, that is to say, that they should have resolutely broken both with anarcho-syndicalist sectarianism and with reformism, the tool of imperialism.

Organize a Party with the best workers' elements, help them to educate themselves through contact with their everyday experiences and in the course of working-class struggle; link this Party, through the labour of each of its members, to the factory, in workers' organizations, in peasant communities, and to the mass of workers and rural labourers; win by your labour the confidence of the workers and thereby the leadership of the workers' organization. Publish an organ of the Party, publicize its thought and action amongst the masses, win their confidence so that they may see their only guide in the Communist Party, be it legal or illegal. We ask you then definitely to abandon all idea of forming a Socialist Party in Peru. If your work to create such a party has advanced to the stage that organizations have already been formed, we ask you to liquidate the Socialist Party, explaining to the masses the reasons for this measure and transforming such organization as may exist into organizations of the Communist Party.

Links with the broad labouring masses

The mistaken idea of creating a Socialist Party stemmed from the good intention of not isolating the Communists from the Peruvian revolutionary masses, to find a means of linking themselves to the masses in order to lead them to action. If you give up the idea of the Socialist Party, how is it possible to achieve this indispensable linking of the Communist Party, even though it may be illegal, with the Peruvian workers' and peasants' masses?

With which masses must the Communist Party link itself most closely? Not with the masses of the petty bourgeoisie of the cities who, perhaps, might easily follow the action of a Socialist Party. The effort of the Communist Party must tend towards linking itself closely, first and foremost, with the industrial proletariat of the great imperialist enterprises, the workers of the mines, oil-fields, textile factories, transport, etc; then directly with the great mass of the agrarian workers of the large plantations of cotton, sugar, rice, rubber, etc.

The Communist Party must immediately link itself with the peasant masses, particularly with the masses of the sierra Indians who are one of the most important factors for the development of the Peruvian revolution, since they have a tradition of revolt against the great feudal landowners. The Party must link itself with the masses of peons in the great feudal latifundia of the sierra, with the Indians of the rural communities and with the peasant smallholders on the outskirts of the cities and in different parts of the coast.

Finally, and only in the third place, the Communist Party should strive to draw the revolutionary petty bourgeoisie of the cities, the artisans, intellectuals, and small traders, into the struggle against imperialism and feudalism, against the dictatorship of the Catholic Church, in a word, against the whole of the capitalist system.

To achieve the linking of the Party with these masses, so that it becomes the guide of the proletariat and of the allies of the working class in the revolutionary struggle, there is no organizational trick by which the work can be facilitated. It is not enough to launch the slogans 'Socialist Party' or 'Workers' and Peasants' Bloc' or any others, to obtain spontaneously the result desired. It is necessary to develop the work of conquering the masses at the base, organizing the proletarians in their mass organizations—unions and Communist Party— organizing the peasants in agrarian leagues, drawing the revolutionary strata of the petty bourgeoisie into the action of the Anti-Imperialist League, the Red Aid, and other organizations sympathizing with the Communist Party. It is necessary for the Communist Party to expand its work and the network of its cells within these mass organizations. Above all, it is necessary that, by means of its cells, it should develop the fighting spirit of the masses, organizing workers' combat committees to carry class warfare into the industrial enterprises and plantations, and organizing peasants' combat committees to occupy the estates and drive out the landowners and to promote risings and agrarian revolution. By means of these struggles, beneath the leadership of the Communist Party, there will be developed the real links with the masses, internally co-ordinated by their cells, unbreakable links forged in revolutionary battle.

It is possible that, in a more advanced stage of the mass movement, it might prove necessary to find organizational forms for this alliance of the peasants' and workers' masses in their common struggle. In a situation like this a workers' and peasants' congress might be summoned to unify the struggle led by the workers' and peasants' revolutionary organizations to give them a fresh impulse and a broader base. The Communist Party should be sure to keep for itself the leadership of the Workers' and Peasants' Bloc which might be the outcome of such a congress. But an eventuality of this sort must be the result of serious work on behalf of the Party; since it has the confidence of the masses, its active cells must be the framework or backbone of this. It is essential to reject the idea of a Workers' and Peasants' Bloc which is nothing more than a label or electoral façade of the Communist Party, or a new name for a second party, broader and less revolutionary than the Communist Party, a dangerous pseudonym for the Socialist Party or *Aprismo*.

In all our mass work, it is necessary to clarify our position with respect to the revolutionary petty bourgeoisie which plays a considerable political role in Peru as in other Latin American countries, on account of the youth of the working class and its dispersal far from the great political centres of the country. The petty bourgeoisie does not constitute a homogeneous class possessing common interests. It is composed of various social strata and widely differing interests, and the most opposing tendencies; it is composed above all of the remnants of classes in process of disappearance, representing the vestiges of economic systems and social relations in process of liquidation—artisans, small traders, smallholders, etc. These strata can participate actively in the struggle against imperialism, as they feel their existence to be menaced by it. But their struggle is not 'revolutionary' in its fundamental orientation, since it tends to a return to an economic system and a social order already superseded by technical and economic progress itself. It has its eyes fixed on the past, which it would like to revive, and not towards the future, towards Communism, which represents the only economic system and social order higher than imperialism. The only class which is in essence really revolutionary in Latin America is the industrial and agricultural proletariat, which may draw after it the dispossessed peasants struggling for land. This is the class which must be the driving force of revolution. The struggle against imperialism of certain strata of the petty bourgeoisie can and must be an important support for the revolution led by the proletariat; it is only within this historical framework, as a part of the revolution led by the working class, that this struggle of the petty bourgeoisie against imperialism takes on a 'revolutionary' character. But the experience of the Kuomintang, the experience of the Mexican Revolution led by the 'revolutionary' petty bourgeoisie, as that of Ayora's Government in Ecuador, and the Fascism of Ibáñez in Chile, are other perfectly clear demonstrations that the petty bourgeoisie leads the revolution to bankruptcy, capitulates to imperialism, places itself in its service in order to suppress the true movement of the working and peasant masses in the hour of proletarian revolution. The *soi-disant* revolutionary petty bourgeoisie is most liable to slide into Fascism when, after realizing it is powerless to revive a liberal petty-bourgeois regime, it puts itself at the service of big capital or imperialism in order to combat the revolutionary workers' movement.

These truths, illustrated by historical examples, which are every day more frequent, from China, Mexico, Ecuador, Chile, and Peru itself, should form the centre of your action against APRA.

It is in the measure that the working masses realize these fundamental truths that they will definitely detach themselves from APRA and set resolutely to work creating and developing their class organization, their class party, the Communist Party, and take the leading position in Peru's revolutionary struggle.

The ideological struggle against APRA is thus one of the first conditions for the complete enlightening of the Peruvian proletariat's conscience, an enlightening which is indispensable if you wish to avoid your future work being permanently sterilized by vestiges of *Aprista* ideology surviving in the workers' movement.

The process of liquidating APRA, both abroad and in Peru, has made serious headway thanks to the political action you have taken. Ideologically and organizationally, APRA is in retreat, whilst proletarian ideology and organization are emerging clearly in place of its confused ideology. Nevertheless, this process needs to be intensified by your action and political work. APRA was, in the interior of the country, more of a current of opinion than an organization, an ideological and political influence in the heart of the masses of the petty bourgeoisie and the working class. There is no doubt that, despite the success of your propaganda, APRA still preserves a certain authority and maintains certain illusions amongst the masses. You must therefore continue to develop your action against APRA, specially in the heart of the organizations and of the working masses.

Workers' struggles and the immediate tasks

The first task of your group then is to form a Communist Party, liquidating the ideology of APRA and grouping together the best workers' forces throughout the whole country. You must, at the same time, work out a programme of action based on the decisions of the 6th Comintern. This programme of action should be approved by your congress. This essential work, which we are discussing in detail, must go hand in hand with a drive for organization and propaganda, that is to say, the creation of a party organ to convey its thought, watchwords, and directives to the worker and peasant masses. To avoid repression by the Government, this organ can be outwardly presented as a workers' daily, but your action amongst the masses should make it known as the organ and mouthpiece of the Communist Party, and its contents should be absolutely Communist.

Besides this fundamental task, which consists of organizing the Communist Party and the means of linking it with the organizations of the mass of the proletariat and the peasants, it is necessary to give the highest priority to trade union work. It is in the trade union movement that you will obtain the best forces for the Party. It is there that the masses will be organized to lead the class battle against the imperialism which is dominating and exploiting the country.

In the present situation of Peru, as in Latin America as a whole, the development of great worker struggles is inevitable. Stemming from the exploitation to which workers are subject, forced by a violently repressive regime to provide profits by the sweat of their brow for the foreign imperialists and the national bourgeoisie who participate in their exploitation, these struggles may initially take on the character of a struggle for immediate demands (higher wages, reduction of the working day, payment in cash, freedom to make purchases elsewhere than at company stores, etc) but they will rapidly assume a revolutionary character by virtue of their anti-imperialist scope and by forms of struggle intensified by police repression and the dictatorial regime (e.g. the strike in the Colombian banana zone, etc).

The Party must keep this perspective in view and prepare for these proletarian struggles; it must create at the right moment an organ of combat for the workers—factory agitation, and action committees—and draw on the whole mass. The struggle must also be prepared by intensifying the trade union organization at the base, amongst the masses. The fact that you have developed a great labour force for the creation of the Peruvian CGT[1] should not lead you to overlook that the fundamental work is not the organization of a centre or the creation of a CGT, but the organization of workers everywhere they are exploited, and the creation of mass unions in enterprises.

In this important field, your tasks are as follows:

(*a*) To be actively concerned with the organization of those categories of workers who are most exploited in the country's basic industry and in the great

---

[1] *Confederación General de Trabajadores.*

imperialist enterprises (oil, mines, sugar, etc). It is absolutely necessary to begin to organize the masses of agricultural workers, the coastal plantations (sugar, rice, cotton, etc) and of the feudal latifundia of the sierra, using the existing native organizations (Regional Native Federation of Peru), but above all, by specially training certain comrades to be sent to the great enterprises with the special task of working in them and organizing the working masses there, and raising the demands appropriate to each branch of industry. This is one of the most important and urgent tasks, though it offers great difficulties which Communists and union militants must at all costs strive to overcome.

(*b*) Work of this kind presupposes a prolonged study of the work and life of the workers in the different industries, and the establishment of concrete demands which directly interest the agricultural and industrial working masses.

(*c*) Attempts must be made to organize trade unions on an industrial basis, organizing a union branch in every factory. But still more must efforts be made in every strike movement for the preparation of some action, that the organized and unorganized workers should together nominate action committees, strike committees, factory committees, representing the workers as a whole in which the trade union section and the Communist cell—if they perform their duty—must become the centre and moving spirits of the same.

(*d*) The CGT must try to consolidate and broaden the existing organizations adhering to it—textile, railways, transport, etc.—introducing a system of regular subscriptions, minimal at first, so as not to alienate the workers, but making them realize the need for having regular resources with which to tackle the tasks of organization, propaganda, agitation, and solidarity.

(*e*) A trade union journal needs to be created, either by transforming *Labor* into a fighting organ of the Peruvian CGT or else by creating a special organ for the trade union movement.

Apart from this trade union activity, which ought to claim your best efforts during the present period, we also deem it important that the Party should concern itself with work amongst the native masses of the sierra Indians of the agrarian communities and those of the latifundia who live in conditions of feudal exploitation, and are one of the most important revolutionary factors in Peru. Native revolts to defend the land of the communities or to re-establish the agrarian community in place of the great feudal estate which has dispossessed them, are incessantly renewed. It is essential to link this movement and its demands to the proletarian movement of workers in the cities and the great enterprises. The well-grounded suspicion of the natives with respect to 'white' workers must be overcome by utilizing native workers from the cities and mines for liaison and propaganda, and by developing a systematic work in the army which is formed almost exclusively of Indians. The disrupting of the governmental army and the linking of the workers' revolutionary movement with the peasants of the sierra are two fundamental tasks, and relatively easy ones, of your military work.

To these tasks must be added that of developing the anti-imperialist movement into a revolutionary mass movement.

Peru is one of the Latin American countries most thoroughly controlled and harshly exploited by Yankee imperialism; yet Hoover's tour did not provoke there any mass manifestation against imperialism. The party itself must remedy this situation, and not leave a monopoly of the anti-imperialist struggle to APRA and other agents of English imperialism. It must create the Anti-Imperialist League and give it a clearly revolutionary content, drawing into it the workers' and peasants' masses at the same time as the intellectual and petty-bourgeois elements which want to struggle against imperialism by the side of the workers and peasants.

We do not believe that what has been said above covers all the multiple tasks devolving on your group in the present Peruvian situation. We have drawn your attention to those we consider essential and primordial at the present moment. To organize the Communist Party and the Trade Union Confederation, the exploited proletariat of the great industrial and agrarian enterprises, to link them to the mass by means of systematic and persistent work of propaganda, organization and agitation, to give to this mass work a clear and solid ideological basis—such are the fundamental tasks facing you. We do not doubt that you will resolutely pursue them and that the Peruvian revolutionary movement will rapidly acquire an important place in the Latin American movement and the international movement in general.

8 Brazil

49. Assessment of the revolutionary prospects by a Brazilian Communist: speech by 'Keiros' [?Queiroz] at the 3rd Congress of the CPs of South and Caribbean America, October 1934:[1] excerpts (*p. 19*)

The National Conference of the Communist Party of Brazil took place in July 1934, with 45 comrades participating. After hearing reports of the Party leadership, the Conference recognised that Brazil is rapidly moving towards a deep revolutionary crisis. The next few months may be decisive for the unfolding of great events in Brazil.

These conclusions were drawn, not merely on the basis of the analysis made by the Thirteenth Plenum of the Executive Committee of the Communist International, but chiefly on the basis of the analyses of the struggles organized by us, as well as the spontaneous activities which have broken out and which the Communists are not leading as yet.

At the present time so many strikes are taking place in Brazil that it is impossible to give accurate figures. . . . The agrarian crisis is rapidly sharpening. The

[1] *The Communist International*, 20 May 1935, pp. 577–88.

peasant masses are taking up the armed struggle. These struggles in the village meet with response in the towns, link up with the movement of the proletariat, and, in its turn, the urban movement is meeting with response in the villages of the Northeast. Not so long ago a strike of agricultural labourers, which was linked up with strikes of textile workers and paper workers took place. . . .

The partisan movement is also growing, but here also new methods are employed in the struggle. Now the partisans are not alone in their struggle. The struggle also has the support of the toilers in the villages. The partisan *cangaceiros*[1] are calling for struggle, are uniting the poor peasants in their battle for bread and for life. The government can no longer successfully deal with this movement. It is no longer a small peasant uprising against which it was enough to dispatch a hundred soldiers. In the Bahia province alone, the partisans represent a detachment of approximately 1,500 men, armed with machine guns, equipped with motor trucks, etc. . . .

The army in Brazil is demoralised from the top to the bottom. It is not an army like that in the Argentine. In no other army is there such bad discipline as in the Brazilian army. This army does not resemble the German, the French, nor the army of any other country. Military schools were always strongholds of the revolutionary struggle for democratic liberty. In 1922 I was myself a soldier. At that time our discipline was such that we had only to be given a few cartridges, and we would immediately ask for a light from the officers. The soldiers took part in the uprisings.

The majority of the officers are from the petty bourgeoisie. They are young people who were unsuccessful in becoming officials, unsuccessful in winning their bachelor degrees, and who entered the army, because officers are paid salaries. What has been happening in the army recently? There has been a strike in the military school, organized by our youth nucleus. The young men protested against compulsory drill, for better food, etc.

Now we have Communist organisations in the majority of the corps. The army is sympathetic towards strikers. The soldiers came to a textile factory and said: 'We are not against the workers and will support you, have no fear.'

A constant struggle is going on in the barracks. In the North the soldiers are reading the Party manifesto calling upon them to organise soviets and telling them about the Soviet Union.

In Pernambuco in 1931 the soldiers organized, arrested their officers and took the government into their own hands. They seized the palaces and banks, took control of the tax apparatus, the post and the telegraph. And then they did not know what to do next. They then appealed to the officers who claimed to be in solidarity with the soldiers and released some of these officers. But the officers organized the forces of counter-revolution and despite their strong resistance the soldiers were crushed. . . .

What will happen if we link up with the broad masses of the North-east? We must not fear that we shall be called golpists,[2] putshchists. The peasants want to fight with arms in hand. The soldiers want to fight for a better life. The

---

[1] Traditional Brazilian bandits or guerrillas.
[2] Those who attempt a *golpe* or coup d'état.

broad masses of the people are joining the struggle. We shall fight, arms in hand, for the improvement of their material conditions, against imperialism, against the reactionary government of Vargas, against the latifundia owners. Enough of this trailing at the tail end of the movement! The movement must be properly organised.

50. Report after visiting Pernambuco by the Comintern's representative Arthur Ewert on preparations for an armed rising, June 1935:[1] excerpts (*p. 19*)

The struggle in the region of the S. Francisco river. At the time of our arrival, all preparations were in train for the rising in a region comprising six municipalities, some 20,000 square kilometres, and a population of 135,000. Aim of the rising: seizure of power, with the prospect of shortly afterwards setting up soviets and establishing Soviet power. Our comrades in Pernambuco had already drafted the decrees of the future Soviet Government and sent them on to the S. Francisco river. It is clear that the instructions to set up Soviet power on such a narrow basis were completely wrong. Such instructions were also contrary to the directives of the Central Committee. These directives, moreover, were given little importance by the leading comrades in those parts, and they declared that something had to be done since the masses and their leaders there wanted to fight. Comrade Silo sought to defend these tactics by reference to the decisions previously taken. It was difficult to get him to agree to the change of tactics (creation of national revolutionary government) and that the setting up of soviets at the S. Francisco river was wrong. However, we convinced the comrades that their conduct had been irregular, and after a thorough discussion the following points were agreed upon:

(*a*) Send off a telegram at once postponing the rising,

(*b*) send Cajt to the S. Francisco river at once,

(*c*) start a great peasant movement in that region, and develop bodies of volunteers out of that movement as a means of support for it, and begin the struggle with a number of regular volunteer groups. The aim of the struggle should be to achieve the peasants' demands. Action should not be taken in the name of the Party or of the National Liberal Alliance. Soviets should not be set up, but peasant leagues and committees. Other fighting nuclei should be formed in other regions of Pernambuco, as well as in other states. They should enter into relations with the *cangaceiros* already in existence. Some work has already been done in this direction and liaison may already be established, or will be shortly.

51. Comintern commendation of the Brazilian Communists for using the National Liberation Alliance as a means of seizing power: statement by Wang Ming, rapporteur for Latin America, at the 7th Comintern Congress, 17 August 1935:[2] excerpt (*p. 19*)

In Brazil, a broad, democratic organisation has been formed with the participation of the Communist Party, the 'National Freedom Alliance', and has

---

[1] *Relatorio . . .*, pp. 394–0.   [2] *Inprecorr*, xv/36, 17 Aug. 1935, pp. 938–9.

been joined even by many officers of the army and navy. At numerous meetings our comrade Prestes, the hero of the Brazilian people, was elected honorary president of this Alliance. During the Vargas government, whilst the rights of the people and all freedom were being trodden underfoot on direct imperialist orders, Prestes issued on behalf of the whole Brazilian people the slogan: 'All power to the National Freedom Alliance.'

As part of its task of conquering state power by the Alliance, the Communist Party of Brazil must intensify its endeavours for securing the national united front, must overcome the sectarianism of some individual Communists, and go forward to the highest forms of the struggle for power. The winning over of the masses of the peasantry and the further extension of the anti-imperialist People's Front are amongst the chief pre-requisites of success. A government of the National Freedom Alliance to which this movement can lead, will not yet be a revolutionary democratic dictatorship of the workers and peasants, but above all, it will be an anti-imperialist government. The Communists will fight in it for national independence, but at the same time they must use it as the vehicle for achieving widespread social measures in the interests of the workers and peasants and of the middle classes of the towns. The work accomplished by the Brazilian comrades evidences excellent beginnings towards the formation of the anti-imperialist united front. I wish and hope for their victorious accomplishment of this difficult task.

52. Statement by Dimitrov at the 7th Comintern Congress urging the formation of a people's revolutionary army, August 1935:[1] excerpt (*p. 19*)

In Brazil, the Communist Party having laid a correct foundation for the development of the United anti-Fascist front by the establishment of the National Liberation Alliance, has to make every effort to extend further this front by drawing into it first and foremost the many millions of the peasantry, leading up to the formation of units of a people's revolutionary army completely devoted to the revolution and to the establishment of the rule of the National Liberation Alliance.

53. Instructions to the Brazilian Communists to accept Prestes as their leader: letter from Rodolfo Ghioldi and Arthur Ewert to Antonio Maciel Bomfim, member of the Brazilian CP national secretariat, 6 October 1935:[2] excerpt (*p. 18*)

It will in practice be necessary for the Secretariat to have the collaboration of two reliable and informed persons who need not be members of the Central Committee or even of the Communist Party. . . . We propose that Garoto[3] should be accepted as a member of the Central Committee and elected on to the Politburo. We would like to say a few words to justify this proposal. This is something we have for some time past been meaning to propose to you. The

---

[1] *Inprecorr*, 1935, no. 37, p. 971.   [2] *Relatorio . . .*, pp. 46–7.
[3] Luiz Carlos Prestes.

postponement of the [meeting of the] Central Committee from September to October gave us time, and in the meantime there has also been held the Seventh Congress whose deliberations facilitate a solution of this question. You will learn from Lacerda's[1] report that Garoto was elected on to the Executive Council of the Third Communist International. But even if this had not been the case, the situation in Brazil, the special role and work accomplished by Garoto up to now necessitate his election to the Central Committee and the Politburo. (It would not of course be fitting, for conspiratorial reasons, for him to visit all the [Party's] sections.) The more we now manage to build up a firm and unbreakable unity between the Party's proletarian leadership and the popular national leader, the easier it will be to overcome the difficulties which may arise at different stages of the Brazilian revolution. Garoto's election to the Central Committee will serve as a demonstration of this [unity]. The Party and its leadership recognize that he is entitled to share in running it. Party and leadership will know that Garoto's special role does not mean a weakening, but rather a great positive help and strengthening of the Party. Party and leadership will appreciate the evolution of LCP[2] from petty-bourgeois revolutionary to bolshevism and popular national leader, a path which thousands of national-revolutionary leaders and elements will take in the course of the Brazilian revolution.

54. Prestes issues a call to arms: communiqué by Luiz Carlos Prestes published by 'A Manhã', organ of the National Liberation Alliance, 27 November 1935 (*p. 19*)

The Revolutionary Committee, under my direction, in face of the events which are taking place in the north of the country and of the menace of a reactionary dictatorship, resolves that all the forces of the Revolution should be ready to fight for popular liberties and to give the decisive blow to Getulio Vargas's Government of national treason.

The day and hour will be announced in due course.

55. Outbreak and suppression of the rising: Comintern report, 21 December 1935:[3] excerpts (*p. 19*)

In Natal and Recife, the two capitals respectively of the Brazilian states, Rio Grande do Norte and Pernambuco, the military forces which were stationed in the two cities rose, on November 22, supported by broad masses of the people, and in particular by the entire working class of those places.

While the revolutionists in Natal succeeded, after a twenty-four hours' battle with the military police, in capturing Natal and several other towns in the State of Rio Grande, and in setting up the first national-revolutionary people's government (which however, was able to retain control for only four days), a

---

[1] Fernando Lacerda, Brazilian CP leader, delegate to the 6th Comintern Congress, and representative of the S. American CPs on the ECCI.
[2] Luiz Carlos Prestes.
[3] *Inprecorr*, xv/70, 21 Dec. 1935, pp. 1718–20.

12

like success was lacking in Recife. The revolutionists were not able to gain the centre of the city and the port against the military police. But the workers, after occupying the Villa Militar and the most important working-class suburbs, did however gain a most advantageous strategic position along the railway line which leads inland. This enabled them later to retire inland with all their arms and munitions.

The main revolutionary forces in Rio Grande do Norte were enabled to make a similar move, after the national-revolutionary government had been forced to retire by the much stronger forces of the federal government and of the government of the State of Bahia. The first organised, armed national-revolutionary forces, consisting of soldiers and workers, have unfolded the banner of Luiz Carlos Prestes and the National Liberation Alliance. The first national-revolutionary people's government in Brazil has fallen, but the national revolution has set out along the path of struggle, and has undergone its first battles with great concrete gains. . . .

The national-revolutionary leadership came to the decision to launch a general rising of the people by means of a revolt in the barracks at Rio de Janeiro. The revolutionary forces here were considerable in number and were armed, and the organised active participation of the working class of Rio de Janeiro (both of the capital and the State of that name) in an extended struggle on behalf of the national-revolution could be depended on. Revolutionary officers and soldiers examined the situation together with working-class leaders, and they were mutually agreed on the decision for the uprising. They hoped to seize the initiative by a bold stroke, and then to develop their full forces in the struggle. In the event of victory, or of a struggle with good prospects of victory, in Rio de Janeiro, the other centres of the national-revolutionary movement were to swing into the struggle.

Undoubtedly, here we had a case of the over-estimation of the strength of the national-revolutionaries, and an under-estimate of the forces still at the disposal of their opponents, in the capital.

The revolutionary troops of the Third Infantry Regiment and of the Flying School were beaten by superior forces after a battle lasting from seven to nine hours. Despite the heroic efforts of revolutionary officers and soldiers, they were unsuccessful in winning over to their side other important military units, such as mechanised artillery, and so on. By the early morning of November 27, the revolutionary leaders realised clearly that the uprising would be unsuccessful, even with the aid of the workers' shock-brigades. They had, then, no choice but to surrender to their opponents, as the particular circumstances in Rio de Janeiro rendered it impossible to break through and make for the interior. The government took prisoner 2,500 soldiers and 50 officers, ranging from lieutenants to colonels.

III WAR, COLD WAR, AND PEACEFUL COEXISTENCE

1 Latin America

56. 'Pravda' interview with Stalin, who accuses the Latin American countries of furthering US aggressive policies at the UN, February 1951:[1] excerpts (*p. 21*)

The United Nations, created as the bulwark for preserving peace, is being turned into an instrument of war, into a means of unleashing a new world war. Its aggressive core is represented by ten member-countries of the aggressive North Atlantic Pact and twenty Latin American countries. The representatives of these countries now decide the fate of war and peace in the United Nations. It was they who carried the shameful decision on the aggressiveness of the Chinese People's Republic.

It is characteristic of the present regime in the United Nations that, for instance, the small Dominican Republic, whose population hardly amounts to two millions, has the same weight as India, and much more weight than the Chinese People's Republic, which is deprived of the right to vote in the United Nations. Thus, being turned into a tool of aggressive war, the United Nations is at the same time ceasing to be a world organisation of nations enjoying equal rights. It is more an organisation for the Americans, an organisation acting on behalf of the requirements of the American aggressors.

Not only the United States and Canada are striving to unleash a new war. The same stand has also been taken by twenty Latin American countries, the landowners and businessmen of which are craving for a new war somewhere in Europe or Asia, in order to sell goods to the belligerent countries for excessively high prices and to earn millions from this sanguinary business. It is no secret for anyone that their representatives now represent the most solid and obedient army of the United States in the United Nations.

---

[1] *The Times*, 17 Feb. 1951, quoting the official version published in the *Soviet Monitor* (London).

57. Bulganin, in a press interview, enunciates the policy of peaceful coexistence as applied to Latin America, January 1956[1] (*p. 21*)

Q: Does the Soviet Union intend to establish diplomatic relations with those countries of Latin America with whom such relations do not exist at present?

A: The Soviet Union, it stands to reason, is also ready to establish diplomatic relations with those countries of Latin America with which it does not yet have such relations. We stand for the development of international links and co-operation with all states, including the countries of Latin America.

Q: What benefit does the Soviet Union receive from the existence of diplomatic relations with Argentina, Mexico, and Uruguay?

A: The relations which the USSR has with Argentina, Mexico, and Uruguay are of benefit, it seems to us, to both parties. They facilitate the co-operation of these states on questions relating to the maintenance and strengthening of peace. They promote the development of economic, cultural, and other links between the USSR and these countries. Thus trade between the Soviet Union and Argentina has recently been expanded considerably. It may be hoped that our relations with the countries of Latin America will continue in the future to be developed to the mutual advantage of the parties, in the interests of strengthening international co-operation.

Q: What assurances would the Soviet Union give with regard to non-interference in the political life of the countries of Latin America?

A: The USSR does not interfere in the internal affairs of other states and considers that other states also should not interfere in the internal affairs of the Soviet Union. The Soviet Union's foreign policy is built on respect for the sovereignty of all states, both large and small, on the recognition of the right of all peoples to an independent national and state development. Peaceful coexistence and the friendly co-operation of states regardless of the difference n their social structures—this is the most important principle of our foreign policy.

Naturally, all this remains completely valid in the Soviet Union's attitude towards the countries of Latin America.

Q: Does the Soviet Union plan to increase its trade with countries of Latin America, and what steps will be taken in this respect?

A: The Soviet Union stands for the development of trade with countries of Latin America on the basis of mutual advantage.

Q: Does the Soviet Union intend to participate in other industrial fairs in countries of Latin America such as that recently held in Buenos Aires? Will they include exhibits on the development of atomic energy along with manufactured goods?

A: The Soviet industrial exhibition in Buenos Aires in 1955 was one of the many exhibitions organized recently by the USSR in other countries. The Soviet Union will continue to hold such exhibitions and to participate in international fairs in the future, taking into account in this matter the desires of the Governments of the countries concerned and the mutual interests. It is

---

[1] Interview given by N. A. Bulganin, Chairman of the Council of Ministers, to a correspondent of *Visión*, *Pravda*, 17 Jan. 1956.

not excluded that exhibits on the utilization of atomic energy for peaceful purposes may be presented at exhibitions and fairs. The Soviet Union has already presented such exhibits at exhibitions in Geneva and Delhi in 1955.

Q: What goods could the Soviet Union offer to countries of Latin America, and what would the Soviet Union desire to purchase in these countries?

A: The Soviet Union exports a wide variety of goods, given a mutual interest in this. In particular, the Soviet Union might deliver to Latin American countries various types of industrial equipment and machinery, including equipment for the oil industry, complete equipment for individual enterprises, lathes, instruments, automobiles, and agricultural machinery. If necessary, the Soviet Union might give technical aid and the aid of specialists, and also might exchange experience in the field of industry, energy, construction, transport, and agriculture. In addition to equipment and machinery, the Soviet Union also exports a large number of other goods which may be of interest to countries of Latin America, for example timber and cellulose articles, oil and oil products, rolled ferrous metals, cement, asbestos, paints, and chemicals and other goods. In turn, our country might import from Latin America products of agriculture, animal husbandry, and the mining industry. The practice of trade between the USSR and many other countries has confirmed the mutual advantage and expediency of this exchange.

Q: Would the Soviet Union, in its trade with countries of Latin America, prefer to deal with Governments or with private corporations and individuals?

A: In its foreign trade, the Soviet Union deals with state organizations and with private companies and individuals.

Q: Does the Soviet Union intend to encourage an exchange of visits with countries of Latin America?

A: Yes, it intends to do this.

Q: Will the Soviet Union not examine the question of permitting the airlines of Latin America which pass through Europe at present to extend their routes to cities of the Soviet Union?

A: This question requires special consideration, for here the concrete conditions and requirements of the contracting parties play the decisive role.

58. Khrushchev, in a press interview, calls for closer trade and diplomatic relations, March 1958:[1] excerpts (*p. 21*)

With goodwill on the part of the peoples who trade, one can without difficulty find forms of economic relations acceptable both to the Soviet Union and to the countries of Latin America. The problem lies not in the form but in the essence. The main thing, the essential prerequisite for increasing the economic ties between the countries of Latin America and the Soviet Union, is the desire to trade in fair and mutually advantageous conditions. . . .

The Soviet Union has trade relations with several Spanish-American countries at the present time. The Soviet Union's trade with these countries has increased considerably since the war. Nevertheless, the volume of trade with

---

[1] Interview granted to Manuel Mejido, *Excelsior* (Mexico City), 13 Mar. 1958.

the Spanish American Republics is still not sufficient. The possibilities of increase between my country and your countries have not been exploited as fully
as they should. For example, the Soviet Union could supply Spanish America
with a wider assortment of industrial tools and machinery for your industrialization, and also various raw materials, in exchange for the traditional
export merchandise of the countries of Spanish America.

At the present time, of all the Spanish-speaking countries the Soviet Union
trades most actively with Argentina and Uruguay. With these countries we
have trade-and-payments agreements. It is sufficient to say, for example, that
during the last four years alone Argentine-Soviet trade reached a figure of
$180 million. . . .

Starting from its peace policy and the well-known principles of peaceful
coexistence, the Soviet Union is prepared to establish commercial, diplomatic,
and all kinds of relations with the countries with which, for different reasons,
she has no relations at the moment.

The Soviet people show great interest in the old and splendid culture of the
Latin American peoples and are prepared to establish the widest possible
cultural ties with all those countries.

59. Growth of Soviet interest: the founding of the
Latin American Institute, 1961[1] (*p. 21*)

Latin America is playing an increasingly important role as one of the leading
fronts in the national-liberation fight of the peoples against imperialism, for
their independence and democracy. The national-liberation movement which
has developed in Latin America, the triumph of the people's revolution in Cuba,
the growth of the workers' movement and the increase in the influence of the
Communist parties call for a profound study of the socio-economic and
political processes which are developing in this part of the world.

However, up to the present time scientific investigation into the problems of
the present-day economics, politics, national-liberation and workers' movements in Latin America, in spite of certain advances, has been inadequate and
has been carried on largely in an unsystematic way. The selection of subjects
by the investigators has been largely a subjective process and a number of
writings have had little connection with the present day. One of the serious
defects in this field has also been the poor co-ordination of the work of various
Soviet specialists—economists, historians, philosophers, etc.

There was practically no co-ordination of the efforts of Soviet scholars in
the study of Latin America with the studies of the scholars of other Socialist
countries.

To effect a serious improvement in the study of present-day Latin American
problems, a specialized, comprehensive, scientific research centre, the Latin
American Institute, has been set up within the framework of the Department of
Economic, Philosophical, and Legal Sciences of the Academy of Sciences of
the USSR. The Institute has been given the task of carrying out a scientific
investigation into the main socio-economic and political processes which are

[1] *Novaya i noveyshaya istoriya*, no. 2, 1962.

proceeding in modern Latin America. The Institute is also charged with the co-ordination of scientific investigation into the problems of Latin America. Courses are being arranged for post-graduate students by the Institute to train qualified specialists in the present-day problems of the Latin American countries.

The creation of the new Institute within the system of the Academy of Science of the USSR will advance the further improvement in research work into the problems of Latin America in our country.

Support for the 'struggle against imperialism'

60. Statement by S. R. Rashidov, head of the Soviet delegation, at the Tricontinental Conference, Havana, 6 January 1966:[1]
excerpts (*p. 28*)

. . . I wish to stress that the Soviet delegation has come to this conference with the objective of facilitating in every way the unification of the anti-imperialist forces of the three continents to lend still greater scope and still greater effectiveness to our common struggle against imperialism and neo-colonialism headed by the United States of America. . . .

. . . The Soviet delegation wholeheartedly supports the suggestion about the establishment of a three continent solidarity organization at this Conference. . .

We express fraternal solidarity with the armed struggle waged by the patriots of Venezuela, Peru, Colombia and Guatemala for freedom against the puppets of imperialism.

We express our solidarity with the struggle of the people in British, French and Dutch Guianas and the Antilles, with the struggle of the people of Puerto Rico. We are certain that the struggle of these peoples will lead them to their cherished goal, national independence. . . .

Our Conference should unite the anti-imperialist forces into a single movement of the peoples of three continents and hoist the militant spirit of Havana as its banner.

The Soviet delegation proposes also to proclaim, in commemoration of the First Solidarity Conference of the peoples of Asia, Africa and Latin America, an International Week of Solidarity of the peoples of the three continents in the struggle against colonialism, neo-colonialism and imperialism and to observe this Week annually from January 3rd to January 10th.

The Soviet delegation issues an urgent appeal to all the national organizations and movements represented at this Conference to unite in the struggle for this great goal. May this Conference be a new step on this road; may it multiply and strengthen the unity of our ranks and give new strength to the liberation struggle throughout the world.

---

[1] OAS, Council, Special Committee to Study Resolutions II.1. & VII of the 8th Meeting of Consultation of Ministers of Foreign Affairs, *Report . . . on the First Afro-Asian-Latin American People's Solidarity Conference . . .*, ii. 65–75.

61. Report by Brezhnev to the CPSU CC on the 'internationalist duty' of the CPSU to support the struggle against imperialism, March 1966:[1] excerpts (*p. 29*)

Special mention must be made of the courageous liberation struggle of the peoples of Latin America. Only recently the USA regarded Latin America as a reliable bastion. Today in every country of that continent the people are waging a struggle against US imperialism and its accomplices—the local military, feudal lords and bourgeoisie, who are linked up with foreign monopolies. This struggle is headed by the working class and the Communist Parties.

An important factor of our day is the consolidation of the unity of the Asian, African and Latin American peoples in the struggle against imperialism. The Afro-Asian solidarity movement, the movement for the unity of the Arab peoples and for the unity of the peoples of Africa, and the solidarity movement of peoples of the three continents are in line with the vital interests of these peoples and we actively and ardently support them.

Comrades, the Communist Party of the Soviet Union regards as its internationalist duty continued all-round support of the people's struggle for final liberation from colonial and neo-colonial oppression.

Our Party and the Soviet state will continue to:

render utmost support to the peoples fighting for their liberation and work for the immediate granting of independence to all colonial countries and peoples;

promote all-sided co-operation with countries that have won national independence and help them to develop their economy, train national cadres and oppose neo-colonialism;

strengthen the fraternal links of the CPSU with the Communist Parties and revolutionary democratic organisations in Asian, African and Latin American countries.

62. View of the revolutionary process in Latin America by the Director of the Latin American Institute, Professor Volsky, March 1968[2] (*p. 57*)

The revolutionary and progressive forces of Latin America recently celebrated the 50th anniversary of the founding of the first Marxist party on the continent, the Communist Party of Argentina. In this half-century, the organized workers' movement and the liberation struggle of the peoples of Latin America have traversed a long and complicated path.

Especially important and truly historic changes have taken place in the third stage of the general crisis of capitalism. In conditions of the general weakening of imperialism and the emergence of the world system of socialism, the influence of the ideas of October in Latin America has intensified immeasurably. The struggle of all the forces of imperialism and reaction has grown sharper.

[1] *Kommunisticheskaya Partiya Sovetskogo Soyuza*, 23rd Congress, *Report* (Moscow, Novosti Press Agency, 1966).
[2] *Pravda*, 19 Mar. 1968 (*CDSP*, 10 Apr. 1968, pp. 19–20).

In this new situation in the Western Hemisphere, the Cuban revolution triumphed. Generated by the internal laws of the country's development, it was at the same time a concrete consequence of the new balance of forces in the world arena, of the continued growth of the forces of socialism and the continued weakening of the world system of capitalism.

The revolutionary process in Cuba was characterized by a close intertwining of national-liberation and social tasks, graphic confirmation of the proposition that a popular movement 'originally directed toward national liberation turns against capitalism and imperialism' (V. I. Lenin, 'Complete Collected Works,' Vol. XLIV, p. 38).

The experience of the Cuban revolution shows that in our time, in conditions of socialism's mighty impact on the development of all social and political processes in the modern world, the leadership of people's anti-imperialist revolutions in the developing countries can be assumed by revolutionary-democratic strata reflecting the interests and sentiments of the broadest popular masses. However, the realization of the far more complex goals and tasks of the socialist revolution and the profound reconstruction of the whole society on new principles calls for leadership on the part of the vanguard party of the working class, well armed with Marxist-Leninist theory.

Cuba itself chose socialism, without any interference from outside. This is the best reply to those who shout about the 'export of revolution.' At the same time, this choice became possible thanks to the existence of the Soviet Union. The Soviet Union has given and is continuing to give Cuba comprehensive support and assistance; this has doomed to failure attempts at the military strangulation of the revolution and economic blockade. Both the friends and enemies of socialism in Latin America have had an opportunity to see for themselves that the USSR does not interfere in the internal affairs of any country but always acts resolutely in defence of the right of peoples to self-determination.

Every genuine revolution is, beyond question, the internal affair of the people concerned. Marxists are convinced that the implantation of revolution from outside will not produce the desired effect. A revolution can be victorious and its results lasting only if the ideals of the revolution ripen in the country itself and eventually come to be held by the majority of the people.

But it is also perfectly obvious that no liberation movement and no genuine revolution, even though it has ripened on national soil, can or should be isolated or nationally exclusive. The very internationalism of revolutionary ideas emphatically poses the question of the solidarity of the peoples who are fighting for their freedom and of the necessity of consolidating all the international revolutionary forces fighting against the common enemy of imperialism and for the achievement of common ideals. The history of Latin America has many outstanding examples of solidarity—from the joint struggle of the newborn nations for independence to the present-day movement in defense of revolutionary Cuba.

The constantly growing influence of the ideas of national liberation and of socialism is demonstrated best of all by the feverish attempts of reactionary forces to curb the spread of these ideas by any means possible. Of course, it is

American imperialism that exerts itself to the greatest extent along these lines. Since the assassination of Kennedy, the stick has again taken first place in the American 'carrot and stick' policy in Latin America, as, incidentally, it has in other parts of the world as well. Military missions, the implantation and support of military dictatorships, schools for 'antiguerrillas,' the intervention in the Dominican Republic, the provocations against Cuba, the hammering together of 'inter-American' armed police forces—these are the main elements of current US policy in Latin America.

It is impossible to put an end to the domination of imperialism without destroying the social and economic forces on which it rests in each country. The owners of latifundia, big merchants, financiers and middlemen, who are closely linked with foreign monopolies and reactionary generals and officers —these are the main local forces that are hostile to new trends and social changes and are the chief allies of imperialism.

The bourgeoisie of the Latin American countries has proved incapable of leading the implementation of even those social changes that would have cleared the way to the more rapid development of capitalism. In most of the countries, even isolated, irresolute and half-hearted steps taken against the oligarchies and foreign monopolies by the ruling bourgeois parties, afraid of relying on the masses, have led only to the mobilization and coalescence of internal and external reaction. The military coups in 1964–1966 in Argentina, Brazil, Boliva and other countries and the terror and repression against the working people and progressive forces are vivid manifestations of the profound crisis of Latin American capitalism.

The liberation movement of the peoples of Latin America is now entering a new stage. In the 1950s, when the struggle of the popular masses was on the upswing and the third stage of the general crisis of capitalism was developing, the working people still believed in the possibility of progressive social changes under the leadership of the national bourgeoisie and in the latter's constructive potential and were still willing to support it in many ways and to follow it. Now the national bourgeoisie, which in some countries has been crushed by the oligarchic cliques and the military and in others has been frightened by the Cuban revolution, is incapable of independently implementing any serious social and economic transformations. It is becoming still more obvious that this can be accomplished only through the struggle of the popular masses. In the present stage, as never before, the progressive forces, first of all the Communist Parties, are setting themselves the primary task of assuming full leadership in this struggle of the peoples and of rallying around themselves all forces that in one form or another oppose the oligarchies and imperialism and stand for progress and democracy.

Needless to say, the conditions for implementing this task are far from identical in the various countries of Latin America; this gives rise to a great diversity of methods and techniques in the struggle of the revolutionary forces and to the necessity for the vanguard of the working people in each country to take specific national features into account.

In some countries of Latin America (Chile, Mexico, Uruguay, Costa Rica and others) an activation in the struggle of the democratic forces can be observed, a process of their consolidation is taking place, albeit slowly, and stubborn class battles are developing. In other countries, especially following coups d'état, reactionary and pro-imperialist forces have succeeded in bringing about a temporary weakening in the liberation movement.

For the revolutionary forces in many Latin American countries, the 1960s have been a time of testing of their ideological, political and organizational maturity. Lessons were drawn from the Cuban revolution not only by the progressive forces but also by American imperialism and the local ruling classes. Striving to arrest the expansion and deepening of the revolutionary struggle, they make use of all means available to them, from the direct export of counterrevolution to active attempts to split the progressive forces from within.

The Communist Parties of the Latin American countries, ardently support- ing all anti-imperialist revolutionary actions on the part of the popular masses, at the same time are exerting substantial efforts aimed at preventing the stereotyping of revolutionary tactics and the elevation of any one form of struggle to the status of an absolute and at the correct combination at any given moment of armed struggle with the development of all other forms of struggle.

The Communists of Latin America are conscious of their responsibilities to their peoples, work constantly on the ideological and organizational strengthening of their parties and make wide use of the experience of the struggle of other fraternal parties, including that of the Communist Party of the Soviet Union.

Viewing the liberation movement on the continent in inextricable connection with the basic contradiction of our time—the contradiction between socialism and capitalism—the Latin American Communists are active propagandists of the ideas of proletarian internationalism and of the close unity of all currents in the world revolutionary process. These ideas were brilliantly expressed by the representatives of the Communist Parties of the Latin American countries in their speeches at the Meeting in Budapest.

Having as an example the successes achieved by the countries of the world socialist system, the peoples of Latin America are realizing more and more the historical hopelessness and sterility of the path that the local oligarchies and the US imperialists are trying to impose on them (and in many countries are imposing). The working class of Latin America is one of the most active combat detachments of the international proletariat. Suffice it to say that although it constitutes only about 9 % of the working class of the capitalist world, in the last few years it has provided between 30 % and 50 % of all strikers in the capitalist countries.

In these conditions, as the revolutionary forces emphasize in their program- matic statements, the successful development of the liberation movement will depend on many factors, including:

—the strengthening and consolidation of the revolutionary political van- guard and its ability creatively to elaborate a correct strategy, a clear-cut and principled political line and flexible tactics;

—the struggle for unity of action of the working class and the overcoming of dissociation into various trade union associations;

—the overcoming of the gap between the struggle of the working masses of the city and those of the countryside and the organization of an effective alliance of workers and peasants;

—the enlistment in active political struggle on the side of the revolutionary forces of broad strata of the population that are potential allies of these forces;

—the expansion of cooperation between the progressive forces and those political trends that are followed by quite broad strata of the working population. The platform of such cooperation could be the struggle for profound social reforms, against the dominance of imperialism and for the broadening of relations with all countries in the world.

In Latin America today the anti-imperialist, patriotic and liberation currents are making ever broader paths among almost all classes of society.

The strength of these currents lies in the fact that, taken together, they embrace the majority of the people. Many of their weaknesses are connected with the absence of unity and the presence of friction and contradictions among them. However, there is no doubt that there is an objective basis for the fusion of all the currents of the liberation movement in the first stage into a united anti-imperialist people's-democratic front, and in subsequent stages for the fusion of genuinely revolutionary forces into a united anti-imperialist and anticapitalist front, which would ensure the development of the revolution and the complete success of its historic mission. The rate at which these prospects are realized will depend to a very great degree on the establishment first of mutual understanding and then of firm unity of action of all progressive forces.

Trade relations

63. Soviet policies and prospects, March 1967[1] (*p. 22*)

The opportunities and prospects for the development of trade and economic ties between the Soviet Union and the countries of Latin America become broader each year.

Economic ties between the Soviet Union and the Republic of Cuba, the first socialist state in the Western Hemisphere, are developing successfully. These relations, based on the principles of fraternal cooperation and mutual aid, correspond to the interests of the building of socialism and communism in our countries and constitute a new type of economic relations.

As for trade and other economic ties between the USSR and the other Latin American countries, the Soviet Union in these relations invariably proceeds from the principles of mutual advantage, equality and respect for the national sovereignty of other countries.

Latin America is the source of deliveries of many valuable raw materials and semimanufactured goods which the Soviet Union imports for its national economy. These items include coffee, cacao, sugar, wool, cotton, nonferrous

[1] *Pravda*, 5 Mar. 1967 (paras. 1–12 & 19–22: *CDSP*, 22 Mar. 1967, pp. 20–1; paras. 13–18 trans. by the editor).

metals, rice, vegetable oil, hides and semiprocessed leather, fruit, etc. Soviet foreign trade organizations can also on certain conditions buy some types of industrial goods in the Latin American countries.

On the other hand, the economic development of the Latin American countries requires large amounts of various types of machinery and equipment, semimanufactured goods, raw materials and other commodities. The Soviet Union, which possesses vast economic potential and a comprehensively developed industry, can supply many of these commodities.

The development of trade can undoubtedly be of great assistance in strengthening the economies of the Latin American countries, first of all in increasing their industrial potential. Trade with the Soviet Union means for the Latin American countries an expansion of markets for their goods and an improvement in the commodity structure of their exports through the addition of new commodities, and it can be an important element in stabilizing their currency and financial position.

Recently more and more Latin American countries have begun to realize the expediency of developing trade and economic ties with the Soviet Union. Whereas ten years ago only three countries in Latin America—Argentina, Mexico and Uruguay—carried on direct trade with the Soviet Union, at present the number of trade partners of the USSR in Latin America has risen to nine. The new USSR trade partners include Brazil, Chile, Colombia and other states. Soviet foreign trade organizations carry on small-scale trade operations with Guyana and Jamaica.

According to preliminary data, the Soviet Union's goods turnover with the countries of Latin America approximated 900,000,000 rubles in 1966, as against 28,000,000 rubles ten years ago.

Soviet-Brazilian trade has undergone substantial development recently. In 1966 the volume of Brazil's trade with the Soviet Union was more than 50,000,000 rubles. For such large countries as the USSR and Brazil, of course, this is not such a large figure. But it must be taken into account here that trade between these two countries had its beginning, for all practical purposes, only seven years ago.

Brazil supplies the Soviet Union with coffee, cacao beans, cacao-seed oil, cotton, vegetable oil, sisal, hides and semi-processed leather and other goods.

The Soviet Union ships mainly petroleum to Brazil, as well as some non-ferrous metals and small amounts of machinery and equipment. In August, 1966, a protocol on the delivery of Soviet machinery and equipment to Brazil was signed by the two countries.

A noteworthy feature of this protocol is the commitment assumed by the Soviet side to use 25% of the actual receipts from the sale of Soviet machinery and equipment for the purchase of Brazilian manufactured and semimanu-factured goods. For Brazil, which is interested in expanding its exports, especially of manufactured goods, this condition in the protocol is very important, since it opens up one possible way for marketing the output of its young and developing industry. This condition also represents a new step by the Soviet Union in the practical implementation of the recommendations of the UN Conference on Trade and Development, in the section dealing with promoting the export of manufactured goods by the developing countries. Naturally, the exertion of considerable effort on the part of both sides is called for to ensure the practical implemention of this protocol.

Argentina is an important partner in trade with the Soviet Union. Like Brazil, this country has great economic potential. However, trade between the USSR and Argentina is developing extremely unevenly. Last year there began talks between USSR and Argentina about a new trading agreement, and later about a protocol for the supply of Soviet machinery and equipment to Argentina. These talks were stopped by the Argentine side. The new Argentine government has still not taken practical measures to continue talks.

In January of this year between USSR and Chile there were signed a trade agreement, an agreement about the delivery to Chile of Soviet machinery and equipment and an agreement that the Soviet Union would give technical help to Chile in the construction of industrial and other plant and would offer commercial credits for these purposes. These were the first trade and economic agreements in the whole history of Soviet-Chile relations. They create favourable conditions for economic collaboration between the two countries.

Recently those Latin American countries which do not have diplomatic relations with us have begun to show interest in developing trade with the Soviet Union. One of these countries is Colombia.

The Soviet Union buys coffee from Colombia and in exchange supplies the popular GAZ 69 cars and also certain other goods.

The development of Soviet-Colombian trade could be much more rapid if the Soviet forcign trade organizations and Colombian business circles disposed of better information about the export possibilities and import requirements of both countries, about the specific peculiarities of their markets, and if they had more stable business links.

Last year for the first time Ecuador showed interest in trade with the Soviet Union. Last September talks between Soviet and Ecuadorean trade delegations took place in Moscow. The two sides agreed to complete these talks in the spring of this year.

Other Latin American states too are showing an interest in trade with the Soviet Union. True, in a number of cases this has been manifest only in timid steps and feeble soundings.

Opponents of the development of trade and economic ties between the Soviet Union and Latin America, trying to discredit these ties, advance against them highly primitive arguments which cannot stand up under criticism. The monopolies of the Western countries, first of all the American monopolies and groups in Latin America connected with them, are afraid that an expansion of trade with the Soviet Union will undermine their domination of the Latin American market and prevent them from dictating prices there, and attempt to persuade business and official circles in these countries that the Soviet Union is allegedly incapable of supplying many of the commodities in which they are interested, that the quality of Soviet goods does not meet market requirements, etc. However, they pass over in silence the fact that many developing countries of Asia and Africa carry on extensive trade with the USSR, making use of all the advantages this trade offers. For instance, India, Pakistan, the

UAR and other countries buy hundreds of millions of rubles' worth of machinery and equipment in the USSR and in exchange deliver not only their traditional raw-material export commodities but also many manufactured goods.

The opponents of the development of trade between the USSR and the Latin American countries do not limit themselves only to statements against this trade. Taking advantage of their connections in the government and financial circles of certain Latin American countries, they seek to bring about the imposition of bans on trade with the Soviet Union by these countries, extend unfavorable terms in obtaining bank credits to firms showing an interest in Soviet goods, block the issuance of licences for importing Soviet commodities and create difficulties for trips to the USSR by representatives of business circles and trips by representatives of Soviet foreign trade organizations to the countries of Latin America.

No matter what obstacles may be erected in the path of the development of trade and economic relations between the Soviet Union and the countries of Latin America, life will have its way. The economic prerequisites for the expansion of these relations, the desire of the Latin American countries to find new markets for their goods, the example of other countries—all this exerts an important influence on the positions of the Latin American countries.

64. A vindication of Soviet policies: article in 'Pravda', December 1967[1] (*p. 22*)

A substantial majority in the business circles of Latin America, as well as broad strata of the Latin American public, believes that the development of trade ties with the Soviet Union is for the Latin American countries a means of relieving their difficult economic situation, promoting industrial development, expanding markets for their export goods and weakening their shackling economic dependence on foreign monopoly capital, above all the capital of the USA. One of the most recent manifestations of these views took place at the meeting, held recently in Bogota, of the special Latin American coordinating commission for working out a unified policy for the Latin American countries at next year's international UN Conference on Trade and Development. The delegates sitting on this commission unanimously called for the maximum stimulation of trade with the socialist countries, in particular with the USSR.

At the same time, the most reactionary circles in the Latin American countries, which act in concert with the foreign monopolies—in the first place American monopolies—that have penetrated deeply into the economic life of these countries, are trying to prove that the development of trade ties with the Soviet Union is fraught with danger for the countries of Latin America, since it may lead to the dissemination of communist ideas and to an undermining of the capitalist system of the economy in these countries. These circles do not limit themselves to statements in the newspapers and on radio

[1] *Pravda*, 15 Dec. 1967 (*CDSP*, 3 Jan. 1968, pp. 15–16).

and television. They use a considerably broader arsenal of means in seeking to attain their goals, which are aimed against the development of trade ties with the Soviet Union. Making use of their connections with governmental and financial circles in several Latin American countries, they strive for bans and restrictions on trade with the USSR, place firms that show an interest in Soviet goods in unfavorable conditions for obtaining bank credits and even resort to blackmail and threats with respect to firms that trade or intend to trade with the Soviet Union; they endeavor in every way to create unfavorable conditions for Soviet foreign-trade organizations and erect financial, economic and administrative barriers to Soviet goods. . . .

The fact that the USSR has trade ties with the countries of Latin America, needless to say, does not in the last mean that we agree with the policies of the governments of the countries concerned. It would be an equally profound mistake to regard such relations as an expression of any support or assistance whatsoever on the part of the Soviet Union to the oligarchical reactionary regimes in a number of Latin American countries.

In 1966 the total volume of trade between the Soviet Union and the countries of Latin America came to 867,000,000 rubles, as against 222,000,000 rubles in 1960.

At present the Soviet Union trades in Latin America with Cuba, Brazil, Argentina, Mexico, Uruguay, Chile, Colombia, Ecuador and several other countries.

The Soviet Union's chief trade partner is Cuba, which accounts for about 80% of the total goods turnover between the USSR and the countries of Latin America. Cuba satisfies more than one-half of its requirements in imported goods through trade with our country. The volume of Soviet-Cuban trade is growing continuously.

This growth is the result above all of the Soviet Union's desire to render fraternal assistance to the Cuban people. The bulk of Soviet exports to Cuba consists of industrial goods, which account for 75% to 80% of all deliveries. . . .

In exchange for its goods, the Soviet Union buys from Cuba sugar, products containing nickel, alcohol and several other commodities.

The trade volume of the USSR with the capitalist countries of Latin America amounted to 178,000,000 rubles in 1966. The development of trade ties with these countries on a fair commercial basis is a matter of substantial interest to the Soviet Union.

These countries export to the Soviet Union goods needed by Soviet industry and for supplying the population, items such as wool, hides, coffee, cacao beans, rice, cotton, vegetable oil and other commodities. The Soviet Union has been buying these goods in Latin America for several years now, and it should be noted that the purchases of some goods by the Soviet Union are very important for the Latin American countries. For example, in some years our country has bought from Brazil as much as 24% of its export resources of cacao beans, 18% of its cotton and 10% of its vegetable oil; from Argentina, it has bought up to 20% of its large-size hides and 30% of its linseed oil; and from Uruguay, it has purchased up to 17% of its large-size hides and up to 30% of its wool.

The Soviet Union buys goods in Latin America at fair prices and thereby assists the peoples of the Latin American countries in combating the foreign monopolies, which try to dictate their own prices on many types of export goods.

Needless to say, the volume of the Soviet Union's purchases of goods in the capitalist countries of Latin America could be substantially increased. For this, it is necessary above all for these countries in turn to expand their purchases in the USSR since, as is frequently said in Latin America, he who buys must also sell. Only in this event can trade be mutually advantageous.

The observance of this just principle is a major condition necessary for an increase in the volume of trade between the USSR and the countries of Latin America, inasmuch as all the earnings from the sale of Soviet goods to these countries are used, as has been repeatedly stated, to buy goods from them.

The Latin American countries, which need many commodities for their economic development, can find much to buy in the Soviet Union. With its mighty economy and highly developed industry, the Soviet Union is able to deliver to these countries a wide range of goods that they either do not produce or produce in insufficient quantities and so are forced to buy from the Western countries, first of all the USA.

The Soviet Union can deliver to the countries of Latin America various kinds of industrial and power-engineering equipment, metal-cutting machine tools, automobiles, tractors, road-building machinery, excavators, airplanes, ships, rolled ferrous metals, lumber and paper products, petroleum, petroleum products and many other goods.

With a view to creating favorable trade and political conditions for the development of trade between the Soviet Union and several capitalist countries of Latin America, trade and payments agreements have been concluded with Brazil, Chile and Colombia in the past few years.

The Soviet Union has also concluded with Brazil and Chile agreements on the delivery to these countries of machinery and equipment on terms that are the usual practice in international trade in these goods. . . .

The Soviet Union has also concluded with Brazil and Chile agreements on the delivery of complete sets of industrial equipment. . . .

The conclusion of the above-mentioned agreements has contributed to a certain increase in trade between the USSR and the countries of Latin America, in particular to deliveries of Soviet machinery and equipment to these countries. However, the full implementation of the agreements is complicated by the increasing counteractions being taken by the Western monopolies and reactionary circles in the countries of Latin America, which believe that each Soviet tractor, automobile, machine tool or any other kind of machine delivered to Latin America carries with it the truth about the Soviet Union and shows the peoples of Latin America the enormous successes the Soviet Union has achieved in a brief historical period thanks to the socialist system. The American monopolies and the reactionary circles in the Latin American countries are doing everything possible to prevent the setting up of economic ties between the Latin American countries and the Soviet Union.

The deliveries of Soviet machinery, equipment and other goods to the

13

countries of Latin America and the Soviet Union's purchases of goods from these countries correspond to the latter countries' vital national interests, since they further a weakening of their dependence on the imperialist powers, first of all the USA. They are aimed at promoting the development of industry in the Latin American countries. The development of trade with the USSR creates conditions enabling some of the Latin American countries to withstand pressure from the imperialist states. Trade ties between the USSR and the Latin American countries also present an obstacle to the aggressive aspirations of the USA with respect to Latin America.

The Soviet Union does not use its trade ties with the Latin American countries to impose on them any kind of one-sided obligations or to make political demands on them. The Soviet Union intends to continue developing trade ties with the countries of Latin America on a mutually advantageous commercial basis. . . .

2 *Argentina*

The Perón regime

65. Soviet denunciation of the regime for its pro-German and Fascist tendencies: article by F. Glibovsky, August 1944:[1] excerpts (*p. 32*)
The so-called United Group of officers which led this revolt consists of senior army officers closely connected with Germany and its network of agents in Argentina. The present Minister for War, General Perón, the foremost representative of this group, is a former pupil of the German military school and an admiring product of the German army. Many others who took part in the coup had completed their military training by taking a course in Germany, where they became agents of Hitlerism. . . .

Argentina is the country where the German Fascists are trying to establish themselves most firmly. It is no coincidence that the choice of the German Fascists should have fallen on Argentina. In the first place, it is one of the most developed Latin American countries both in the field of industry and in that of agriculture. Secondly, Argentina is more weakly bound to the United States than the other countries in the western hemisphere. Her export of grain

[1] *Voina i rabochni klas*, no. 16, 15 Aug. 1944.

and cattle products are directed towards Europe, principally to Great Britain. . . .

The foreign policy of Argentina, as is particularly shown in all pan-American conferences, has always been one of lining up the strongest South American states against the United States. The bloc formed by Argentina, Brazil, and Chile (the so-called ABC bloc) has held together not so much out of the common interests of those states, but from the endeavours of Brazil and Chile to enlist Argentina's support against the short-sighted policy of the powerful North American firms monopolizing all industrial growth, which has been aptly described as the Big-Stick policy.

In so far as the Good-Neighbour policy announced by the Roosevelt administration has latterly lessened this impact of the American monopolists on the interests of local circles in those countries, specially in time of war, their incentive to preserve the 'ABC bloc' has diminished. Brazil, for instance, after receiving million dollar credits for the development of many branches of industry and also a great quantity of war material on lend-lease terms, has now completely left that bloc. With regard to Chile, where the basic wealth remains in the hands of big American firms, that country still endeavours to keep in with Argentina.

Hitler's plan for the penetration of Latin America is wholly based on the special position of Argentina and on the calculation of exploiting, on the one hand, the absence of close links between her and the United States, and on the other hand, on certain great-power ambitions harboured by Argentina's ruling circles.

66. Statement by Vyacheslav Molotov at the UN Conference on International Organization opposing Argentina's participation in the San Francisco Conference, 30 April 1945[1] (*p. 32*)

The Soviet Delegation consider the question of inviting Argentina to the Conference an important one. . . . It is quite natural therefore that the Soviet Delegation, desiring to acquaint itself with this question and to let all the other members of the Conference do likewise, suggest that its discussion be postponed for a few days. Everyone knows that in the war against our common enemy Argentina has held a special place; it is equally well known that for these past years of war, neither the foreign nor the domestic policies of the Argentine regime has met with the other United Nations' approval. . . .

I understand that certain representatives of the Latin American countries hold the view that the situation has changed for the better there. All I should like to ask of you is that the Soviet as well as the other delegations be given a chance to acquaint themselves at length with the facts and to satisfy themselves that the situation in Argentina has really improved. . . . Imagine what would happen if we acted rashly and invite Argentina to this Conference although in the present war she has been assisting the Fascists who are our enemies. and failed to invite Poland which is an ally. . . . It may be argued that Argentina

[1] *UNCIO*, i. 345–7.

has sinned, but that her sins may be forgotten. This may be true; perhaps we should really forget Argentina's sins. But let me ask you; if certain sins committed by Argentina may be forgotten, why should we forget Poland's services?

67. 'New Times' article describing Allied recognition of the Argentine Government as 'appeasement', June 1945:[1] excerpts (*p. 32*)

The Farrell-Perón government declared war on Germany and Japan on March 27, 1945, when the clock of history was already on the stroke of twelve—less than six weeks before Hitler Germany's unconditional surrender and the termination of the war in Europe. In return for this gesture, the Argentine ruling clique secured the restoration of normal diplomatic relations with the United States, Great Britain and other democratic countries, and then received a ticket of admission to the San Francisco Conference. The price was exorbitant, the more so that there has been no change in the Farrell-Perón policy. Numerous facts go to show that Argentina's declaration of war on Germany was nothing but a tactical manoeuvre made in agreement with the Hitlerites. . . . As we know, Argentina was invited to San Francisco in a great hurry. The initiators of this diplomatic step declined to postpone the decision even for a few days, thus depriving the conference delegates of the opportunity of acquainting themselves with the true state of affairs in that country. . . . The Buenos Aires correspondent of the New York Tribune reports that the arrests and persecution of anti-Fascists are continuing all over Argentina on an unprecedented scale. In the light of these facts, the policy of recognizing the Fascist Farrell-Perón regime, like the continued tolerance of the Fascist Franco regime, is reminiscent of the deplorable policy of 'appeasement' pursued by the leaders of a number of the democratic countries in the period preceding the Second World War.

68. Communiqué on the establishment of Soviet relations with the Perón regime, 6 June 1946[2] (*p. 32*)

The Government of the USSR and the Government of the Argentine Republic, inspired by the high principles of international co-operation and understanding, state that as from today they have decided to establish full diplomatic relations between both states. Both Governments have decided to appoint their Ambassadors within the shortest possible time. . . .

Negotiations that have reached this satisfactory conclusion were carried out in Buenos Aires between Russian Envoy Plenipotentiary, H. E. Konstantin V. Shevelev, and the President of the Argentine Nation, General Juan D. Perón and Minister for Foreign Affairs, Dr Juan A. Bramuglia. . . .

[1] L. Volinsky, 'The role Argentina is playing', *New Times*, 1 June 1945, pp. 27 & 30.
[2] *Pravda*, 7 June 1946.

69. Soviet press comment on the establishment of relations, June 1946[1] (*p. 32*)

The Governments of the USSR and the Argentine Republic have declared their decision to establish full-scale diplomatic, consular, and commercial relations with each other. This decision was taken as a result of negotiations in Buenos Aires between the plenipotentiary of the Soviet Union and the leaders of the new Argentine Government. The establishment of diplomatic relations between these two countries is a sure investment in the cause of strengthening postwar peace.

Argentina, second in size and third in population of the Latin American countries, was one of the few states which, twenty-eight years after the October Revolution, had not established diplomatic relations with the USSR. This fact, however, could not prevent the growth of the Soviet Union's popularity among the broad strata of Argentine society. The popularity of the Soviet Union rose especially during the war of liberation of the nations from Fascism. It was the Soviet Union which bore the brunt of this war.

Recently the movement in Argentina to establish diplomatic relations with the USSR assumed especially large proportions. The arrival in Buenos Aires of a Soviet commercial mission gave strong impetus to this movement. The Argentine newspaper *Noticias gráficas* wrote: 'The largest state in the world, Russia, will trade with our country to the advantage of both. Public opinion cannot understand what motives and what concealed forces or influences stand in the way of establishing correct and normal diplomatic relations with Russia.'

A resolution was introduced in the Argentine parliament recommending that the Government establish diplomatic relations with the Soviet Union. The demand for establishment of such relations assumed a national character. Many meetings were held throughout Argentina, in which various political parties, trade unions, public, cultural, and other organizations participated. It was noticeable that supporters of the new President of the Republic, Perón, took an active part in these meetings.

Concerning one of these thousands of meetings, the Argentine newspaper *La Hora* wrote: 'The scale of these meetings shows that the people realize that the establishment of official friendly links with the Soviet Union in the present circumstances has great significance for the future of Argentina.' Many papers emphasized that the establishment of diplomatic relations with the USSR will result in the growth of the Argentine's international influence and will aid in consolidating her independence.

The Soviet Union, true to her constant wish to support normal relations with all states, received favourably the proposal of the Government of Argentina that diplomatic relations be established between the USSR and Argentina. This decision of the Soviet Government was greeted with satisfaction by the entire Soviet public.

The international reactions to the establishment of diplomatic relations

[1] *Pravda*, 9 June 1946.

between the USSR and Argentina indicate that this act will have real significance not only for the two states but for general peace.

The decision of the Soviet and Argentine Governments begins a new stage
in the relations between the two countries. Let us hope for the rapid and
fruitful development of Soviet-Argentine relations to the good of both peoples.

70. Soviet article on the suppression of the Slav Union,
November 1949:[1] excerpts (*p. 64*)

Argentina's ruling circles have closed down the progressive newspapers
published in the languages of the Slav peoples, dissolved the Third Slav
Congress, and arrested the leaders of the [Slav] Union. The police have struck
against the Argentine-Soviet Institute for Cultural Relations. According to
an Associated Press report, the Argentine police recently raided the said
Institute whilst the writer A. Varela was giving a lecture. The police seized
300 people attending the lecture and threw them into jail. Some of those who
were locked up were tortured. Peaceful citizens were subjected to this monstrous
repression simply because they went to listen to a lecture about the Soviet
Union and its heroic people. . . .

According to official figures, about 3 million immigrants are living in
Argentina, some 800,000 of whom are estimated to be of Slav origin. All of them
came from different European countries, particularly the Western Ukraine,
Bulgaria, Poland, and Czechoslovakia, at a time when their native lands were
under regimes which condemned the broad masses to a life of starvation.

Those times have gone for ever. The Soviet Union, where man's exploitation
of man has been for ever abolished as a result of the great October Socialist
Revolution, and the countries of people's democracy, where a new social
structure is being built, enjoy enormous sympathy on the part of Argentina's
Slav workers. The struggle of the progressive Slavs to establish friendly
relations between Argentina and the USSR and people's democracies, the
struggle against her subjection to the American imperialists, aroused furious
rancour and fierce repression on the part of the Argentine reaction. . . .

Whilst the progressives of Slav origin were being subjected to fierce repression, every turn-coat and traitor to his country fleeing from the people's
democracies found a warm welcome and protection here. Furthermore, the
Argentine reaction looked beyond the seas to find in the Tito–Ranković
band[2] their partners in the struggle against the democratic powers in the
international arena. Tito's agents found in Argentina willing support for
their action as provocateurs and became veritable accomplices of the local
police. Thus, on the day appointed for the opening of the Third Slav Congress
in Buenos Aires, some of Tito's men wormed their way into the groups of
delegates and, in order to provoke an incident, smashed the window-panes in
the premises where the Congress was being held. At the moment when this
attack on the Slav Congress was being perpetrated, not a policeman was to

---

[1] *Slavyane* (Moscow), Nov. 1949, pp. 32–3.
[2] President Tito and Vice-President Alexander Ranković. Yugoslavia was denounced by
Moscow and expelled from the Cominform in 1948.

be seen near the spot. But as soon as Tito's provocateurs had made off, the police at once appeared and began to arrest the delegates and guests.

Anti-Soviet incidents

71. 'Izvestiya' on attacks on the Soviet Embassy in Buenos Aires, June 1961[1] (*p. 33*)

The Soviet public is deeply indignant at the bandit provocational attacks made on the building of the USSR Embassy in Buenos Aires. Three such attacks have been made in the past five weeks. Moreover, they have been made with the obvious connivance of the Argentine authorities. . . .

Here, for example, is how the attack was made on May 18. In the evening on that day, a group of hooligans, about 15 or 20 of them, appeared at the USSR Embassy. The participants in the attack hurled bottles of an inflammable substance at the Embassy door, covered the street around the Embassy with anti-Soviet leaflets and opened fire with weapons at the Embassy building.

It is characteristic that half an hour before the attack began, the policemen guarding the building were forewarned about it by a photographer from the newspaper La Razon who had arrived there ahead of time. However, at the moment of the attack there was not even one policeman on guard at the Embassy. Police detachments arrived only after the hooligans had already disappeared.

On May 31 the building of the press department of the USSR Embassy in Argentina was also subjected to a provocational attack. The bandits hurled bottles of an inflammable substance at the press department buildings, broke the glass in the doors and windows, opened fire at the building from the street and scattered leaflets demanding a break-off of diplomatic relations with the Soviet Union and containing threats against Soviet diplomats.

The attack on the building of the press department of the Soviet Embassy in Argentina was made only 12 days after a similar attack on the Embassy itself, after which, as is known, the USSR Ministry of Foreign Affairs lodged a strong protest with the Argentine government and demanded that Soviet institutions in Argentina be protected from provocations and that normal conditions for their operation be created.

The repetition of these bandit actions against the USSR Embassy attests to the fact that certain circles in Argentina, unobstructed by official authorities, are with impunity continuing their provocations aimed at kindling a campaign hostile to the Soviet Union in the country and at spoiling Soviet-Argentine relations; this is stressed in the note from the USSR Ministry of Foreign Affairs that V. V. Kuznetsov, USSR First Deputy Minister of Foreign Affairs, handed to Mr Olive Dez, the Argentine Republic's Charge d'Affaires in Moscow, on June 3.

[1] *Izvestiya*, 6 June 1961 (*CDSP*, 5 July 1961, pp. 18–19).

It should be emphasized that the complicity of the Argentine authorities in the provocational attacks against Soviet diplomatic institutions in Buenos Aires is occurring at a time when the movement of peoples for a relaxation of international tension and for improving relations between states is gaining force in the world. The government of Argentina clearly is swimming against the current. While a tendency to strengthen trade, cultural and other relations with the Soviet Union manifests itself in other countries of Latin America, the opposite can be observed in Argentina. The Argentine authorities clearly are conniving in the actions of the circles that are attempting to damage Soviet-Argentine relations.

Such a policy cannot be of benefit to the Argentine people or to the country's national interests. This policy plays into the hands of the 'cold war' proponents.

The Soviet Union has lodged the strongest protest in connection with the provocational attacks upon the building of the press department of the USSR Embassy in Argentina and has demanded that measures be taken immediately to ensure the safety of the USSR Embassy in Buenos Aires. It also demands compensation for damage to the Embassy and strict punishment for the guilty persons.

We would like to hope that the Argentine authorities will show a proper realization of the need to observe the elementary norms of international law and diplomatic ethics with respect to a country with which Argentina has been maintaining normal relations for many years.

72. 'Izvestiya' on further attacks on the Embassy, October 1961:[1] excerpt (*p. 33*)

... Provocational raids on the USSR Embassy have been carried out in Argentina for several months now. In the brief period between April and the end of September there have been five attacks.

Despite vigorous protests by the USSR Ministry of Foreign Affairs—in oral statements and in a June 3 note to the Embassy of the Argentine Republic in Moscow—against the outrages perpetrated in Buenos Aires, the attacks on the USSR Embassy continue.

The Argentine authorities have promised repeatedly to take measures for the protection of the USSR Embassy against provocational raids, but they have not gone beyond promises. Thus, in effect they are condoning the anti-Soviet provocations.

In whose interests are the anti-Soviet provocations in Buenos Aires perpetrated? Undoubtedly, in the interests of reactionary circles that seek a deterioration in Soviet-Argentine relations. According to information in the press, the participants in the raids on the USSR diplomatic mission in Buenos Aires themselves have stated that they are acting on orders from Roy Rubottom, the US Ambassador to Argentina, and from the US Central Intelligence Agency.

Arturo Frondizi, President of Argentina, has made quite a number of

[1] *Izvestiya*, 11 Oct. 1961 (*CDSP*, 8 Nov. 1961, p. 27).

statements recently to the effect that Argentina must pursue a policy of peaceful coexistence with all countries and must cooperate in solving disputed international questions. How can these statements be reconciled with the regular bandit attacks on the USSR Embassy in Buenos Aires, committed with the connivance of Argentine authorities?

It is believed in the Soviet Union that, in the interests of peace and of peaceful coexistence, it is absolutely necessary that the government of the Argentine Republic take immediate and effective measures to halt the provocational actions, to guarantee safety and to create conditions for the normal operation of the Soviet Embassy in Buenos Aires. The continuation of the provocational actions against the USSR Embassy may cause serious consequences, for which the government of the Argentine Republic undoubtedly will bear all the responsibility.

73. 'International Affairs' (Moscow) on the Soviet attitude to Arturo Illia's Government, December 1963:[1] excerpt (*p. 33*)

Arturo Umberto Illia, the new President of Argentina, has taken up residence in the Pink Palace in Buenos Aires. . . .

In foreign policy, Dr Illia went on record as favouring peace and more extensive trade with all countries. He said that the Moscow Treaty has produced real possibilities of establishing peace on earth. . . .

The Soviet Government, true to its policy of equal co-operation and support of popular aspirations for national independence, took a profoundly understanding attitude to the policy announced by Dr Illia. The arrival of a Soviet Government delegation to attend the ceremony of Dr Illia's installation as President was regarded by Argentine opinion as a manifestation of the Soviet attitude.

N. S. Khrushchov's message wishing the new President every success was resonant both in Argentina and in the other Latin American countries. It was taken as yet another mark of the Soviet desire to develop relations with the Latin American countries on the principles of peaceful co-existence, mutual benefit, and profound respect for national sovereignty.

74. Soviet protest over the 'Michurinsk' incident, July 1967[2] (*p. 33*)

On July 23 the USSR Ministry of Foreign Affairs, on instructions from the Soviet government, sent a note to the Embassy of the Argentine Republic in Moscow stating the following:

'The Soviet government calls the attention of the government of Argentina to an instance of flagrant high-handedness and lawlessness perpetrated on July 22, 1967, by the Argentine authorities with respect to the Soviet ship Michurinsk in the port of Buenos Aires. At about 4 p.m., local time, details of marines numbering about 200 persons and accompanied by watchdogs arrived at the dock where the ship was moored and surrounded the Soviet

---

[1] *International Affairs*, no. 12, Dec. 1963.
[2] *Pravda & Izvestiya*, 25 July 1967 (*CDSP*, 16 Aug. 1967, p. 20).

vessel. Representatives of the customs authorities of Argentina, accompanied by a military escort, came aboard the ship and demanded of its captain that they be allowed to examine the diplomatic mail on the ship. During this episode a Soviet seaman was wounded by a bayonet.

'These provocational actions on the part of the Argentine authorities constitute a brazen flouting of generally recognized norms of international law and of the 1961 Vienna Convention on diplomatic relations. The flagrant arbitrariness of the representatives of the Argentine authorities can only be regarded as a premeditated act having as its goal the exacerbation of relations between the Soviet Union and Argentina.

'The Soviet government lodges a resolute protest against the unlawful actions of the Argentine authorities with respect to the ship Michurinsk, demands the immediate cessation of these actions and expects that those guilty of perpetrating them will be strictly punished. The Soviet side reserves the right to demand compensation for the damage inflicted by the unlawful actions of the Argentine authorities.

'The USSR Ministry of Foreign Affairs requests the Embassy of the Argentine Republic to transmit the contents of this note to the Argentine government without delay.'

75. Argentina condemns the Soviet invasion of Czechoslovakia, August 1968[1] (*p. 33*)

The Argentine Government, shocked by the intervention of the Soviet Union and other member countries of the Warsaw Pact in Czechoslovakia, regrets and energetically condemns this act which involves a violation of Czechoslovak sovereignty and transgresses the principles of the United Nations Charter and the principle of non-intervention which has been set out in Resolution 2131 of the General Assembly.

The action of the Soviet Union, which cannot be disguised by the futile excuses offered, seriously affects world peace and is clear evidence of the disregard for the principles of coexistence between states which have been so frequently proclaimed by the same intervening power.

In advance of learning that the Security Council has been called to deal with these events, Argentina undertakes already to give her full support to every effort which is made to re-establish normal conditions in Czechoslovakia and to guarantee the right of her people to decide their own destiny without foreign intervention.

Commercial relations

76. The Argentine-Soviet trade agreement, 5 August 1953[2] (*pp. 22, 32*)

On Aug. 5 a trade and payments agreement between the USSR and the

[1] Argentine Government press release, Buenos Aires, 21 Aug. 1968.
[2] *Izvestiya*, 15 Aug. 1953 (*CDSP*, 26 Sept. 1953, p. 25).

Argentine Republic was signed in Buenos Aires. The large volume of trade between the two countries envisaged by the agreement, as well as the wide assortment of mutual supplies, indicate that great prospects are opening up for Soviet-Argentine economic cooperation.

The Soviet Union will send Argentina coal, oil, metal products, chemical and medical goods, etc. In addition, the USSR will sell Argentina, with payment on installments, equipment and materials for the oil-drilling, coal-mining and electrical industries, railroad equipment and tractors and agricultural machines. Argentina will supply the Soviet Union with linseed oil, wool, cowhides, sheepskins, pig fat and other goods.

During the Soviet-Argentine trade negotiations, which were begun in Moscow and now successfully concluded in Buenos Aires, various prophets of the American and pro-American press foretold their failure. Someone even claimed that the USSR-Argentine trade negotiations were 'empty propaganda'. Now all these by no means disinterested persons, ill-disposed towards Soviet-Argentine economic cooperation, who do not want a strengthening of mutual understanding and friendly relations between the Soviet Union and Argentina, have had to stop talking.

The USSR-Argentina trade agreement has been signed, has gone into force and, it can be confidently stated, will serve the well-being of both countries.

The Argentine public and press, which greeted conclusion of the trade agreement with great satisfaction, are taking special note of those features which favorably distinguish it from the trade conditions ordinarily foisted on Argentina and the various other Latin American countries by their North American 'neighbor'. Not to mention the fact that the USA is trading solely in dollars, the American monopolies refuse to supply the countries of the American continent, less developed industrially, with industrial equipment and thus deliberately hinder their national industrial development. When these countries try to break away from the American market and obtain needed goods elsewhere, the reactionary press raises the cry that this is a violation of 'hemisphere solidarity', and Wall Street threatens the recalcitrant country with economic sanctions.

The Argentine public has soberly evaluated the state of affairs. It understands well who is dissatisfied with the development of trade between Argentina and the Soviet Union and why. As the newspaper Crítica stated July 1, the essence of the matter is that the Soviet Union agreed to promote development of Argentine industry by means of its supplies. It is clear that Argentina's American imaginary 'friends' cannot, as Crítica emphasized, 'look calmly upon this turning of our trade toward countries which offer us what we need and which buy what we can sell'.

On Aug. 9, after the signing of the Soviet-Argentine trade agreement, another Argentine newspaper, El Debate, stated: 'We must give up thinking about the USA. Present-day reality tells us that we must trade with everyone. He who buys from us is a friend. He who, like the USA, keeps us from trading with others who are imposing no economic sanctions on us, is an enemy.'

It is realized in Argentina that under the agreement with the USSR Argentine industry will receive equipment it could never obtain otherwise. Oil equipment in particular is meant. The newspaper Propositos writes that 'the peaceful policy of the Soviet Union, which does not impose agreements and is not attempting to infringe on the economy of other countries, is exemplified by the Soviet Union's desire to sell, for example, oil equipment, which the USA has repeatedly refused us, since it does not want us to develop our own national production.'

The Soviet-Argentine trade agreement, based, like all other USSR trade agreements with foreign countries, on principles of equal rights and mutual interest, has stirred widespread reaction in the other Latin American countries. They are beginning more and more to take account of the fact that discriminatory measures which restrict their foreign trade strike at their national interests, that the need to restore normal international trade is long since ripe.

The press of Uruguay, Brazil, Chile and Mexico more and more frequently carries articles demanding restoration and development of trade with the USSR and other countries in the democratic camp. Uruguayan newspapers emphasize that the interdict imposed by the USA on sale of woollen products by Uruguay is leading to a market crisis in the textile industry, which would not be the case 'if we sold to all who wish to buy from us'. Baltazar Castro, a member of the Chilean Congress, spoke out in favor of restoring economic ties with the USSR. In Brazil a national meeting of Brazilian industrialists unanimously supported demands for the establishment of trade relations with all countries without exception.

The desire of business circles in a number of Latin American states to expand their countries' foreign trade is understandable and timely. As for the Soviet Union's viewpoint on development of international economic ties, it is known that the Soviet public considers them an important way to strengthen peace. The Soviet government, as was stated at the fifth session of the USSR Supreme Soviet, intends still more persistently to pursue a policy of developing trade between the Soviet Union and foreign countries.

77. Visit of Soviet delegation to Buenos Aires, 6 May 1958:[1] extract (*p. 32*)

The Soviet government delegation, which has come to Argentina to attend the inauguration of President Arturo Frondizi, gave a press conference May 5 for local and foreign newsmen. M. P. Tarasov, head of the delegation and Vice-Chairman of the Presidium of the USSR Supreme Soviet, made a statement at the press conference expressing profound gratitude to the government leaders and the people of the Argentine Republic for the gracious hospitality and attention accorded the delegation during its stay in Argentina. . . .

The head of the Soviet delegation emphasized that there had been and are no points of contention between the Soviet Union and the countries of Latin America which would impede the development of friendly relations between them. The Soviet Union is prepared to develop economic, cultural, scientific and sports relations with all the Latin American countries. This would

[1] Tass, 6 May 1958 (*CDSP*, 11 June 1958, p. 24).

correspond to the interests of the peoples of all the countries and of the Soviet Union. The Soviet Union can export machinery and equipment to Argentina and other Latin American countries, particularly equipment for the oil industry, electrical and road-building equipment, metalworking machine tools, various instruments and tools, and transportation equipment. The Soviet Union can be a steady buyer of the traditional export commodities of the Latin American countries.

The head of the Soviet delegation noted the development of trade, cultural and other ties between the USSR and Argentina. We hope, he said, that cooperation between the USSR and Argentina will continue to develop successfully in all spheres, in the interests of the peoples of our countries and of universal peace. . . .

78. Agreement for the supply of Soviet oil equipment, October 1958[1]
(*p. 32*)

Negotiations were conducted in Moscow recently with an Argentine trade delegation, appointed by decree of the President of Argentina, on the conclusion of an agreement on Soviet deliveries of oil equipment for the development of the Argentine oil industry.

These negotiations, which took place in a friendly atmosphere and in the spirit of mutual understanding, culminated in the signing Oct. 27 of a corresponding agreement.

In order to cooperate in the development of the Argentine oil industry, Soviet machinery for prospecting work, drilling work and for the operation of oil wells will be delivered from the Soviet Union to the Argentine Republic. The machinery will include drilling rigs, seismographic stations, turbodrills, beam pumps, pumps, compressors, electrical equipment, motors and trucks.

To make it easier for the Argentine Republic to finance purchases of the above equipment in the USSR, the USSR is granting the Argentine Republic a credit of 400,000,000 rubles at 2·5% annual interest. The credit is good for three years. The credit will be repaid in deliveries of Argentine goods over a seven-year period in equal annual deliveries beginning three years after shipment of the specified machinery. The agreement is subject to ratification.

The agreement on deliveries of machinery for the Argentine oil industry from the USSR was signed for the USSR government by N. S. Patolichev, USSR Minister of Foreign Trade, and for the President of Argentina by José V. Liseaga, Envoy Extraordinary and Minister Plenipotentiary and Deputy to Parliament.

[1] *Pravda*, 28 Oct. 1958 (*CDSP*, 3 Dec. 1958, p. 18).

3 Brazil

79. Statement by Prestes, Secretary of the Brazilian CP, at a meeting of civil servants, affirming that the Party would fight for the USSR in the event of a conflict with Brazil, March 1946:[1] excerpt (*pp. 25, 34*)
[*In reply to a question as to the attitude of the Party if Brazil should go to the aid of any imperialist nation which declared war on Russia.*]
We should act like the forces of resistance in France and Italy when they rose against Pétain and Mussolini. We should resist an imperialist war against Soviet Russia and we should take up arms to oppose in our own country a reactionary Government of those who seek to return to Fascism. But we believe that no Government will try to raise the Brazilian people against the Soviet people which is fighting for progress and for the welfare of the poor. If any Government committed this crime, we Communists would fight for the transformation of an imperialist war into a war of national liberation.

80. 'New Times' on anti-Soviet trends in Brazil, January 1947[2] (*p. 34*)
In December 1946 alone the newspapers of the Brazilian capital printed more than four hundred articles and other items containing slanderous fabrications against the Soviet Union. The palm in this undignified contest belongs to the newspaper *A Vanguardia*, which printed as many as fifty items of this sort in December. The newspaper *A Manha* is a close second, with forty-four, and the *Correio da Manha* third, with thirty-five articles and other items hostile to this country.
This campaign, obviously organized and directed from some definite source, is not confined to newspapers.
On December 20, Arruda Camara demanded in the Chamber of Deputies that the Soviet Ambassador be deported from Brazil and that diplomatic relations with the Soviet Union be broken off. Camara spiced his demands with slander and insults against our country and the Soviet people. That same day the Fascist Integralist organization held an anti-Soviet meeting. The police permitted that meeting to be held in the centre of the city 'in view', as the newspaper *Folha Carioca* says, 'of the patriotic and non-partisan character of that affair.'
The Brazilian reactionary press and the Brazilian Fascists are obviously doing their utmost to work up hostile sentiments amongst the Brazilian people against our country. Neither the Soviet people nor the Soviet press have ever displayed the slightest unfriendliness or suspicion in regard to the Brazilian people. The policy of the Soviet State towards Brazil, as well as towards other Latin American states, is one of peace and a desire for friendly cooperation.

[1] *Tribuna popular* (Rio, founded by Brazilian CP), Mar. 1946.
[2] *New Times*, 24 Jan. 1947, p. 28.

The attempts to spread in Brazil suspicion and hostility towards our country are dictated by interests that have nothing in common with the interests of the Brazilian people. They are part of the machinations of the enemies of peace and can only arouse a feeling of indignation amongst the Soviet public.

81. A Soviet view of Brazil's army and President: article in the 'Literaturnaya Gazeta', 4 October 1947: excerpts (*p. 34*)

For many years Mr Dutra's military career was remarkably colourless. At the age of 43 he was still a major, though the Brazilian army, not distinguished for a superabundance of soldiers, swarms with generals.

But in 1931 Mr Dutra moved up to the fore through Napoleonic exertions. Within three years he became general, then successively commander of the garrison of the capital, Minister of War, and President of the Republic.

How did that come about? Did Mr Dutra spectacularly reveal military talents on the field of battle? But Brazil was not at war with anyone. And in Brazil generals are not generally born on the battlefield. In Brazil, generals are born in the coffee plantations.

Knowing this strategic truth, 'our trusty and devoted friend' formed strong links with those oligarchical, landowning cliques which rule the country. Some thousand powerful coffee-planters own 91 per cent of Brazil's land. This was the case in 1937 under Brazil's President, the Fascist Vargas, who destroyed the last remnants of democratic liberty in the country and set up a regime of military dictatorship with the help of Mr Dutra. In this sense, General Dutra may be said to have been reared on coffee-beans.

In these same years he energetically developed some links or other with the Axis states. Mr Dutra's frequent visits to the German embassy culminated in an arms order for $60 million which Mr Dutra placed with the firm of Krupps, through Hitler's personal representative in Brazil. This, it is true, was before 1939. But that date in no way abated Mr Dutra's morbid passion for Fascist Germany. . . . The Fascist decoration sent to Mr Dutra by Hitler in recompense for the political sympathies of 'our trusty and devoted friend' was presented to him by the attaché nominally in charge of 'cultural affairs'. True, this was before 1939. But the march of history did not stop at that date. History has the unfortunate habit of marching on.

1941 arrived. German bombers were barbarously bombing British towns. England was ablaze. Precisely at that dramatic moment Brazil's War Minister General Dutra found it most opportune to take an open stand against any rapprochement with England, and publicly confirmed his pro-Hitler sympathy. In the same year—two years after 1937—'our trusty and devoted friend' had the audacity to threaten in demonstrative fashion that he would resign if the preparations then afoot for Brazil to break with the Axis states were carried into effect.

The same General Dutra contrived to make his way to Washington and there solemnly to declare, with many expressions of tropical exuberance, that Brazil would take her place beside the United States of America. It is true that he was in no hurry to specify the date by which the Brazilian army would take the front. We in the Soviet Union were not greatly put out by this delay. We resolved that we would somehow go on fighting—without Brazil.

As for General Dutra, he apparently came to the conclusion after visiting Washington that there was still a little time before the 'second front' was opened in Italy. . . .

With the smell of gunpowder still in their nostrils from the battles they had been fighting against their own compatriots, the Brazilian regiments left for the front in Italy. They were under the command of the 'coffee general', General Eurico Gaspar Dutra himself. . . . But whoever said that the Brazilian army had to fight? It had plenty to keep it busy, not on the field of battle in Europe, but at home. That at least is what General Dutra thought. Returning from the 'Italian campaign' crowned with the victor's laurels, he firmly resolved to be elected to the Presidency. And although the Constitution does not give the right to vote to the Brazilian army the latter has arrogated to itself the right to 'make' the elections. With this end in view, General Dutra placed his officers in the censorship and all other key posts. In those days, whilst the Soviet army was fighting on the field of battle, the Brazilian army strictly forbade any Soviet newsreels to be shown. Apparently the famous 'coffee general' was scared of our Red Army men even when they appeared on the screen.

The army joined the battle of the elections. . . . So General Eurico Gaspar Dutra became President of Brazil. Not suffering from any excess of modesty, he proclaimed the day on which he took office a national holiday. For the Brazilian people it was a day of national woe. . . . Dutra issued a decree banning 'extremist ideas', suppressed the slightest manifestation of freedom of thought. He clamped the mind in fetters. He sent the best of the nation to prison or to the block. He outlawed the Communist Party. He filled the whole of fair Brazil with mourning. . . .

82. Statement by the Brazilian Minister for Foreign Affairs breaking off diplomatic relations with the USSR, 21 October 1947 (*p. 34*)

The *Literaturnaya Gazeta* inserted an extremely insulting and even calumnious article against the Head of the State and the Armed Forces of Brazil.

It is a matter of universal notoriety that the Soviet press is strictly controlled by the Government which is therefore virtually responsible for everything which is printed in that country. In consequence, the Ministry for Foreign Affairs instructed the Brazilian Ambassador in that capital to present to the Soviet Minister for Foreign Affairs a note protesting against the insult and demanding satisfaction, together with a declaration that if the latter were declined it would be impossible to continue diplomatic relations, at least correctly, between the two Governments.

This note was returned without reply under the false pretext that it had been drafted in unfriendly terms.

In view of these facts the Brazilian Government decided to break off relations with the Soviet Union. The note of rupture dispatched by the Itamaraty [Foreign Office] to the Brazilian Embassy in Moscow was presented yesterday at 7.15 p.m. in the following terms:—

'Brazilian diplomatic relations with Russia go back to the year 1830 when, first of all South American countries, we established a Legation in St Petersburg. These relations remained correct and friendly until the day when they were interrupted by the revolution and by the vicissitudes resulting from the consolidation of the new regime set up in Russia.

'At the end of the last Great War, which saw our two flags united on the same field of battle, we wished to reactivate this union in homage to the heroism with which the Russian people fought, as well as to the work of co-operation which Russia devoted to the common effort of the victorious countries for the establishment of peace and for the reconstruction of the devastated territories. Between two countries, so distant from each other and without appreciable economic relations—as is the case between Brazil and Russia—this collaboration would have to take place primarily in the sphere of the United Nations Organization. With this in mind we established an Embassy in Moscow and we received in the capital of Brazil a Soviet Embassy, both installed in the course of the year 1946.

'We were soon disillusioned by the failure to accord reciprocal treatment to the two Missions: whereas in Rio de Janeiro the Soviet Ambassador and his staff received the courtesy, the privileges, and facilities which are traditionally accorded to the representatives of friendly countries, the Brazilian Ambassador in Moscow and his staff suffered every kind of restriction, some of which were vexatious to a degree. The Brazilian Government suffered such unequal treatment so as not to take up a discriminatory or exceptional point of view, since the majority of diplomats accredited to the Soviet capital find themselves in an identical situation. Moreover, we entertained the hope that this state of affairs might be transitory and that, when confidence and mutual understanding had been patiently established between the Soviet Government and the Governments of the democratic States, it would be agreed in Moscow that our representatives should enjoy the liberty of movement without which neither their functions could be efficiently discharged nor their daily life be rendered tolerable.

'This forbearance and understanding were, however, badly repaid. The Soviet press, so strictly controlled by the Government, recently attacked us strongly and without reason.

'And so a few days ago, in spite of the repeated votes cast by the Brazilian delegation in favour of a member of the USSR in a closely-fought election for membership of the Security Council, the head of the Brazilian delegation, Dr Osvaldo Aranha, who was President of the Assembly at the time, was brutally attacked by the Moscow press and offensively accused of being in the pay of the United States Government. These votes moreover were given in opposition to the United States delegation, and they had at least the merit of freedom and independence. This fact was forgotten and insults were showered upon us, only because the President, merely observing the procedural regulations of the Assembly, did not allow intemperate speech by the Soviet delegate!

'It would seem, further, that there was a deliberate intention to provoke us gratuitously for, next, a newspaper insulted and gravely slandered the Head of the State and the Armed Forces of Brazil. It was essential that we should issue
14

a vehement protest and demand satisfaction for this abuse. We did so in such terms that we should be able to continue to maintain relations of any correctitude with the Government of the USSR.

'The note of the Brazilian Ambassador although steeped in just indignation against the offending journalist, and energetic in its claims, was phrased in modest terms in regard to the Soviet Government.

'Nevertheless the latter refused to accept it with the pretext that the tone was unfriendly. If the Soviet Government supported the journalist and felt itself implicated by the retaliation, it only made the situation worse and in any event by the unjustified return of the note practically refused to give the satisfaction which Brazilian susceptibilities made indispensable.

'The Soviet Government thus gave to this lamentable incident a solution which implies contempt for the relations which we earnestly tried to maintain and cultivate.

'In these circumstances all that remains for me is to notify Your Excellency, in the name of and under instructions from my Government, that as from this date diplomatic relations between Brazil and the USSR have ceased.'

Yesterday at 18 hours the Embassy of the United States of America, which had kindly agreed to the request of the Brazilian Government to take over the protection of their national interests in the Soviet Union, made the requisite communication to the Russian Ministry for Foreign Affairs.

83. Message from Khrushchev and Brezhnev to Jânio da Silva Quadros, August 1961[1] (*p. 35*)

It is with great satisfaction that we seize the favorable occasion of the trip by the Soviet good-will mission to Brazil to send the present message and, in the name of the peoples of the Soviet Union, the Presidium of the USSR Supreme Soviet and the Soviet government, to transmit to you and to the large and industrious populace of Brazil greetings and wishes of happiness and good fortune.

We in the Soviet Union are following with great understanding the vigorous efforts of the Brazilian people toward ensuring a firm defense of Brazil's national interests in international relations and toward developing cooperation with all the countries of the world. You personally, Mr President, can take a large part of the credit for determining this position. We are thoroughly familiar with your repeated declarations in favor of strengthening the general peace, in the defense of the national sovereignty of states and the right of all peoples to self-determination and for the final liquidation of colonialism.

The Soviet public appreciated highly your statement that Brazil will not agree to any form of colonialism or imperialism and will work for the un-delayed granting of independence to all colonial peoples without exception. This statement strengthens the certainty that Brazil will fight actively for the realization of the historic declaration on granting independence to colonial countries and peoples adopted at the 15th session of the UN General Assembly.

We have noted with satisfaction that recently the Brazilian government has

[1] *Pravda*, 26 Aug. 1961 (*CDSP*, 20 Sept. 1961, p. 21).

been speaking out decisively for a broad development of cooperation with all countries on an equal basis, which undoubtedly serves the interests of preserving and strengthening peace.

We are convinced that you share the view that there are only two paths of international development. Either the policy of the arms race will continue, and then mankind will not be free of the danger of being plunged at any moment into a devastating nuclear and rocket war. As a snake can only beget a snake, the arms race can only beget war. This path is rejected by the peoples of all countries and by the governments of the peaceloving states. Or the policy of peaceful coexistence of states with different social systems will triumph. In our time, when science and technology have achieved unseen heights, the peaceful coexistence of states has become an urgent demand of life itself. The objective course of history and irrefutable facts of contemporary life demonstrate that the ensuring of peace on earth is fully realistic and realizable within the lifetime of our generation. Now that man has conquered the earth's gravity and has penetrated into cosmic space, there can be no doubt that he can just as successfully break the chains of distrust and prejudice that separate peoples.

The principles of peaceful coexistence lie at the basis of the foreign policy of many peace-loving states in Europe, Asia, Africa and Latin America. The Soviet Union fights consistently and untiringly so that these principles will become the premise for the policy of all countries on our planet. Then international relations will have a good and solid basis for the development of peaceful and effective cooperation among states.

Brazil, the largest country in Latin America, is taking an increasingly firm hold on its rightful place in the family of peace-loving peoples. The Soviet people entertain feelings of deep and sincere sympathy for the gifted Brazilian people, have a great interest in their history and value their freedom-loving traditions. They study the rich national culture of the Brazilian people and appreciate highly Brazil's contribution to the treasury of world culture.

The Soviet people understand well the Brazilian people's strivings to strengthen their national economy and to free it from foreign influence. We know from our own experience that this is the only course capable of ensuring an upsurge in the nation's welfare. We sincerely wish Brazil success on this path.

The negotiations with the Brazilian trade delegation headed by Mr Leao de Maura [Moura], recently conducted in Moscow, which led to positive results, permit us to hope that mutually advantageous trade relations between our countries will develop successfully. We have no doubt that in the future there may be new prospects for expanding economic cooperation and trade between our countries. The Soviet Union, for its part, expresses readiness to promote this in every possible way.

We recently received in the Soviet Union, with complete cordiality and as friends, emissaries of the Brazilian people, a Brazilian parliamentary delegation headed by Mr Clemilio de Lemos. We view these visits as a good beginning in the further expansion of contacts and cooperation between our countries in various fields of human endeavor.

We want to point out, Mr President, that your statements to the effect that

there are no obstacles to the resumption of diplomatic relations between Brazil
and the Soviet Union have met full understanding here. The resumption of
diplomatic representatives will undoubtedly create more favorable conditions
for the development of relations of friendship and confidence between our
countries, based on noninterference in one another's domestic affairs, respect
for sovereignty and dignity, equality and fruitful cooperation.

Mr President, we recall with pleasure your trip to the Soviet Union in the
summer of 1959 and our interesting and useful talks with you. We hope that
we shall have the pleasant occasion of a new encounter with you, an outstanding statesman, the President of the United States of Brazil, in our hospitable
land. . . .

84. President Quadros's reply to the message from Khrushchev and Brezhnev, August 1961[1] (*p. 35*)

I am profoundly grateful to the peoples of the Soviet Union, to the Presidium
of the USSR Supreme Soviet and to the Soviet government for their magnani-
mous display of interest in the present and future of my country.

The good-will mission met with me and other officials in the young Brazilian
capital and departed on a trip through the interior regions of the country. This
trip enabled the members of the mission to form a detailed and comprehensive
impression of what today's Brazil represents and to transmit their impressions
to Your Excellencies.

I have no intention of anticipating the undoubtedly very accurate conclusions that your compatriots will draw. Nevertheless, it is of interest to me
that the Soviet Union pays attention to the specific problems of a huge country
that is developing at an extremely rapid rate, a country that is fighting for
progress, at the price of enormous but noble efforts, over vast territories where
misery reigns, some of which are overpopulated while others are almost
uninhabited. This picture gives some idea, even though an incomplete one, of
the gigantic task confronting the Brazilian people.

The Russian people are in a position to understand us. Their recent history
is characterized by struggle, which they carried on under other historical and
social conditions, to attain the present prosperity of their country.

The situation in Brazil is different. We have no religious, racial or ideological
prejudices. The Brazilian people, being a Christian and peace-loving people
distinguished by an unflinching devotion to democratic freedoms, are at
present inspired by progressive aspirations connected with their great civilizing
mission.

Poor or underdeveloped countries often encounter a lack of understanding
at certain stages of their struggle for liberation. This lack of understanding
increases when the time comes for them to assert their independence firmly.
Brazil is now passing through such a period.

It is pleasant for me to note that such powers as the Soviet Union have
recognized the active and independent participation of our country in international life. It remains for me to hope that our activity and position will be

---

[1] *Pravda*, 26 Aug. 1961 (*CDSP*, 20 Sept. 1961, pp. 21–2).

correctly interpreted and that at the present moment, which calls for broad and fraternal mutual understanding among all states, the door will be opened to us for sincere and fruitful cooperation with the peoples from whom we are separated by great distances.

It is important for Brazil to develop exchanges with the Soviet Union. We have something to offer and much to learn. The scientific and technical knowledge and resources accumulated by the USSR in the course of its immensely rapid movement toward progress may contribute to the development of my country precisely at the moment when Brazil has decided to break the chains of poverty, illness and ignorance. We have received valuable help from other sources, but it is insufficient from the standpoint of our requirements and our potentials for expanding production.

The message from Your Excellencies made me completely certain that you understand Brazil's national tasks. Our activity in international politics will be intensified constantly in the interests of peace, progress and the liberation of all peoples.

Brazil, for all practical purposes an unarmed nation, ardently desires that the great powers' statements in favor of disarmament be carried into action; this will lead to purposeful activity by world public opinion and will sow universal hope that our generation will live to see the day when peace reigns on earth.

It remains for me to comment on some other specific problems touched upon in the message from Your Excellencies.

As for the resumption of relations between Brazil and the Soviet Union, I can inform you that this question is successfully under consideration on the Brazilian side, and I am convinced that its study will lead quite soon to positive results.

I accept the invitation of Your Excellencies to visit the Soviet Union as head of state. I retain the most pleasant memories of my previous trip to your country. We shall be able, in due time and with mutual consent, to set the date when I am to avail myself of this invitation, which is an honor to me.

I would like to inform Your Excellencies of the wonderful impression I gained from meetings with the Soviet good-will mission. . . .

85. Reply by Khrushchev to questions by the Director of 'Ultima Hora', predicting close political and economic relations between the USSR and Brazil, March 1963:[1] excerpt (*p. 35*)

. . . Between our countries there are no questions at issue that could hamper the development of friendly relations between them. We are convinced that Brazil and the Soviet Union can be good friends and that such friendship would make a great contribution to the cause of promoting international co-operation and preserving world peace. It is primarily here, in our view, that lies the positive significance of the resumption of diplomatic relations between our countries.

It is true that there are some who do not like it when the Soviet Union

[1] *Pravda*, 30 Mar. 1963.

establishes good relations with the Latin American countries, and not with them only indeed. But the question is, can anyone who really wants genuine international co-operation fear good relations between the Soviet Union and other nations? We for our part do not object to, say, the United States of America building their relations with other states on the basis of the principles of the United Nations Charter—of living at peace with each other, as good neighbours, without interfering in domestic affairs, respecting the independence and sovereignty of states. On the contrary, we welcome this in every way.

We ourselves follow a policy aimed at maintaining good relations also with your northern neighbour, the United States, and with other countries. To take the opposite viewpoint would mean to adopt the road of setting some states on a collision course with others, of sowing the seeds of suspicion and mistrust among states, among peoples. But this is not the road towards peace, towards ensuring the security of the peoples, and we do not doubt that in Brazil too the opinion is the same on this score.

The beneficial effect of the friendly relations established between the Soviet Union and Brazil have already found expression in the development of trade between our countries. Since we restored relations, a little more than a year ago, the exchange of trade between our countries has increased more than fifty per cent as compared with 1961. We hope that the new trade-and-payments agreement currently being negotiated in Rio de Janeiro will lay the foundations for further considerable expansion of Soviet-Brazilian trade relations.

We are ready to facilitate an increase in the volume of mutual trade. The Soviet Union is a major exporter of machinery and equipment. Our trading agencies are in a position to offer Brazil a broad range of engineering products. We also have good possibilities for trading in such commodities as oil and oil products, grain, and many other things. At the same time, we could increase purchases of traditional Brazilian exports, in particular coffee, cacao, and other things. In other words, the possibilities for developing trade between our countries are far from being exhausted.

We note with satisfaction that in the past year Soviet-Brazilian contacts become somewhat more lively in other fields as well. Exchanges of delegations of political figures, scientists, artists became more and more free. We were pleased with the interest displayed by Brazilians in the Soviet industrial and trade fair in Rio de Janeiro. Our people enthusiastically acclaimed the performances of talented Brazilian artists in the Soviet Union where the rich original culture of the Brazilian people is highly appreciated.

The resumption of diplomatic relations between the Soviet Union and Brazil has thus opened up broad prospects for friendly co-operation between our countries. The meaning of the policy of peaceful coexistence is that states with differing social systems search and find such ways of co-operation which bring benefits and advantages to both. We are in favour of such co-operation. . . .

The Soviet Government is ready to discuss with the Government of Brazil the problem of economic co-operation and to find mutually acceptable ways of promoting Brazil's industrial development. An understanding could be reached, for instance, on the deliveries of necessary machinery and equipment from the

USSR, on the dispatch of Soviet specialists to Brazil, on the training of Brazilian specialists in the USSR.

I think that the Soviet people, too, could learn much that is useful from what is being done in Brazil, for instance, in construction and architecture. Thus, in our opinion, there is quite a sound foundation for the development of economic co-operation between our countries.

86. 'Izvestiya' complains of anti-Soviet acts by Brazilian authorities, May 1964:[1] excerpts (*p. 35*)

Police operations have developed on a broad scale in Minas Gerais. . . . The sale of all Soviet publications is prohibited, including those on science and art; this measure is all the more strange since the sale of these publications has been based on a Soviet-Brazilian agreement that no one has officially cancelled. . . .

The 'ideological' offensive is accompanied by an unbridled anti-Soviet campaign that has seized a considerable part of the press. Slander against the Soviet Union is pouring forth in streams, insulting fabrications concerning the USSR Ambassador in Brazil and other Soviet officials are being published. More than that, an attempt is being made to deprive our embassy of the possibility of normal use of means of communications. Even urgent telegrams often arrive here after several days' delay.

Economic relations

87. Communiqué on the Soviet-Brazilian trade agreement,[2] December 1959:[3] excerpt (*pp. 22, 34*)

Following negotiations in Moscow from Nov. 28 to Dec. 9, 1959, the Soviet trade delegation, headed by Deputy Minister of Foreign Trade N. N. Smelyakov, and the Brazilian trade delegation, headed by Ambassador E. P. Barboza da Silva, reached agreement on the general aim of creating the bases on which mutually advantageous trade between the USSR and Brazil might be re-established and developed.

The agreed volumes of trade between the two countries provide for deliveries of goods in 1960 in the sum of $25,000,000 on each side. It is expected that this total will increase to $37,000,000 in 1961 and $45,000,000 in 1962.

The chief Brazilian export to the USSR will be coffee. Cocoa beans, vegetable oil, raw hides and certain other goods will also be shipped from Brazil to the USSR.

The chief Soviet exports to Brazil will be oil and petroleum products, wheat, machinery and equipment, metals and chemical and other goods. . . .

[1] *Izvestiya*, 5 May 1964 (*CDSP*, 27 May 1964, pp. 26–7).
[2] For full text of the agreement see Rl Inst. of International Affairs, *Documents on International Affairs 1959*, p. 403.
[3] *Pravda*, 11 Dec. 1959 (*CDSP*, 13 Jan. 1960, p. 23).

88. Khrushchev receives the head of a Brazilian trade delegation,
  May 1961:[1] excerpt (*p. 34*)

On May 3 N. S. Khrushchev, Chairman of the USSR Council of Ministers, received Paulo Leao de Maura [Moura], head of a special Brazilian trade delegation with the rank of minister, who is in Moscow.

In the course of the talks Mr Leao de Maura declared that the purpose of his present negotiations with Soviet representatives is to search for ways and means to develop Soviet-Brazilian trade relations and to raise the trade between the Soviet Union and Brazil to a level more befitting the great economic importance of these two countries and their possibilities for complementing one another economically.

Mr Leao de Maura also transmitted personal greetings to the Chairman of the USSR Council of Ministers from Mr Janio Quadros, President of the United States of Brazil.

N. S. Khrushchev declared that he wished Mr Leao de Maura great success in his mission, because he fully agreed with the view that the Soviet-Brazilian trade must reach a high level. He added that to attain this end and to improve over-all relations between the Soviet Union and Brazil, diplomatic relations between the Soviet Union and Brazil should be restored, since this would constitute a major spur to expanding trade. . . .

89. 'Izvestiya' on the Soviet-Brazilian trade agreement,
  April 1963:[2] excerpts (*p. 34*)

. . . The first trade and payments agreement for our two countries was signed in a ceremonious atmosphere on Saturday in the ancient hall of the Ministry of Foreign Affairs in Rio de Janeiro. . . .

. . . The agreement, calculated for five years, provides for a sharp increase in the volume of trade between the Soviet Union and Brazil. For example, this year the trade turnover will double in comparison with 1962, reaching a volume of approximately $125,000,000. In 1964 it will reach $200,000,000 and in 1965 will rise to $225,000,000. This growth is all the more impressive in that as late as 1958 Soviet-Brazilian trade was practically nil. Enormous significance is attached here to the signing of the agreement. In recent times Brazil has been experiencing growing difficulties in trade with the United States and West European countries. Brazilian goods have more and more trouble forcing their way into these markets, and prices for them are falling steadily, which causes the country colossal economic losses. From 1955 through 1961 alone, for example, Brazil lost $1,500,000,000 on this.

In these conditions Brazil has turned to a search for new markets.

A special agency for arranging trade with the socialist countries of Eastern Europe was formed in December, 1962, by decision of the Brazilian government. It has launched into vigorous activity, furthered, in particular, by the success of the Soviet-Brazilian trade negotiations.

[1] *Pravda*, 4 May 1961; *Izvestiya*, 5 May 1961 (*CDSP*, 31 May 1961, p. 18).
[2] *Izvestiya*, 23 Apr. 1963 (*CDSP*, 15 May 1963, p. 28).

It must be said that Soviet-Brazilian trade has its violent opponents. It pleases not everyone that Brazil has refused to subordinate itself to commercial dictation and now is deciding for itself with whom and what goods it will trade. The arrival here of the Soviet trade delegation caused distinct uneasiness in certain circles. Some newspapers, including the most reactionary press organs, have launched a hostile campaign.

What will the ill-wishers say now as they read the text of the agreement? Brazil is going to deliver coffee and cotton, cacao beans and oranges, rice and vegetable oil and raw leather to the Soviet Union. Brazil will receive from the Soviet Union wheat, oil, petroleum products, machines and equipment, rolled ferrous metals, nonferrous metals, fertilizer, pulp and newsprint. Our countries have something to offer one another. There are big prospects for Soviet-Brazilian trade.

In welcoming the successful conclusion of negotiations, President Joao Goulart of Brazil said in a special statement for the readers of Pravda and Izvestia: 'I want to express my delight in connection with the signing of the trade and payments agreement between the Brazil and the Soviet Union. This is an important stride forward along the path of developing relations between our two countries.'

90. Soviet-Brazilian trade protocol, August 1966:[1] excerpt (*p. 34*)

A protocol on deliveries from the Soviet Union to Brazil of $100 million worth of machinery and equipment on commercial credit terms for 1966/9 has been signed here. The protocol was signed on behalf of the Soviet Government by N. S. Patolichev, Minister of Foreign Trade of the Soviet Union, and on behalf of the Government of Brazil by Roberto de Oliveira Campos, Minister of Planning and Economic Co-ordination. . . .

The correspondents of *Pravda* and APN requested Comrade Patolichev to evaluate the importance of the new protocol for the further development of trade between the two countries.

'Trade has always promoted mutual understanding between nations', Patolichev said. 'The Soviet Union trades with a great many countries in the world. Our country, therefore strictly adheres to the principles of equality, non-interference in the internal affairs of other countries, and the mutual advantage of the countries concerned. These principles lie at the base of our trade with Brazil.'

Trade between the Soviet Union and Brazil is increasing. The level so far attained does not, in our view, correspond to the possibilities which exist. Of course, our countries, which enjoy immense economic potentialities, could exchange to mutual advantage a considerably greater quantity of goods, both raw materials and manufactures.

The new protocol envisages supplying Brazil in the course of the next four years with Soviet machines and tools. The extension of our exports will enable us not only to increase purchases of Brazil's traditional exports, but also to begin to purchase semi- and fully manufactured goods.

[1] *Izvestiya*, 11 Aug. 1966; *Pravda*, 14 Aug. 1966.

We consider that the signing of the protocol can play an important role in the further development of mutually beneficial Soviet-Brazilian trade. But much still needs to be done to bring this to a successful conclusion. It is to be hoped, for instance, that more visits by representatives of Soviet foreign trade organizations will be paid to Brazil, and by representatives of Brazilian firms and organizations to the Soviet Union, for a deeper study of the market and the commercial possibilities of our countries.

4 Bolivia

Economic relations

91. Statement by Dr Marcial Tamayo, Bolivian delegate to the UN General Assembly, accusing the USSR of 'economic aggression', 2 October 1958:[1] excerpt (*pp. 24, 39*)

At the present time, my country is faced by Soviet economic aggression, which aims at the gradual destruction of the world tin market. The fearful prospect of armed aggression with modern weapons of war tends to overshadow the fact that economic aggression also breaches the innermost defences of the country attacked and spreads ruin and intolerable misery in its midst. The Soviet Union's aim in dumping huge quantities of tin on the world markets can only have been to demoralise the peoples which live by the export of that mineral and to capitalize on the resulting discontent and social unrest.

My country has effected far-reaching political, economic and social changes. The people is free, and the country is sovereign. No form of oligarchy exists. If the Soviet Union's conduct was consistent with its own propaganda, it would respect this country which has made such efforts to emancipate its people and regain its dignity. The reason for the present Soviet attitude is that our revolution was accomplished without foreign tutelage and without invoking any doctrine alien to the Christian tradition of its supporters. The fact is that my people is today the victim of an economic war unleashed by distant enemies which have selected Bolivia as the latest target of their many-sided world-wide offensive. I appeal to the free countries to ponder this grave situation which has arisen. . . .

[1] *GAOR*, 13th sess., 767th mtg., p. 287.

92. Soviet rebuttal and counter-charge in 'Izvestiya', 10 October 1958[1] (*pp. 24, 39*)

In recent times American propaganda has been conducting a slanderous campaign to blame the Soviet Union for the economic difficulties Bolivia is experiencing. The pages of the US monopoly press constantly carry articles about the mythical 'Soviet economic aggression' against Bolivia, charging that 'Soviet tin dumping' is responsible for the crisis in Bolivian tin exports, which provide 80% of the country's total currency receipts. Recently The New York Times devoted an entire page to this myth.

However, the facts completely expose the fabricated nature of this American propaganda and offer convincing proof that the true stranglers of the Bolivian economy are the very organizers of this slanderous campaign, the US monopolies.

Specifically, there is an abundance of facts to support this in the book 'The Mining Problem in Bolivia,' which was published recently in that country. The author of the book, Prof. Gualberto Pedrasas, exposes in many examples the complete baselessness of the myth of USSR 'economic aggression' against Bolivia. The pamphlet describes in detail the fatal consequences of the control held over the Bolivian economy—particularly the tin industry—by the American monopolies, which impede in every way the country's economic development and keep Bolivia in a state of backwardness and poverty. 'Bolivia's mining wealth,' Pedrasas writes, 'is completely in the hands of American imperialism.'

Having made Bolivia dependent on the American market, the USA arbitrarily imposes low prices on Bolivian raw materials and limits raw materials exports at its discretion. As a result the price of Bolivian tin has fallen from $1·83 per pound in 1941 to $0·80 per pound today. Bolivia has lost $50,000,000 a year on sales of tin to the United States.

Prof. Pedrasas shows the absurdity of the allegation that 'the sale by the Soviet Union of 10,000 tons of tin on the world market' has resulted in a sharp 'reduction in export quotas of tin and has created an acute economic and social problem in the countries that produce this metal.'

The author points out that the 10,000 tons of tin, which, by the way, were not dumped but sold at normal prices, could not exert such a major influence on the world market. The main reason for the crisis, he points out, is that 'the USA, having accumulated vast stocks of tin amounting to 200,000 tons, does not wish to make new purchases and is obstructing the marketing of this metal by Bolivia.'

The way in which the USA is smothering the Bolivian economy has once more been made glaringly apparent by the American authorities' recent decision to cut imports of lead and zinc by 20%. As the Bolivian press has pointed out, the result of this restriction will be to reduce Bolivian exports by an additional $6,000,000 a year. The Chamber of Deputies, lodging an official protest against the decision of the American authorities, described it as 'US economic aggression against Bolivia.'

[1] *CDSP*, 19 Nov. 1958, p. 20.

Is it not clear to all that the slanderous campaign waged by American propaganda over 'Soviet economic aggression' against Bolivia is simply a clumsy attempt to divert attention from the real economic aggression of the USA against this Latin American country?

93. Official communiqué on Khrushchev's offer of a tin smelter, October 1960[1] (*pp. 24, 39*)

Public opinion is aware that the Prime Minister of the USSR, Mr Nikita Khrushchev, on 5 October last, offered the Bolivian representative at the United Nations to give a tin smelter to the country.

The smelting of tin in Bolivia—a long-standing national aspiration—will serve to enable the industrial cycle of mining production to be completed in its own country, so that our chief export product could be sold not only in the form of simple concentrates, but as metal, and furthermore, a certain quantity of this would then become available for building up secondary industries.

The Supreme Government has therefore received this information with the serious attention which is due to it, and has carried out a preliminary study by means of a commission of politicians, economists, and mining technicians.

The Soviet offer, moreover, fits in with the plans previously worked out by the Government of the National Revolution to achieve the complete rehabilitation of the mining industry.

In order to finance the above-mentioned plans, which envisage the raising of the production indices of the nationalized mining industry, the setting up of plant for the concentration of low-grade ore, and finally, the construction of smelting furnaces, the Supreme Government has begun negotiations with the different international banks, specially the Inter-American Development Bank, and is also studying the suggestions put forward by various European countries, to which the offer of the USSR must now be added.

With these considerations in mind, the Executive has decided to send a commercial mission to visit France, Germany, Holland, Czechoslovakia, and the USSR in the course of the next month.

This mission will formalize the negotiations already under way to achieve the desired rehabilitation of our principal export industry and will study the technical and economic aspects of the implications of the Soviet offer.

94. Letter from Brezhnev to Víctor Paz Estenssoro reaffirming Soviet readiness to establish economic and political relations, December 1960:[2] excerpt (*p. 24*)

... The peoples of the Soviet Union harbour sentiments of deep respect and sympathy for the Bolivian people, who have a great tradition of struggling for freedom. The Soviet people follow with sincere sympathy the efforts of the people and Government of Bolivia to consolidate the independent development of their country.

[1] *Bolivia* (La Paz), no. 6, 30 Nov. 1960 (published by the Dirección General de Informaciones).
[2] Ibid., no. 8, 30 Dec. 1960.

We are well aware of the success achieved by the working people of Bolivia in the exploitation of the national oil and mining industries, who, in the possession of very rich natural resources and capable national cadres, aim at making progress in building up a healthy national industry.

This is gratifying to the Soviet people, whose sympathies are ever with those countries which have entered the path of independent national development and the creation of their own industry as the basis for consolidating their complete economic independence.

The Soviet Union has always shown that it is ready to develop economic and commercial relations with all countries on principles of mutual benefit. Our country is providing disinterested help to the countries of Asia, Africa, and Latin America in the cause of the development of their economy and culture, regardless of any conditions of a political or military character.

Between the Soviet Union and Bolivia there have not existed, and do not exist, any problems under discussion which might hamper the development between them of collaboration of mutual benefit in the political and economic field, and likewise in the development of cultural, scientific, and other relations. Our countries have diplomatic relations, and the Soviet people have received with satisfaction the well-known decision of the National Congress of Bolivia regarding the establishing of Bolivian diplomatic relations in Moscow and your statement, Mr President, that this decision of the Legislative branch will be executed by the Bolivian Government.

We note with pleasure that the USSR and Bolivia hold the same opinions regarding a number of most important international problems concerned with the strengthening of the general peace.

All this, Mr President, in our opinion creates a very good basis for the consolidation of Bolivian-Soviet relations. The future development of relations between our countries, the spirit of mutual understanding and friendship, will answer the interests of our peoples and will be a positive contribution to the cause of strengthening peace throughout the world.

Relations between Communist Parties

95. 'Pravda' report on visit of Bolivian Communist leaders to Moscow, July-August 1965:[1] excerpts (*p. 27*)

Upon the invitation of the CPSU Central Committee, a delegation of the Communist Party of Bolivia, headed by Comrade Jorge Kolle, Secretary of the Bolivian Communist Party Central Committee, was in the USSR in July and August, 1965. . . .

The delegation met with Comrade B. N. Ponomarev, Secretary of the CPSU Central Committee, in the CPSU Central Committee. In the course of the conversation, which proceeded in an atmosphere of fraternal friendship, an exchange of opinions took place indicating the coincidence of the two parties'

[1] *Pravda*, 3 Sept. 1965 (*CDSP*, 22 Sept. 1965, p. 27).

views on questions of the world Communist movement and the national-liberation movement. . . . The representatives of the two parties declared their support for the struggle of the Dominican people in defense of their legitimate right of independently deciding their own destiny and noted that the armed intervention of the American imperialists is a hopeless attempt to restrain the upsurge of the liberation movement in Latin America. The two sides expressed ardent solidarity with the people of revolutionary Cuba, who are building socialism. . . .

The Bolivian CP delegation emphasized that this solidarity contributes to the strengthening of the revolutionary struggle of the Bolivian people and is a concrete manifestation of the support rendered by the CPSU to national-liberation movements regardless of the path of development of the revolution, which is determined by each party on the basis of the situation obtaining in the country in question.

The representatives of the CPSU and the CPB reaffirmed their loyalty to the line of the Communist movement collectively worked out at the 1957 and 1960 Conferences and unanimously emphasized the urgent necessity of an active struggle for strengthening the unity of the international Communist movement.

5 Chile

96. Note from the Chilean Government to the Soviet Government breaking off relations, 21 October 1957[1] (*p. 35*)

The Government of Chile has reached the conviction that the events which have disturbed public peace in Chile of recent months have been caused by the instigations of international Communism acting directly through Chilean groups of like nature. These instigations stem from a whole system of political action and international penetration directed from the USSR.

This conviction, together with the inescapable obligation of maintaining public order and the rule of democratic institutions which the Chilean people has freely embraced do not allow my Government to continue maintaining relations with a country which has inspired such grave blows against the political independence of the Republic and has endangered the very life of the nation.

It is therefore my duty to inform your Excellency that, from this date, the Government of Chile considers her diplomatic and consular relations with the USSR to be severed.

[1] *El Mercurio* (Santiago), 29 Oct. 1947.

97. Letter from the Chilean representative to the UN Secretary-General complaining against Soviet intervention in Czechoslovakia and proposing that the Czechoslovak representative should be heard by the Security Council, March 1948:[1] excerpts (*p. 35*)

I have the honour, on behalf of Chile, which I represent before the United Nations, on personal and direct instructions from the President of the Republic, to request you to refer the question raised by the permanent representative of Czechoslovakia to the Security Council. . . .

Chile cannot remain indifferent before the events described by the representative of Czechoslovakia. No country which is a Member of the United Nations, however small or however remote from the theatre of events in question, can evade the responsibilities of solidarity deriving from the Charter. . . .

But there is another moral reason which leads my Government to sponsor the Czechoslovak delegate's request that the country's case should be investigated and considered. In October last Chile was obliged to sever diplomatic relations with the Union of Soviet Socialist Republics and with Yugoslavia, because those countries were interfering in her internal affairs (trying to disrupt and hamper production of the basic raw materials such as copper and nitrates, which Chile exports to friendly countries) through the illegal revolutionary action of a national group working in their interest. The objects of this action, which coincide completely with those of her intervention in Czechoslovakia, demonstrate the extent and nature of the Union of Soviet Socialist Republic's plans and prove that neither geographical situation nor greater or lesser degrees of strength or size, or a country's love of peace or indifference to it, are factors which can have any influence in enabling a country to avoid being involved in a conflict such as a great power like the Union of Soviet Socialist Republics might undertake.

98. The Security Council debate on the Chilean proposal, 17–22 March 1948:[2] excerpts (*p. 35*)

Mr Gromyko (USSR). I am instructed by the Government of the USSR to object categorically to the Chilean communication being placed on the Security Council's agenda. That communication is nothing other than a pure invention which unmistakably betrays both its own authors and their backers, whose orders they subserviently obey.

Everyone understands that we are not concerned here with Chile or the ostensible 'anxiety' felt by the clique now in power in Chile for the maintenance of peace. The personal opinion of that clique is of little interest to us, since strictly speaking, it has no opinion of its own in the sphere of international politics. That is borne out by a number of facts. It is simply a puppet controlled, as we all know, by influential foreign circles, who feel that it is sometimes advantageous to act through their lackeys rather than directly. . . .

[1] S/694, *SCOR*, 3rd yr., suppl. for Mar. 1948, pp. 32–3.
[2] Ibid., 3rd yr., pt. 1, Jan.–Mar. 1948, pp. 90, 95–6, 100, 196, 208–9, 255–60.

Mr López (Colombia). . . . . I have just read over the letter of the representative of Chile, and I fail to find anything in it that warrants the very aggressive, and I should say, unbecoming, terms in which Mr Gromyko has seen fit to refer to Chile and to the document it submitted. He said it was an 'unclean' document. Furthermore, he did not hesitate to call Chile a 'lackey' of some other Power.

I believe it is high time that somebody should question the propriety of using this kind of language when referring to some of the non-permanent members of the Security Council or to other Members of this Organization, and I, for one, should like to register my protest against that kind of language in the Security Council. . . .

Mr Gromyko. I do not intend to take lessons in language from the representative of Colombia . . . or anybody else. I would add that I did not and do not intend to say things that are agreeable to the authors of that dirty and slanderous document, the so-called Chilean document, or to those who stand behind them. . . .

[By 9 votes to 2 the Council accepted the Chilean proposal and Mr Papanek, the Czechoslovak representative, addressed the Council.]

Mr Tarasenko (Ukrainian Soviet Socialist Republic). Despite a number of objections the Chilean letter has come before the Security Council for discussion. Willy nilly we are obliged to turn our attention to this extraordinarily dirty and calumnious document.

Mr Santa Cruz (Chile). Since I have been invited to sit on the Council in accordance with Article 31 of the Charter, I think that I have the right to the protection enjoyed by all the members of this Council against insolent language and insults.

I therefore request formally to be informed in what manner the Council intends to protect my country's right, and my right as a representative to the United Nations. Or else let us be told clearly if we are to be given free rein in our choice of adjectives in expressing our opinions concerning certain countries, their leaders and their representatives. I should not be at any loss for adjectives nor do I lack the desire to use them.

Mr Gromyko. The Chilean representative should be asked not to interrupt. . . . All the assertions that the Government of Chile, in taking this step, has been guided by noble motives for the maintenance of peace completely lack foundation and mislead only people who are naive and inexperienced in politics.

One might say that no attention should be paid to this Chilean concoction, since there is no difficulty in understanding its intention. But such a conclusion would not be quite correct, as the problem lies not in Chile but in those influential foreign circles without whose encouragement the present ruling clique in Chile could not have raised the question.

It is clear to everyone acquainted with some of the latest facts concerning the foreign policy of the present Chilean Government that it has no foreign policy of its own—nor does it lack only a foreign policy—and that this clique is playing the role of a puppet of the financial and industrial kings of Wall Street, who hold in their grip all the principal levers of Chilean economy and completely control her domestic and foreign policies. What that leads to is also known. It leads to the enrichment, at the expense of the Chilean people, of the American monopolies, accustomed to profiteering on the sweat and blood of their peoples. . . .

. . . The stain of disgrace which will fall upon Chile because of the guilt of her present venal rulers will not be washed out for a long time to come. There can be no doubt that the working people of Chile, like every honest man in the world, will feel only disgust for the actions of the present Chilean rulers. The Chilean people know that only a few individuals who have sold their skins to the foreign masters can profit from such actions and that the people themselves will gain nothing, because the relations between Chile and those who actually hold in their grip economic and political control over that country are governed by the law of the jungle. . . .

Mr Santa Cruz (Chile). . . . I wish to say first of all that in sponsoring the accusation of the permanent representative of Czechoslovakia we were well aware that we should bring upon ourselves the ire of the Union of Soviet Socialist Republics, and we therefore carefully weighed the step we were about to take. The Union of Socialist Soviet Republics has come to regard the United Nations merely as a great loudspeaker through which to broadcast propaganda to the whole world and as a solid platform from which to thunder forth, in safety, against democracy. A most cold-blooded cynicism has been displayed with absolute disregard for truth, elemental standards of decency, and the interests of this Organization. It was consequently logical to expect the USSR to react with surprise at a small nation venturing to remind the United Nations that the Organization had been established to defend peace in an effective manner; to intervene in the aggression of one country against another; to defend the dignity and worth of the human person, democratic forms of government, the equality of nations large and small, and respect for the obligations arising from treaties and other sources of international law. . . . We therefore knew that our action would seem intolerable to a brazen aggressor, unfitted by tradition and by the congenital incapacity of the regime under which it is living to maintain an appearance of democratic discussion and a democratic attitude even in this Organization. . . .

This is not the first time that the representatives of the USSR have called the Latin American countries puppets of the United States. Others have previously been so characterized, and it is now our turn.

In addition to the usual amount of deliberate bad faith contained in this statement, it may also have been prompted by that total misconception of human and national conduct which inevitably affects the thinking of persons born and reared with a limited view of the world and humanity, who are absolutely sealed off from outside influence and are imbued with a de-humanized mistrust of any person who thinks and acts freely.

The idea behind the Inter-American system must appear as a legend or fable to the representatives of the USSR who are accustomed to see their own Government enslaving all the small countries on its borders. A Government that has made bad faith its principal rule of conduct in international relations cannot possibly comprehend the existence of twenty independent republics,

15

with populations varying between one million and 45 million inhabitants, living together with the richest and most powerful country in the world in an international system of free determination and democratic discussion of common problems, and subject to a judicial system which is an example to the world. . . .

. . . We needed no outside encouragement whatsoever to feel deeply concerned over the Czechoslovak question or to use our limited means for calling the attention of the world to the great danger threatening all the free peoples of the world, especially all small countries. Despite our distant geographical position, we had the misfortune to suffer in our own flesh an attempt to carry out this gigantic and cunning plan for world domination and the destruction of western civilization, undertaken by the Union of Soviet Socialist Republics assisted by its fifth columns—the Communist Parties. . . .

Just as the Government of the Union of Soviet Socialist Republics changed its colours during the fight against Fascism and proclaimed its intention of pursuing a common aim with the democratic countries, so also did the Chilean Communist Party, from 1938 on, proceed to conform to the universal instructions and to evidence a willingness to collaborate with the democratic parties. The Third International announced its dissolution in order to tranquilize the democracies. . . . The Communist Party in Chile agreed to join the democratic parties in a government the programme of which included these same principles and also the principles of continental brotherhood and friendship towards all the peoples of the earth. . . .

The Government had not been in office six months when the President of the Republic became convinced that the Communist Party had no interest whatever in collaborating to solve the serious economic and social problems resulting from the war. Just as in France and just as in the tragic example of Czechoslovakia, so eloquently expounded by Mr Papanek, the Communist Party in Chile had entered the Government only to use it as a means of strengthening the international position of Soviet Russia. Thus, there was once more demonstrated how absolutely incompatible it is for democracy to join with elements seeking only its destruction and following orders from abroad. The orders in this case were to eliminate every possibility of economic collaboration with the United States, even at the sacrifice of the vital interests of the country. The Communist ministers were accordingly forced out of the Government, and very shortly, just as was the case in France, a wave of revolutionary strikes flared up in the mining and industrial centres where the trade unions were controlled by the Communist Party. All of this culminated in a revolutionary strike in the coal mines, vital centres where the Communist Party had gained absolute domination due to a relentless trade union dictatorship. Even though the Government succeeded in having the economic conditions of the workers improved, the strike continued. To the amazement of the entire country, it was then shown that there existed a far-reaching plan for revolution and sabotage, a plan directed and fostered by the embassies of the Union of Soviet Socialist Republics and of Yugoslavia, and by agents planted in the diplomatic service of their country who served the group which seized power in Czechoslovakia. The principal objectives of this plan—which was merely part of the vast world wide plan—were to paralyse the national economic life by immobilizing transportation and by obstructing exports of copper and nitrates, which account for 90 per cent of our foreign exchange. All of this was intended to force the Communist Party back into the Government, this time in key positions, in order to prevent shipment to the United States of basic products such as copper, iron and nitrates, in the case of a possible war with the Union of Socialist Soviet Republics. The same objective and the same methods were employed by the French Communist Party two or three months later with an identical lack of success, but unfortunately, they were successful in Czechoslovakia owing to the direct assistance of the Union of Socialist Soviet Republics. The situation had become so serious that if the Government had not acted with extreme dispatch, we should have seen in that far-off corner of Latin America a dramatic prefigurement of the tragedy which took place in Czechoslovakia.

99. Statement by A. P. Kirilenko, member of the CPSU Presidium and delegate to the 13th Chilean CP Congress, on fraternal relations between the two Communist Parties, October 1965:[1] excerpts (*p. 36*)

... Between the Communist Party of the Soviet Union and the Communist Party of Chile [Comrade Kirilenko said] truly fraternal relations have developed over the course of decades, based on the principles of the Marxist-Leninist teaching which guides us, on the common ideals of the world proletariat, on fraternal revolutionary solidarity and at the same time on complete noninterference in one another's domestic affairs. We wish the Chilean Communists success in implementing the important decisions adopted by the 13th Congress of the Communist Party of Chile. ...

100. 'Pravda' article disclaiming responsibility for Chile's labour troubles, March 1966:[2] excerpts (*p. 36*)

... The reactionary press and radio of Chile, in justifying the reprisals, turns to the most ridiculous falsehoods. Such as, for example, that it is possible to find references to the connection alleged to exist between the strikes in the copper mines and the decisions of the Havana Conference of the Solidarity of the Peoples of the Three Continents. ... All these false arguments have only one aim—to lay a smoke-screen of a slanderous campaign against the progressive forces, and to try to lay the blame on them for the sad events. ...

These tragic events have deepened the crisis which the Christian Democrat Party of Chile is undergoing. ...

Chile's true friends cannot but regret the situation which is coming about in the country. They were pleased from the bottom of their hearts at the prospects which were opened up by the reforms proposed by the Frei Government and rejoiced at Chile's independent foreign policy. The efforts of reactionary forces to deflect Chile from these policies cannot but harm the national interest of the country.

[1] *Pravda*, 19 Oct. 1965 (*CDSP*, 10 Nov. 1965, p. 27).
[2] By Borovsky, *Pravda*, 17 Mar. 1966.

101. Statement at press conference by Ambassador Anikin on the development of Chilean-Soviet relations, 29 November 1967:[1] **excerpts** (*p. 36*)

Ambassador Aleksandr Anikin yesterday held a press conference to mark the third anniversary of the re-establishment of diplomatic relations between Chile and the Soviet Union.

'In a few words', said Anikin, 'I can say that we are pleased with the state of Soviet-Chilean relations and with their rhythm of development. Our collaboration is based on the principles of equality, mutual respect, and non-intervention in internal affairs. I should like to make special mention of the favourable conditions in which the Soviet Embassy in Santiago has been working. We have succeeded in exchanging opinions with Chilean statesmen regarding the main international problems and Soviet-Chilean relations. We have noted with satisfaction, for example, that the Chilean delegation actively supported the Soviet proposal at the 20th General Assembly of the United Nations for non-intervention in the internal affairs of states.'

Anikin stressed the important role played by the interchange of parliamentary delegations, the visit of members of the Chilean Government to the USSR, and the elaboration of three agreements: on trade, on the supply of Soviet machinery and equipment, and on technical and economic assistance.

Further to the above, Anikin pointed out that the total envisaged in the agreements amounted to $42 million. 'There is the possibility', he said, 'of building a copper rolling plant with an annual capacity of 60,000 tons and a plant for lubricants, and for the passing on of experience in the exploitation of molibdenum.'

The credits extended to Chile by the USSR carry a 3–3½ per cent rate of interest per annum, as against the 6–7 per cent which is general for international credits. Furthermore, one clause in the agreements includes a provision which is unusual in Soviet agreements: the USSR undertakes that 30 per cent of its purchases will be of articles manufactured in Chile. A plant for prefabricated houses is also under study. . . .

'If Chile wants technicians, they will come', he said. 'For the moment, it is only a question of projects. But the USSR has 30,000 technicians working in developing countries.'

The agreements with Chile have been mostly concluded through state organizations.

Anikin observed with pleasure that in the last two years 1,000 Chileans visited the USSR, whilst 500 Soviet citizens came to Chile, most of them members of artistic ensembles. He underlined the scientific collaboration between the Soviet Academy of Sciences and the University of Chile, and the work carried out by Soviet astronomers on Cerro Calán and the setting up of the modern observatory on Cerro El Roble.

The Ambassador said that Chilean artists in the Soviet Union met with the same warm applause as Soviet artists in Chile. He announced that the great

[1] *El Siglo* (Santiago), 29 Nov. 1967.

poet Yevgeny Yevtushenko and a Georgian group would shortly arrive on a visit. He stressed the agreement for pairing the cities of Valparaiso and Novorossiisk and Temuco and Stavropol.

He added that 200 young Chileans were studying at the Patrice Lumumba University, with scholarships awarded by the Chilean-Soviet Cultural Institute, and that the USSR would be very pleased to conclude an intergovernmental agreement for cultural and scientific collaboration which would open up new possibilities of interchange.

The Soviet Ambassador said that in the three years he had been in Chile, 'he had come to feel a perfect Chilean', and that 'he did not know which part of the country was the most beautiful, for he knew it all from the northern desert to Patagonia'. He said that in all his travels through Chile he had never encountered any difficulty and had everywhere been warmly received.

'The doors of the USSR are open to everyone, and In-tourist is represented in the Chilean travel agencies', he said. 'Men of the Right and of the Left have been made equally welcome.'

Anikin stated that the delays in implementing the agreements were due to the complexity of the situation and to inexperience, but that in every case the solutions most favourable to Chile were being sought. . . .

The Ambassador remarked that there were twenty-five officials employed at the Embassy, plus their wives and children, and in addition that there were three correspondents and two professors of language, but that the number of the latter would be increased at the request of the cultural organizations.

'Above all', concluded Anikin, 'we are interested in developing and broadening our commercial and cultural relations and we believe that there will be interest in this on the Chilean side too.'

6 *Colombia*

102. Tass denial of Soviet involvement in the Bogotá riots, April 1948[1] (*p. 37*)

Referring to reports from Bogotá, the New York radio and the BBC have for the last two days been spreading reports that the Colombian Government has announced the rupture of diplomatic relations with the Soviet Union. The same announcement was repeated by a representative of the United States State Department in Washington. Moreover, rumours are being released alleging that the events of the last few days in Colombia are the result of the

[1] Communiqué of 14 Apr. 1948.

activity of Communist agents, including 'two Soviet' agents or, according to another report, 'two Russians'.

According to information received by Tass, the Ministry of Foreign Affairs of the USSR has been unable for the last few days to establish contact with the Soviet Mission in Bogotá, from which no answers to inquiries from Moscow have been coming in for several days now.

Tass is authorized to state that any rumours about the participation of any 'Soviet' or 'Russian' agents in events in Bogotá are a ridiculous fabrication and are being circulated for aims hostile to the Soviet Union.

103. Soviet protest to the Colombian Government, 3 May 1948[1] (*p. 37*)

As reported on April 14 by the Soviet Press, communications between the Soviet Legation in Colombia and the Foreign Ministry of the USSR were interrupted. It was only on April 21 that, for the first time after the interruption of communications, a report was received from the USSR chargé d'affaires in Colombia stating that on April 12 an armed raid had been made on a house in which members of the Soviet Legation resided in Bogotá.

In this connection, Mr E. Fedin, USSR chargé d'affaires in Colombia, was instructed to address the following statement to the Colombian Foreign Minister Zuleta:

'In the evening of April 12, an armed raid was made on the house occupied by the Third Secretary and other officials of the USSR Legation in Colombia. Officials of the Mission were searched and their documents, money and personal property were seized and carried away by the persons who participated in the raid.

'The Soviet Government learned of this atrocious fact only 10 days later, since from April 10–21 communications between the Soviet Legation and the Foreign Ministry of the USSR were interrupted by the Colombian side.

'There is no doubt that the above-mentioned criminal act against Soviet diplomatic representatives in the capital of Colombia, Bogotá, is the result of the violent campaign against the Soviet Union which is being conducted in Colombia with the direct connivance of the Colombian authorities, who even facilitated the dissemination of an obviously fabricated and provocative report alleging that 'Soviet agents' or 'Russian agents' had participated in the recent events in Colombia.

'The Soviet Government lodges a protest with the Colombian Government against the deliberate deprivation of the USSR Bogotá Legation's communication with Moscow and against the open encroachment on the immunity of Soviet diplomatic representatives.

'The Soviet Government insists on an investigation of the circumstances of the raid on the house of members of the Legation, on the restoration of the stolen documents, valuables and property of members of the Legation and on the bringing of the culprits of these criminal actions to strict account.'

---

[1] *Soviet Monitor*, 3 May 1948.

104. 'Izvestiya' on attempts to stimulate trade relations,
1 March 1964:¹ excerpts (*p. 37*)

... Fresh new winds are now blowing over Colombia. There is much talk
here that Colombia's politics needs new horizons, and there is talk of the
need for restoring diplomatic relations with the Soviet Union. . . .

The Soviet Union has an irresistible attraction for the business world of
Colombia as a trade partner. It seems that the example of Brazil, which has
set up broad and constantly growing, mutually advantageous trade with the
USSR has become contagious. Some people here are already beginning to act
without waiting for the official establishment of economic relations with the
Soviet Union. A new company has just been formed in Bogota. It includes
three energetic local entrepreneurs who, considering the situation of the
country, are brazen. They began trading with the Soviet Union at their own
risk and have already concluded the first bargains: We shall receive the famous
Colombian coffee and they expect GAZ-69 trucks. . . .

105. The Soviet attitude towards the Colombian guerrillas:
Aleksandr Lebedev's view of the Communist Youth Movement,
October 1966:² excerpt (*p. 38*)

The leader of the Communist Youth Movement in the USSR, Aleksandr
Lebedev, . . . denied that the Communist Party in his country had sent a
greeting to the guerrillas or political leaders in Colombia, and said that the
only message sent conveyed greetings to those attending the Congress of
Colombian Communist Youth which is now meeting.

The young Communist leader expressed surprise at the report which appeared
last night in *El Vespertino* to the effect that the party representing his country
is giving moral support to the Colombian guerrillas.

'My people, my organization, and Soviet young people', he said, 'have
the greatest sympathy for all national-liberation movements in the world. It
is natural that we should extend our greatest sympathy to the countries which
are fighting for social progress, and in this sense we support their social struggle,
morally and politically.

'This is our position in principle. To us, it is completely obvious that each
people is defending its existence on the basis of the conditions prevailing in
each country, and there is no question but that each people can and should
define this struggle. This is a matter', he added, 'which is the responsibility of
each separate people, and I reiterate once again that our position in regard to
any such problem is based on respect for countries—is based on non-interference. Any movement of liberation struggle is a national matter. That we
sympathize with it is another thing, which we do not conceal. But we insist,
in this matter, on the principle of non-intervention.'

Moreover, Aleksandr Lebedev stated that 'we have never proclaimed the
principle of exporting revolution'.

¹ *CDSP*, 25 Mar. 1964, p. 30.   ² *El Espectador* (Bogotá), 15 Oct. 1966.

106. Cuban criticism of the Soviet attitude to Colombia: Castro's closing speech to the Latin American Solidarity Organization, 10 August 1967:[1] excerpts (*p. 37*)

With regard to our position criticizing the problem of financial and technical assistance to the Latin American oligarchies. . . .

Our position does not refer to trade. It has never related to trade. And this position of ours is known to the Soviets. They are points of view which we have expressed to them.

We are referring to the problem of financial and technical aid by any Socialist state to those countries. These two things are not to be confused, and should not be confused. Even some Socialist states went so far as to offer loans in dollars to Señor Lleras Restrepo since he had got into difficulties with the International Monetary Fund. And we asked ourselves: how could this be? It is absurd! Dollar loans to an oligarchic Government which is repressing the guerrillas—which is persecuting and murdering guerrillas! And war is waged amongst other things, by means of money. Above all, the oligarchs have nothing else for waging war save the money with which to pay mercenary soldiers.

To us this seems absurd. Everything which implies financial and technical aid to any of the countries which are repressing the revolutionary movement —countries which are accomplices of the imperialists against Cuba—we condemn. . . .

If internationalism exists, if solidarity is a word worthy of utterance, the least we can expect from any state of the Socialist camp is that it should not lend financial or technical assistance to any of these Governments.

107. Approval of Soviet policy by the Colombian CP at the Tricontinental Conference, Havana, January 1968[2] (*p. 37*)

1. In the third committee of this conference a proposed resolution[3] was presented condemning the trade relations of the Socialist camp with Latin American countries. Our delegation opposes such a proposal for the following reasons:

(*a*) For many years now US imperialism has maintained a strict monopoly over the commercial life of our country, preventing in fact trade with the Socialist countries.

(*b*) The opening of Colombian trade with Socialist countries reduces the total dependence which we now have on US imperialism, principal enemy of our people, and weakens the dominion which the Yankee monopolies hold over the country to an all-inclusive extent.

(*c*) Colombia's trade with Socialist countries is no Mephistophelian manoeuvre agreed upon between imperialism and the Socialist countries, as some try to picture it, but the product of real contradictions within Colombian

[1] *Granma*, 10 Aug. 1967.
[2] *Documentos políticos* (Colombian CP bi-monthly), Jan. 1968.
[3] The resolution referred to has not been made public.

society. In Colombia it is precisely the most reactionary forces which register opposition to such relations under the pretext of the 'Communist peril'.

(*d*) The solution of the Colombian organizational problem will not be achieved except by means of the assumption of power which in our country cannot be attained except through violent means, by the use of force. But by reducing the economic power of US imperialism through economic competition the Socialist camp contributes to the struggle which we anti-imperialist militants are letting loose in the country.

2. For all these reasons our representatives, the delegation of the PCC and the FARC,[1] are directly opposed to such a proposed resolution. And the Colombian delegation which, had it been integrated would have been able to vote, was unable to integrate itself, elect a president and, for the reasons exposed in our statement, was unable to vote for such a proposal.

108. Broadcast by Carlos Lleras Restrepo on the resumption of diplomatic relations with the USSR, 24 January 1968:[2] excerpt (*p. 38*)

Our decision is the culmination of a process. We have sent commercial missions to the Soviet Union and received Soviet commercial missions in Colombia, we have also visited other Socialist countries in an effort to broaden our relations. We must realize that we live in a world made up of not just the Western countries alone, with which we naturally have closer connections. This link, however, cannot make us shut our eyes to the fact that there is yet another part of the world, even though that other part may have adopted political and economic systems different from those we defend and shall continue to defend and uphold in our country.

Everyone accepts the convenience of commercial relations, not because those commercial relations may mean the solution to Colombia's problems. . . . I myself pointed out in a book I wrote on international trade that I did not consider trade with the Socialist nations a definite panacea, although for many years, whilst participating in international meetings and in technical seminars on international trade such as those held to prepare the Geneva conference, my opinions supporting the maintenance and intensification of commercial relations with Socialist nations and favouring efforts to increase such trade manyfold were never liked. Furthermore, my administration did not invent those relations with Socialist nations. Previous governments made bilateral commercial compensation agreements, including agreements with Russia, with reciprocal credits. It is just that those agreements were not managed actively. Besides, it is somewhat abnormal for commercial agreements to be governed by agreements signed by the Coffee Federation or the Bank of the Republic and for the government which has to promote trade to remain aloof, pretending to be ignorant that bodies in which its officials and employees are participating are making agreements with a nation. I believe that it is more normal for us to have a diplomatic representation that can give more

---

[1] *Fuerzas Armadas Revolucionarias Colombianas.*
[2] Verbatim monitoring of broadcast of 24 Jan. 1968; shortened version in *El Espectador* (Bogotá), 25 Jan. 1968.

unity and efficiency to the expansion of our trade. However, this has no political significance. I have always supported a thesis which, I believe, also has the traditional support of the country. It is that the fact of maintaining diplomatic relations does not mean that one agrees with either the political or the economic systems of that nation, nor that one is inclined to adopt them or prefers them to others. I believe that one has to coexist in the world with all systems without this meaning that one agrees with or approves of them. . . .

We have faith—at least I have much faith—in my ideas. I am not afraid to have them compared with other systems, nor do I believe, as I said in my message to Congress last year, that customs houses can be established for ideas. . . . Furthermore, the fact that Communist propaganda is made does not depend on whether diplomatic relations exist or not. Communist magazines now come into Colombia, Communist propaganda is made, there are scholarships for Colombian students in Russian universities and in those other East European nations. Fortunately, Colombia has not also established its iron curtain to prevent people from entering and leaving. It is managing its system democratically, and this will not change course because of the existence of a diplomatic mission.

In speaking with the Russian mission that was studying trade with Colombia, I was very emphatic in stating that Colombia wanted to strengthen her relations with the Socialist nations on the basis of mutual respect, that agents of foreign nations must abstain from all political activity, as they should abstain; and we resumed relations on that basis.

109. Statement by the Colombian CP CC on the renewal of diplomatic relations: Tass report of 26 January 1968[1] (*p. 38*)

Twenty years after the scandalous rupture of relations provoked by the Ospina Pérez regime, under the insolent pressure of the Yankee imperialists, the Government has resumed diplomatic relations with the Soviet Union at the request of large sectors of the nation.

The renewal of Colombia's diplomatic relations with the Soviet Union, this time at the ambassadorial level, is an important step which has been well received by numerous social and political groups throughout the country. Those who favour the Government's decision are in the majority, an eloquent contrast to the isolated individuals who have expressed their anachronistic conformity with outworn anti-Communist arguments.

Renewing diplomatic relations with the Soviet Union will benefit the vital interests of Colombia, whose development has been held back and distorted by United States monopolies which increasingly impose unfair trade agreements upon us. And while they loot our natural riches and drain the physical energies of our people they export more and more profits, to the detriment of our national economy.

Normal relations with the Soviet Union could mean Colombia's key step to progress as commercial, cultural, and scientific exchanges between the countries increase.

[1] *El Siglo* (Santiago), 27 Jan. 1968.

Nevertheless, it must be borne in mind that although relations with the Soviet Union and other Socialist countries may stimulate national forces interested in the country's independent development, they will not be able to substitute the urgent need for basic changes in Colombia's social and economic structures. These inevitable historic changes can occur only through courageous popular struggles, through the worker-peasant alliance, and through the united action of the revolutionary forces.

7 Cuba (Pre-Castro)

110. Cuban note of protest to the Soviet Legation in Havana, 3 March 1949[1] (*p. 36*)

The Ministry of State present their compliments to the Soviet Legation and have the honour to express the following points:

1. The Government is profoundly disturbed by the unprecedented, reiterated, and simultaneous public statements made by the leaders of some minority groups in different countries, whose prime object is the destruction of the world democratic system, declaring what the attitude of those minority groups will be in the event of war.

2. This association of groups disloyal to their respective countries, and which by their conduct separate themselves from the democratic group of nations, undoubtedly follows an international plan tending to disturb international peace.

3. The imminent seriousness of this joint mobilization, which seeks to emphasize the potential strength of these disruptive forces, must necessarily arouse the defensive and energetic response of all nations who are members of the United Nations Organization and the Organization of American States in joint defence of the postulates and sacred principles contained in their respective charters.

4. The resulting situation is unacceptable to all democratic Governments, who are obliged to avoid and prevent by every means, even the most serious, this propaganda and these activities, whatever their real origin or pretext, from contributing to create a state of moral confusion as a first step in a perfectly thought-out and sinister plan.

5. The Legation of the Soviet Union does not limit itself to natural interchange of cultural ideas and commercial propaganda by means of periodic bulletins and other activities, but has on certain occasions, under the protection

[1] Havana press, 10 Mar. 1949.

of the liberties offered by our democratic regime and certainly in abuse of those liberties, reached the point of disseminating ideologies harmful to our own regime, and even reproducing pamphlets insulting certain high personages, in such a way that retaliation is ruled out, since the system of government obtaining in the Soviet Union prevents the free expression of thought.

6. This situation cannot go on, and the Government is obliged to take strong measures to prevent its continuation, which is now openly aggressive; nor can it permit groups subject to totalitarian ideas and to foreign political orders to find either direct or indirect support in diplomatic missions which enjoy privileges and immunities so long as they do not infringe the democratic principles of the states to which they are accredited. . . .

111. Speech by Blas Roca, Secretary-General of the Cuban CP, on the Communists' attitude to the USSR, 21 December 1949:[1] excerpts (*p. 36*)

The seventieth birthday of Stalin is a festival celebrated throughout the world wherever men have their habitation, from the frozen polar regions to the burning tropic equatorial zones. . . . In our little country, too, in our beloved Cuba, we celebrate the festival, we make our modest contribution, and join in this universal homage to Stalin. In doing so, we know that we not only express the feelings and conscience of the Communists, militants, and members of our *Partido Socialista Popular*, but we also embody and represent the feelings of the toiling masses, the anti-imperialists, in a word, of the democrats of the Cuban people.

The Cuban people must feel affection and gratitude towards Stalin for the extraordinary contribution he made to the recent war to vanquish our enemies, the worst enemies of mankind, the powers of the Nazi-Fascist-Japanese axis. . . .

Every Cuban who loves liberty, hates Fascist slavery, loves his country and people, must feel admiration and gratitude for Stalin; they must feel as their own this homage we pay him today.

The Cuban people must feel affection and gratitude towards Stalin for his struggle for peace, for what the Soviet Union represents and does as the bulwark of the peoples in the struggle to prevent the conflagration of a new world war. . . .

We feel for Stalin profound admiration, respect, and affection.

We see in Stalin the purest, fullest incarnation of our ideals and aspirations.

We see in Stalin the leader of valour and genius of the working class, the wise master, staunch and sagacious guide, in whose word we can always trust and through whose guidance we can always find the sure way to struggle and triumph. . . .

Today, one cannot be a Communist without being a Stalinist, for Stalin is the greatest Communist of the present day. . . . We are proud to be called Stalinists, and only sorry not to be so more fully; we are only sorry not to

[1] *Fundamentos* (Havana), no. 95, Feb. 1950.

be good enough Communists, good enough Marxist-Leninists, to deserve with full justification that honourable title. . . .

In the greetings sent by our *Partido Socialista Popular* to Comrade Stalin there are three short sentences which sum up what the great leader means to us:

His life inspires us:
His example strengthens us:
His teachings guide us.

We would like our life to be like his, our actions like his actions, and our whole activity the correct application of his teaching.

112. Speech by Juan Marinello to the 6th Assembly of the PSP, Havana, February 1950:[1] excerpt (*p. 36*)

We salute the Soviet Union on the Day of the Red Army with profound Cuban love. There is no contradiction or paradox in saying that our devotion to the Soviet Union stems from our deep sense of being Cubans. For we Cubans want what is best for Cuba, and Cuba can only attain what is best by way of peace. And the Soviet Union is the pure and powerful vanguard of the universal movement for peace. For we want a free and happy Cuba, and this she can only be if her sovereignty and political development are respected, as this is understood, proclaimed, and practised by the Soviet Union. For we want a Cuba fraternally united to all peoples, and not subservient to the interests of the great power which exploits her. We want a Cuba free of imperialist exploitation, as the Soviet Union wants every people to be free. We want, in short, a Socialist Cuba, without acts of oppression to excite her ingratitude or acts of discrimination to provoke her wrath; a Cuba in friendship and brotherhood with the Soviet Union.

113. Soviet press statement on breaking off relations with Cuba, March 1952[2] (*p. 37*)

On 21 March 1952 the Cuban authorities grossly violated the generally accepted norms of diplomatic relations between countries, forbade the entry into Cuba of Soviet diplomatic couriers who had arrived with the diplomatic pouch for the Soviet Legation in Havana. With the knowledge and on the instructions of the Government of Cuba, the Cuban authorities prevented the chargé d'affaires of the Soviet Union in Cuba from meeting the diplomatic couriers at the airport on arrival, and the diplomatic couriers, in spite of the fact that they had visas for entry into Cuba, were told to leave the country at once.

On 3 April 1952 Comrade Fomin, chargé d'affaires of the Soviet Union in Cuba, called on the Cuban Vice-Minister of Foreign Affairs and, on instructions from the Soviet Government, handed him the following note:

'The Legation of the Soviet Union in Cuba, on instructions of the Soviet Government, considers it necessary to state the following:

'In view of the fact that on 21 March of this year the Cuban Government

[1] *Fundamentos*, no. 97, Apr. 1950.　　[2] All Moscow papers, 5 Apr. 1952.

refused to allow diplomatic couriers of the Soviet Union to enter Cuba and thereby deprived the Legation of the Soviet Union in Cuba of normal diplomatic contact with the Government of the Soviet Union, in violation of generally accepted diplomatic norms, the Soviet Government is withdrawing the chargé d'affaires of the Soviet Union in Cuba and terminating relations with the Cuban Government.'

114. A Soviet view of Cuba: article by Yu. Yartsev in the 'Literaturnaya Gazeta', 8 April 1952 (*p. 37*)

Let us recall O. Henry's well-known pamphlet 'Cabbages and Kings'. In the banana republic of Ancuria a 'revolution' has just taken place. In this connection two emissaries of the American Vesuvius company, which domineers there, exchange impressions:

'How fine it is in our time', says the first one enthusiastically, obviously the less experienced, 'to be able to overthrow presidents and to put others in their place according to one's own choice.'

'Oh, it's a purely business operation', confidently remarks the other, who knows the ropes.

Such a lightning 'operation' was done recently in one day in the capital of the republic of Cuba, Havana. On 10 March, President Carlos Prío Socarrás yielded his place to General Fulgencio Batista i Zalvidar.

The reactionary Cuban newspaper *Diario de la Marina* observed knowingly that the coup 'was carried out in an organized fashion'. There was an obvious advantage on Batista's side. A certain officer of the American army in full-dress uniform was present in his headquarters in Campo Columbia, a suburb of Havana, on the morning when the question of the seizure of power was decided upon. Prío Socarrás, being sure, as his minions stated, that Washington 'knew what was going on', divested himself of his powers and the above-mentioned officer congratulated the conspirators on their success.

What is known about ex-President Carlos Prío Socarrás? His close personal contacts with gangsters, the assassinations of trade unionists, the savage persecutions of progressive organizations and, primarily, of the *Partido Socialista Popular* of Cuba, are well known. All this gave rise to especially sharp indignation in the masses of the Cuban people. Therefore it was decided for the time being to replace Prío Socarrás, who had been thoroughly compromised. Now, as is perfectly logical, he has turned up in the United States, in Florida, at the fashionable health resort of Miami—this refuge for idlers where he will have the chance to while away the time peacefully until his American masters consider him a suitable candidate for a routine coup.

Well, and what is known about General-President Fulgencio Batista? He is no newcomer to the political scene. His career began already in the years of the terrible dictatorship of Machado, an out-and-out American puppet. In 1933, heading the coup d'état, Batista himself seized power and was the *de facto* dictator of Cuba right up to 1944. The name of Batista also calls to mind the activity in Cuba of the American Ambassadors Wallace and Caffery who, though they were not military men, commanded this general at one time.

Finally, one must not pass over in silence such an eloquent fact in his biography as a trip in 1938 to the United States, where Batista established business relations with the Washington military and the Wall Street financiers.

And so one President has taken over the place of another. What, it may be asked, has changed? Cuba remains as before a colony of the American monopolists, and both Presidents, the old one and the new, are only obedient puppets in their hands. The boss pulls the string—there is a coup in Havana; he pulls again—there is another coup and the next President turns up. There is almost no difference between the Presidents—it is a question of a struggle inside the Cuban ruling clique.

It is characteristic that the day after the coup the *Wall Street Journal* stated: 'The reaction of the sugar industry may serve as the best pointer.' The fact is that Cuba is one gigantic sugar-cane plantation. Cuban sugar is exported. The true masters in the country are the American and mixed Cuban-American companies—the Cuban-American Sugar, the General Sugar Estates, the United Fruit Company, and others. They control over two-thirds of the output of the sugar factories, a substantial part of the arable lands, the electric-power stations, mines, and oil deposits. They own the Consolidated Railroads of Cuba and they do what they like in the Cuban National Bank as if it were their own pocket. Generally speaking, the sugar magnates in Cuba feel like the banana kings and rubber princes described by O. Henry.

The sugar kings hope that under the new American viceroy the number of strikes will be reduced and profits will increase still more. It is not surprising that their reaction was not long in coming and turned out to be favourable in the highest degree. The Association of Sugar Plantation Owners gave their support to the newly-made President. American business men, the *Wall Street Journal* authoritatively explained, consider that they are going to 'prosper under Batista'.

Washington officials and US newspapers are encouraging General Batista. They are extolling him to the skies and showering him with compliments. It was suddenly 'remembered' in the State Department that during his first period in office Batista gave a good account of himself in the eyes of the Yankees from the very best standpoint; he gave the Wall Street capitalists truly unrestricted opportunities for the investment of capital and wrought fiercer vengeance on the trade unions than other Cuban dictators.

The New York *Daily News* appealed to Batista to 'keep a tight grip on the Communists' and not allow a breakdown in supplies of sugar and rum to the USA.

The general chorus of instructions and congratulations to the new President was completed by a compliment from the former US Ambassador in Cuba, Braden, who is connected with the biggest Wall Street monopolies and who called Batista a 'strong man'. The Yankees, by the way, were followed by Franco; he was the first in Western Europe to recognize General Batista's regime.

The first steps of the 'strong man' showed that he will not lag behind the real powers that be. He is faithfully serving his Washington masters; after all, it depends on them how long Batista will remain in the role of dictator of Cuba.

He immediately promised them everything he could and everything that was demanded of him. First of all, he publicly guaranteed the 'fullest protection' for all old American capital investments in Cuba and also promised to throw the doors wide open to new ones. Then he dissolved parliament. Thirdly, he imposed a ban on strikes, to the great satisfaction of the sugar kings and the Yankee employers who are exploiting other branches of the Cuban economy. Finally, in a fit of sincere gratitude, to those who had again made him a splendidly functioning puppet, Batista announced that he would send troops to Korea 'if necessary'.

Cuba is a colony. It is not surprising that the institutions there are colonial too. They are indeed savage and outrageous to the last degree. The escapades of the rampant American supervisors from the sugar plantations set the model of behaviour for the local Cuban gentry. The followers of Prío Socarrás and Batista assiduously imitate the jargon and manners of those thugs. Moreover, the Cuban rulers set them in motion not only in the gangsterish company to which they are so accustomed, but also in those cases when they have to act, so to speak, on the international arena. You do not have to go far for examples.

Grossly flouting the commonly accepted norms of diplomatic relations between countries, the Cuban authorities, on 21 March 1952, forbade the entry into Cuba of Soviet diplomatic couriers who had arrived with the diplomatic mail for the Soviet Legation in Havana. Despite the Cuban entry visas possessed by the diplomatic couriers, they were asked to leave the country immediately and the chargé d'affaires of the Soviet Union, with the knowledge and on the instructions of the Cuban Government, was prevented from meeting them at the airport. In view of this the Soviet Government broke off diplomatic relations with the Government of Cuba.

Thus the new Cuban Government's act, hostile towards the Soviet Union, received its proper assessment.

This act is by no means unique in the chain of anti-Soviet provocations organized recently by the Cuban authorities and inspired by their sponsors. In this respect both Presidents, the former and the present one, are of the same calibre. Let us recall that in July last year an unexploded bomb was found in the garden of the Soviet Legation in Havana, thrown there by 'unknown terrorists'.

At the same time, in the summer of 1951, the Minister of the Interior, Lomberto Diaz, by way of developing the anti-Soviet campaign that had begun, delivered obviously provocative statements.

In February this year the Cuban Chief of Police Peras Alfonso, who is in the service of the American Embassy, sent out an anti-Soviet circular letter to all police administrations.

Such are these brazen provocations and wild fictions. In this connection it will be pertinent to point to some of the people who are behaving in Cuba as if they were in Anchuria, who are interfering shamelessly in its domestic affairs. Let us mention, for instance, the American Embassy official Anderson who was the organizer of the plot directed against the leaders of the *Partido Socialista Popular*, or John Bonds, also an official of the United States Embassy, who quite recently demanded of the Cuban supreme electoral tribunal, an official government organ, that it should give him 'information about the activity of Communists in Cuba', in other words, that it should communicate data about the political views of a specific section of the Cuban population. Moreover, the Yankees, apparently, imagine that all this is quite in order. Is it not they who are sovereign masters in this colony? This is what is happening in Cuba, which has fallen into the power of the 'Anchurian' dictators.

8 The Dominican Republic

115. Soviet insistence that sanctions against the Trujillo regime are a matter for the UN, not the OAS: letter from the First Deputy Minister for Foreign Affairs to the President of the Security Council, 5 September 1960[1] (*p. 42*)

As stated in document S/4476 dated 1 September 1960, the Organization of American States (OAS), at the Meeting of the Ministers of Foreign Affairs of the States members of the OAS held on 20 August 1960, adopted a resolution condemning the acts of aggression and intervention committed against the Republic of Venezuela by the anti-popular Trujillo regime in the Dominican Republic. The resolution provides for the application of enforcement action against this regime including the breaking of diplomatic relations of the member States of the OAS, and partial interruption of economic relations, with the Dominican Republic.

On the basis of Article 53 of the Charter of the United Nations, the Security Council should consider this question and endorse the decision of the Organization of American States, in that it is designed to remove the threat to peace and security created by the actions of the Dominican authorities. Article 53 of the Charter provides that the Security Council shall utilize 'regional arrangements or agencies for enforcement action under its authority' and that 'no enforcement action shall be taken under regional arrangements or by regional agencies without the authorization of the Security Council.'

In consideration of the foregoing I have the honour to request you, on behalf of the Soviet Government, immediately to convene a meeting of the Security Council for the purpose of considering the decision taken by the Organization of American States concerning the Dominican Republic and with a view to the speedy adoption by the Council of an appropriate resolution.

---

[1] S/4477, *SCOR*, 15th yr., suppl. for July, Aug., and Sept. 1960, pp. 134–5.

116. Statement by V. V. Kuznetsov in the Security Council,
9 September 1960:[1] **excerpts** (*p. 42*)

The representatives of some countries, in their statements before the Council, have argued that the measures taken by the Organization of American States against the Trujillo régime are not in the nature of enforcement action and consequently do not come within the scope of Article 53 of the Charter. Such arguments are completely untenable. . . .

. . . The United States representative—obviously in order to distract the Council's attention from the essence of the matter under consideration—made so bold as to attack the Soviet Union and the People's Republic of China by making the banal and outworn assertion to the effect that these Powers are supposedly interfering in the affairs of the American republics. If we are to speak of foreign interference in the affairs of the Latin American States, we must name precisely the United States as a Power which has been and still is flagrantly interfering in the affairs of those States and is threatening intervention in the countries which do not wish to subject themselves to the orders of the United States monopolies. . . .

. . . Finally, the United States representative has tried here, somewhat obscurely, to make it appear as though the USSR were taking advantage of the Security Council and had it in mind to veto some future resolution. Our aims are perfectly clear: we support and will continue to support the struggle of all peoples who are seeking to strengthen their independent existence. I shall not, however, conceal from the United States representative that by analogy with this case of the Dominican Republic, it would, of course, unquestionably be necessary, in certain other cases, for the same kind of discussion to be held and the same kind of decision adopted with respect to the aggressive policy pursued by the United States in regard to certain Latin American countries. In such cases, however, they apparently consider that they are the masters and that such decisions would not be permitted.

The 1965 crisis

117. Letter from the Soviet representative to the President of the
Security Council denouncing US intervention, 1 May 1965[2] (*p. 42*)

The world has witnessed another aggressive act of United States imperialism. This time the object of the armed intervention was a Latin American country—the Dominican Republic, where a reactionary junta which enjoyed the support of the United States has been deposed.

On 28 April 1965 the President of the United States of America, Mr Lyndon B. Johnson, ordered the landing of United States troops on the territory of

---

[1] *SCOR*, 15th yr., 894th mtg., pp. 11 & 14; 895th mtg., p. 3.
[2] S/6317, *SCOR*, 20th yr., suppl. for Apr., May, and June 1965, pp. 71–2.

the Dominican Republic. On the same day 400 United States marines—part of the contingent brought to the shores of the Dominican Republic beforehand by United States warships—invaded that territory. The very next day the strength of the United States troops had reached 1,700.

As the colonialists always did in the past, the United States is conducting its intervention under the hackneyed pretext of "ensuring the safety" of United States citizens in the Dominican Republic. It is perfectly clear, however, that the landing of United States marines in the Dominican Republic is nothing but an act of direct aggression against the people of that small country, a gross interference in its internal affairs and another attempt to keep in power a reactionary, anti-popular dictatorship which is to the liking of the United States and to crush a people's striving for freedom and independence.

Of late, ruling circles in the United States are resorting more and more frequently to direct interference in the internal affairs of other countries in the struggle against the national liberation movement in many parts of the world, particularly in the countries of Latin America. From giving open support to the reactionary military in a number of Latin American countries, following the bloody reprisals against the Panamanian patriots who defended the national sovereignty of their country, the United States has gone on to make direct use of its armed forces against the Dominican people who are striving to assert their national dignity and independence.

In order to cover up its armed intervention in the Dominican Republic, the United States is once more trying to retreat behind the screen of the Organization of American States, which it long ago placed in the service of its imperialist designs. They are very much mistaken at Washington, however, if they hope that by such means they can mislead world public opinion about the real aims and the true character of the actions of the United States in the Dominican Republic. Even within the Organization of American States itself, voices are being raised in protest against the United States policy of dictation and violence.

There can be no justification for the invasion of the territory of a sovereign State by United States armed forces.

Such an act of undisguised arbitrariness is a cynical violation of the elementary norms of international law and of the United Nations Charter, which forbids the threat or use of force against the territorial integrity or political independence of any State in international relations.

The intervention against the Dominican Republic is a new manifestation of the United States policy of arbitrariness and aggression. In these days, one aggressive act by the United States follows another: the expansion of the armed intervention in South Viet-Nam, the barbarous bombings of the territory of the Democratic Republic of Viet-Nam, the piratical raids on towns and villages in Laos, the landing of United States-Belgian paratroopers in the Congo and now the armed invasion of the territory of yet another sovereign State—the Dominican Republic.

All these are links in the United States imperialist policy, which is creating hotbeds of conflict now in one, now in another area of the world and is raising international tension to a still higher level.

The attempts of the Government of the United States to assume the role of the ruler of the destinies of peoples, to dictate its will to them and to crush the national liberation movements are evoking just indignation and protest all over the world. All those who cherish the cause of peace, freedom and independence for the peoples resolutely condemn the disgraceful actions of the United States imperialism and demand that the aggressors be curbed.

As is known, the Soviet Government has instructed its representative to the United Nations to request an urgent meeting of the Security Council to consider the question of the armed interference by the United States in the internal affairs of the Dominican Republic.

118. Soviet Government statement to the President of the Security Council alleging that OAS action violated the UN Charter, June 1965[1] (*p. 42*)

The United States of America, after perpetrating overt military intervention against a sovereign State—the Dominican Republic—and thereby grossly violating very important principles of the United Nations Charter and the generally accepted rules of international law, is using the Organization of American States as a smokescreen for its aggressive acts. On 6 May, the Meeting of Consultation of Ministers of Foreign Affairs of the States members of the OAS, despite the vehement objections of a number of Latin American States participating in the meeting, adopted, under direct pressure from the United States of America, a resolution on the formation and the use in the Dominican Republic of a so-called 'inter-American Force'.

This resolution of the OAS is in flagrant contradiction with the Charter of the United Nations.

The OAS resolution violates Article 2 of the United Nations Charter, which prohibits the threat or use of force in international relations 'against the territorial integrity or political independence of any State, or in any other manner inconsistent with the purposes of the United Nations'.

The resolution violates Article 39 of the United Nations Charter, which states that the Security Council alone shall determine 'the existence of any threat to the peace, breach of the peace, or act of aggression' and decides what measures shall be taken 'to maintain or restore international peace and security'.

The OAS resolution is contrary to Article 53 of the United Nations Charter, which states that no enforcement action shall be taken under regional arrangements or by regional agencies 'without the authorization of the Security Council'.

Consequently, the OAS resolution violates fundamental provisions of the United Nations Charter and is therefore illegal.

The United States has also disregarded the obligations it assumed under the Charter of the OAS and other inter-American agreements. Under article 15 of the Charter of the OAS, no State or group of States has the right to intervene, directly or indirectly, for any reason whatever, in the internal or external affairs of any other State.

[1] S/6411, *SCOR*, 20th yr., suppl. for Apr., May, and June 1965, pp. 225–7.

Following the formation of the 'Inter-American Force', which is being used for intervention in the internal affairs of the Dominican Republic, the United States is now endeavouring to organize a permanent inter-American force, an endeavour that is fraught with great danger for the other countries of Latin America. It means in practice that the imperialist forces in the United States are trying to arrogate to themselves the right to intervene under the OAS flag in the internal affairs of other Latin American States for the purpose of dealing with Governments that are not to their liking and with the democratic forces that are seeking to strengthen their freedom and independence.

The Soviet Government deems it essential to draw the attention of the States members of the Security Council and of all States Members of the United Nations to the serious consequences which may result from the actions taken by the United States to make use of the Organization of American States for its aggressive purposes, in violation of the United Nations Charter.

It is obvious that these actions of the United States are a further manifestation of that country's aggressive foreign policy. The United States armed intervention in the internal affairs of the Dominican Republic has followed the United States aggression in Indo-China, the intervention of the colonial Powers in the Congo and the intervention of the imperialist forces in the affairs of sovereign States in other parts of the world.

The Soviet Government calls on the Security Council and all States Members of the United Nations to repulse the attempts to bring about arbitrary rule and lawlessness and high-handedly to violate very important principles of the United Nations Charter. It is essential to put an end to the United States aggression against the Dominican Republic and to bring about the immediate withdrawal of United States armed forces and of all foreign troops from that country. It is essential to prevent further use of the Organization of American States by the United States for the attainment of its imperialist aims and for intervention in the affairs of sovereign States.

9 *Ecuador*

119. An Ecuadorian Communist view of Soviet trade with Ecuador, January 1968:[1] excerpt (*p. 22*)

The *Dolmatovo* was at the Guayaquil maritime terminal 5 to 10 January. This was a historical event, not only because trade relations with the USSR were

---

[1] *El Pueblo* (Guayaquil), 13 Jan. 1968.

directly and greatly expanded, but because it is the first Soviet trading vessel to dock at our port.

Trade relations between Ecuador and the Socialist countries, particularly Czechoslovakia, the USSR, the German Democratic Republic, and Poland, are expanding greatly, in spite of attempts by unpatriotic individuals in key positions in the Government and imperialism, particularly Yankee imperialism, whose monopolies in our country are breaking up, to prevent increased trade relations. Thus, we now have the opportunity of freeing ourselves from the economic plunder to which we have been subjected traditionally by the imperialist monopolies, particularly in our foreign trade which they have controlled actively by setting prices, creating markets and shipping space for our exportable products based on their interests. They have even told us, as in the case of the banana, what we should produce and in what quantity.

Trade with the Socialist countries, to which should be added the establishment of diplomatic and cultural relations, has been and is a goal of our party, of the labour movement, the students and democratic and patriotic Ecuadorians, because it is a step forward in the achievement of our independence, because it decreases the extreme poverty of our people, and because it creates hope for the independent development of the economy of our country.

On 5 January the Soviet trading vessel *Dolmatovo* arrived at the maritime terminal in Guayaquil. For five days the ship's hold was loaded with 100,000 quintals of cacao which the USSR bought from the Ecuadorian firm Ultramares Corp., headed by Luis A. Moboa. In one fell swoop Ecuador exported $3 million worth of cacao to the USSR. This is 17·3 per cent of our total export of cacao for 1966. And this shipment is only the first of many to be made this year until tens of thousands of tons of cacao are exported. This, of course, will surpass our cacao exports for the last few years. Furthermore, in the transactions, the Ecuadorian exporters have not been subjected to the oppressive taxes they are subjected to by the imperialist monopolies. The agreement was made freely, under mutually beneficial conditions. As can be seen, with this one transaction, Ecuador gains in every sense: millions of sucres will be added to the treasury; a buyer has been assured, and one with unlimited buying power since the population of the USSR is over 240 million; Ecuadorian farmers will again be able to grow cacao which was replaced by bananas because of the continuous low prices set by imperialists and by the lack of markets; Ecuador now has relations with a provider of industrial machinery, scientific and technical instruments, etc., all of the highest quality, and with a country whose economy is not undergoing a crisis and which has no objectives which counter human solidarity; and, finally, Ecuador is free from the stifling effects of imperialism.

The Yankee imperialists used their agents, the Ecuadorian Federation of Free Workers of Guayas (FETLIG), particularly the divisionist agent Luis Villacres Arandi, to prevent the shipment of cacao on the *Dolmatovo*, and thus to obstruct the beginning of trade relations between Ecuador and the USSR. To do this, they tried to use the old useless trick dictated to their agents in the Maritime Federation of Venezuela. This scheme consists of having the port workers of Latin America boycott the ships of those countries that trade with Socialist Cuba. But the stevedores that loaded the *Dolmatovo*, including the Union of Workers of the Port Authority, associated with FETLIG, and the bourgeois dailies, and leaders of the organizations of business-men, like the Chamber of Commerce of Guayaquil, not only rejected the imperialist scheme, but denounced Yankee imperialism for its aggression against the economy of Ecuador and its attempt to obstruct the development of relations with Socialist countries.

120. Greetings from the CPSU CC to the Ecuadorian CP, August 1968:[1] excerpt (*p. 26*)

The Central Committee of the CPSU expresses its sincere gratitude to the Central Committee of the Ecuadorian Communist Party for the invitation to send its representatives to the 8th Congress of your Party. We are deeply convinced that our visit to your country will be a new step towards the streng-thening of the fraternal unity of the Communists of Ecuador and of the Soviet Union, towards friendship between the people of Ecuador and the peoples of the Soviet Union.

It is for us, dear comrades, a particular pleasure to have been fortunate enough to have the honour of being the first emissaries of the CPSU in all the history of the relations between our Parties to attend a congress of Ecuadorian Communists. . . .

Our people have the greatest friendship for the people of your country. Difficulties are being ironed out and gradually cultural and economic relations are being established between our countries. The Soviet Union always keeps strictly to the principles of non-interference in the internal affairs of other countries, to the principle of mutual respect and mutual advantage in economic relations. Our country is ready to expand its relations with yours to the utmost, on the basis of those principles.

There has never been any disagreement between our two parties. . . . The Ecuadorian comrades and their general staff, the Central Committee of the Party, headed by Comrade Pedro Saad, an illustrious son of the Ecuadorian people, enjoy tremendous sympathy within the international Communist movement.

[1] *El Pueblo*, 31 Aug. 1968.

10 Guatemala

121. Note from the Foreign Minister to the UN Secretary-General denying that Guatemala is becoming an 'advance-post of Soviet Communism', April 1953:[1] excerpt (*p. 40*)

Since the advent of the Guatemalan Revolution of 1944, newspaper chains in the United States, important newspapers in other countries, and the largest North American news agencies have been carrying out a systematic publicity campaign of false and tendentious news designed to portray Guatemala as 'an advance-post of Soviet Communism in the American continent', 'an instrument of Moscow', and a 'spear-head' of the Soviet Union against the United States of America.

The campaign even went to such extremes that a well-known English journalist dared to assert that there was a secret base for Soviet submarines in Guatemala.

It was also asserted that Guatemala had made an agreement with Czechoslovakia for the supply of arms in exchange for coffee. . . .

The Government of Guatemala is not the satellite of the Soviet Union, the United States, or any other country. Guatemala maintains diplomatic relations with very many countries, including the USSR. The Soviet Union does not intervene, directly or indirectly, in the internal affairs of Guatemala, as Guatemala does not intervene or wish to intervene in, or disturb the peace of any other country. . . .

122. A Soviet view of the Arbenz Government: article in 'Komsomol Pravda', 26 February 1954: excerpts (*p. 40*)

The present Government of Jacobo Arbenz is a bourgeois Government. But it differs from other bourgeois Governments by the fact that its activities are not based on the support of the semi-feudal barons who formerly enslaved the people and bit by bit sold the country to the United Fruit Company. The present Government has legalized the trade unions, which during the period of the dictatorship were deep underground, has restored to the working people the right to strike, guaranteed civil freedoms, and established a system of social insurance. It is carrying out agrarian reform in order to save peasant families from hunger and to limit the rapacious activities of the United Fruit Company. . . .

The acts of the Guatemalan Government, which is treading the road of defending the country's national sovereignty, have caused a storm of reaction in the camp of the American monopolies. And although there is no mention in the programme of the present Government of Guatemala of Socialism or

---

[1] Guillermo Toriello, *La Batalla de Guatemala* (Mexico, 1955), pp. 289–97.

Communism, the USA has accused its activities of constituting a 'Communist threat'. . . .

On US initiative the Tenth Pan-American Conference is to be held in March in the capital of Venezuela, Caracas. The Latin American press reports that the US delegation intends proposing a resolution at the Conference clumsily accusing Guatemala of aggressive designs towards the United States and the other Latin American countries. Such a resolution could serve as a pretext for direct armed intervention by the USA in Guatemala. To this end, so-called 'liberation detachments', comprising mainly reactionary emigrant dregs, are being assembled at present on the territory of Nicaragua, Honduras, and the Dominican Republic.

123. OAS declaration of solidarity against the intervention of international Communism, March 1954[1] (*p. 40*)

Whereas:

The American republics at the Ninth International Conference of American States declared that international communism, by its antidemocratic nature and its interventionist tendency, is incompatible with the concept of American freedom, and resolved to adopt within their respective territories the measures necessary to eradicate and prevent subversive activities;

The Fourth Meeting of Consultation of Ministers of Foreign Affairs recognized that, in addition to adequate internal measures in each state, a high degree of international cooperation is required to eradicate the danger which the subversive activities of international communism pose for the American States; and

The aggressive character of the international communist movement continues to constitute, in the context of world affairs, a special and immediate threat to the national institutions and the peace and security of the American States, and to the right of each state to develop its cultural, political, and economic life freely and naturally without intervention in its internal or external affairs by other states.

The Tenth Inter-American Conference

I

Condemns:

The activities of the international communist movement as constituting intervention in American affairs;

Expresses:

The determination of the American States to take the necessary measures to

[1] Inter-American Conference, 10th, Caracas, 1954, *Final Act* (Washington, Pan-American Union, 1954, mimeo), pp. 94–5.

protect their political independence against the intervention of international communism, acting in the interests of an alien despotism;

Reiterates:
The faith of the peoples of America in the effective exercise of representative democracy as the best means to promote their social and political progress; and

Declares:
That the domination or control of the political institutions of any American State by the international communist movement, extending to this Hemisphere the political system of an extracontinental power, would constitute a threat to the sovereignty and political independence of the American States, endangering the peace of America, and would call for a Meeting of Consultation to consider the adoption of appropriate action in accordance with existing treaties.

II

Recommends:
That, without prejudice to such other measures as they may consider desirable, special attention be given by each of the American governments to the following steps for the purpose of counteracting the subversive activities of the international communist movement within their respective jurisdictions:

1. Measures to require disclosure of the identity, activities, and sources of funds, of those who are spreading propaganda of the international communist movement or who travel in the interests of that movement, and of those who act as its agents or in its behalf; and

2. The exchange of information among governments to assist in fulfilling the purpose of the resolutions adopted by the Inter-American Conferences and Meetings of Ministers of Foreign Affairs regarding international communism.

III

This declaration of foreign policy made by the American republics in relation to dangers originating outside this Hemisphere is designed to protect and not to impair the inalienable right of each American state freely to choose its own form of government and economic system and to live its own social and cultural life.

124. Guatemalan rejection of the declaration of solidarity, March 1954[1] (*p. 40*)

The Delegation of Guatemala, in signing the Final Act of the Tenth Inter-American Conference, makes express reservation to Resolution XCIII, entitled 'Declaration of Solidarity for the Preservation of the Political Integrity of the American States against the Intervention of International Communism', and rejects all its implications because it believes that it follows the tendency to intervene, sooner or later, in the internal affairs of the American States, on the pretext of combating communism, and with the aim of hampering the economic and social development of its peoples who are struggling for their complete liberation.

The Delegation of Guatemala, on the basis of Article 15 of the Charter of the Organization of American States, reiterates its condemnation of any form of intervention, and declares that any attempt at intervention in its internal affairs, politically or economically, unilaterally or collectively, whether by American or extracontinental states, or by any international organization, regardless of the reason for which it is invoked, shall be immediately denounced before the Security Council of the United Nations, as an imminent threat to the peace and security of the states and to their political independence.

125. Soviet insistence that the Guatemalan problem should be handled by the Security Council rather than the OAS: statement by S. Tsarapkin in the Security Council, 20 & 25 June 1954:[2] excerpts (*p. 41*)

The Security Council has before it the protest of the Guatemalan Government against the armed aggression committed by neighbouring States. . . .

. . . At this critical moment when there is not only a threat of aggression against a Member of the United Nations, but when aggression has already occurred, it is intolerable that the Security Council should wish to refuse to take immediate steps to end aggression and to refer the question to the Organization of American States. The United States of America, which dominates the Organization of American States and bends it and controls it at will, has already stated—the State Department said so yesterday—that it wants the question of Guatemala to be referred to the Organization so that its accounts with Guatemala can be settled there. Guatemala's sin has already been explained to the Council by the Guatemalan representative: its sin was to dare to set a limit to the appetites of an American fruit company, the United Fruit Company. . . .

. . . The United States representative asked with emotion what was the reason for the Soviet Union's present attitude in the Security Council; why it was interesting itself in the Western Hemisphere. He even voiced the suggestion that

[1] Inter-American Conference, 10th, Caracas, 1954, *Final Act* (Washington, Pan-American Union, 1954, mimeo.), p. 111.
[2] *SCOR*, 9th yr., 675th mtg, 20 June 1954, paras. 108, 113, 176; 676th mtg, 25 June, paras. 147-8.

the Soviet Union, it would appear, had certain intentions in the Western Hemisphere. . . .

I must once again stress that the Soviet Union considers that wherever aggression occurs, be it in the Northern or the Southern Hemisphere, the Eastern or the Western Hemisphere, it must be stopped. The Charter binds each Member of the United Nations, and particularly the permanent members of the Security Council, to take all steps in the Council to end aggression even if it occurs in the Western Hemisphere; even if it occurs in Central America against the minute Republic of Guatemala. Tomorrow aggression may be committed against Honduras; the day after tomorrow Nicaragua may be the victim—who knows, the marines may again be sent to that country to lord it there as they once did in the past. . . .

. . . Today Guatemala is the victim of aggression. Tomorrow it may be Honduras, and the day after it may be Colombia, which has previously been the victim of aggression. The representative of Colombia will remember how the Republic of Panama came into existence. I am sure he has not forgotten.

That is what history tells us, and very recent history too, but an attempt has been made here to reproach the Soviet Union with making use of the veto. The reason why the Soviet Union voted against the transfer of the question of an act of aggression to the Organization of American States was that it believes that the question of putting a stop to aggression should be dealt with by the Security Council, the body upon which Article 24 of the Charter lays primary responsibility for the maintenance of peace and security. . . .

11 Mexico

126. A Mexican editorial on A. I. Mikoyan's visit to Mexico, 24 November 1959:[1] excerpts (*p. 31*)

In connection with the Soviet Exhibition and the visit of the Soviet Vice-Premier Anastas Mikoyan, propaganda in favour of the Communist way of life is being carried on in the very heart of our Mexico. We live in a land where certain fundamental human liberties are respected, and it is logical and natural that Soviet apologists should make propaganda in this Republic. . . .

We do not criticize the Deputy Head of the Soviet Government for speaking about Communism and praising it, as is natural in his position. But what we do reproach him for—and in this we reflect public opinion—is for making a practice of praising Russia by criticizing the United States. . . .

[1] *Excelsior* (Mexico City), 24 Nov. 1959.

Mr Mikoyan has little understanding, or has been badly informed, of the psychology of the Mexican people. He tries to revive old resentments against the United States, forgetting that the man in the street in Mexico does not want somebody else to do his thinking for him nor to be used as a tool in the cold war. The Russian official who has come to visit us may continue to enjoy Mexican hospitality and to say whatever he likes; but without trying to involve us in useless conflicts and misunderstandings with those who are now good neighbours and friends.

127. Mikoyan's statement on Mexican relations with the USSR and the USA on his visit to Mexico, November 1959:[1] excerpts (*p. 31*)

... If for the time being the development of trade between Mexico and the Soviet Union is weak and inadequate, I think the responsibility for this rests with the exporters and importers of both countries. They evidently do not do enough to look for new ways, new customers, and they work in a somewhat old-fashioned manner.

There is sometimes talk that the Soviet Union allegedly wants to provoke a quarrel between the Latin American countries and the USA and to cause a deterioration in the relations between them. This is not true. We Soviet people ourselves want a radical improvement in relations with the USA and friendly relations with all other countries. Some allege that we want to undermine your Mexican trade with the USA. But this does not make the least bit of sense. Mexico and the USA are neighbors with a huge common border; traditional trade connections have been established between you, and a large part of Mexico's foreign trade is with the USA. But we do not believe this means that you should not trade with other countries. There are many goods for Mexico to trade with the Soviet Union.

It is known that there are certain influential persons in the USA who are against the USSR's trading with the Latin American countries. I do not wish to take issue here in Mexico with certain US leaders. I am obliged to do this only in line with defending the interests of our foreign trade policy. . . .

I was very much surprised by an article I read in your newspaper Excelsior. On the eve of our arrival in Mexico this newspaper published an article by its commentator Carlos de Negri. . . . He stated in particular: 'In concluding a treaty or agreement with the USSR, it can be foreseen that we shall give something and receive nothing in exchange.' . . . Of course everyone knows that when traders give something, they also receive something in exchange.

I can say to you officially that there is no instance in which Soviet foreign trade organizations would not fulfill their obligations. . . .

[1] Speech by Mikoyan at banquet given by National Association of Importers and Exporters, *Pravda*, 30 Nov. 1959 (*CDSP*, 30 Dec. 1959, pp. 22–3).

128. Joint Mexican-Soviet communiqué on the Mexican Foreign Minister's visit to Moscow, May 1968:[1] **excerpt** (*p. 31*)

On the invitation of the Soviet Government, Antonio Carrillo Flores, Minister for Foreign Affairs of the United States of Mexico, paid an official visit to the Soviet Union from 21–29 May 1968. He was accompanied by Alfonso de Rozenweig Díaz, Director-General for Bilateral Relations of the Ministry of Foreign Affairs of Mexico, and Manuel Sanchez Cuen, Ambassador with special mission.

The Minister paid a visit to N. V. Podgorny, President of the Presidium of the Supreme Soviet of the USSR, and conveyed to him a friendly message from Gustavo Díaz Ordaz, the President of the United States of Mexico.

The Minister visited A. N. Kosygin, Chairman of the Council of Ministers of the USSR.

The Mexican Foreign Minister had also a number of detailed talks with A. A. Gromyko, the Soviet Minister for Foreign Affairs.

All meetings and talks were held in a cordial and friendly atmosphere. They gave the chance of exchanging views on the development of Soviet-Mexican relations, as well as on urgent international problems of mutual interest to both countries, and confirmed the coincidence or proximity of the stands of both countries with reference to various issues.

Both sides stressed the urgent necessity of a treaty on the non-proliferation of nuclear weapons, the draft of which is under discussion at the UN General Assembly. They declared that they would go on supporting the non-proliferation treaty and expressed their conviction about this treaty being an important stride towards implementing other disarmament measures.

In the course of the exchange of views, the Mexican Foreign Minister declared that in accordance with the decision of President Gustavo Díaz Ordaz, approved by the Congress of Mexico, the country's territory, territorial waters, and air space were a zone completely free of nuclear weapons.

The Soviet Foreign Minister confirmed that the Soviet Union supported the idea of establishing a non-nuclear zone in Latin America, just as in other areas of the world, considering this to be an effective means for limiting the sphere of the proliferation of nuclear weapons. Here the Soviet Union proceeds from the fact that commitments on the establishment of non-nuclear zones may apply both to whole continents or geographic areas and to individual countries.

Appreciating highly the efforts undertaken by Mexico in this sphere the Soviet Union is prepared to respect Mexico's status as a non-nuclear zone, bearing in mind that other nuclear powers, too, would commit themselves to respect this status.

Both sides agreed to continue the exchange of opinions with the purpose of successfully concluding talks on this issue in a form that is mutually acceptable to the Governments of the USSR and Mexico.

Both sides confirmed that the Soviet Union and Mexico would continue

[1] *Pravda*, 30 May 1968.

promoting the efforts of the states which, on their part, strive to turn their territories into zones fully free of nuclear weapons.

During the talks opinions were exchanged on urgent international problems. It was pointed out that the preservation of peace is the most important task which conforms to the interests of all peoples. The sides confirmed that relations between states must be based on profound respect for independence, sovereignty, territorial integrity, and strict observance of the principle of non-interference in the internal affairs of each state.

Both sides stressed the important role the United Nations is called upon to play as an instrument for the maintenance of peace and international security and declared their striving to strengthen this international organization and increase its effectiveness on the basis of the strict observance of its Charter.

The Foreign Ministers came out in favour of the speedy and complete abolition of the remnants of the colonial system and vigorously condemned the racialist regimes still existing. The very existence of such regimes is a challenge to the United Nations and its basic principles.

In the course of the talks questions were discussed pertaining to bilateral relations between the USSR and Mexico. It was noted with satisfaction that Soviet-Mexican relations continue to develop in a spirit of traditional friendship and mutually beneficial co-operation.

Both Ministers stressed the importance and mutual benefit of the trade and economic ties that exist between the two countries. They noted the considerable growth of cultural relations between the Soviet Union and Mexico and confirmed the mutual interest in developing them further.

While the Mexican Foreign Minister was in the Soviet Union an agreement on cultural and scientific exchange was signed which will help to further strengthen Soviet-Mexican friendly relations.

129. Telegram from the Presidium of the Mexican CP CC to the CPSU CC deploring Soviet intervention in Czechoslovakia, 21 August 1968[1] (*p. 31*)

The Presidium of the Mexican Communist Party deplores the intervention of the armies of the Soviet Union and other Warsaw Pact countries in Czechoslovak territory and requests the immediate withdrawal of troops and the normalization of relations with the Czechoslovak Party and Government on the basis of the principles of equality, mutual respect and non-interference in internal affairs.

(signed) Arnaldo Martínez Verdugo.

[1] *La Voz de México* (Mexico City), 27 Aug. 1968.

12 Panama

130. 'New Times' article deprecating Panamian pretensions to play an international role, 28 March 1947

Until now the Panama Republic has not laid claim to a decisive say in the post-war settlement. Its half million inhabitants are too busy battling the jungle and cultivating those patches of their native soil which are still not built over with American bases and airfields.

However, concern for the prosperity of the banana export trade has proved to be too commonplace a preoccupation for some of Panama's statesmen. They have been seized by an urge to astonish the world and have undertaken an impressive international demarche. The Ministry of Foreign Affairs of the Panama Republic has announced that Panama does not agree with the Italian peace treaty and refuses to adhere to it.

One of O'Henry's heroes, the president of the imaginery South American Republic of Anchuria, was distinguished for his immoderate ambition. He almost succeeded in converting Anchuria into a power with which all the nations of the world had to reckon. He failed only because of his amazing and extravagant vanity.

The same thing has happened in Panama. Its Ministers have also devised a rather extravagant way of drawing attention to themselves. But there is method in this extravagance. Panama's ministers do not find it necessary to protest against acts which arouse the legitimate concern of the peoples, but which are favourably regarded in Washington.

131. Overtures for the establishment of commercial and diplomatic relations: press interview with V. L. Bazykin, Soviet Ambassador to Mexico, May 1959:[1] excerpts (*p. 22*)

'The Soviet Union is ready to establish commercial and cultural relations with the Republic of Panama', His Excellency Vladimir L. Bazykin, head of the Delegation of Soviet observers to the Economic Commission for Latin America Conference and Ambassador Extraordinary and Plenipotentiary of the Soviet Union in the Republic of Mexico, told this newspaper. . . .

'We believe that this would be useful and profitable for both countries. If there is a desire also on the side of Panama, we are ready', he said. . . .

He declared that the Soviet Union was disposed to establish with these Governments [i.e. of Latin America] an exchange of Soviet machinery and equipment in return for export products from those countries which had the same desire to foster commercial relations with Russia.

'As you know', declared Bazykin, 'Russia has no interest in capitalizing her investments in other countries. We simply sell tools and machinery, we help in

[1] *El Día* (Panama), 20 May 1959.

the construction of industrial plants and factories, in exchange for products and primary materials which we need for our own industry.' He said, finally, that there is no danger of these industries and production being Russian property.

Turning to the possibility of technical assistance, he showed that the Soviet Union has not only given economic support to these plans for industrialization but has educated a very large number of foreign technicians, engineers, and scientists. He cited the case of Argentina, a country for which the Soviet Union has recently opened a credit for several million dollars in exchange for a number of basic products. He spoke of India, China, and France, and said that the same thing could be done in Latin America.

Detailing the possibilities of commercial exchanges with Panama, Bazykin stated that it would be for relevant institutions in both countries to establish what products Russia needs and the industries and types of machinery in which our Government is interested. In this respect, he added that naturally the establishment of diplomatic relations between both countries would greatly facilitate the realization of any such plan.

The Soviet Delegate stressed the possibility of vigorous artistic and cultural exchange between both countries. He believed that positive results would ensue from an interchange of artists, university professors, sportsmen, men of letters, agricultural, scientific, and industrial exhibitions.

On saying goodbye, the Ambassador promised that on his return to Mexico he would ask his Government to secure the translation into Russian of the best literary productions of Panamanian authors, and that if possible these would visit Moscow at the invitation of the Soviet Union.

13 Paraguay

Paraguayan CP pro- and anti-Soviet factions

132. Statement by the Paraguayan CP Commission for Defence and Reorganization denouncing the anti-Soviet faction, August 1965:[1] excerpts (*p. 26*)

At a meeting of the Central Committee [of the Paraguayan Communist Party] n March 1956, immediately following the XX Congress of the Communist Party of the Soviet Union and the denunciation of Stalin's personality cult

[1] *Pravda*, 13 July 1967.

17

and its consequences, Creydt[1] made a partial and formalist self-criticism of his grave mistakes in the leadership of the party. Today, in the light of facts, it can be clearly seen that this 'self-criticism' was a manoeuvre designed to attenuate criticism and prevent his dismissal under the influence of the ideas of the XX Congress of the Communist Party of the Soviet Union. . . .

Now Creydt has passed over to the enemy territory of calumnies and insults against the Central Committee of the Soviet Union, and to acts of provocation. He made use of Arturo López, anti-Soviet provocateur, to fabricate a farcical 'enlarged Central Committee' comprising three titular members and one candidate member of the vanished Central Committee, together with a number of 'guests'. In a meeting on 11 July of this fabricated Central Committee, following the directives of Creydt, the provocateur Arturo López hurled against the Communist Party of the Soviet Union and other fraternal parties the infamous accusation of 'intervention' in the affairs of our Party, and of 'conspiring to impose a change in its political line'.

The truth is quite the opposite. What has really happened is that there has been a fractional conspiracy by Creydt in order to destroy the Paraguayan Communist Party. What has really occurred is Creydt's ideological and practical rupture with proletarian internationalism and the international Communist movement. Invoking the mendacious slogan of 'intervention' and appealing to the ideological arsenal of bourgeois nationalism, Creydt claims to pose as the champion of the 'independence' of the Party. Crawling through the mire of this path of treachery, he spreads vile calumnies against the Communist Party of the Soviet Union, the United Party of the Socialist Revolution of Cuba, against Comrade Fidel Castro and many other leaders and fraternal parties.

The Paraguayan Communist Party indignantly rejects this provocative campaign and expresses to the Communist Party of the Soviet Union and to all Communist Parties its deep gratitude for the manifold help and solidarity which they have given, and are still giving, to the just struggle for the national liberation of the Paraguayan people. . . .

The Committee for the Defence and Reorganization of the Party will immediately take the necessary measures for the full restoration of normal and fraternal relations of the Paraguayan Communist Party with the Communist Party of the Soviet Union and all Marxist-Leninist parties, on the basis of the principles of proletarian internationalism, equality, independence, and mutual aid.

133. 'Pravda' report of support by the CPSU for the pro-Soviet faction, 13 July 1967: excerpts (*p. 26*)

On 11 July a meeting took place in the Central Committee of the CPSU between M. A. Suslov, members of the Politburo, the Secretary of the CPSU Central Committee, and a delegation from the Paraguayan Communist Party (PCP) headed by Hugo Campos, members of the Political Commission of the PCP Central Committee.

[1] Oscar Creydt, for many years the Secretary-General and leading figure of the Paraguayan CP.

The PCP delegation spoke of the selfless and heroic struggle of the Paraguayan Communists and the whole people of Paraguay against the military dictatorship, stressing that in this struggle the PCP uses all the forms and methods available to it, according to the development of the given situation. The Party has recently been subject to a grave ordeal on account of the infiltration into its ranks of hostile elements who have striven to change its militant revolutionary line and who are responsible for the deaths of a number of staunch and active Communists.

The Paraguayan comrades state that the National Conference held recently for preparations for the 3rd Party Congress outlined a programme for the Party's continued struggle and reaffirmed the Paraguayan Communists' inviolable loyalty to Leninist principles and norms in party life.

The delegation emphasized that the Paraguayan Communists, inspired by the successes of the USSR in the building of Communism, fully support the firm and consistent policy of the CPSU Central Committee and the Soviet Government. . . .

The conversation was attended by A. S. Belyakov, Deputy Director of the CPSU Central Committee's International Department.

The meeting took place in an atmosphere of cordiality and friendship characteristic of the relations between the PCP and the CPSU.

Support of Castro's purge of the Cuban 'microfaction'

134. Statement by the Paraguayan CP supporting Cuban action and accusing the USSR of 'brutal intervention', 13 February 1968:[1] excerpts (*p. 26*)

The Paraguayan Communist Party (Secretary—Oscar Creydt) has expressed full support for the Cuban Party in connection with the measures taken by the Cuban party against the micro-faction headed by Aníbal Escalante. It also describes as correct Cuba's decision not to take part in the international Communist meeting in Budapest.

In a message addressed to Fidel Castro . . . the Paraguayan Communist Party says among other things that 'it appears clear, in the light of Comrade Raúl Castro's report, that the opportunist divisionist group was in touch with officials of the CPSU and that the objective of the factional manoeuvre was to take advantage of the economic and technical aid that the Soviet Union gives Cuba in order to exercise political pressure on the Cuban Government and on the leadership of the Communist Party of Cuba to make them change their strategic and tactical line and substitute an opposite line.'

The Paraguayan Communist Party statement says: 'It was not difficult for us Paraguayan Communists to understand this abnormal situation, despite the fact that it is totally inadmissible from the viewpoint of the principles of

[1] Prensa Latina agency report from Montevideo, broadcast from Havana, 14 Feb. 1968. Verbatim monitoring of broadcast.

Marxism-Leninism and of the sacred duties of proletarian internationalism. As is known, our Party has been subjected to brutal intervention, tending to change its line to one of opportunism. Foreign intervention used as its instrument for this purpose a group of renegades ready to sell the Party line in exchange for promises of "unlimited support". This manoeuvre began immediately after the Central Committee of the Paraguayan Communist Party had begun to approach the sister party of Vietnam fraternally in order to study the experiences of the people's war.'

The Party statement adds that 'in past years, we have committed serious errors, starting out from the unfounded position that divergences and divisionism within the international Communist movement came from the Communist Party of China. Long and painful experience has helped us to understand that the profound causes of divisionism lie in vacillation when facing the desperate aggressiveness of US imperialism and the resulting errors of the right. The recent Latin American Solidarity Organization Conference demonstrated where divisionism within the international Communist movement really comes from. At that conference, the group of renegades whom the leaders of the CPSU officially recognized as the "Paraguayan Communist Party" attacked Cuba, accusing it unjustly of negotiating with the monarchy in England and the Fascist tyranny in Spain. This divisionist group, naturally, supported all the rightist positions which oppose the development of the guerrilla struggle in the Latin American countries.

'Our own experience makes it easy for us to understand the firm reaction of the Central Committee of the Communist Party of Cuba against the divisionist manoeuvres and the pressures tending to sway the Cuban Revolution, forcing it to give up its international role.'

The Paraguayan Communist Party document declares further that Cuba's position in refusing to attend the international Communist meeting is correct.

14 Uruguay

135. 'Pravda' report of visit of Soviet delegation to Montevideo and an increase in Soviet-Uruguayan trade, 25 August 1958: excerpt
(*p. 29*)

Last night the head of the delegation from the Supreme Soviet of the USSR which has been visiting Uruguay, A. F. Gorkin, gave a press conference on the results of the visit of the Soviet parliamentarians to this country.

Referring to the contact which the members of the Soviet delegation had been having in Uruguay during their visit with those concerned with economic and social affairs, and with representatives of business circles, acquainting themselves with the development of the industrial and agricultural economy of the country and paying visits to a number of economic organizations and cultural institutions, A. F. Gorkin declared:

'We have listened with satisfaction to the statements of Uruguayan officials to the effect that they are keenly interested in the question of the further development of friendly relations with the Soviet Union. We are also convinced that the Uruguayan people nourish feelings of sincere sympathy for the Soviet people. And we can state that the Soviet people and Government are sincerely striving to strengthen all sorts of friendly links with Uruguay, as with other countries of Latin America.

'It is gratifying to state that recently there has been a development in the economic, cultural, sporting, and other links between our countries. To this the direct contacts established between representatives of our parliaments have made a substantial contribution.

'Of great significance for the relations between our countries', continued A. F. Gorkin, 'is the successful development of Soviet-Uruguayan commercial links. Interchange between the Soviet and Uruguayan people in the fields of culture, learning, and sport are increasing. The Soviet people are keenly interested in the literature and achievements of the Uruguayan people.'

In conclusion, A. F. Gorkin expressed the conviction that the visit of the delegation of the Supreme Soviet of the USSR would serve the cause of the further development of friendship and cooperation between the peoples of the Soviet Union and Uruguay, and expressed gratitude for the warm welcome extended to the delegation.

136. Decree by Uruguayan National Council to limit the size of the Soviet diplomatic mission in Montevideo, 5 October 1961: excerpts (*p. 29*)

The Minister of Foreign Affairs will fix the number of members of the staff which the Legation of the USSR in the Republic may comprise, taking into account the staff of other European Missions. . . .

Any proposed movement of the staff of the Legation of the USSR outside a radius of forty kilometres from the centre of the capital must be notified to the Ministry of Foreign Affairs two working days in advance. . . .

It is strictly forbidden to approach nearer than forty kilometres from the land frontier of the Republic unless it should be necessary to travel along international routes, for which a special permit must be obtained in the same form and on the same conditions as stipulated in the previous paragraph.

137. Press report of decree of National Council expelling four members of the Soviet diplomatic mission, 5 October 1966[1] (*p. 30*)

Four of the officials of the Soviet Embassy in Uruguay were yesterday declared

[1] *La Mañana* (Montivideo), 5 Oct. 1966.

personae non gratae by a Decree of the National Council of Government which fixed a time-limit of 48 hours for them to leave the country.

When the 'Tricontinental Conference', attended by delegations from countries in Asia, Africa, and America, was held at La Havana last year, the speech made by the leader of the Soviet delegation was considered by the Uruguayan Government to be an open exhortation to subversion. For this reason the Soviet Ambassador in Uruguay was called to explain the terms of the speech, *qua* an official expression of the views of the Government of the USSR. The Soviet Ambassador replied that this speech did not emanate from any Soviet Government organ and that, therefore, it could only be considered as being the opinion of important sectors in his country, without the character of a government policy statement.

Soviet offensive. Of late the Soviet Union have reinforced their efforts to increase their relations with Latin America and Uruguay. Within this field the following facts should be underlined: the grant of a $US100 million credit to Brazil for which an important delegation travelled to Rio de Janeiro, headed by the Minister of Foreign Trade, who signed the relevant agreement together with the Brazilian representatives; the offer of a similar credit of $20 million to Uruguay; the appointment by the Uruguayan Government of a committee, under the chairmanship of Contador Enrique Iglesias, to study the terms of a future agreement; the visit of the Soviet Ambassador to Salto where he was invited by the International Committee for the Salto Grande dam; the visit to Montevideo of the Leningrad Ballet and the Moscow circus, as well as an exhibition of plastic arts, the visit of Soviet doctors, the gift of medical materials and of books to the University, etc.

Fears of infiltration. Nevertheless, the Uruguayan Government redoubled its vigilance so as to prevent possible Communist infiltration into the country. On the occasion of the 19th Congress of the Communist Party, which was held last month, and in view of the fact of the announcement that foreign delegations would attend, President Alberto Heber stated in a political speech in Tacuarembo, that 'only Uruguayans are allowed to enter here'. Shortly after that there followed a draft regulation on the issue of visas, prepared by the Ministry of Foreign Affairs, the Ministry of the Interior, and the Directorate of Migration, and addressed to Uruguayan consular authorities in Communist countries, with a view to preventing the entry into the country of persons opposed to the ideological principles on which the Uruguayan system of government is based. The list of countries affected by this ruling, which has antecedents in a decree passed at the time when Dr Juan José de Amézaga was President, includes all countries under a Communist regime.

Likewise a commercial mission from North Korea was expelled from the country and similar measures are under study in regard to the commercial mission from the Democratic German Republic; and the visa for the representative of the Tass Agency has been cancelled, and up to the present no visa has been granted to the new representative of this agency.

Subversive action. On Monday last the Soviet chargé d'affaires *a.i.*, Mikhail Muzhin was summoned by President Heber and the Minister of the Interior,

Dr Storace Arrosa, who raised with him the intervention of officials from his Embassy in subversive activities in the trade union field.

Yesterday, at a meeting of the (Blanco) Majority group of the National Council of Government, also attended by the Ministers of National Defence (General Moratorio), Foreign Affairs (Señor Vidal Zaglio), and the Interior (Dr Storace Arrosa), the decree of expulsion was approved, after study of a confidential memorandum on the activities of the Soviet officials. . . .

Memorandum on subversive activities. The memorandum circulated to the Councillors is entitled 'Subversive activities of USSR diplomatic officials in political and trade union fields in Uruguay', and reads as follows:

'Since 15 September last a new escalade of labour activity has been initiated which has resulted in a wave of strikes and trade union stoppages in most public and private spheres, for the normal functioning of the democratic institutions of the Republic.

'The principal origin of this new wave springs from the Uruguayan Communist Party Congress held in the middle of August last, which was attended by an important and outstanding delegation of the Soviet Communist Party. This Soviet delegation brought with it important decisions and documents prepared at the highest level in the headquarters of the Western Hemisphere Department in Moscow, the contents of which are concerned with the immediate fulfilment of major objectives in political and trade union fields in this Republic.

'These objectives are guided, controlled, and regulated in an invisible and clandestine, but certain way by key diplomatic officials of the Soviet Embassy. In broad lines, the objectives to be carried out by the Communist political organs and their associated forces, the execution of which has rapidly been set in motion, are as follows:—

(*a*) to weaken and split the principle of authority throughout the whole hierarchical ladder, in every institution, be it public or private;

(*b*) to unleash disorder, and discouragement regarding the possibilities of progress, among the working classes, encouraging them to violence and aggression;

(*c*) to break the will to work among work forces, bringing about paralysis of labour by constant holding up of work through stoppages and strikes;

(*d*) to aggravate the economic and financial crisis which the country is experiencing by making deep-laid use of disorganization of work, sabotage of industrial production, and the application of expert techniques of economic subversion;

(*e*) to reaffirm more thoroughly the strong predominance of Communist agents in the direction of the trade unions;

(*f*) to undermine the prestige of the republican and democratic institutions which rule us, by means of lying, slanderous, and aggravating propaganda;

(*g*) to encourage hate and permanent tension between social classes, provoking continued antagonism and opposition. . . .'

The text of the decree is as follows:—

'In view of the information given, the National Council of Government resolve:

(1) to declare *personae non gratae* the officials of the Soviet Embassy, Messrs Sergey Alekseyevich Yangalkin, Nikolay Iosipovich Ivanov, Aleksey Alekseyevich Zudin, and Vladimir P. Shvetz;

(2) to allow a time-limit of 48 hours for them to leave national territory.'

The preceding resolution will be transmitted to those concerned today at 10 a.m. in the premises of the Soviet diplomatic mission, and as from that moment the time-limit granted will be in force.

Exchanges between the Soviet and Uruguayan CPs

138. Address by Aleksey Rumyantsev, member of the CPSU CC and Chairman of its delegation, to the 18th Uruguayan CP Congress, July 1962:[1] excerpts (p. 31)

Allow me cordially to thank the Central Committee of your Party, headed by Comrade Rodney Arismendi, for having invited a delegation from the CPSU to the Congress. The participation of your party in the Congresses of the CPSU has become a fine tradition. Today we note with tremendous satisfaction that this tradition, a testimonial to the indestructible friendship between our two Marxist-Leninist Parties, has been even further strengthened, and for the first time a delegation from the CPSU has been offered the opportunity of being present at a Congress of the militant Communist Party of Uruguay. . . .

The Soviet Communists and all the Soviet people know and have deep affection for the veterans of the Communist movement of Uruguay, Comrades Julia Arévalo and Francisco Pintos—the only Uruguayan who personally knew the great Vladimir Il'ich Lenin—Felix Ramírez, Juan Mujica, Julio Baccino, Ramón Benutti, Alejandro Caccia, Teófilo Godoy, and other heroic fighters who dedicated many years of their lives to the cause of struggle for the Uruguayan people. . . .

For many years there have been relations between our two countries. The Soviet people hold the Uruguayan people in high esteem. The Uruguayan people have given humanity magnificent writers, educators, artists, and scientists, who have contributed greatly to the cause of world science. There have never been any contentious problems between our peoples.

We highly appreciate the great work which the Uruguayan Communists are doing to strengthen the friendship between the Soviet and Uruguayan peoples. . . . The role played by the international communist movement is now becoming more important. The Communist Party of Uruguay is one of the fighting arms of the world army of Communists fighting for peace, work, freedom, equality, fraternity, and happiness of all peoples. It is engaged in a systematic Marxist-Leninist policy, a policy of internationalism. It is fighting adamantly against revisionists, dogmatists, sectarians, and other opportunists. It enjoys well-deserved prestige in the family of brotherly parties. Fully fraternal relations

[1] *El Popular*, 2 July 1962.

exist between the Communist Party of the Soviet Union and the Communist Party of Uruguay.

139. Article by a member of the Soviet delegation to the 45th anniversary celebrations of the Uruguayan CP, September 1965:[1] excerpts (*p. 31*)

During September and October of this year I had the opportunity to attend the 45th anniversary celebrations of the Communist Party of Uruguay as part of a CPSU delegation. . . .

It is impossible for words to convey what happened when we read out the greetings of the Central Committee of the CPSU and, in the name of the Central Committee of our Party, presented a gift to our Uruguayan comrades—a magnificent portrait of Vladimir Il'ich Lenin, painted by the skilled craftsmen of the village of Fedoskino. Long-sustained applause rang forth, and there were exclamations of 'Long Live the party of Lenin!' 'May the friendship between the Uruguayan and Soviet peoples grow stronger!'

The participants at the rally adopted a note to the CPSU Central Committee and presented to the CPSU delegation a bust of José Artigas, Uruguay's national hero. . . .

The ordinary workers did not conceal their feelings of gratitude to the Soviet Union for its tireless struggle in defence of the sovereignty of peoples. Uruguayan Communists have a high regard for the role of the CPSU in the struggle for unity within the international Communist movement, angrily condemn those who bring dissension into it, and express their steadfast loyalty to the principles of Marxism-Leninism.

140. 'Pravda' on meeting of the First Secretary of the Uruguayan CP, Rodney Arismendi, with leaders of the CPSU, 27 March 1968 (*p. 31*)

Leonid Brezhnev, General Secretary of the CPSU Central Committee, had a meeting on 25 March with Rodney Arismendi, First Secretary of the Central Committee of the Communist Party of Uruguay.

During the meeting, which proceeded in an atmosphere of friendship and comradeship characteristic of relations between the Communist Party of the Soviet Union and the Communist Party of Uruguay, opinions were exchanged on a wide range of questions of interest to both sides.

Boris Ponomarev, Secretary of the CPSU Central Committee, took part in the talk.

The representatives of the CPSU and the Communist Party of Uruguay unanimously noted that United States imperialism, which is the centre of world reaction, strives by every means, including force of arms, to hamper the progressive development of mankind, to retard the liberation struggle of the peoples. The aggressive policy of the United States ruling circles, their interference in the internal affairs of other countries, cynical support of the

[1] V. Stepakov in *Pravda*, 30 Dec. 1965.

reactionary and dictatorial regimes in Latin America constitute a serious threat to universal peace and contradict the national interests of the peoples of Latin America and all the countries.

The representatives of the CPSU and the Communist Party of Uruguay have once again vigorously condemned the piratical aggression of United States imperialism in Vietnam and voiced their militant solidarity with the heroic and just struggle waged by the Vietnamese people.

The representatives of the CPSU and the Communist Party of Uruguay hold that in the present conditions the struggle for rallying and uniting the Communist movement on the principled basis of Marxism-Leninism acquires special significance. In the opinion of both parties conditions are growing ripe for holding an international meeting of representatives of Communist and Workers' Parties. They assess the new meeting as a serious contribution to the active struggle for uniting the Communist movement, for its militant cooperation, for the triumph of the principles of Marxism-Leninism, the ideas of proletarian internationalism, for the unity of all the anti-imperialist forces.

In the course of the talk Arismendi noted that the purposeful struggle waged by the Communist Party for strengthening the unity of all the Left forces of the Uruguayan people is yielding positive results. The influence and prestige of the Communist Party of Uruguay is growing among the masses. The Communist Party of Uruguay is consolidating the unity with the Communist Parties of Latin America, is launching an ever broader movement of solidarity with the struggle of the people of Vietnam, with the Cuban Revolution, with all the revolutionary movements. It is developing energetic solidarity actions with the Latin American peoples' struggle which it regards as inseparable from the patriotic and liberation aspirations of the people of Uruguay.

Arismendi stressed the world historic role of the CPSU and the Soviet Union towards which the working people of Uruguay entertain great sympathies. Extensive preparations are now under way in Uruguay for the 50th anniversary of the Great October Socialist Revolution, the holiday of the revolutionaries of all countries.

In their turn the CPSU representatives spoke about the building of Communism in the USSR, about the activities of the CPSU, about the political and labour enthusiasm with which the Soviet people are preparing for the glorious 50th anniversary of the October Revolution. The CPSU representatives expressed solidarity with the struggle waged by the Uruguayan Communists for peace, democracy, and social progress, and highly assessed the contribution made by the Communist Party of Uruguay to the struggle for the unity and solidarity of the international Communist movement.

The representatives of both Parties stressed their loyalty to the conclusions drawn by the 1957 and 1960 meetings of the Communist and Workers' Parties and reaffirmed their striving to develop comradely and fraternal relations between the CPSU and the Communist Party of Uruguay on the basis of the principles of Marxism-Leninism and proletarian internationalism.

141. Declaration of the Executive Committee of the Uruguayan CP issued in Montevideo supporting Soviet intervention in Czechoslovakia, 29 July 1968: excerpt (*p. 31*)

The Uruguayan Communist Party totally shares the preoccupation expressed in the Warsaw Pact and gives its unshakeable support to the decision contained therein to help the Czechoslovak patriots to defend a Socialist regime threatened by counter-revolution. It is thus consistent with its permanent internationalist position expressed particularly when we proclaimed as our principal duty solidarity in the defence of Cuba *vis-à-vis* imperialism. The Uruguayan Communist Party in particular expresses once again its total solidarity with the Soviet Union, which, shedding the generous blood of its soldiers, carried the principal weight of Nazism and which today, in the heart of Europe as in its help to the people of Vietnam, and its support for revolutionary Cuba, is the bastion of world revolution and the powerful protecting shield which defends the peoples from imperialist aggression.

Exchanges between Uruguayan and Soviet Governments

142. Note by Soviet Government in reply to Uruguayan note rejecting accusations of having fomented subversion at the Tricontinental Conference, Havana, 11 February 1966[1] (*p. 29*)

The Soviet Government has been informed that recently in certain Latin American countries certain circles have been mounting a propaganda campaign concerning the results of the 'First Conference of Solidarity Between the Peoples of Three Continents' in which the representatives of social bodies from many countries in Asia, Africa, and Latin America examined jointly the question of the people's struggle against imperialist, colonialist, and neo-colonialist exploitation. In particular, versions are being put about that the representatives of the Soviet social bodies who took part in the work of this conference called for the realization of 'subversive activity' in the countries of Latin America, and for intervention in these countries' internal affairs, etc. Shamelessly falsifying the facts there are persons who have been making statements as though it were representatives of the Soviet Government itself, and not of Soviet social bodies, who took part in the 'Conference of Solidarity between the Peoples of Three Continents'. As may be seen from press reports, these malignant attacks on Soviet foreign policy regarding the Conference have been taken up in addition in the Organization of American States.

The Soviet Government sees no special need to make an official denial of such inventions, the inconsistency of which is clear to anyone who looks without preconceived ideas at the Solidarity Movement of the peoples of Asia, Africa, and Latin America, which has the noble objectives of favouring the struggle of the peoples for their internal independence against the forces of

[1] *La Mañana*, 16 Feb. 1966.

imperialism, colonialism, and neo-colonialism. As regards the essence of the Soviet Union's policy towards the Latin American countries (which the organizers of the said propaganda campaign are now trying to discredit) this policy, the thinking of the Soviet Government, is well known to the Government of the Oriental Republic of Uruguay.

In this policy towards all states, including naturally the countries of Latin America, the Soviet Union, in full conformity with the Charter of the United Nations, starts from the principles of the equality of all states, big and small, and of mutual respect of sovereignty and independence, and rigorously observes the principles of non-intervention in the internal affairs of states. The recognition of the right of each people to determine its own destiny has been, since the first days of the birth of the Soviet state, one of the fundamental principles of its foreign policy. The Soviet Union rejects and always has rejected the so-called 'exportation of revolution' and in the most decided manner declares itself against any attempt at 'exportation of counter-revolution'. Throughout all the years of its existence, the Soviet state has demonstrated by hard facts that it strictly respects and observes the sovereign rights of states, and establishes its relations with them on a basis of sincere goodwill and mutual advantage.

It is well known that on the initiative of the Soviet Union in the 20th Session of the United Nations General Assembly, there was approved the Declaration on the inadmissibility of interference in the internal affairs of states and on the protection of independence and sovereignty. The Soviet Government notes with satisfaction that when the said question was considered in the General Assembly by the Soviet Delegation and those of a number of Latin American countries, useful contacts were established which favoured mutual understanding and a positive solution of the question as a whole. In the opinion of the Soviet Government the task now consists in working to fulfil the just demands included in the United Nations Declaration on the inadmissibility of interference in the internal affairs of states, in order to secure strict observance by all states of what has been laid down in the Declaration. In this respect the Soviet Government is disposed to collaborate with the Governments of the Latin American countries and other states.

The Soviet Union has always shown its willingness to develop collaboration with all countries, including the countries of Latin America, to resolve international questions, especially those concerned with the objective of strengthening peace in general. The Soviet Government has declared itself in favour of the strengthening and extension of relations in the economic, commercial, cultural, scientific, sporting, and other peaceful fields with all states, considering that such relations are a matter of reciprocal interest. The Government of the Oriental Republic of Uruguay is well aware of the steps taken systematically in this field from the Soviet side.

By putting into practice, consequently, on the international scene, the policy of strengthening peace and reinforcing the independence and sovereignty of all states, and of non-intervention in their internal affairs, the Soviet Union has lent and continues lending the necessary support to those states who are victims of aggression on the part of the forces of imperialism. Our country helps and will go on helping the Democratic Republic of Vietnam and the Vietnamese people, who are defending their freedom and independence in the struggle against the North American aggressors. The Soviet Union declared itself decisively in support of the people of the Dominican Republic whose territory was invaded by the North American interventionists. The Soviet Government decisively supports the people of the colonial countries who are making efforts to secure their freedom and national independence.

The Soviet people feel a sense of friendship and of profound solidarity towards all the peoples who are carrying out the struggle for their national freedom. It was precisely in this sense that the Delegation of the Soviet social bodies spoke in the 'Conference of Solidarity of the Peoples of Three Continents'. At the same time the Soviet Delegation declared itself decisively in favour of the application of the principle of peaceful coexistence (one of the fundamental principles of the foreign policy of the Soviet Union) in relations between states with different social regimes.

Bearing all this in mind there naturally arises the question: what ends are served by the attempts which are now being made to present in a distorted form the political line of the USSR with regard to the countries of Latin America? The Soviet Government is convinced that the hostile anti-USSR campaign now being waged in the United States of America and in a series of Latin American countries serves only the interests of the very forces who are carrying out a policy of aggression and of shameless interference in the internal affairs of other states. These forces—and it is a secret to no one that foremost among them are certain circles in the United States of America—want at any price to distract the attention of the peoples from their criminal acts in Vietnam, in the Dominican Republic, and in many other nations of the world. It is no casual coincidence that the alleged complaint against the Soviet Union was taken up in the Organization of American States precisely at the moment when the United States of America was preparing the renewal of the barbaric bombing raids on the peaceful cities and villages of North Vietnam.

It is impossible not to see that with the help of this campaign the United States thinks it can disorientate public opinion in the Latin American countries so as to be able with greater ease to intensify still further its pressure on the countries of Latin America, including armed intervention in their internal affairs, which as is well known, is openly called for by the widely known resolution of the House of Representatives of the North American Congress on 20 September 1965.[1]

Such are the considerations which the Soviet Government has thought it necessary to set out with regard to the attempts of certain circles to cast a shadow on the objectives and principles of the policy of the USSR towards the countries of Latin America. The Soviet Government expresses the hope that, in spite of the intrigues of the said circles, which would wish to prevent the fruitful development of relations between the Soviet Union and the Latin

---

[1] Res. no. 560 justifying action in the Western hemisphere 'which could go so far as to resort to armed force . . . to forestall or combat intervention . . . by international Communism' (*Congressional Record*, H.R., 20 Sept. 1965, no. 24347).

American states, these relations are going to develop successfully in the interests of both sides.

143. Official reply of the Uruguayan Government rejecting Soviet assurances, March 1966[1] (*pp. 28, 29*)

The Government of the Republic has taken cognisance of the reply of the Ambassador of the USSR to the statement recently made by the Minister of Foreign Affairs, regarding the resolutions adopted at the so-called Tricontinental Conference of Havana.

1. First, to avoid any misunderstanding, the Government of Uruguay wishes to point out that its statement was intended to clarify a situation originating in the resolutions of the Havana Conference which constitutes a serious undermining of the juridical bases of harmonious international relations, an inadmissible intervention in the internal affairs of various states, an intolerable violation of the principle of self-determination, extremes that are recognized and affirmed as such in positive international law in force. There is nothing in Uruguay's statement that represents either a 'propaganda campaign' or a 'malicious attack against Soviet foreign policy'; neither is there any intended 'misrepresentation of Soviet policy on the Latin American countries'.

If these attitudes are attributed even indirectly to Uruguay, the Government not only cannot accept them, but also firmly and completely denies them. They have nothing to do with Uruguay's position, which was only to point out that it is seriously and inadmissibly irregular for an international conference, participated in by citizens and Governments of states with which Uruguay maintains diplomatic relations, to proclaim and incite internal subversion and to promise aid to subversive movements—all in violation of the clear standards of international law.

2. The Government of Uruguay takes due note of the fact that—with regard to the USSR—according to the statement of its Ambassador, only representatives of 'Soviet social organizations' took part in the Havana Conference; in other words, there was no official Soviet delegation at the Conference and its resolutions in no way bind the Government of the USSR, which therefore disavows them.

In reaching this conclusion, which naturally and logically derives from the Soviet reply, the Uruguayan Government considers it a duty to point out that those social organizations—some of whose representatives are members of important agencies of the Government of the USSR, agencies among whose responsibilities is the foreign policy of the country—have contributed with their vote to the approval of a resolution that openly violates the Charter of the United Nations, the aforementioned resolution adopted by the 20th Session of the United Nations General Assembly, and the principles that the USSR claims as fundamental to its foreign policy.

3. The Uruguayan Government has demonstrated its adherence to the principle of non-intervention, its clearly leading role in the defence of self-determination of the peoples, and its will to fight for an international code of

[1] *Boletín para el servicio exterior del gobierno del Uruguay*, yr. 3, no. 104, 20 Mar. 1966.

peace and justice, based on the maintenance of friendly relations and co-operation with all states.

But, for that very reason, it cannot tolerate the fact that a conference, lacking qualifying credentials of any kind, should proclaim an interventionist and aggressive policy, and that participating in this conference with impunity are persons or organizations, whether or not official representatives, of states with which Uruguay maintains diplomatic relations.

4. In taking note of the assertion that the USSR 'complies strictly with the principle of non-intervention in the internal affairs of the states'—a principle also fully observed by Uruguay with a precision that allows for no distortion whatever—this Government must observe that such a view obligates and commits the USSR to adopt necessary measures to condemn all attitudes leading to the repudiation or violation—direct or indirect—of what it claims to be a cardinal principle of its foreign policy.

15 Venezuela

144. Venezuelan communiqué on an incident over two Soviet couriers, 10 June 1952 (*p. 39*)

On the 7th inst. there arrived at Maiquetia airport on board an aircraft of the KLM company Soviet citizens Nicolay Yukushev and his wife Aleksandra Yukusheva, who were briefly detained in custody pending their immediate re-embarcation, as they were suspected of illegal political activities. At the same time there appeared in the offices of the National Security Department two persons who, without making their identity known, said that they were members of the staff of the Soviet Embassy in Venezuela, and who took it upon themselves to oppose this measure aggressively and violently, showing disrespect for the authorities to the point of trying to force the door of the room where the two aforementioned foreigners were lodged. They refused to recognize the identification badges of the Venezuelan authorities and they insisted that the persons held in custody should be handed over to them, still using a similar tone to that mentioned in the foregoing sentence.

These two officials were later identified as the Honourable chargé d'affaires *a.i.* of the Embassy of the Union of Soviet Socialist Republics and the attaché of the same Mission, Messrs Lev Krylov and Mikhail S. Alyabiyev, respectively.

The Government of Venezuela considers that the attitude adopted by these Soviet officials does grave harm to the relations between the two countries and constitutes an unacceptable breach of the elementary standards of conduct which diplomatic representatives should observe.

In consequence, the Ministry of Foreign Affairs has given instructions to the Venezuelan chargé d'affaires in Moscow that he shall, in the name of the Government, enter a strong protest with the Government of the USSR and at the same time request the immediate withdrawal of Messrs Krylov and Alyabiev.

145. Venezuelan communiqué on the rupture of relations with the USSR, 13 June 1952 (*p. 39*)

In execution of the instructions sent him on the 10th instant by the Ministry of Foreign Affairs, the Venezuelan chargé d'affaires in Moscow addressed to the Government of the USSR a note of protest concerning the events referred to in the Ministry's communiqué of that date.

Without making an explanation, and in disregard of the respect due in dealings between sovereign states, the Government in question has refused to receive the Venezuelan note of protest.

In contrast with this attitude, the Ministry of Foreign Affairs of Venezuela, before the Soviet authorities had taken up this attitude of negation, had arranged for one of its high officials to receive the chargé d'affaires of the USSR when on the 9th instant the latter requested an interview to present his complaint. The interview was granted the same day. On this occasion Mr Krylov explained his own version of the events which had occurred and was given a promise that these matters would be investigated. Not only, therefore, was a hearing given to his explanation, of which he also handed in a memorandum, but he received at the hands of the Government of Venezuela the attention due to the representative of a country with which relations are maintained.

The Council of Government of the United States of Venezuela consider the negative attitude of the Soviet Government as an insult to the Venezuelan nation and, in consequence, with effect from today declare that their relations with the Government in question are broken off and have given instructions to the chargé d'affaires in Moscow to return immediately to Venezuela.

146. Tass communiqué giving the Soviet account of the incident, 18 June 1952 (*p. 39*)

In connection with the unjustified arrest by the Venezuelan police of Comrade N. P. Yakushev, a member of the Soviet Embassy, and his wife, and in connection with the acts of hooliganism committed against Comrade L. V. Krylov, the acting chargé d'affaires in Venezuela, the Soviet Government has severed relations with the Government of Venezuela, as announced in the Soviet Note published on 14 June.

According to information received, the Venezuelan Government has taken a number of new illegal measures in regard to the Soviet Embassy. It has surrounded the Soviet Embassy by police armed with machine-guns. It has cut off the Embassy's links with the outside world, deprived the Embassy of connections with the Soviet Foreign Ministry, and has deprived the members of the Embassy of the possibility of obtaining food supplies.

In view of the continued violent excesses committed by the Venezuelan authorities *vis-à-vis* the Soviet Embassy, the Soviet Government has, through the medium of the Czechoslovak Government acting through the Czechoslovak Ambassador in Venezuela, demanded the Venezuelan Government to revoke its illegal measures regarding the Soviet Embassy, and has warned that it holds the Venezuelan Government fully responsible for the consequences of its illegal actions.

The Soviet Government has also warned the Venezuelan Government that retaliatory measures will be taken in regard to the Venezuelan Embassy in Moscow if the Venezuelan Government does not cease its illegal actions.

Relations between Communist Parties

147. Statement by the Politburo of the Venezuelan CP on its attitude to the USSR, February 1967:[1] excerpt (*p. 27*)
Within the international Communist movement there have arisen, and are now tending to intensify, certain anti-Soviet currents which openly offend against the postulates of proletarian internationalism and contribute to weaken a united mobilization against the imperialist offensive. The Venezuelan Communist Party cannot remain indifferent to such manifestations, which obviously do harm to the revolutionary movement as a whole, and therefore deems it necessary to make known its attitude in this matter.

The Soviet Union, born of the great Revolution carried out by the Russian people and the party of Lenin in 1917, is without doubt the strongest bulwark of the revolutionary movement on a world scale and an extraordinary example of the immense conquests of the socialist system and a palpable demonstration of its superiority over capitalist regimes. Furthermore, the Soviet Union is objectively one of the basic points of support for the movements of national liberation. . . . We Venezuelan Communists have been trained—and we are training our people from the very moment the Party was constituted—on the example of the Russian revolutionaries and of Socialist development, likewise in the understanding of what the USSR meant yesterday as the only example of the Socialist world then coming to birth, and of what it means today as an essential part of this camp for the triumph, the consolidation and the further development of the Venezuelan Revolution.

It is thus with pain and disquiet that we have seen anti-Soviet feelings arise within the revolutionary camp itself, for we consider that whatever tends to lower the prestige of the Soviet Union and to pour scorn on the aid which it has so generously offered and continues to offer to the movements of national liberation and to other Socialist countries, has a negative effect on the inter-

[1] Boletín de Información, ed., *Paz y Socialismo* (Prague, July 1967).

national revolutionary movement of which the Venezuelan Communist Party forms part. . . .

There is nothing in common, nor can there be, between anti-Sovietism and revolutionary action. To foment friendship and brotherhood with the great Soviet people and its well-tried Party, and to admire what they have achieved, is today more than ever the primordial duty of all who put the defeat of imperialism above every secondary consideration, above all differences of judgement and all national antagonism which must be radically rejected.

Neither can anti-Sovietism be concealed beneath the mantle of ideological difference and the struggle of opinions within the revolutionary movement. The way to deal with these discrepancies has been clearly laid down in the Declaration of the Communist and Workers' Parties signed in Moscow in 1960 by the overwhelming majority of the detachments forming the world Communist movement.

May this be a propitious opportunity to reaffirm the friendship and gratitude of our Party towards the Soviet people and the Communist Party of the Soviet Union which is building Communism with growing success and forms the vanguard of all the peoples of the world; and to reject energetically the calumnies launched against that great people and that great party.

16 Cuba under Fidel Castro

148. Letter from Marshal Voroshilov to Dr Manuel Urrutia announcing Soviet recognition of the Provisional Government, 10 January 1959[1] (*p. 43*)

The Government of the Union of Soviet Socialist Republics, guided by the generally recognized principles of peaceful coexistence and by the interests of international co-operation, herewith announces its official recognition of the Provisional Government of the Republic of Cuba.

The peoples of the Soviet Union warmly wish the Cuban people success and prosperity.

[1] *Pravda*, 11 Jan. 1959.

149. Speech by Severo Aguirre, Cuban delegate, at the 21st CPSU Congress reporting on Fidel Castro's advent to power, 31 January 1959:[1] excerpts (*p. 43*)

... When, twenty-five months ago, the rebel detachments of Fidel Castro, and of other patriots and fighters against imperialism, began an armed struggle, our Party deemed that its first duty was to show help to the insurgents by gving them correct guidance and assuring them of the support of the popular masses. The Party led the peasants' struggle for land, and that increased its authority amongst the peasantry.

Our Party played an active part in the rebel movement in so far as it had the character of a partisan struggle and nothing in common with putschism or individual terrorism. It called on the popular masses to give all possible backing to Fidel Castro, and by all the means at their disposal to unmask the Government's brutal repression against the partisans and the peasant population of the partisan areas. The Communists showed great valour in taking part in the armed struggle and earned the love and esteem of their comrades by being in the front line of the battle.

The armed struggle ended by overthrowing Batista's dictatorship and liquidating the military clique with whose help the leading circles in the USA had been attempting to save the old reactionary regime from complete collapse.

The theses published by the National Committee of our Party declared: 'The tyranny has been overthrown, thanks to the resistance of the whole nation who took active part against it in all fields, and by using all possible forms [of struggle]; armed struggle, work-stoppages, the general strike, the patriotic movement, the action of the working and peasant masses, propaganda and agitation, the boycott of the faked elections, the struggle against the agents of tyranny in different organisations.'

At the present time power has passed into the hands of the rebel forces, headed by Fidel Castro, and his 26 July organization, consisting 90 per cent of peasants, rural and urban workers, and students of different revolutionary trends. This is a new Government. The whole of the old state and military apparatus has been destroyed; nothing remains of the Government or organized forces which might represent the fallen regime. The armed forces are being completely rebuilt under the control of the rebels and their key-posts filled by the Partisans or their loyal supporters. The old army no longer exists.

On the proposal of the leader of the movement, Fidel Castro, a Provisional Government has been set up. This Government enjoys such a powerful backing both inside the country and abroad, that the Washington Government has to take its existence into account. The country has been freed from oppression; it has won independence and become self-governing.

Comrades! It is difficult to describe the revolutionary spirit which today animates the Cuban people who have risen to defend their country and to destroy the political hegemony of foreign imperialism.

What do the events in Cuba show? The events in Cuba, like those in

[1] Kommunisticheskaya Partiya Sovetskogo Soyuza, Congress, 21st, Moscow 1959, *Stenografichesky Otchet* (1959), i. 489–92.

Venezuela, have confounded the assertions of those who made out that, because of their proximity to the United States, the successful struggle of the countries of Latin America is impossible. When a whole nation takes to armed struggle and takes the destiny of its country into its own hands, victory is certain.

Little Cuba has inflicted a defeat on the powers of reaction and imperialism. This victory has proved possible thanks to the new alignment of forces in the international arena, thanks to the growth of the Socialist camp and the successful struggle of the oppressed nations of Asia and Africa. . . .

Comrades! Allow me from this historic tribune to express gratitude to all the Communist and Workers' Parties of the world for their solidarity with what the Cuban people have achieved. All of you, with your greater experience, must realize that the struggle of the Cuban people is not over, and that after this first struggle, it has embarked on a new stage, which is still harder and more dangerous. And we must tell you, with all clarity, that we need still more support from the Socialist world.

150. Joint communiqué on Soviet-Cuban commercial agreement, February 1960:[1] excerpt (*p. 44*)

. . . Considering the interest of both sides [the USSR and Cuba] in an expansion of trade relations on terms of equality and mutual advantage, the USSR agrees to buy 425,000 tons of Cuba's 1960 sugar harvest and to purchase a million tons of sugar in each of the four following years. In addition, the Soviet Government grants a $100 million loan at 2·5 per cent annual interest to the Cuban Government for the purchase of machinery and materials and, on account of this loan, will offer whatever technical aid may be required in 1961–4 in the construction of plants and factories undertaken by the Cuban Government. With a view to extending and consolidating the contacts already established in the field of economic co-operation, technical aid, and cultural interchange to the advantage of both peoples, the two Governments, acting as fully sovereign Governments, agree to consider at an opportune moment the question of resuming diplomatic relations on terms of complete equality and independence.

151. 'Pravda' interview with Mikoyan before his return to the USSR from Cuba, 16 February 1960: excerpts (*p. 44*)

Q. Will Soviet technicians be coming to Cuba?

A. Only in case we receive such a request. . . .

Q. Will the Soviet Union export the Cuban sugar it purchased to other countries?

A. Why should we speculate? We are buying for ourselves so that our people will consume more sugar. . . .

Q. Will Cuba have to use Soviet credit to buy commodities in the Soviet Union?

[1] *Pravda*, 15 Feb. 1960.

A. Yes. . . .
(One of the American journalists at the press conference asked whether the credits granted to Cuba by the Soviet Union envisaged the sale of military planes at present, or in the future).
A. No. This is not envisaged. No one raised this question with us.
Q. Or armaments either?
A. No. The credits granted to Cuba will be used exclusively to purchase machinery. You seem extremely interested in arms. . . .

152. Announcement of renewal of diplomatic relations between the USSR and Cuba, 8 May 1960[1] (*p. 44*)
The Governments of the USSR and the Republic of Cuba announce that they have decided to re-establish formal diplomatic relations at Embassy level.
It should be borne in mind that these relations were in effect resumed by virtue of the recognition extended to the Government of the Republic of Cuba in January 1959 by the USSR, which was subsequently confirmed by the visit to Cuba of the first Deputy Chairman of the Council of Ministers of the USSR, A. I. Mikoyan.
As a result of this visit there was signed on 13 February 1960 a commercial and payments agreement and an agreement on the granting of credit which signified the establishment from that time of normal trade relations between both countries.

153. Broadcast statement of 15 July 1960 by Capt Antonio Núñez Jiménez, Executive Director of the Cuban Institute for Agrarian Reform, on the reception by Khrushchev of a Cuban delegation in Moscow in June 1960:[2] excerpts (*p. 45*)
We went to the Soviet Union and to some other Socialist countries as instructed by the Revolutionary Government in order to initiate, or rather to increase, cultural and commercial interchange with the different countries which I have mentioned. . . .
We visited Prime Minister Khrushchev. When we passed through the door into the office of the Prime Minister of the USSR and were about twenty yards away, and when the Head of the Government caught sight of the first delegation from the Revolutionary Government of Cuba to visit his country he courteously came towards us, greeted us with a formal handshake, but at once cast aside all formality and embraced us fraternally with every mark of sympathy towards us. He took the arm of two of us 'bearded ones' in the delegation and began to laugh, saying that he was delighted to have the bearded revolutionaries of Cuba around him.
He was very affable towards us and spoke most generously of our Revolution, which he described as the most portentous historical event of recent times,

[1] *Pravda*, 8 May 1960.   [2] *Obra revolucionaria*, 25 July 1960.

one of the most notable events of modern history. He spoke of Fidel and his leadership in really historic words. He referred to Fidel as a great national leader, a great liberator of his people, and as the hope of all peoples groaning under tyranny, as had been the case of our country until Fidel forged the national unity of the country in its struggle against the foreigner.

Khrushchev displayed a great knowledge of the historic events which culminated in the triumph of the Revolution. He told us that the statements he had made in Paris had assisted our country in the defence of its sovereignty when he protested against the imperialist attacks on Cuba, and he said: 'The imperialist aggressors will not dare to attack Cuba openly because they know that world public opinion will not let them in present circumstances.' He described to us how the Soviet Union paralysed the aggression of the English and French imperialists against the Suez Canal when they invaded Egypt, when Khrushchev declared that Soviet rockets could be sent up over Great Britain, the nation sponsoring the attack on the Egyptians, who were struggling like ourselves for national independence, so that the people might gain control over the natural resources of their country. So it was that an imperialist aggression was paralysed by the serious responsible declarations of Nikita Khrushchev.

When we raised the matter, or rather asked him how the Soviet Government would reply to an aggression of this nature against our country, Nikita again recalled his declarations at the time of the Suez affair, and the following days confirmed the great and disinterested friendship which this great fighter for world peace has for the defence and sovereignty of the Cuban Fatherland, and we must be enormously grateful for the way he has defended, in the name of the Soviet Government and people, the threatened sovereignty of our Fatherland. He repeated that the Soviet Union neither wished nor saw any necessity—nor should we permit it—for a foreign power to set up here new military bases, new aggressive bases against other peoples. The Soviet Union, he said, had no need of bases anywhere, though the imperialists make out that the Soviet Union wanted to have bases in Cuba. In the first place, the establishment of such bases is not Soviet policy, and secondly, the Soviet Union has only to press a button in any part of the Soviet Union for rockets from that country to fall on any other part of the planet. . . .

154. Address by Khrushchev to the All-Russian Teachers' Congress, Moscow, threatening to use rockets in support of Cuba, 9 July 1960:[1] excerpt (*p. 45*)

The time when the United States could dictate is over. The Soviet Union is raising its voice for, and offering help to, the peoples of Cuba fighting for their independence. . . .

The socialist states and all peoples who stand on positions of peace will give the Cuban people support in their just struggle, and no one will succeed in enslaving the Cuban people. It should not be forgotten that the United States are not now at such an inaccessible distance from the Soviet Union as formerly.

[1] *Pravda*, 10 July 1960 (*AFP*, 1960, p. 207).

Figuratively speaking, in case of need, Soviet artillerymen can support the Cuban people with their rocket fire should aggressive forces in the Pentagon dare to start intervention against Cuba. And let them not forget in the Pentagon that, as the latest tests have shown, we have rockets capable of landing precisely on a given square at a distance of 13,000 kilometres; this, if you wish, is a warning to those who would like to settle international business by force and not by sense.

155. Promise of economic and military help for Cuba: Soviet-Cuban communiqué following an exchange of opinions between Raúl Castro and Khrushchev, July 1960:[1] excerpt (*p. 45*)

On behalf of the Soviet Government and the Soviet people, N. S. Khrushchev expressed warm support for the noble struggle waged by the Cuban people. He told Raúl Castro that meetings were being held throughout the Soviet Union at which millions of working people protested angrily against the economic blockade of the Republic of Cuba by the ruling quarters of the US and other countries and against their threats of an armed intervention against Cuba. N. S. Khrushchev reaffirmed that the Soviet Union would use everything to prevent US armed intervention against the Republic of Cuba.

Firm confidence was expressed that all the peoples would support the Republic of Cuba and help it break the ring of economic blockade. The forces of the countries of the Socialist camp are so great today and they are so strong economically that they can fully take upon themselves, on the basis of the development of normal trade relations, the provision of Cuba with all the necessary goods which are denied her by the US and some other capitalist countries today. The Government of the Soviet Union, N. S. Khrushchev said, is prepared to deliver oil and other goods in amounts fully meeting the requirements of Cuba, in exchange for Cuban goods.

156. Khrushchev's message to Fidel Castro on the anniversary of 26 July 1960:[2] excerpt (*p. 45*)

Allow me, Mr Prime Minister, to send my cordial congratulations to you and the peace-loving Cuban people on the occasion of the revolutionary festival of 26 July.

The armed rising which you and your comrades launched seven years ago against foreign imperialist oppression and internal reaction marked the beginning of the people's revolution in Cuba. The Cuban people boldly raised the flag of struggle for national independence and drove out Batista, the foreign capital's dummy, and proclaimed their right to be free and to dispose freely of the fruits of their labour.

The Soviet people greeted with great joy the birth of the free Cuban state and watched with deep sympathy the unbreakable resolution which it displays in defending the conquests of the Revolution.

[1] *Pravda*, 21 July 1960.   [2] *Obra revolucionaria*, 26 July 1960; *Pravda*, 26 July 1960.

Your selfless struggle for the liberty and honour of the nation places you, Mr Prime Minister, and your country in the forefront of the fighters against imperialist slavery.

The Cuban Revolution has created the new prerequisites for further development of the national-liberation movement in the countries of Latin America. The cause of heroic Cuba, which staunchly pursues a policy of defending her national interests, has today become the banner of all progressive forces of Latin America rising to struggle for liberation from imperialist oppression.

The Cuban people is not alone in its struggle for this just cause. The struggle of the Cuban people is intimately bound up with the general struggle of the forces of peace and progress for the maintenance of peace and the defence of the interests of the peoples struggling for their freedom and independence. The Soviet Union will offer Cuba the necessary support in her just struggle, and if armed intervention is undertaken against Cuba, will offer Cuba the necessary aid.

I assure you that in this work the Soviet Union will not lag behind.

I wish you, Mr Prime Minister, and all the people of Cuba, success in your noble and selfless struggle for the independence of your country.

157. Declaration of San José: Final Act of the OAS 7th Meeting of Consultation, 29 August 1960:[1] excerpt (*pp. 41, 45*)

The Seventh Meeting of Consultation of Ministers of Foreign Affairs

1. Condemns energetically the intervention or the threat of intervention, even when conditional, by an extracontinental power in the affairs of the American republics and declares that the acceptance of a threat of extracontinental intervention by any American state endangers American solidarity and security, and that this obliges the Organization of American States to disapprove it and reject it with equal vigor.

2. Rejects, also, the attempt of the Sino-Soviet powers to make use of the political, economic, or social situation of any American state, inasmuch as that attempt is capable of destroying hemispheric unity and endangering the peace and security of the hemisphere.

158. Declaration of Havana, vindicating Cuba's association with the USSR, September 1960:[2] excerpts (*p. 45*)

1. The Assembly condemns roundly, and in all its aspects, the so-called Declaration of San José, a document dictated by American imperialism. . . .

4. The National Assembly of the People declares that the aid spontaneously offered Cuba by the Soviet Union, in the event of our country being attacked by the imperialist military forces, could not be considered as an act of intervention but that, on the contrary, it manifestly constitutes a gesture of solidarity. This aid offered to Cuba in the imminent face of attack by the Pentagon does as much honour to the Government of the Soviet Union as the cowardly

[1] OAS, doc. OEA/Ser. F/11.7 (English), p. 4.
[2] *Obra revolucionaria*, 6 Sept. 1960; *Pravda*, 8 Sept. 1960.

and criminal aggressions unleashed against Cuba dishonour the Government of the United States. The General Assembly of the People therefore accepts this aid and, before America and the world, expresses their gratitude to the Soviet Union for its offer to support Cuba with the aid of rockets in the event of her soil being invaded by the military forces of the United States.

5. The National Assembly of the Cuban People categorically denies that there is any pretension on the part of the Soviet Union and the People's Republic of China to 'make use of the economic, political and social position of Cuba to shatter continental unity and imperil the unity of the hemisphere'. ...

159. 'Pravda' report of the first meeting between Fidel Castro and Khrushchev, 21 September 1960: excerpts (*p. 46*)

On 20 September the leader of the Soviet delegation to the Fifteenth Session of the General Assembly of the United Nations, Nikita S. Khrushchev, visited the leader of the Cuban delegation, Fidel Castro, at the Theresa hotel in Harlem.

This meeting between the leaders of the Governments of the USSR and the Republic of Cuba was warm and friendly. N. S. Khrushchev and Fidel Castro exchanged opinions on a number of leading questions relating to the international situation and the current session of the United Nations General Assembly. It was with the greatest satisfaction that they noted that they shared the same views on these questions. Fidel Castro warmly thanked N. S. Khrushchev for the Soviet Union's support for the struggle of the Cuban people for freedom and independence. He also thanked the head of the Soviet delegation for paying him a visit at his modest lodgings in Harlem. ...

In front of the microphone of the American radio N. S. Khrushchev said that he was very glad to meet and talk with Cuba's national hero, Fidel Castro. 'I considered', said N. S. Khrushchev, 'that I just had to meet the heroic man who had raised the standard of the Cuban people's struggle for liberty and independence, the struggle of poor against rich, and ensured the victory of the working people. The Soviet people warmly welcomes that victory and wishes the Cuban people and their national leader Fidel Castro every success.'

160. Interview granted by Khrushchev to a group of Cuban journalists headed by Carlos Franqui: the 'symbolic' nature of the rocket pledge, 22 October 1960:[1] excerpt (*p. 45*)

Franqui. The imperialists claim that the Soviet Government's statement on the possibility of using rocket weapons in the event of armed aggression against Cuba is of purely symbolic significance. What do you think of this?

Khrushchev. I should like such a statement being made by the enemies of the Cuban Revolution to be really symbolic. This requires that the imperialists' threat of intervention in Cuba does not turn into military operations. There

[1] *Pravda*, 30 Oct. 1960.

would then be no need to test the reality of our statement on armed aid to the Cuban people against aggression. Is that clear?

Franqui. We too shall use it as a figurative expression if they refrain from attacking us.

Khrushchev. Right.

Franqui. I want you to understand me correctly that it would be a fine thing if the threat were not carried out.

Khrushchev. Yes.

Franqui. But if the threat should be carried out, if the threat materializes, I gather that there are ample rockets in readiness for this?

Khrushchev. Undoubtedly. Your understanding is correct. It would be good if there were no aggression. And we are doing our utmost to avoid launching combat rockets, because the main thing is that people should not be destroyed, that they go on living, that life flourish.

161. Economic relations: joint communiqué signed at Moscow by Mikoyan and 'Che' Guevara, 19 December 1960:[1] excerpts (*p. 46*)

The Cuban mission appreciates the sincere efforts of the Soviet Union to attain world peace, which found their principal expression in the concrete proposals on peaceful coexistence between states with differing social systems and in the clear-cut proposals on general disarmament made by N. S. Khrushchev, Chairman of the USSR Council of Ministers, in the United Nations. All this is of still greater importance if one bears in mind that the country making these proposals on peaceful coexistence and disarmament is the mightiest country on earth, whose successes in the production of the newest and most awesome types of weapons substantially surpass the results achieved by the bloc of all militaristic states.

The economic mission of the Revolutionary Government of Cuba conveys warm feelings of gratitude from their people and their government to the people and government of the Soviet Union for the assistance offered by an independent country that is in the vanguard of the countries of the socialist camp.

The mission notes that this aid is being effected in three ways:

First, through commitments in the building of industrial complexes to ensure the supply to Cuba of the basic types of raw materials necessary for the industrial development of Cuba, such as an iron-and-steel mill and an oil refinery, and also through commitments in the development of the country's oil and ore deposits and the generation of electric power.

Second, rendering aid through deliveries of vitally important goods when Cuba was first blockaded by the United States of America, and especially deliveries of oil, which required a great effort on the part of the Soviet Union and was proof of its present economic might. This has also found expression in the purchase of 700,000 tons of Cuban sugar (over and above the 1,000,000 tons of sugar provided for by the Soviet-Cuban agreement), which the North

---

[1] *AFP, 1961*, pp. 278–80 (*Hoy*, 20 Dec. 1960).

American government unjustly withdrew from the quota it had established for Cuba as part of an international agreement.

The third and most important aspect of assistance was the statement made by N. S. Khrushchev, Prime Minister of the Soviet Union, on the readiness of the USSR to render Cuba full support in defending its independence against aggression.

The mission also notes the efforts by the Soviet Union aimed at protecting the interests of Cuba in international organizations at a time when this small republic has become one of the most sensitive spots in the question of safeguarding world peace. The Soviet Union and Cuba have thus fulfilled their agreement to fight together for world peace, which was announced in Havana. . . .

The Soviet side warmly supports the Havana Declaration expressing the Cuban people's aspirations for new achievements in economic and social development, which is a just reply to the colonial San José Declaration adopted at Costa Rica.

The Soviet side recognizes as just the foreign policy by which Cuba seeks to maintain its ties with the fraternal American republics. Cuba is conducting a foreign policy independent of the colonial bloc the United States of America is knocking together in that part of the world and has sided with the countries waging a just struggle for their freedom and independence. It has sided with the countries of the camp of peace.

Full agreement was reached during the talks on economic questions. A protocol on trade between the USSR and the Cuban Republic in 1961, providing for substantial increase in the volume of trade between the two countries, was signed.

Under the protocol, Cuba will export to the Soviet Union raw sugar, nickel oxide, fresh and canned fruit, juices, tanned hides and other goods.

The Soviet Union will export to Cuba petroleum and petroleum products, rolled ferrous metals, tin plate, wheat, fertilizers, chemicals, machinery and equipment, foods and other goods necessary to ensure the uninterrupted functioning of Cuba's industry, the successful development of its economy and the supply of the population with necessary goods.

An agreement was signed stipulating that the Soviet Union, in conformity with the wishes of the Cuban side, will render technical assistance to the Cuban Republic to be paid for out of the loan granted under the Soviet-Cuban agreement of Feb. 13, 1960: in geological prospecting for iron ore, chromites, petroleum and other minerals, including the delivery of the necessary equipment and devices; in building a new steel mill and in enlarging the capacities of existing steel mills; in the construction of thermal power plants with the necessary transmission lines; and in building a new oil refinery.

Technical assistance in the building and enlarging of the listed enterprises will be rendered by Soviet organizations through carrying out designing and prospecting work, supplying equipment, machinery and materials that cannot be found in Cuba, assembling the equipment and starting up the enterprises.

The sides signed an agreement on aid by the Soviet Union to the Republic of Cuba in the preparation and training of Cuban specialists for various branches of Cuba's national economy. Under this agreement the USSR will accept Cuban students to be trained as engineers of various specialties and prepared for scientific work; it will also accept highly skilled factory workers and technicians to whom it will give industrial and technical training at Soviet enterprises. . . .

The problems created for the Cuban economy by economic aggression on the part of the United States were also discussed. The Soviet Union agreed to take all measures within its power to ensure the supply of vitally important goods for the Cuban economy when they cannot be purchased in other countries and also expressed readiness to buy 2,700,000 tons of Cuban sugar if the United States of America carries out its threat not to buy Cuban sugar.

If the United States of America purchases some quantity of Cuban sugar, the Soviet Union will reduce its purchases of Cuban sugar correspondingly while bearing in mind the existing agreement that the Soviet Union will purchase 1,000,000 tons of Cuban sugar annually and that the deliveries of certain Soviet exports—oil, for instance—for which a special agreement exists will be paid for by deliveries of Cuban sugar.

The price of raw sugar has been set, with due consideration for the interests of the Cuban people, at four United States cents per British pound (free alongside ship). The Cuban side notes with satisfaction both this fact and the spirit of solidarity shown by the Soviet Union and other socialist countries in helping Cuba while it is faced with economic aggression. . . .

The atmosphere at the talks, which had as their purpose the carrying out of a number of measures and the resolute condemnation of the actions of imperialism, was characterized by a desire to preserve peace throughout the world and to struggle in every way so that international disputes may be settled through peaceful negotiations. In this connection, the Soviet Union and Cuba declare themselves staunch supporters of peaceful coexistence of states with different social systems and firmly uphold the proposals on disarmament and the changing of the structure of the United Nations to conform with the new world situation that N. S. Khruschev outlined to the UN members.

Both sides declare emphatically that world peace will never be endangered or violated in any way by actions of the Soviet Union or Cuba.

162. Statement by Khrushchev denying that rocket bases have been, or will be, established in Cuba, January 1961:[1] excerpt (*pp. 46, 49*)

Today, alarming reports are reaching us from Cuba that an imminent invasion of Cuba is under preparation by the most aggressive monopolists of the United States. As a pretext for this they are trying to make out that the Soviet Union is constructing, or has constructed, rocket bases in Cuba against the United States. It is well known, however, that this is a loathsome slander. Everyone knows very well that the Soviet Union has no military bases in Cuba or in any other countries.

[1] *Pravda*, 3 Jan. 1961.

163. Statement by Fidel Castro, 2 January 1961:[1] excerpt (*p. 46*)
Those very people who have surrounded our nation with atomic bases are
now, in order to justify an aggression, inventing [reports of] rocket-launching
pads in a neighbouring country. That is to say, they are inventing the very
thing they have been doing *vis-à-vis* the Soviet Union, inventing and fabricat-
ing a lie which, on the other hand, is a true description of what they themselves
have been doing in a number of countries.

What would have become of the world if the Soviet Union had argued in
the same way? What would have happened if, when the imperialists installed
dozens of atomic bases on her very borders, the Soviet Union had said: 'In
the face of such an obvious act of aggression we are going to invade those
countries'? If the Soviet Union had argued like the imperialists, the world
would have seen itself involved in an infernal conflagration.

**164. Speech by Fidel Castro qualifying the Cuban Revolution as
'Socialist', 18 April 1961:[2] excerpt (*p. 47*)**
This is what they [the United States] cannot forgive us; that we are here, under
their very noses, and that we have carried out a Socialist Revolution under their
very noses! This Socialist Revolution we are defending with our rifles. This
Socialist Revolution we are defending with the valour with which our anti-
aircraft crews yesterday riddled the aggressor's aircraft with gunfire. . . .
This, comrade workers and peasants, is the Socialist and democratic Revolution of the common people.

**165. The Bay of Pigs invasion attempt, 1961: draft resolution submitted
by the Soviet delegation at the UN, 18 April 1961[3] (*p. 47*)**
The General Assembly,
    Deeply concerned about the armed aggression against the Republic of Cuba
and viewing this aggression as a grave threat to general peace and security,
    1. *Condemns* the aggressive actions of the United States and other countries
on whose territories counter-revolutionary bands are being formed, trained
and armed, and from whose territories invasion of the territory of the Republic
of Cuba is being carried out;
    2. *Demands* the immediate disarming of all counter-revolutionary bands on
the territory of the United States and other countries, where they are being
prepared for aggression against Cuba;
    3. *Demands* that the Governments of all States Members of the United
Nations cease to give assistance of any kind to such bands and to allow
their territory to be used by them for the preparation and execution of aggressive actions against Cuba;
    4. *Calls* on all States Members of the United Nations to tender the necessary

[1] *Obra revolucionaria*, 4 Jan. 1961.
[2] Ibid., 16 Apr. 1961.
[3] A/4744, Report of First Committee, *GAOR*, 15th sess., Ann., agenda item 90, para. 8.

assistance to the Government of the Republic of Cuba, should it so request to repel the aggression.

166. Khrushchev's message to J. F. Kennedy, 22 April 1961:[1] excerpt (*p. 47*)

As for the Soviet Union, I have said many times and I affirm again: Our Government does not seek any advantages or privileges in Cuba. We have no bases in Cuba and do not intend to establish any. This is well known to you, and to your generals and admirals. If despite this, they still insist on scaring people with inventions about 'Soviet bases' in Cuba, they do it for the benefit of simpletons. . . .

The Soviet Government has always consequently defended the freedom and independence of all nations. It is obvious, then, that we cannot recognize any US rights to decide the fate of other countries, including the Latin American countries.

167. Joint communiqué following the visit of Osvaldo Dorticós to the USSR, signed by Brezhnev and Dorticós, 21 September 1961:[2] excerpts (*p. 47*)

. . . The two sides reaffirmed the community of positions of the Soviet Union and the Republic of Cuba on all the international questions discussed: the ensuring of a stable peace, peaceful coexistence, the achievement of an agreement on general and complete disarmament, the signing of a peace treaty with Germany and the solution on this basis of the West Berlin question and the immediate and final liquidation of the colonial system in all its forms and manifestations. . . .

The Cuban side expressed once again the appreciation of the Cuban people for the manifestation of solidarity and for the help and cooperation rendered to Cuba by the Soviet Union and the whole socialist camp without any demands or conditions whatever of a political or economic nature that would affect, directly or indirectly, its independence and sovereignty, its unqualified right to dispose of its own natural resources or its right to self-determination.

Cuba has achieved its revolution independently and has freely chosen the path of socialist development, which is best suited to ensure its rapid and effective development and the highest material and spiritual living standards for its people. . . .

Soviet-Cuban trade is developing successfully in 1961.

The Soviet Union gives Cuba technical assistance in geological surveys for iron ore, oil and other minerals. Design work is being done for a metallurgical plant, an oil refinery and two thermal power plants that will be built with technical assistance from the Soviet Union. Machine plants are being designed. Questions of assistance in the development of the chemical industry and the construction of pulp-and-paper enterprises will be studied. The Soviet Union is giving Cuba technical assistance in the development of the nickel industry.

[1] *Department of State Bulletin*, 8 May 1961, pp. 664–6.
[2] *Pravda*, 21 Sept. 1961 (*CDSP*, 18 Oct. 1961, pp. 21–2).

The two sides discussed and proposed measures for further expanding economic cooperation and Soviet-Cuban trade.

An accord was reached on conducting negotiations toward the signing of a long-term trade agreement providing for a further increase in deliveries of raw sugar from Cuba to the USSR.

The Soviet government declared its readiness to continue to render comprehensive assistance in the development of the national economy of the Republic of Cuba and of the basic branches of its industry and agriculture and to exchange with Cuba achievements in science, technology and culture.

An accord has been reached on substantially increasing the capacity of the oil refinery and the metallurgical plant that are being designed by Soviet organizations.

The two sides agreed on the advisability of concluding an agreement on scientific and technical cooperation between the Soviet Union and the Republic of Cuba. . . .

168. Speech by Fidel Castro declaring himself to be a Marxist-Leninist, 1 December 1961:[1] extracts (*p. 48*)

When I was recently looking through my books, I found that, in my student days, I had read as far as page 370 of *Capital*. That is as far as I got. I plan, when I have time, to continue studying Karl Marx's *Capital*.

In my student days I had studied the Communist Manifesto and the selected works of Marx, Engels and Lenin. It is naturally very interesting to re-read now what I read in those days. Very well; do I believe in Marxism? I believe absolutely in Marxism! Did I believe in it on the first of January (1959)? I believed in it on the first of January! Did I believe in it on 26 July (1953)? I believed in it on 26 July! Did I understand it then as I understand it today, after ten years of struggle? No, I did not understand it then as I understand it now. Compared with what I understood then and what I understand now, there is a great difference. . . . Do I have some doubt about Marxism, and believe that some interpretations are mistaken and ought to be revised? No, I have not the slightest doubt. . . . The more we confront the reality of a revolution and the class struggle, and see what the reality of the class struggle is in its revolutionary setting, the more we are convinced of all the truths written by Marx and Engels, and the truly masterly interpretation which Lenin gave to Scientific Socialism. . . .

We are at the stage of constructing Socialism. And what sort of Socialism must we apply? Utopian Socialism? We must simply apply Scientific Socialism. That is why I began by saying in all frankness that we believed in Marxism, that we believed it to be the most correct, the most scientific, the only true, the only really revolutionary theory. I must say with full satisfaction and full confidence; I am a Marxist-Leninist, and I shall be a Marxist-Leninist until the last day of my life!

[1] *Obra revolucionaria*, 2 Dec. 1961.

169. Official Soviet statement reaffirming that the USSR has established no military base in Cuba, February 1962:[1] excerpts (*p. 49*)

... The Soviet government cannot disregard the fact that government figures of the USA, in asserting that Cuba is all but a conveyer belt for 'extra-hemispheric' intervention, are plainly pointing at the Soviet Union. They even go so far as to say that Cuba has become a military base of the Soviet Union. But then let them say where, in what part of the island, there is a Soviet military base and what kind of base it is: rocket, air force or naval. Let them find just one platoon of Soviet soldiers. Finally, let them show any request the Soviet Union has made to set up a military base on Cuba. No one is able to do this, because there are no Soviet military bases on Cuba and there never were. But it is possible to indicate precisely the location of an American military base. ...

... The Soviet Union has taken a stand and will continue to do so on the side of the Cuban people in their just struggle, has given them aid and will continue to do so. ...

... The Republic of Cuba, as N. S. Khrushchev, the head of the Soviet government, has clearly stated, can always rely on the help and support of the Soviet people. The well-known warnings by the Soviet government, addressed to the enemies of Cuba, remain in force today. ...

170. The development of Soviet-Cuban relations, May 1960–May 1962: article by Jacinto Torras, June 1962[2] (*p. 48*)

On 8 May of the current year, the second anniversary of the restoration of diplomatic relations between Cuba and the Soviet Union was commemorated.

Before the restoration of diplomatic relations, firm economic and commercial relations had been established between both countries. On 13 February 1960, during the visit of Vice-Premier Mikoyan to Cuba, a trade and payments agreement for five years (1960–4) and an agreement granting a credit of $100 million on the part of the Soviet Union, lasting until 1975 and with the low interest rate of 2·5 per cent p.a., were signed in Havana.

As the Soviet writer Kaminin pointed out in the newspaper *Izvestiya*: 'In these two years there have occurred—as all the world knows—dozens, perhaps hundreds, of moving manifestations of friendship and cooperation between the two peoples.'

This is indeed a fact. The relations between the Soviet Union and Cuba in these two years offer a lofty example of friendship and fraternal collaboration shown by a great country, whose people did away with capitalism more than forty-four years ago, built Socialism, and have begun to build Communism, after routing the Nazi invader, towards a country like Cuba which lived through more than four and a half centuries of colonialism, and whose people won their liberty and the right to follow the path of Socialism by dint of courage and heroism.

[1] *Pravda*, 19 Feb. 1962 (*CDSP*, 14 Mar. 1962, p. 35).
[2] *Cuba socialista*, no. 10, June 1962.

The collaboration and friendship of the Soviet Union towards Cuba have manifested themselves in all fields—economic, cultural, technical, in public health, and in the decisive help which brought the aggressive plans of Yankee imperialism to a halt on more than one occasion.

The trade and payments agreement on 13 February laid the foundations for the development of a commercial interchange based on a true reciprocity, exempt from marginal conditions, the freezing of tariffs, the concession of preferences, and the prohibition of free trade with other countries, as happened with the agreements imposed by North American imperialism. By the same treaty, the Soviet Union pledged itself to buy from Cuba 1 million metric tons of sugar annually for each of the five years that it remains in force, paying 20 per cent of the value in freely convertible currency and the rest with Soviet goods freely chosen by Cuba and at international prices, which in many cases proved lower than those which Cuba had been forced to pay previously to the imperialist monopolies.

On the basis of this agreement there has been an intensive development in Cuban-Soviet trade. In 1960 the total volume of commercial interchange reached a figure of somewhat less than $100 million. In 1961 this figure was increased five and a half times, and in 1962 it will be seven and a half times greater than in 1960, or about 40 per cent higher than in 1961, reaching a volume of $750 million.

These global figures, which show the rapid increase of Cuban-Soviet trade, cover various great and decisive aspects of the friendly collaboration of the Soviet Union towards Cuba.

The year 1960, when the trade agreement with the USSR entered into force, was the year of the great economic offensive by means of which Yankee imperialism aimed to overthrow the Cuban Revolution. This economic offensive, a real war against our country, threw into relief the Cuban people's degree of awareness and unity and their decision to struggle to the death in defence of their freedom and revolutionary conquests, and at the same time served to display the Soviet Union's firm attitude of friendship and co-operation.

The first great episode of this fraternal collaboration occurred—as we all remember—when Cuba, in a sovereign act, decided to buy petroleum offered by the Soviet Union through the trade agreement, at a price below that imposed by the international oil monopolies which until then had exercised an absolute control over the importation, refining, and distribution of oil and its derivatives in our country.

The monopolies joined battle with the aim of dealing a mortal blow against the Revolution, bearing in mind that Cuba disposes of no fuel of her own. They refused to sell oil at a reduced price and prevented an inadequate enterprise which was disposed to do so by threats. They later refused to refine the crude oil acquired by the Revolutionary Government in the Soviet Union, which led to the refineries and the distributive apparatus being taken over.

This was the first dramatic battle of the Cuban Revolution against Yankee imperialism in the economic and commercial field. This battle was won with the help of the Soviet Union, which brought into action her economic, technical, and organizational resources and regularly transported oil to Cuba, over great distances, despite the threats of reprisals launched by the monopolies. The collaboration of the Soviet Union was so efficient that not for a single minute was the supply of petrol to our country affected.

Yankee imperialism's second great economic aggression against Cuba took place in July 1960, when the Government of the United States arbitrarily and unilaterally suspended our sugar quota in that market, forbidding the import of some 700,000 tons of Cuban sugar which still needed to be supplied in that year. The patent purpose of this measure was to deprive Cuba of her essential source of foreign exchange, and to provoke a sharp economic crisis with the object of routing the Cuban people and their Revolution.

The Soviet Union immediately gave another sign of her fraternal collaboration by announcing her decision to acquire those 700,000 tons of sugar. This friendly collaboration developed in 1961 and 1962, when the United States totally suppressed their purchases of sugar from Cuba and the Soviet Union went on to acquire increasing quantities of Cuban sugar at a price well above that prevailing on the world market. In the present year, the Soviet Union will buy from Cuba 2,880,000 metric tons of sugar, and has furthermore shown her readiness to acquire up to 3,200,000 metric tons, which Cuba has not been able to meet on account of a reduced sugar harvest.

Imperialism launched its third commercial and economic offensive in 1960 when, in November of that year, it placed an embargo on North American exports to our country with the obvious aim of paralysing our supplies of spare parts and raw materials and also of consumer goods. In this battle, the co-operation of the Soviet Union was decisive for Cuba. Our country made a great effort to switch its trade rapidly from the US to the USSR and other Socialist countries since, among other things, the shortage of freely convertible currency limited her purchases from other capitalist powers. To achieve this change-over of imports in a short space of time, overcoming the previous ignorance of the market, distance, and other technical factors, the help

Geographical distribution of foreign trade
(In percentages of total foreign trade)

Exports to

	1958	1959	1960	1961	1962 (est.)
Socialist countries	2·6	2·2	24·4	74·7	86·7
United States	66·8	69·4	52·8	4·6	1·0
Other countries	30·6	28·4	22·8	20·7	18·3

Imports from

	1958	1959	1960	1961	1962 (est.)
Socialist countries	0·3	0·3	—	86·1	80·3
United States	69·8	67·9	—	1·1	0·0
Other countries	29·9	31·8	—	12·8	19·7

of the Soviet Union of the countries of the Socialist world was once again decisive.

The figures for the geographical distribution of our foreign trade reflect the magnitude of the change, as can be seen from the table on p. 268.

During 1960, and following the signing of the trade and payments treaty with the Soviet Union, Cuba signed commercial agreements with the other Socialist countries which contributed to the development of her foreign trade and which were, at the same time, instruments for expressing the friendly co-operation of all those countries with our country.

A very recent and clear manifestation of the Soviet Union's co-operation with Cuba has been the supply of food products, raw materials, and other goods to the value of tens of millions of dollars, with a view to improving the Cuban people's sources of supply, in addition to the deliveries envisaged under the Trade Protocol signed the present year and on credit. Amongst the additional foodstuffs with which the Soviet Union will supply us are large quantities of rice, potatoes, beans, vegetable oils, wheat-flour, tinned meat and fish, condensed milk, maize, and other products. Other Socialist states are also lending their fraternal and valuable co-operation to Cuba in the matter of foodstuffs and important offers have been received from Hungary, Bulgaria, and Poland.

In the field of financial and technical aid, the collaboration of the Socialist states has been extraordinary during these two years of diplomatic relations. The $100 million loan granted by the Soviet Union to Cuba on 13 February 1960 was intended for industrial plant, equipment, and technical assistance according to contracts being worked out by the competent organs of both countries. On the basis of this agreement, Cuba has signed contracts under which she is receiving technical aid and equipment from the USSR for carrying out geological exploration for the development of the nickel and chemical industries. She is also receiving the USSR's technical assistance in studies for the establishment of a steel industry.

In the field of technical assistance for the training of specialist and qualified cadres, there are at present some 1,500 young Cubans studying in universities, specialized colleges, and factories in the USSR, as well as some 1,000 young men, most of them farmers, finishing a specialized course in agriculture. Technical assistance has been extended to cover the setting up of teaching centres for training qualified workers for our country's industry. At the same time, the Soviet Union has lent Cuba the help of hundreds of technicians of various specialities who have come to our country.

The Soviet Union's technical assistance to Cuba is of such magnitude that we cannot claim to cover it entirely in this article. But the nature of the truly fraternal collaboration of this technical assistance deserves to be stressed. Whereas the immense majority of the technicians who came to Cuba before the Revolution, very inferior in quantity and quality to those we now receive from the USSR and other Socialist countries, were specialists in the service of the great capitalist enterprises whose object it was to exploit our people, the Soviet specialists and technicians, and those from the other Socialist countries, come to offer us their skills, to work shoulder to shoulder with us with the sincere aim of helping towards the speediest solution of our problems, the quickest development of our economy, and the best training of our technical cadres. This is the spirit and practice of the Soviet Union's and the other Socialist countries' collaboration with Cuba.

The fraternal collaboration of the Soviet Union has also manifested itself in the field of culture and sport. The interchange between the two countries of artistic ensembles and of outstanding artists is well known. It is enough to mention the visits to Cuba of the Red Army Ensemble and the Moiseyev Popular Dance Ensemble, and the visit to the USSR of the Cuban Ballet, the Modern Dance Ensemble of the National Theatre, and of well-known artists.

In the field of sport, different Soviet and Cuban teams have exchanged visits, and there has recently taken place the great international chess tournament in which the most prominent figures for the Soviet Union and the Socialist states took part.

In the field of public health, the Soviet Union has also shown her fraternal collaboration towards Cuba. Two outstanding instances in this sphere have been the sending of anti-polio vaccine which makes possible the eradication of this terrible disease from our country, and the gift of a hospital now under construction in Holguín. Outstanding Cuban doctors and specialists have visited the USSR and in Cuba we have received visits from notable Soviet specialists, and also exhibitions which have brought us the latest advances in medical science.

Together with this vast economic, cultural, artistic, and scientific collaboration, the USSR has given her decisive support to the liberty and independence of Cuba in the face of the constant threats and aggression of Yankee imperialism. The whole world knows, and we Cubans can never forget, the categorical warning to the United States Government given by the Soviet Union, in the words of Nikita S. Khrushchev, when they were putting the finishing touches to their plans to attack our country at the end of 1960. When the bands of mercenaries armed by imperialism landed in Playa Girón in April 1961, the Soviet Union again stretched out her brotherly hand to the Cuban people. And recently, when North American imperialism endeavoured, with aggressive intent, with the help of its Latin American puppets at Punta del Este, to isolate Cuba from the other countries of the continent, the Soviet Government once again raised its voice in energetic condemnation and warning in its declaration of support for Cuba made on 18 February of this year.

These moving instances of solidarity in all fields are the target of distortions by imperialist propaganda which desperately wants to prevent the example of this new type of relations between the peoples being known in all its greatness by the peoples of Latin America and the other peoples of the world. The contrast between the type of relations imposed by the United States on Latin America, based on inequality and the plundering of its riches and of its peoples, and the type of the fraternal relations on the part of the Soviet Union and all the Socialist camp, based on the principles of peace, self determination of peoples, and the independence and sovereignty of all countries, enrages the imperialists, the great monopolies and their lackeys.

North American imperialism also strives to make out that these fraternal relations between the Socialist camp and Cuba were inspired by objectives of military aggression against the United States. By these lies the imperialists are simply seeking to justify their own aggressive designs against our country.

Thanks to the revolutionary unity and firmness of the Cuban people and to this sort of relations between the USSR and all the Socialist camp towards our country, our Revolution has been able to advance and the power of the workers and peasants to consolidate itself. That is why the Cuban people, in drawing up the balance sheet of their two years of relations with the Soviet Union, manifests their delight in knowing that their great cause of freedom, national independence, and Socialism can count on friends as disinterested and powerful as are the countries of the Socialist camp headed by the great Soviet Union.

171. Joint statement issued in Moscow by representatives of the Soviet and Cuban Governments on additional Soviet economic and military aid to Cuba, 2 September 1962:[1] excerpts (*p. 49*)

Comrade Ernesto Guevara Cerna [Serna], Minister of Industry, and Comrade Emilio Aragones Navarro, both members of the National Leadership of the Integrated Revolutionary Organizations of Cuba, were in the Soviet Union from Aug. 27 to Sept. 2, 1962. . . .

During these friendly negotiations, the two sides agreed on the construction in Cuba, with the assistance of the Soviet Union, of the metallurgical plant provided for in the Soviet-Cuban agreement of Nov. 16, 1960, which is of great importance for the development of the economy of the Republic of Cuba.

The two sides agreed that Soviet organizations would work out, in as short a time as possible, a technical and economic report relating to the construction of a metallurgical plant with a complete metallurgical cycle, using iron ore reserves available in the Republic of Cuba, and would submit it to the government of the Republic of Cuba by the middle of 1963.

At the same time the two sides deemed it advisable, in view of additional potentials discovered, to rebuild three existing metallurgical plants and to raise their combined capacity from 110,000 to 350,000 tons of steel a year.

The two sides also agreed to continue the exchange of experience between the Soviet Union and the Republic of Cuba in the field of agriculture by working out individual agricultural problems as well as by dispatching specialists to Cuba for work on irrigation, soil reclamation, hydrotechnical construction and practical questions of the Soviet Union's assistance to Cuba in agriculture, including the sending of Cuban citizens to the Soviet Union to study the various branches of agricultural production.

The two sides noted with great satisfaction that the successful conclusion of the negotiations in Moscow would contribute to the further development

[1] *Pravda*, 3 Sept. 1962 (*AFP, 1962*, pp. 368–9).

of fraternal friendship and close economic cooperation between the USSR and the Republic of Cuba.

During the visit of Comrades Ernesto Guevara Cerna and Emilio Aragones Navarro in the Soviet Union, there was also an exchange of opinions in connection with the threats by aggressive imperialist circles with respect to Cuba. In view of these threats, the government of the Republic of Cuba asked the Soviet government for aid in the form of armaments and the appropriate technical specialists to train Cuban servicemen. The Soviet government was attentive to this request by the Cuban government and an accord was reached on this question. As long as there are threats from the above-mentioned circles with respect to Cuba, the Republic of Cuba has every reason to take measures necessary to ensure its security and the defense of its sovereignty and independence, and all genuine friends of Cuba have the full right to respond to this legitimate request.

172. Statement by the Soviet Government admitting that arms were being sent to Cuba 'for defensive purposes', 11 September 1962:[1] excerpts (*p. 50*)

... We can say to these people that these are our ships, and that what we carry in them is no business of theirs. It is the internal affair of the parties engaged in this commercial transaction. We can say, as the popular saying has it: 'Don't stick your noses in where you have no business.'

... As is known, a certain amount of armament is also being sent to Cuba from the Soviet Union at the request of the Cuban government in connection with the threats by aggressive imperialist circles. The Cuban statesmen have also requested the Soviet government to send to Cuba Soviet military specialists, technicians to train the Cubans in mastering up-to-date weapons, because modern weapons now require high qualifications and considerable knowledge. It is natural that Cuba does not yet have such specialists. This is why we took an understanding attitude toward this request. It must be said, however, that the number of Soviet military specialists sent to Cuba can in no way be compared with the number of agricultural and industrial personnel sent there. The arms and military equipment sent to Cuba are intended solely for defensive purposes. The President of the USA and the American military, like the military of any country, know what means of defense are. How can these means menace the United States of America?

... The Government of the Soviet Union has authorized Tass to state also that there is no need for the Soviet Union to set up in any other country—Cuba, for instance—the weapons it has for repelling aggression, for a retaliatory blow. The explosive power of our nuclear weapons is so great and the Soviet Union has such powerful missiles for delivering these nuclear warheads that there is no need to seek sites for them somewhere beyond the boundaries of the Soviet Union. We have said, and we repeat that if war is unleashed, if the aggressor attacks one or another state and the state asks for help, the Soviet Union has

---

[1] *Pravda*, 12 Sept. 1962 (*AFP, 1962*, pp. 371–2; para. 1 trans. by the Editor).

the capacity to extend help from its own territory to any peace-loving state, and not only to Cuba. And let no one doubt that the Soviet Union will give such help, just as it was ready in 1956 to render military assistance to Egypt at the time of the Anglo-French-Israeli aggression in the Suez Canal area. . . .

The Soviet government will not follow in the path of the USA, which is calling up 150,000 from the reserves. If we were to repeat the actions of the USA we would be doing apparently exactly what certain American circles want—helping them to inflame the situation. But we cannot disregard the United States' preparation of an act of aggression. The Soviet government considers it its duty to display vigilance in this situation and to instruct the Minister of Defense of the Soviet Union and the Soviet Army Command to take all measures to place our armed forces at peak military preparedness. . . .

173. The October 1962 missile crisis: address by J. F. Kennedy to the nation announcing that the existence of offensive missiles in Cuba has been confirmed, 22 October 1962:[1] excerpts (*p. 50*)

This Government, as promised, has maintained the closest surveillance of the Soviet military buildup on the island of Cuba. Within the past week unmistakable evidence has established the fact that a series of offensive missile sites is now in preparation on that imprisoned island. The purposes of these bases can be none other than to provide a nuclear strike capability against the Western Hemisphere.

Upon receiving the first preliminary hard information of this nature last Tuesday morning [October 16] at 9:00 a.m., I directed that our surveillance be stepped up. And having now confirmed and completed our evaluation of the evidence and our decision on a course of action, this Government feels obliged to report this new crisis to you in fullest detail.

The characteristics of these new missile sites indicate two distinct types of installations. Several of them include medium-range ballistic missiles capable of carrying a nuclear warhead for a distance of more than 1,000 nautical miles. Each of these missiles, in short, is capable of striking Washington, D.C., the Panama Canal, Cape Canaveral, Mexico City, or any other city in the southeastern part of the United States, in Central America, or in the Caribbean area.

Additional sites not yet completed appear to be designed for intermediate-range ballistic missiles capable of travelling more than twice as far—and thus capable of striking most of the major cities in the Western Hemisphere, ranging as far north as Hudson Bay, Canada, and as far south as Lima, Peru. In addition, jet bombers, capable of carrying nuclear weapons, are now being uncrated and assembled in Cuba, while the necessary air bases are being prepared.

This urgent transformation of Cuba into an important strategic base—by the presence of these large, long-range, and clearly offensive weapons of sudden mass destruction—constitutes an explicit threat to the peace and security of all the Americas, in flagrant and deliberate defiance of the Rio Pact of 1947, the

[1] *AFP, 1962*, pp. 399–402.

traditions of this nation and hemisphere, the Joint Resolution of the 87th Congress, the Charter of the United Nations, and my own public warnings to the Soviets on September 4 and 13.

This action also contradicts the repeated assurances of Soviet spokesmen, both publicly and privately delivered, that the arms buildup in Cuba would retain its original defensive character and that the Soviet Union had no need or desire to station strategic missiles on the territory of any other nation.

The size of this undertaking makes clear that it has been planned for some months. Yet only last month, after I had made clear the distinction between any introduction of ground-to-ground missiles and the existence of defensive anti-aircraft missiles, the Soviet Government publicly stated on September 11 that, and I quote, 'The armaments and military equipment sent to Cuba are designed exclusively for defensive purposes,' and, and I quote the Soviet Government, 'There is no need for the Soviet Government to shift its weapons for a retaliatory blow to any other country, for instance Cuba,' and that, and I quote the Government, 'The Soviet Union has so powerful rockets to carry these nuclear warheads that there is no need to search for sites for them beyond the boundaries of the Soviet Union.' That statement was false.

Only last Thursday, as evidence of this rapid offensive build-up was already in my hand, Soviet Foreign Minister Gromyko told me in my office that he was instructed to make it clear once again, as he said his Government had already done, that Soviet assistance to Cuba, and I quote, 'pursued solely the purpose of contributing to the defense capabilities of Cuba,' that, and I quote him, 'training by Soviet specialists of Cuban nationals in handling defensive armaments was by no means offensive,' and that 'if it were otherwise,' Mr Gromyko went on, 'the Soviet Government would never become involved in rendering such assistance,' That statement also was false.

Neither the United States of America nor the world community of nations can tolerate deliberate deception and offensive threats on the part of any nation, large or small. We no longer live in a world where only the actual firing of weapons represents a sufficient challenge to a nation's security to constitute maximum peril. Nuclear weapons are so destructive and ballistic missiles are so swift that any substantially increased possibility of their use or any sudden change in their deployment may well be regarded as a definite threat to peace.

For many years both the Soviet Union and the United States, recognizing this fact, have deployed strategic nuclear weapons with great care, never upsetting the precarious *status quo* which insured that these weapons would not be used in the absence of some vital challenge. Our own strategic missiles have never been transferred to the territory of any other nation under a cloak of secrecy and deception; and our history, unlike that of the Soviets since the end of World War II, demonstrates that we have no desire to dominate or conquer any other nation or impose our system upon its people. Nevertheless, American citizens have become adjusted to living daily on the bull's eye of Soviet missiles located inside the USSR or in submarines.

In that sense missiles in Cuba add to an already clear and present danger— although it should be noted the nations of Latin America have never previously been subjected to a potential nuclear threat.

But this secret, swift and extraordinary buildup of Communist missiles—in an area well known to have a special and historical relationship to the United States and the nations of the Western Hemisphere, in violation of Soviet assurances, and in defiance of American and hemispheric policy—this sudden, clandestine decision to station strategic weapons for the first time outside of Soviet soil—is a deliberately provocative and unjustified change in the *status quo* which cannot be accepted by this country if our courage and our commitments are ever to be trusted again by either friend or foe.

The 1930's taught us a clear lesson: Aggressive conduct, if allowed to grow unchecked and unchallenged, ultimately leads to war. This nation is opposed to war. We are also true to our word. Our unswerving objective, therefore, must be to prevent the use of these missiles against this or any other country and to secure their withdrawal or elimination from the Western Hemisphere.

Our policy has been one of patience and restraint, as befits a peaceful and powerful nation, which leads a worldwide alliance. We have been determined not to be diverted from our central concerns by mere irritants and fanatics. But now further action is required—and it is underway; and these actions may only be the beginning. We will not prematurely or unnecessarily risk the costs of worldwide nuclear war in which even the fruits of victory would be ashes in our mouth—but neither will we shrink from that risk at any time it must be faced.

Acting, therefore, in the defense of our own security and of the entire Western Hemisphere, and under the authority entrusted to me by the Constitution as endorsed by the resolution of the Congress, I have directed that the following *initial* steps be taken immediately:

First: To halt this offensive build-up, a strict quarantine on all offensive military equipment under shipment to Cuba is being initiated. All ships of any kind bound for Cuba from whatever nation or port will, if found to contain cargoes of offensive weapons, be turned back. This quarantine will be extended, if needed, to other types of cargo and carriers. We are not at this time, however, denying the necessities of life as the Soviets attempted to do in their Berlin blockade of 1948.

Second: I have directed the continued and increased close surveillance of Cuba and its military buildup. The Foreign Ministers of the OAS in their communique of October 3 rejected secrecy on such matters in this hemisphere. Should these offensive military preparations continue, thus increasing the threat to the hemisphere, further action will be justified. I have directed the Armed Forces to prepare for any eventualities; and I trust that, in the interest of both the Cuban people and the Soviet technicians at the sites, the hazards to all concerned of continuing this threat will be recognized.

Third: It shall be the policy of this nation to regard any nuclear missile launched from Cuba against any nation in the Western Hemisphere as an attack by the Soviet Union on the United States, requiring a full retaliatory response upon the Soviet Union.

Fourth: As a necessary military precaution I have reinforced our base at Guantanamo, evacuated today the dependents of our personnel there, and ordered additional military units to be on a standby alert basis.

Fifth: We are calling tonight for an immediate meeting of the Organ of Consultation, under the Organization of American States, to consider this threat to hemispheric security and to invoke articles 6 and 8 of the Rio Treaty in support of all necessary action. The United Nations Charter allows for regional security arrangements—and the nations of this hemisphere decided long ago against the military presence of outside powers. Our other allies around the world have also been alerted.

Sixth: Under the Charter of the United Nations, we are asking tonight that an emergency meeting of the Security Council be convoked without delay to take action against this latest Soviet threat to world peace. Our resolution will call for the prompt dismantling and withdrawal of all offensive weapons in Cuba, under the supervision of UN observers, before the quarantine can be lifted.

Seventh and finally: I call upon Chairman Khrushchev to halt and eliminate this clandestine, reckless and provocative threat to world peace and to stable relations between our two nations. I call upon him further to abandon this course of world domination and to join in an historic effort to end the perilous arms race and transform the history of man. He has an opportunity now to move the world back from the abyss of destruction—by returning to his Government's own words that it had no need to station missiles outside its own territory, and withdrawing these weapons from Cuba—by refraining from any action which will widen or deepen the present crisis—and then by participating in a search for peaceful and permanent solutions.

This nation is prepared to present its case against the Soviet threat to peace, and our own proposals for a peaceful world, at any time and in any forum in the OAS, in the United Nations, or in any other meeting that could be useful—without limiting our freedom of action. . . .

Post-missile-crisis relations

174. Speech by Fidel Castro, 1 November 1962:[1] excerpts (*p. 51*)

It must be said that, in the course of this crisis, and as the crisis developed, there arose some differences between the Soviet Government and the Cuban Government. But I wish to say something to all Cubans. This is not the place to discuss these problems. This is not the place—where it could be of use to our enemies who might take advantage of the discussions. This must be discussed with the Soviets, at Government and Party level. We must sit down and discuss with them everything which may be necessary, by the light of reason and by the light of principles. For it must be said that we are, first and foremost, Marxist-Leninists, and we are friends of the Soviet Union! Nothing shall come between the Soviet Union and Cuba!

I wish to say something else; that we have confidence in the principles under-

---

[1] *Cuba socialista*, no. 16, Dec. 1962, pp. 28–30.

lying the Soviet Union's policy, in the leadership of the Soviet Union, that is to say, in the Government and the leading Party of the Soviet Union.

If my fellow countrymen ask my opinion at this time, what should I say—what advice should I give them? In the midst of confused situations, of matters which have not been, or are not, fully understood—what should be done? I should say that what needs to be done is to have confidence—to realize that these international problems are extremely complex, extremely delicate, and that our people, which has shown signs of great and extraordinary maturity, should give proof of it now. That is to say: be careful to analyse things, to avoid premature judgements, to be disciplined, and above all, to have confidence—full confidence—in the Revolutionary Government, in the leadership of the Revolutionary Government; full confidence that everything—all problems, all questions—will be discussed at the right time. Bear in mind that there may not be sufficient grounds for passing judgement on certain things, and let it not be forgotten under what dramatic and urgent circumstance events took place. . . .

There is another and still more moving thing. On me, at least, it makes an extraordinary impression; the Soviet men whom we have known here, the technicians of every type who have come to work with us in our fields, school-masters, professors, engineers, planners. The interest and persistence with which they have striven to help us, the affection with which they have helped us! Furthermore, the military technicians—men who have been prepared to die here with us, who have helped us in instruction, training, preparation of our combat forces, who have laboured with us for months—for years—teaching our men to fight, to organize the formidable army we now have.

The basic arms of our forces are arms which the Soviet Union sent, and which the Soviet Union has not withdrawn.

I must tell you that some months ago the Soviet Union decided to write off all the debt incurred by our country so far as arms are concerned.

Above all, there are things I wish to say with absolute sincerity, at this time when a certain displeasure may have been caused as a result of these mis-understandings and differences it is good to remember, above all, what the Soviet Union has done for us. It is good to remember, above all, what it did for us in all the emergencies we have experienced in the face of the blows aimed at us by the Yankees; the economic aggression, the suppression of the sugar quota, the cancellation of oil supplies to our country; how, in the face of each of these aggressions, the friendly arm of the Soviet has been with us. We are grateful, and this we must state here for all to hear.

There are some questions of a military nature which must be treated with the greatest care. Now, as an example, I am going to explain something to you. The strategic arms required for our defence were not Cuban property. This is not the same case as tanks, and a whole series of other arms which are indeed our own property. The strategic arms were not our property.

In the agreements by virtue of which they were sent to our country to strengthen our defences in the face of threatened attacks, it was agreed that these strategic arms, which are very complex and call for very specialized personnel, should remain under the control of Soviet personnel, and should remain the property of the Soviet state. That was why, when the Soviet

Government decided to withdraw these arms, which were their own, we respected their decision. I am explaining this so that it may be understood why the withdrawal was decided by the Soviet Government.

That is why I said that even when we have some justified grounds for dissatisfaction over some act, some detail, we must now more than ever recall how good and generous, what noble friends, the Soviets have been towards us.

175. Statement by J. F. Kennedy confirming that the missile sites were being dismantled, 2 November 1962[1] (*p. 51*)

My fellow citizens: I want to take this opportunity to report on the conclusions which this Government has reached on the basis of yesterday's aerial photographs which will be made available tomorrow, as well as other indications, namely, that the Soviet missile bases in Cuba are being dismantled, their missiles and related equipment are being crated, and the fixed installations at these sites are being destroyed.

The United States intends to follow closely the completion of this work through a variety of means, including aerial surveillance, until such time as an equally satisfactory international means of verification is effected.

While the quarantine remains in effect, we are hopeful that adequate procedures can be developed for international inspection of Cuba-bound cargoes. The International Committee of the Red Cross, in our view, would be an appropriate agent in this matter.

The continuation of these measures in air and sea, until the threat to peace posed by these offensive weapons is gone, is in keeping with our pledge to secure their withdrawal or elimination from this hemisphere. It is in keeping with the resolution of the OAS, and it is in keeping with the exchange of letters with Chairman Khrushchev of October 27 and 28.

Progress is now being made toward the restoration of peace in the Caribbean, and it is our firm hope and purpose that this progress shall go forward. We will continue to keep the American people informed on this vital matter.

176. Visit of Mikoyan, First Deputy Premier, to Cuba for 'a friendly exchange of views', 2 November 1962:[2] excerpts (*p. 51*)

It is with great pleasure that I am looking forward to coming to the friendly Cuba where I already was in February, 1960, and saw tremendous enthusiasm and the unity of all working people of the Republic of Cuba headed by the hero of the Cuban people, Fidel Castro.

I have heard that the American press and radio, and in particular today's newspapers, venture absolutely groundless guesses and fantasies about the purpose of my visit to Cuba.

I am going there for a friendly exchange of views with our close friend, Premier Fidel Castro, on questions of the international situation.

[1] *AFP, 1962*, pp. 451–2.   [2] *New York Times*, 3 Nov. 1962.

177. Message from Fidel Castro to the UN Acting Secretary-General, 19 November 1962:[1] excerpts (*p. 51*)

The Government of the United States and the most reactionary section of the press of that country are endeavouring to create the impression that the Government of Cuba wishes to hamper and sabotage the possibilities for a peaceful solution of the present crisis.

This attitude is based on two absolutely legitimate decisions of our people. The first; not to accept the unilateral inspection of our land whereby the Government of the United States wishes to decide questions which are entirely within our jurisdiction as a sovereign nation. The second; not to be prepared to permit invasions of our airspace which are injurious to our security and offensive to our national dignity.

The Government of Cuba has not created the slightest obstacle to the negotiations which are taking place. This has been and it is our position. Our attitude to the threats and insults of the Government of the United States is something very different.

The United States has now made the IL-28 medium bombers stationed on Cuban territory the crux of the problem. These planes are the property of the Soviet Government. They were brought to Cuba for the defence of our country when faced with aggression. Owing to their limited speed and low flight ceiling they are antiquated equipment in relation to modern means of anti-aircraft defence. It is clear that the position of the Government of the United States in demanding the withdrawal of these planes merely constitutes a pretext for maintaining tension, prolonging the crisis and continuing its policy of force. Nevertheless, if the Soviet Government considers it desirable for the smooth conduct of the negotiations and the solution of the crisis to withdraw these planes, the Revolutionary Government of Cuba will not object to this decision.

178. Statement by J. F. Kennedy at a press conference on the termination of the crisis, 20 November 1962[2] (*p. 51*)

I have today been informed by Chairman Khrushchev that all of the IL-28 bombers now in Cuba will be withdrawn in 30 days. He also agrees that these planes can be observed and counted as they leave. Inasmuch as this goes a long way toward reducing the danger which faced this hemisphere 4 weeks ago, I have this afternoon instructed the Secretary of Defense to lift our naval quarantine.

In view of this action, I want to take this opportunity to bring the American people up to date on the Cuban crisis and to review the progress made thus far in fulfilling the understandings between Soviet Chairman Khrushchev and myself as set forth in our letters of October 27 and 28. Chairman Khrushchev, it will be recalled, agreed to remove from Cuba all weapons systems capable of offensive use, to halt the further introduction of such weapons into Cuba, and to permit appropriate United Nations observation and supervision to insure the carrying out and continuation of these commitments. We on our part

[1] *AFP, 1962*, pp. 460–1 (UN doc. SG 1379, 20 Nov. 1962).　[2] *AFP, 1962*, pp. 461–3.

agreed that, once these adequate arrangements for verification had been established, we would remove our naval quarantine and give assurances against invasion of Cuba.

The evidence to date indicates that all known offensive missile sites in Cuba have been dismantled. The missiles and their associated equipment have been loaded on Soviet ships. And our inspection at sea of these departing ships has confirmed that the number of missiles reported by the Soviet Union as having been brought into Cuba, which closely corresponded to our own information, has now been removed. In addition the Soviet Government has stated that all nuclear weapons have been withdrawn from Cuba and no offensive weapons will be reintroduced.

Nevertheless, important parts of the understanding of October 27th and 28th remain to be carried out. The Cuban Government has not yet permitted the United Nations to verify whether all offensive weapons have been removed, and no lasting safeguards have yet been established against the future introduction of offensive weapons back into Cuba.

Consequently, if the Western Hemisphere is to continue to be protected against offensive weapons, this Government has no choice but to pursue its own means of checking on military activities in Cuba. The importance of our continued vigilance is underlined by our identification in recent days of a number of Soviet ground combat units in Cuba, although we are informed that these and other Soviet units were associated with the protection of offensive weapons systems and will also be withdrawn in due course.

I repeat, we would like nothing better than adequate international arrangements for the task of inspection and verification in Cuba, and we are prepared to continue our efforts to achieve such arrangements. Until that is done, difficult problems remain. As for our part, if all offensive weapons are removed from Cuba and kept out of the hemisphere in the future, under adequate verification and safeguards, and if Cuba is not used for the export of aggressive Communist purposes, there will be peace in the Caribbean. And as I said in September, we shall neither initiate nor permit aggression in this hemisphere.

We will not, of course, abandon the political, economic, and other efforts of this hemisphere to halt subversion from Cuba nor our purpose and hope that the Cuban people shall some day be truly free. But these policies are very different from any intent to launch a military invasion of the island.

In short, the record of recent weeks shows real progress, and we are hopeful that further progress can be made. The completion of the commitment on both sides and the achievement of a peaceful solution to the Cuban crisis might well open the door to the solution of other outstanding problems.

May I add this final thought. In this week of Thanksgiving there is much for which we can be grateful as we look back to where we stood only 4 weeks ago—the unity of this hemisphere, the support of our allies, and the calm determination of the American people. These qualities may be tested many more times in this decade, but we have increased reason to be confident that those qualities will continue to serve the cause of freedom with distinction in the years to come.

179. Khrushchev's report to the Supreme Soviet on the origins and outcome of the crisis, 12 December 1962:[1] excerpts (*p. 49*)

In view of the intensified threat of attack from the USA, the Cuban government approached the Soviet government in the summer of this year with a request for additional help. Agreement was reached on a series of new measures, including the deployment in Cuba of some tens of Soviet intermediate range ballistic missiles, which weapons were to remain in the hands of Soviet military personnel. . . . Our objective was solely the defence of Cuba. . . .

Favorable preliminary conditions have now been created for the elimination of the dangerous crisis that arose in the Caribbean. It is now necessary to complete the negotiations and seal the agreement reached as a result of the exchange messages between the governments of the Soviet Union and the United States and support this agreement with the authority of the United Nations.

The Soviet government is convinced that it is not in the interest of peace to go slow in settling the crisis in the Caribbean area, and we hope the United States government realizes this, too. From what I have said, certain results of the normalization which has started in the situation concerning Cuba will have become obvious.

In the first place it was possible to prevent the invasion which threatened the Cuban Republic from one day to the next, and consequently to prevent a military clash; it was possible to overcome the crisis which threatened universal thermonuclear war.

In the second place, the United States gave before the world a public statement not to attack the Cuban Republic and to restrain their allies from doing so.

Third, the most rabid of the imperialists calculating to start a world thermonuclear war over Cuba could not do so. The Soviet Union, the forces of peace and socialism, have proved that they are in a position to impose peace on the protagonists of war.

Whose side has triumphed? Who has won? It can be said that it is reason that has won; the cause of peace and people's security has won.

The sides displayed a sober approach and took into account the fact that if steps such as these can help to avert a dangerous course of events are not taken, then a third world war can break out.

As the result of mutual concession and compromise, agreement was reached which made it possible to remove the dangerous tension, to normalize the situation. Both sides made concessions. We withdrew ballistic missiles and agreed to the withdrawal of the IL-28 aircraft. This gives satisfaction to the Americans.

Both Cuba and the Soviet Union have reached satisfaction: the American invasion of Cuba has been averted; the naval blockade has been lifted; the situation in the Caribbean is becoming normal: people's Cuba exists, grows stronger, and is developing under the leadership of its revolutionary government, its fearless leader, Fidel Castro. . . .

[1] *Pravda*, 13 Dec. 1962 (*AFP, 1962*, pp. 468–9).

The Cuban government has raised the question that any settlement of crisis in the Caribbean sea should be of a long-term nature and include guarantees for the Cuban Republic which would protect it against aggression and would secure for the Cuban people the opportunity to build their new life under conditions of peace.

The well-known five points, put forward in the speech by Prime Minister of Cuba Fidel Castro on October 28th, which we fully support, serve this aim. These five points are just demands corresponding to the elementary rights of each sovereign state, are dictated by the concern for the preservation of peace and security of Cuba, and conform to the principles of the UN Charter. . . .

For our part we shall firmly adhere to the agreement that has been achieved as a result of the exchange of messages with the United States President. We would like to issue a clear warning that our pledges remain in force so long as the other side abides by this agreement.

In the event of these pledges not being respected by the other party, we would be forced to take such actions as would be required from us in the circumstances.

180. Report by Malinovsky at ceremonial session of Moscow Soviet on armed forces anniversary renewing Soviet pledge of assistance to Cuba, February 1963:[1] excerpts (*p. 51*)

. . . We want to warn the aggressive circles of the US that an attack on the Cuban Republic would mean the start of the third world war. If such an attack is made, peace-loving forces the world over will not limit themselves to protests and demonstrations. They will move to defend the country that is the victim of aggression, and the Soviet Union will be in the front ranks of those who come to its aid.

The peace-loving forces will come to the aid of the Cuban Republic because they will regard a war against it as a war against all who stand for peace and the sovereign rights of peoples.

Should the aggressive circles of imperialism choose not to observe the principles of the UN and unleash a war, that war will be fought not only on the territory of Cuba but on the territory of the United States of America as well. . . .

181. Official statement that Cuba has no wish to take sides in the Sino-Soviet dispute, March 1963:[2] excerpts (*p. 52*)

The letters exchanged between the Central Committee of the Communist Parties of the Soviet Union and China, and the agreed principles which they reveal for surmounting the divergences which have been the subject of public debate, come as most important and welcome news for the whole world Communist movement and for all who struggle against imperialism, against aggression, and for national liberation, democracy, and peace. . . .

In harmony with our most profound convictions and with the reality confronting the Revolution and the building of Socialism in our country, our guide

[1] *Pradva*, 23 Feb. 1963 (*CDSP*, 20 Mar. 1963 p. 10).   [2] *Hoy*, 16 Mar. 1963.

and maximum leader, Comrade Fidel Castro, has laid down our line in regard to the divergences which have arisen within the world Communist movement: not to feed the flames of the discrepancies but to struggle for unity, at home and abroad, and to work for everything which unites us both at home and abroad.

This has been and remains the line followed by our Party. We have allowed no scope for the diffusion of public polemics, for mutual attacks, or for anything which might mean feeding the flames of the dispute. . . . Our United Party of the Socialist Revolution will make its contribution, as far as it is able and with awareness of its responsibility, to the great task of unity and to the advance and triumph of Socialism and Communism in the world, to the cause of the national liberation of the peoples in thrall to imperialism, and to the cause of world peace.

182. Joint communiqué on Fidel Castro's first visit to Moscow, 23 May 1963:[1] excerpts (*p. 52*)

. . . The two sides note that the construction of the new Cuba is being carried out in difficult and complex conditions. . . .

The firm stand of the Soviet Union and the other socialist countries in the cause of defending revolutionary Cuba, the restrained and sober evaluation by the responsible statesmen of the Soviet Union and Cuba of the situation that resulted, and the support for Cuba from all peace-loving states, averted thermonuclear war. The immediate danger of an armed attack on Cuba was removed.

Today, revolutionary Cuba is an example of unbending courage and staunchness in the struggle for independence, and for the right to create a new life without exploiters.

The two sides note that, although the immediate danger of military intervention in Cuba has been removed, the tension in the area of the Caribbean Sea still remains.

This situation could be normalized on the basis of the implementation of the five points advanced by the Prime Minister of the Revolutionary Government of Cuba, Fidel Castro, which include the ending of all measures of economic pressure; the ending of all subversive activities; the ending of attacks from bases situated in the United States and Puerto Rico; the ending of all intrusions by military planes and ships of the United States into the air space and territorial waters of Cuba; and the removal of the United States naval base at Guantánamo from Cuban territory.

The Soviet government emphatically supports these principles, because they are in full accord with the United Nations Charter and reflect the efforts of the Revolutionary Government of Cuba to find a peaceful solution to the outstanding issues that create tension in that part of the world.

The government of the Soviet Union and the government of Cuba proceed from the premise that revolutionary Cuba does not threaten anyone.

The road of development and social change which has been chosen by the

---

[1] *AFP, 1963*, pp. 269–71; last 3 paras. trans. by the Editor from *Cuba socialista*, June 1963.

Cuban people, is its domestic affair, and no one has the right to interfere in its affairs.

Both governments resolutely state their adherence to the principle of non-interference of states in the internal affairs of other countries, and solemnly confirm that the peace-loving principles of the United Nations, including the principle of respect for the sovereignty of states, have their full support, because they meet the interests of peace and friendship between nations.

The Cuban side declares that the people of Cuba highly appreciate the moral and political support and help rendered by the Soviet Union. The statement of the USSR government and its head, Comrade Nikita Khrushchev, the defence by the Soviet Union of Cuba's interests in the United Nations and in other international forums, the action of mass public organizations in the USSR in support of Cuba, and the economic and military aid of the Soviet Union, played a very important role in the struggle of the Cuban people for its freedom and independence against the external threat from imperialism.

The Soviet Union has rendered, and is rendering, effective aid to Cuba in strengthening her defence potential. At the request of the Cuban government the Soviet Union helped Cuba to create a strong army, well trained, and equipped with modern military material, capable of administering a rebuff to any attempts at encroachment on the sovereignty and freedom of the Cuban state.

In the course of the talks between Comrades Nikita Khrushchev and Fidel Castro, it was confirmed by the Soviet side that, if an attack was made on Cuba in violation of the commitments undertaken by the President of the United States not to invade Cuba, the Soviet Union would fulfill its international duty to the fraternal Cuban people, and would render it the necessary aid for the defence of the freedom and independence of the Cuban republic, with all the means at its disposal.

The organizers of aggression should remember that an invasion of Cuba will confront mankind with a devastating nuclear rocket war.

The two sides considered questions connected with the implementation of the Soviet-Cuban agreements on trade and economic, technical, scientific and cultural co-operation, and noted with satisfaction that these agreements are being successfully implemented.

The Soviet Union is constantly increasing the purchase of goods which constitute Cuba's traditional exports, and, together with other socialist countries, is doing everything to satisfy the pressing requirements of Cuba in equipment and raw materials for her industry, and in goods to supply the country's population.

The Soviet Union is also rendering the necessary aid in transporting the goods purchased or sold by Cuba.

The two sides take note with satisfaction of the fact that economic co-operation between the USSR and Cuba is acquiring a more and more extensive and all-round nature. The Soviet Union is rendering Cuba technical assistance in conducting geological prospecting, in expanding and reconstructing three re-smelting metallurgical works, in the construction of a big thermal power station in the development of the nickel and chemical industries and commercial fishing, and the carrying out of priority irrigation and land improvement projects.

The construction of an engineering plant now under way with the help of the Soviet Union is of great importance.

The Soviet Union is rendering help to the Cuban Republic in creating national cadres, by training Cuban citizens in the USSR, and by setting up training centres in Cuba.

Co-operation between Soviet and Cuban organizations and institutions in the fields of culture, science, education, public health and sports is developing successfully.

Agreement was reached in the course of the talks on measures for the further development of economic, trade and scientific and cultural links between the USSR and the Cuban Republic.

Guided by the desire to help to consolidate the socialist economy of fraternal Cuba, and taking into consideration that in recent years raw sugar prices in the world market have risen considerably, the Soviet government, on its own initiative, proposed to change the existing agreement, and to increase the price of the Cuban raw sugar to be bought in 1963, so as to bring this price into line with the level of world prices.

The Soviet government proceeded from the fact that the production of sugar is one of the staple branches of Cuba's economy, and that an increase of sugar prices will play an effective part in consolidating the economic situation in Cuba.

This proposal by the Soviet government was accepted by the Cuban side.

The Cuban and Soviet sides confirm once again that they will struggle tirelessly for the triumph of the Leninist policy of peaceful coexistence. . . .

The parties[1] stress that the Declarations of Havana have an historic importance for the national liberation struggle of the Latin American peoples and give a correct indication of the course of events. . . .

The parties base their policies on the fact that the chief feature of our present age is the transition from capitalism to socialism, beginning with the great October Revolution. This inevitable historic process, being in principle common to all countries in its essence of economic-social and political-social transformation, occurs differently and under differing forms which depend on the national internal and external conditions of the respective countries. PURS and CPSU consider that the question of the peaceful or the non-peaceful road to socialism in one country or another should be definitely settled by the struggling countries themselves and in accord with the practical correlation of the strength of the parties and with the degree of resistance offered by the exploiting class to the socialist transformation of society.

183. Statement by Dr Carlos Lechuga, Cuban delegate to the UN General Assembly, declining to sign the Test-Ban Treaty, 7 October 1963[2] (*p. 52*)

Cuba supports the Soviet Union's policy of peace which, beyond doubt, led

---

[1] The CPSU and PURS.   [2] *GAOR*, 18th sess., 1231st mtg., p. 17.

the Soviet Union to join in concluding a treaty for a partial nuclear test ban. Cuba is prepared to do everything it can to advance the universal cause of peace. Cuba cannot, however, sign a treaty one of the signatories of which is at the same time encouraging a number of activities and pursuing a policy towards our country which, in the last analysis, create what is in fact an undeclared war.

184. Joint communiqué on Fidel Castro's second visit to Moscow, 22 January 1964:[1] excerpts (*p. 53*)

The complete unity of views with regard to all the problems discussed was confirmed.

Both parties note with great satisfaction that the truly fraternal relations existing between the Republic of Cuba and the Soviet Union, between the United Party of the Socialist Revolution (PURS) and the Communist Party of the Soviet Union (CPSU) were still further strengthened during the period which has elapsed since Comrade Fidel Castro's visit to the Soviet Union.

These relations are based on the great principles of Marxism-Leninism, proletarian international solidarity, unity of objectives, of sincere friendship, comradeship, and whole-hearted collaboration. The Cuban Republic and the Soviet Union and their peoples are united by the aspiration of carrying into effect the luminous ideals of Communism. . . .

Both parties took note that the building of Socialism in Cuba is being carried out under conditions of the constant threat by the US imperialist forces, which have not abandoned their plans to stifle the Cuban Revolution. In this situation, one of the Cuban Republic's most important tasks remains that of raising the defensive capacity of the country and of the state of preparedness to repel any aggression. The revolutionary armed forces of the Cuban Republic, which defend the Socialist conquests of the Cuban people and protect its peaceful labour, have at their disposal today the most modern military technology, which the personnel of the Cuban army are learning to handle successfully. In the course of conversations, the Cuban Party drew particular attention to the fraternal aid offered the Cuban Republic by the Soviet Union and other Socialist countries for the development of its Socialist economy and the strengthening of its defensive capacity.

With regard to the economic relations of both countries, the parties agreed to conclude a long-term commercial agreement.[2] This agreement gives secure protection to the Cuban economy against eventual fluctuations in the price of sugar on the world market, against economic pressures on the part of the US monopolies, and increases the possibilities for the long-term planning of the development of the Cuban Republic's economy and for the ultimate well-being of the Cuban people.

The Cuban and Soviet sides express their full confidence that the revolutionary enthusiasm and capacity for hard work of the Cuban people, the leadership and organizing activities of PURS, and the unbreakable unity of

---

[1] *Cuba socialista*, Feb. 1964.   [2] See no. 185.

Cuba with the great Socialist community will ensure everything necessary for the building of Socialist society in Cuba. . . .

In their international policy, the Cuban Republic and the Soviet Union take as their basis the Leninist principle of peaceful coexistence between states. . . .

The Cuban and Soviet sides note with great satisfaction that, as a result of the persistent and sustained efforts of the Socialist states and of all peace-loving states with different social regimes, as a result of the realization of the Leninist policy of peaceful coexistence, there has recently occurred a certain relaxation of international tension. . . .

The Cuban Government is ready to do everything possible to establish 'good-neighbour' relations with the United States on the basis of peaceful coexistence. But the Cuban Government will not permit anyone to intervene in the internal affairs of its country. The path of development of its state—the path of Socialism—chosen by the Cuban people, is the Cuban people's own, inalienable affair.

Comrade Khrushchev . . . confirmed that the Soviet Government fully supports the well-known Five Points put forward by the Cuban Prime Minister, Comrade Fidel Castro, as a basis for the normalization of the situation in the Caribbean region.

Bearing in mind the continuation of provocations on the part of aggressive military circles in the United States against the Cuban Republic, Comrade N. S. Khrushchev, in the name of the Central Committee of the CPSU and the Soviet Government, confirmed once again that if, in violation of the obligations assumed by the USA not to intervene in Cuba, it should commit aggression against her, in that case the Soviet Union would comply with her international duty and offer her the necessary aid to defend the liberty and independence of the fraternal Republic of Cuba with all the means at her disposal. . . .

Both Governments condemn the massacre committed against the people of Panama and the violations perpetrated against the sovereignty of that state by the North American troops occupying the canal zone. They support the people of Panama in their just demands for sovereignty over the said zone and their right to negotiate or to demand the annulment of the arbitrary treaties imposed by Yankee imperialism on that country by virtue of which she was despoiled of her jurisdiction over a piece of her own territory. . . .

Comrade Fidel Castro expressed his approval of the measures taken by the Central Committee of the CPSU to liquidate the existing differences and to strengthen the unity and solidarity of the ranks of the international Communist movement.

185. Soviet-Cuban sugar agreement, January 1964[1] (*p. 53*)

The Revolutionary Government of the Cuban Republic and the Government of the Soviet Union, having studied in a spirit of sincere and cordial friendship the question of supplies of Cuban sugar for the Soviet Union;

Taking into account that sugar production is the principal branch of the

---

[1] *Cuba socialista*, Feb. 1964.

economy of the Cuban Republic, and with a view to the planned development of the Socialist economy of the Cuban Republic;

Notwithstanding the Soviet Union being in a position to manufacture a quantity of sugar sufficient to meet the requirements of her population and for export, but nevertheless taking into account the relations of sincere friendship existing between the Cuban Republic and the Soviet Union, and basing themselves on the principle of the international division of Socialist labour and the advantages to be obtained from the correct application of this principle in the interests of both countries, they have agreed on the following:

Article 1. The Soviet Union will buy raw sugar from the Cuban Republic during the years 1965–70 to the following annual amounts:

1965	2,100,000 tons
1966	3,000,000 tons
1967	4,000,000 tons
1968	5,000,000 tons
1969	5,000,000 tons
1970	5,000,000 tons

Payment for the sugar will be made according to the terms of the commercial agreements in force between the Cuban Republic and the USSR through deliveries of Soviet goods needed by the Cuban Republic.

Article 2. With a view to eliminating the influence of fluctuations in the price on the world market on the economy of the Cuban Republic and to create a solid basis for planning the development of the economy of the Cuban Republic for a lasting period, both parties have reached agreement to fix a stable price for the years 1965–70 for the sugar which the Cuban Republic will deliver to the USSR at the level of 6 cents of the US dollar for one English pound (f.o.b. Cuban ports).[1]

186. Joint communiqué on Osvaldo Dorticós's second visit to Moscow, October 1964:[2] excerpts (*p. 53*)

The Cuban and Soviet sides emphasize that the building of Socialism in Cuba is being carried on in the teeth of incessant acts of aggression committed by imperialist circles against the Island of Liberty. North American imperialism persists in its policy of economic blockade. The United States finances and supports the organization of bands of mercenaries bent on attacking Cuba. Forcing other Latin American states to participate in its aggressive plans against Cuba, the United States forced the so-called 'Collective Sanctions' against Cuba through the Organization of American States. The OAS agreement constitutes a gross violation of the United Nations Charter, and the full responsibility for the adoption of this illegal resolution, which is a threat to the general peace and security, falls upon the USA and on the Governments of the

---

[1] The price of sugar on the world market was then about 10·84 cents a lb. By July 1965 it had fallen to about 2 cents a lb.

[2] *Cuba socialista*, Nov. 1964.

countries which meekly follow along in the wake of Washington's foreign policy. . . .

The general line of policy of Cuba and the Soviet Union is the policy of peaceful coexistence of states with different social systems. . . .

187. Speech by Fidel Castro asserting the independence of his Party, 2 January 1965:¹ excerpts (*p. 53*)

We live in a complex, changing world. So in each country where there is a Marxist-Leninist revolution every leading Party has to know how to interpret doctrine fully and correctly in every concrete case. And something very important has to be said: what each Party should do in every concrete circumstance must not be laid down by anyone from anywhere! What it has to do must be worked out by each Party, by each people. And I must say straight away that no one has ever tried to tell us what we should do. For, in the first place, that is not the practice of any party; and secondly, should any Party attempt to do this with us, it would meet with a decisive and categorical rebuff.

If there be those who wonder how we ought to be thinking, we must reply without hesitation that we have no need to borrow brains from anyone, or to borrow revolutionary spirit, or heroism, or intelligence! . . .

In the field of ideas and experience we should also be active and creative, and arrive at the fullest interpretation of the ideas of Marx, Engels, and Lenin, and make our contribution too in the new circumstances and conditions.

188. Speech by 'Che' Guevara to the 2nd Economic Seminar of Afro-Asian Solidarity criticizing the economic policies of the Socialist countries towards the underdeveloped countries, 24 February 1965² (*p. 54*)

Each time a country is liberated, imperialism suffers a defeat, but it must be realized that this tearing itself free is not achieved by the mere proclamation of independence or by winning victory in the Revolution by force of arms. It is realized when imperialist domination ceases to be exercised over a people. The Socialist countries thus have a vital interest in seeing them torn truly free, and it is an international duty laid upon us by the ideology we hold that we should contribute by our efforts to make the liberation as rapid and thorough as possible.

From all this we can draw one conclusion: the development of the countries which are now beginning to tread the path of liberation must cost the Socialist countries something. We put it like this, without the least suggestion of blackmail or sensationalism, and without any attempt to ingratiate ourselves thereby with the Afro-Asian group of countries. It is a matter of deep conviction. Socialism cannot exist unless a change of conscience occurs which leads to a new attitude of brotherhood towards mankind, both as regards the individual and the society where Socialism is being built, and also on a world scale in relation to all the peoples suffering imperialist oppression.

¹ *Bohemia*, 8 Jan. 1965.   ² *Hoy*, 25 Feb. 1965.

We believe that it is in this spirit that responsibility for helping dependent countries should be approached, and that there should be no more talk about developing a mutually advantageous trade based on prices imposed on backward countries by the law of surplus value and international relations stemming from inequality of interchange, which is a product of this law.

How can it be 'mutually advantageous' to sell at world market prices the primary materials which cost the underdeveloped countries boundless sweat and suffering, and to buy at world market prices the machines produced in the great automatized factories of the present day?

If we establish this sort of relation between the two groups of nations, it must be admitted that the Socialist countries are, in a certain way, accomplices of imperialist exploitation. It may be argued that the scale of interchange with the underdeveloped countries forms an insignificant part of the foreign trade of those countries. That is quite true, but it does not alter the immoral character of the transaction. The Socialist countries have the moral duty to liquidate their tacit complicity with the exploiting countries of the West.

189. Speech by Fidel Castro: 'we are not anyone's satellite', 13 March 1965:[1] excerpts (*pp. 53, 54*)

In respect of revolutionary conviction and sincerity, we have taken lessons from no one, as our liberators of 1895 and 1898 took no lessons in independence and dignity from anyone, any more than did the nation of the First and Second Declarations of Havana, which were copied out of no documents but were the pure expression of the deeply revolutionary and loftily internationalist spirit of our people. . . . So we certainly have the full and absolute right—which I think no one will deny us—to banish from our country and the bosom of our people such disputes and Byzantine battles.

And it is as well that it should be understood that here propaganda is made by our party and guidelines are laid down by our party, that this is a question which appertains to our jurisdiction and that if we do not wish the apple of discord to come here, because we do not want it, no one can smuggle in to us the apple of discord! Our only enemies are the Yankee imperialists! . . .

We are in favour of all necessary help being given to Vietnam; and this help should be in arms and men! We are in favour of the Soviet camp taking whatever risks may be necessary for Vietnam. . . .

This is our considered position, which stems from our legitimate and inviolable right to adopt the measures and to act in the way we deem most just and most reasonable, without anyone deceiving themselves into thinking that they can give us lessons in revolution.

I hope that the mistake of undervaluing and ignoring the idiosyncracy of our people will be avoided. For masses of errors of this type have been committed by Yankee imperialism, one of whose characteristics is to despise and underestimate other small nations. That imperialism committed great and monumental blunders by underestimating our revolutionary people; it would be lamentable if others were to make similar blunders. Our sincere policy has

[1] *Bohemia*, 19 Mar. 1965.

been, and remains, that of uniting; for we are not anyone's satellite, and we never shall be!

190. Speech by Fidel Castro asserting Cuba's right to interpret Marxism-Leninism in her own way, 3 October 1965:[1] excerpts (*p. 54*)

We can disagree with some Party on one point or other. In the heterogeneity of this contemporary world, in such different circumstances, made up of countries in such dissimilar conditions and at such unequal levels of material, technical, and cultural development, we cannot hope to look on Marxism as something like a church, with one religious doctrine, with its Rome, its Pope, and its Ecumenical Council. It is a revolutionary and dialectical doctrine, not a religious doctrine; it is a guide to revolutionary action, not a dogma. To attempt to confine Marxism within the framework of catechisms is anti-Marxist. The diversity of situations will inevitably produce an infinite number of interpretations. Those who interpret correctly may call themselves revolutionaries. Those who make true interpretations and apply them consistently will triumph; those who are mistaken or inconsistent in revolutionary thought will fail, they will be defeated and even superseded, because Marxism is not a piece of private property to be inscribed on a register; it is a doctrine of revolutionaries, written by a revolutionary, developed by other revolutionaries, for revolutionaries.

We must be characterized by our confidence in ourselves and in our capacity to follow and develop our revolutionary path. And we may disagree over a point or two with some party; disagreements, where honest, are transitory. What we will never do is to insult with one hand and beg with another, and we shall know how to keep our disagreements within the bounds of decency with any Party, and know how to be friends with those who know to be friendly, and to respect those who respect us. And these guidelines will determine our absolute freedom of conduct, and we shall never ask anyone's permission to do anything, go anywhere, or be friends of any Party or nation. We know how transitory problems are. Problems pass, but nations remain. . . . We shall never be able to say that those who have helped us defeat the imperialists are accomplices of the imperialists.

191. Letter from the CPSU CC to the United Party of the Socialist Revolution (PURS) welcoming the formation of the Central Committee, 3 October 1965[2] (*p. 54*)

The Central Committee of the Communist Party of the Soviet Union (CPSU) congratulates all the members of PURS and the whole Cuban people on the formation of the Party's Central Committee, its Political Bureau, its Secretariat, and the Commissions of the PURS Central Committee. Like you, we consider this important political decision a great step forward in building up Cuba's United Party of the Socialist Revolution, the vanguard of the Cuban people.

[1] *Cuba socialista*, Nov. 1965.   [2] *Granma*, 4 Oct. 1965.

We are sure that the creation of the directive organs of the Marxist-Leninist Party, which represent the best of the Cuban Revolution, will serve to consolidate still further all the revolutionary forces and partisans of socialism of the whole heroic Cuban people.

The Central Committee of the CPSU is fully convinced that Cuba's United Party of the Socialist Revolution and its Central Committee, led by Comrade Fidel Castro, will go on fighting decisively for the cause of peace and socialism and for the unity of the international Communist movement on the basis of the principles of Marxism-Leninism and proletarian internationalism.

192. Speech by Fidel Castro criticizing the Socialist countries for their relations with Eduardo Frei of Chile, 26 July 1966:[1] **excerpts** (*p. 55*)

This gentleman [President Frei of Chile], the spoilt child of imperialism, coquettishly feigns independence and talks of economic relations with the Socialist camp.

The Socialist camp is of course independent, and has the right to do what it deems fit; that is its business. But we must say quite clearly that the Frei Government is the accomplice of imperialism against Cuba, the shop-window of imperialism which seeks to smuggle in the goods of 'Christian Democracy' as an antidote to the Latin American Revolution. Frei's flirtations will not take anyone in; they will not take the Socialist camp in. For it would be a mistake to imagine that this gentleman is going to transform his vice into virtue; what he is doing, which is all part and parcel of his anti-Cuban policy and the outcome of that real state of affairs which marks his regime as reactionary and pro-imperialist and the accomplice of imperialism in its blockade of Cuba, is simply to try to cover himself with the fig-leaf of false liberty. And naturally imperialism allows, and even encourages, Frei to do this, for it reckons that if any Socialist country aids Frei, 'Christian Democracy' will cost imperialism that much less.

We said that each country has the right to do what it deems fit, just as we too have the right to express some opinions which we deem fit. And it is our duty to warn the Socialist countries against Frei's hypocrisy, against Frei's flirtations, since the prostitute will not become a virtuous woman simply because attention is paid to some of her flirtations. Let Frei first prove that his is an independent Government. Let Frei first show that he does not obey the dictates of Yankee imperialism. Frei's independence will only be demonstrated as an independent gesture which deserves to be seriously taken into account should he have the courage to establish diplomatic and trade relations with Cuba. And as long as this is not done, we Cubans have every right to feel aggrieved; we Cubans have every right to feel injured by any country that offers technical and economic aid to the Frei regime. . . .

Unfortunately, there are times when the Socialist countries make mistakes. But it is not they who must be blamed for their mistakes so much as the pseudo-revolutionaries who give them mistaken advice and counsel. I do not know whether there is any advice of this sort in the case of Chile. I don't even know

[1] *Cuba socialista*, Aug. 1966.

the opinion of the Chilean Leftists. But it would be interesting—very interesting—to know what the Chilean Leftists think about whether or not technical aid should be offered to the pro-imperialist Government of Señor Frei's 'Christian Democracy'.

193. Speech by Fidel Castro renewing his criticism of the USSR for maintaining relations with the 'oligarchies', 13 March 1967:[1] excerpts (*p. 55*)

With none of these Governments which carry out the orders of imperialism will we re-establish our diplomatic relations; we have no interest nor wish to do so. We will only re-establish diplomatic relations with revolutionary Governments in those countries. . . . Economic relations with those oligarchies who broke them off with us? We have no interest in re-establishing them until there are revolutionary Governments in control of those countries.

We shall not help financially any oligarchy to repress the revolutionary movement in blood. And whoever gives aid to those oligarchies where they are fighting against the guerrillas is helping to repress Revolution, for repressive wars are not waged only with arms but also with the millions of pesos which pay for those arms and which pay for mercenary armies.

We have irrefutable proof of the lack of independence of those Governments in the recent case of Colombia, where some days ago, on account of the guerrillas having attacked a train, the Secretary-General and all the leaders of the Colombian Communist Party who happened to be in their usual domiciles were arrested at 6 in the morning. They did not pay the least attention to the presence at the time of a delegation of high Soviet officials who had come to sign a commercial agreement with the Government of Lleras Restrepo, and an interview was said to be due to take place that very day; and on that same day not only were all the Communist leaders arrested, but what is more—according to newspaper reports—the local office of the Tass agency was also raided. Such is the spirit of friendship of those oligarchies! . . . Not everything is rose-coloured in the revolutionary world. Contradictory attitudes are giving rise to more and more complaints. And whilst someone is blamed for renewing relations with West Germany, a host of others are hurrying to see if they can establish relations with oligarchies like Leoni[2] and company. One should take a stand on principle in all things—but in Latin America as well; a stand on principle in Asia, but a stand on principle in Latin America too.

Let us condemn imperialist aggression in Vietnam! Let us condemn the crime which the Yankee imperialists are today committing against Vietnam, and let us condemn it with all our strength and all our heart! But let us condemn from now on the future Vietnams in Latin America; let us condemn from now on the future imperialist aggressors in Latin America.

What would the Vietnamese revolutionaries think if we were to send delegations to South Vietnam to treat with the puppet delegation in Saigon? What will those who are fighting in the mountains of America think when close

---

[1] *Granma*, 14 Mar. 1967.   [2] President Raúl Leoni of Venezuela.

relations are already being sought with the puppets of imperialism in this part of the continent? . . .

194. Report of Kosygin's visit to Cuba, June 1967:[1] excerpts (*p. 55*)
The Prime Minister of the Soviet Union, Alexey Kosygin, arrived yesterday in Havana and was received by the Prime Minister Fidel Castro, President Osvaldo Dorticós, Organizing Secretary of the Communist Party Armando Hart, and members of the Central Committee Osmany Cienfuegos, Raúl Roa and Vilma Espín.

Kosygin was accompanied by his daughter Ludmila Gvishiani, Press Chief Leonid Zamyatin, and Lev Mendelevich, head of the Latin American Department of the Ministry of Foreign Affairs of the USSR, and eighteen other officials. . . .

Kosygin arrived from New York where he had been attending the 5th emergency special session of the General Assembly of the United Nations summoned at the request of the Soviet Union to consider the situation created by Israel's aggression against the Arab countries. . . .

Yesterday morning a meeting took place in the Palace of the Revolution between the Prime Minister of the Soviet Union Alexey Kosygin and the Prime Minister of the Revolutionary Government, the President of the Republic, the Minister of the Revolutionary Armed Forces, and other members of the Politburo of our Party. . . .

195. Speech by Raúl Castro to the Cuban CP CC on the intrigues of the 'microfaction' with Soviet officials, 29 & 30 January 1968:[2] excerpts (*p. 56*)
. . . The. . . group carried out the following activities: the sounding-out of opinions of long-time militants and former PSP leaders; attempts to sound out several members of the Central Committee; approaches made to Soviet, German and Czechoslovak officials and citizens, including Party members, government representatives and journalists with access to leaders of the Central Committee of the Communist Party of the Soviet Union, with the purpose of informing them of their viewpoint, contrary to the position of the Communist Party of Cuba, in order to create an opinion in the leadership of such parties in favor of their position. They even went so far as to aspire to the application of political and economic pressure by the Soviet Union to force the Revolution to draw closer to that country. . . .

Aníbal Escalante made several attempts to spread to countries abroad the differences that his group had with the Party line, and to that end he took advantage of contacts that he had with foreigners, briefing as to information that should be given them and made attempts to travel to the USSR and other countries where he could explain his position. . . .

Shortly prior to the OLAS (Latin American Organization of Solidarity)

[1] *Granma*, 27 & 28 June 1967.   [2] *Granma* (Engl. ed.), 11 Feb. 1968, pp. 5, 7–10.

Conference, Octavio Fernández met Vadim Lestov, a Soviet journalist, at the entrance of the Party's Central Committee headquarters. Lestov told him that he was going to the USSR and would return to Cuba after the 50th anniversary celebrations.

Octavio Fernández informed Aníbal Escalante of this meeting, and Escalante suggested that he see this Soviet journalist and tell him of what was happening, such as the dismissal of former PSP members, the replacement of Armando Acosta,[1] economic problems, the problem of the labor movement, the anti-Soviet trend, and relations with France, and in addition, that an invitation be sought for Aníbal and his wife to visit the USSR, where, under the pretext of looking into matters of poultry genetics, Aníbal himself would present the situation in the Soviet Union.

Octavio Fernández, together with Inaudi Kindelán, visited the Soviet journalist in the Riomar Building, where he lived, and discussed all of the points indicated by Aníbal Escalante, including his need to visit the USSR to present his views and under what circumstances he wished to go. Vadim Lestov stated that, although he would see that the information and the request reached the director of the newspaper *Izvestia* who is an alternate member of the Central Committee of the CPSU, it was preferable that a written report be prepared and signed by Aníbal Escalante, Octavio Fernández and Inaudi Kindelán. He insisted that the report be presented in writing because various opinions existed in the USSR concerning the problems they were presenting and, for example, the Soviet Ambassador in Cuba, Alexander Alexeiev, did not share these views, so that this could appear to be a personal matter brought up by him; and, therefore, a written report signed by them was necessary.

When Octavio Fernández told Aníbal Escalante of the results of this interview and that the written report must be submitted to Vadim Lestov that same evening, or early the next morning at the airport, before his departure for the Soviet Union, Escalante objected to having to prepare a document to present these views. . . .

Nevertheless, he agreed to help prepare the document by dictating the major points to be dealt with to Octavio, who was to type it on another typewriter, one that was not Aníbal's. Octavio took the notes to the ice cream factory managed by Raúl Fajardo Escalona (in custody), who gave him permission to type the report there. . . . But because of the danger and seriousness of preparing such a report . . . Octavio Fernández decided not to prepare the document. He went to his home and burned the notes. . . .

During interrogation Octavio Fernández Bonis (in custody) reconstructed the document dictated by Aníbal. Its contents read as follows:

'With De Gaulle's new attitude in France after his failures in Vietnam and Algeria, appearing before the world with the same past-century slogan of "liberty, legality (sic) and fraternity" and adopting a correct attitude of peaceful coexistence, of free trade with all countries, even of tactical confrontation with Yankee imperialism, although strategically coinciding with it because of their class position, a new trend has been set in motion in our country,

---

[1] The PURS regional Secretary for Oriente Province.

stimulated by a credit extended by France in an effort to draw us closer politically as well.

'With this aim in view, a series of activities, both cultural and social, have been organized —the Salon de Mai, tourist groups, etc.—thus permitting a rapprochement between groups. This group is headed by Llanusa, Marcelo Fernández, Alfredo Guevara and Carlos Franqui. Logically, this is in keeping with the policy of drawing us farther and farther away from the Soviet Union.

'Recently, the book *Revolution in the Revolution?* by Régis Debray was established as study material for Party nuclei. Debray was expelled from the Communist Youth of France under suspicion of being a member of the French Intelligence Service. His book fails to recognize the Party's role and that of the working class in the struggle for power.

'In keeping with this policy of publishing new material and ignoring the manuals and other books containing certain experiences—philosophical as well as economic—the Editora Política was eradicated, and a new organization, The Book Institute, was created to publish books which do not express fully Marxist concepts.

'Promotion of Party cadres is being carried out among comrades of petty bourgeois rather than proletarian extraction, so that all Party Work reflects concepts and methods which are alien to the working class.

'Party candidates are asked their opinion concerning the USSR in order to determine whether or not they sympathize with it. If the answer is affirmative, discussions are held with the comrade to make certain problems clear to him.

'This policy has, of course, led to the gradual replacement of long-time Communists, because their position is considered pro-Soviet.

'In Latin America we find ourselves practically divorced from the great majority of Communist Parties as a result of our opinion on how the struggle should be carried out. This may cause us serious problems with regard to solidarity toward our Revolution and unity of action against imperialism.

'Our economy at present is running at a deficit. The sugarcane harvest this year, after six months, reached the figure of 6,100,000 tons—making it an unprofitable harvest. The difficulty was lack of cane and organization.

'So far as the prospects of our having a sugarcane harvest of 10 million tons by 1970 are concerned, this is very doubtful, since measures for increasing the industrial capacity of installations are not being put into practice at a pace appropriate to this end; moreover, there is another serious problem that we must face: the cutting of cane will not be conclusively solved by the cane conditioning centers.

'As may be observed, to judge from the present size of our sugarcane crop, the years that remain and the difficulties we have met, it will be almost impossible to reach 10 million tons by 1970.

'Therefore our economy in 1970 will not be able to reach the levels necessary to achieve an adequate solution for the country's problems.

'With respect to production in general,' continues the report, which, according to Octavio, the three were going to send to the Central Committee of the CPSU, 'it too, is below the levels required to meet the needs of the people. The policy applied through all production lines is based on a budgetary system which rests on moral incentives, absolutely setting aside material incentives, failing to recognize the laws of social development.

'This whole situation of not applying self-financing and, therefore, material incentives, has caused a slackening of production. Voluntary work is resorted to to meet the goals of production, and this, when it doesn't produce enough to meet costs, results in production of inferior quality.

'The role of the trade unions in this stage of the building of socialism is overlooked. They have been practically stripped of their role in production, completely underestimating the aid that they can give us as a leadership organization of the working class, helping to plan and organize production, develop socialist emulation and see to it that the workers constantly educate themselves politically and culturally.'

The report continues: 'This underestimation of the workers is reflected not only here but also in the workers' dining rooms, whose food value index is low. All this results in a general malaise in the working class.'

These were the fundamental ideas that Aníbal wanted to send to the Soviet leadership, according to the testimony given by one of his closest collaborators.

Later, Aníbal, intent on his purpose, met with a Soviet adviser of the Ministry of the Interior with whom he was acquainted. The Soviet adviser expressed annoyance with a note from the Revolutionary Government, which appeared in the press, concerning the 200-mile limit arbitrarily established by the reactionary military Government of Argentina with the aim of obstructing the operations of Cuba's fishing fleet. The adviser was of the opinion that the note was damaging to the interests of the USSR, and he tried to explain his country's position in paying the fines levied by the Argentine Government. The conversation passed to other international problems; the Cuban and Soviet positions were discussed, and Aníbal presented the viewpoints expressed in the aforementioned document.

The adviser asked Aníbal if he had discussed these viewpoints in Moscow and if he were willing to do so. Aníbal asked him if such an interest in the matter existed, to please arrange passage to the Soviet Union for him and his wife, as this would be a good opportunity for him to present his viewpoints.

During his interrogation, on December 10, 1967, Aníbal declared that he had met Pedro, who was later named adviser to the Cuban Intelligence Service, at the 19th Congress of the CPSU and that the first time he saw him after the triumph of the Revolution was around November 7, 1965, anniversary of the October Revolution, at a dinner at Pedro's house to which he—Aníbal—had been invited. He declared that he attended the dinner accompanied by his wife and that at no time during the visit did any conversation take place on his opinions or the policy of the Revolution.

On that occasion Aníbal invited Pedro to lunch with him as a gesture of reciprocity.

Some time later, Pedro visited Aníbal at his farm, and, from there, the two men and their wives went to lunch at a country restaurant—where, again, there was no conversation of a political nature.

Later—although the exact date has not been determined—Pedro telephoned Aníbal, inviting him to his home for a farewell dinner, since he was leaving the country. (That is, Pedro had finished his job here, he was ready to leave, and he invited Aníbal to his house for dinner.) Aníbal declared that he attended the dinner without asking if other guests would be present and that Pedro didn't say whether or not anyone else would be present—but that at the dinner (such a coincidence!) he met numerous Soviet citizens, among them the new adviser, Pedro's replacement, who proved to be the husband of a classmate of Aníbal's daughter in the Moscow Conservatory of Music.

On one occasion, when Aníbal was already long involved in all these manœuvers, Comrade Manuel Piñeiro, Vice-Minister of the Interior, happened to drive by the Soviet Embassy, and seeing his Ministry's adviser leaning on an automobile and engaged in conversation with someone inside the car, he decided to play a joke and brought his car to a sudden stop beside the parked automobile. To his great surprise and the embarrassment of the adviser, Piñeiro saw that the tête-à-tête was between none other than Aníbal Escalante and his own adviser.

Aníbal declared that he saw the adviser again when he—Aníbal—went to pick up his grandson at the children's nursery of the Soviet Embassy. It was then the adviser invited Aníbal to a farewell dinner because he, too, was leaving Cuba. (Thus, each adviser put Aníbal in touch with the next.)

Aníbal does not remember this adviser's name. (Although he believes that this man held an official position of less importance than Pedro's and showed less political maturity, or something to that effect, thus indicating that they must have discussed a great deal of politics.)

Aníbal attended the dinner alone, and there the conversation dealt with Aníbal's political opinions and other themes of international politics. . . .

(Aníbal has a grandson in the Soviet Embassy's children's nursery. On that occasion we checked on it, because I spoke with the Ambassador and with the chief of advisers at the Ministry of the Interior. The latter was quite offended because he believed Piñeiro should have told him about it.)

(I said to him: 'You're practically suggesting that I have Piñeiro arrested for not showing respect for you, and I don't intend to do such a thing.' And I made it clear to him: 'We are Piñeiro's superiors, not you.' This was said in a most fraternal tone but also with firmness.)

(He said to me: 'How can you possibly believe that we. . . ?' and I replied: 'We don't believe anything, but if you weren't so obtuse about this, you'd interpret it as a warning, and it would be very painful for us to find some Soviet official here—diplomatic or not—involved in matters of an internal character.')

(We already had other indications. . . .)

Other contacts were made between the microfaction and foreign elements, always with the same purpose, to get their points of view known abroad and seek support for their positions.

In this connection a document was seized from Ricardo Bofill Pagés (in custody), former head of the Publicity Department of the State Fruit Growing Enterprise, which totally distorted the history of the struggle against the tyranny, sustained the infamous accusation that the old Communists were being persecuted, and reiterated the all-too-familiar charlatanry about the bourgeois extraction of the leaders of the Revolution and the existing anti-Sovietism.

The document was found hidden under a seat in Bofill's automobile. He had promised to deliver it to a Soviet citizen within a few days, but his arrest frustrated the plan.

The Soviet citizen to whom Bofill was to deliver the document was Mikhail Roy, a journalist of the Novosti agency, now in Cuba. The same man had also made contact with Edmigio López Castillo (in custody) so as to request information on Comrade García Peláez, who had recently been appointed Ambassador to the USSR. For this purpose, López Castillo approached Octavio Fernández, who worked at the COR[1] and could furnish more detailed information.

The three of them met on a street corner in Vedado and went for a long ride in the automobile owned by the Soviet journalist. During the ride, Octavio Fernández gave Mikhail Roy whatever information he had concerning Comrade García Peláez. Roy asked Fernández if he thought García Peláez was anti-Soviet and if his appointment was due to a change in Cuba-USSR policy.

Later Octavio Fernández told Aníbal about the meeting. . . .

Edmigio López Castillo knew Rudolf P. Shliapnikov, known as Rodolfo, who held the post of Second Secretary in the Soviet Embassy. On one occassion, when Rudolf and Edmigio López Castillo, his brother Ricardo, and José Antonio Caballero, were holding a meeting in Edmigio's house, Félix Fleitas and Alfredo Batista—all microfactional elements—arrived and joined in the conversation, criticizing the revolutionary leadership.

Félix Fleitas said that he had been trying to get in touch with the others for quite some time to learn their opinion on the existing policy, and that there were old-time Communists in Cuba who wished to seek asylum in the Soviet Embassy. Rodolfo, the Second Secretary of the Soviet Embassy, interrupted him, saying that that was not the way, that it was necessary to wait.

In this conversation Félix Fleitas also said that the long-time Communists would never betray the USSR, since they agreed with its positions; that the Soviets had to do something here because the situation was very bad, and that they ought to protest about the policy of citicizing the USSR that had prevailed in recent speeches.

'Rodolfo'—that is, Rudolf P. Shliapnikov—explained to them that if they, the Soviets, were to send a note to Major Fidel Castro he was capable of publishing it, and that this was not desirable. Therefore, they couldn't do anything, for then the same things would be said to the Soviets here as to the Yankees.

Fleitas told Shliapnikov that Cuba intended to buy petroleum, and Rudolf told him that it must be the petroleum of Leoni;[2] Fleitas added—jokingly—that it seemed that Cuba was thinking of breaking with the USSR.

At this, Rodolfo, joking, laughingly replied, 'Look, all we have to do is tell the Cuban Government that repairs are going to be made in the port of

[1] Commission for Revolutionary Orientation.
[2] Raúl Leoni President of Venezuela

W

Baku that will last for three weeks,' setting everybody off in loud laughter. It should be kept in mind that this conversation was held among microfactional elements and a Soviet official at the home of one of these elements.

There are several pages appended here relative to this interview.

At the end of November 1966 Rudolf P. Shliapnikov, 'Rodolfo', was invited to an assembly at the Ministry of Labor. He was invited not by any minister, but by one who will be named later.

Rudolf spoke at the assembly. At the end of the meeting Rudolf, Abel Castaño Speinler, a former organizer of the National Tobacco Workers' Union who had taken a course on trade unionism in the USSR, and José Pereda, who was Secretary General of the Young Communist League in the Ministry of Labor and had also studied in the USSR, had a talk in Pereda's office, where they drank a toast, after which Rudolf stated the following: 'The conditions have been created in Cuba for another Hungary; imperialism is working in an objective manner in accord with the concrete*conditions of the Revolution directed fundamentally by the bourgeoisie and the petty bourgeoisie; notice that there is great internal discontent; that it must be pointed out to this Revolution that in Hungary it was not the peasantry that suffocated the uprising, but that confusion had been very widespread and the task of confronting the situation fell to the Department of State Security and that, nevertheless, here in Cuba even this Department showed manifestations that the petty bourgeoisie was to be found even within that organism.'

(As I recall, it was not precisely the Department of State Security that put down the counter-revolutionaries there.)

Arnaldo Escalona, Orlando Olivera, Félix Fleitas (all in custody) and Escalona's wife, Hilda Felipe, attended a luncheon with two Soviet citizens—the captain and political commissar, respectively, of a fishing vessel—carrying forward their plan to defame the Revolution and influence the opinion of every Soviet citizen in contact with Cuba.

A Soviet citizen of Spanish origin named Rafael García, who works with other Soviet technical personnel at the Fishing Terminal, served as interpreter in this conversation.

Arnaldo Escalona stated: 'Look. Tell them—the Soviets—that the main leaders of this Revolution and this Party do not have a Communist background. The majority were anti-Communists. The Party is rife with petty bourgeois elements. There is a leftish adventurist deviation, and that adventurism is in command; they consider Cuba the hub of the world. From here, we give orientation to the whole world and don't accept advice from anyone, orders from anyone; but we give orders, we want to give orientation. In the 22nd Congress (all of this in a very ironic tone), in the Party Congress of the USSR, the Cubans made speeches telling the Soviets what they had to do. We suppose that the Soviets laughed and said "Ah! These boys! These boys!"'

Orlando Olivera: 'The son teaching the father. Look! the Party, because its leadership is petty bourgeois—which doesn't mean that the Party is backed by the petty bourgeoisie. No? You understand me—its orientation is simply nationalist, reflects a chauvinist class tendency, and that is the problem with the international line.

'The economic resources,' continued Olivera, 'that we have, that are obtained in dollars, are invested to subsidize, to give anti-Communist orientation throughout Latin America and on other continents, to attack the Soviet Union and the Communist Parties of every country. It is not that we hold these ideas, but recently we spoke with two members of the Central Committee of the Dominican Communist Party—one of them is Justino del Orbe—and they told us that in their country there are two organizations that are anti-Communist but call themselves Marxist: the 13th of June Movement and the MPD.'[1]

Olivera continued: 'That is, that the daily effort and sacrifice of our workers are being invested to carry out anti-Soviet and anti-Communist campaigns throughout the world.

'The problem is that Fidel wants Cuba to be the hub of the whole world and he himself to become more important than Marx. And for that we have to invent in philosophy, we have to invent in economy, we have to invent in everything, so that he can achieve a stature greater than that of Marx, Engels and Lenin.'

Arnaldo Escalona speaks again:

'I was saying that here the highest political organization in our country does not meet, and, moreover, within the Central Committee the old leaders of the Communist Party of Cuba are in total disagreement with the policy that is worked out here by one man, because here policy is made by no one but Fidel Castro; the highest organism exists but has no opportunity to discuss or express its opinions. And months go by and the former leaders of the Party don't even see Fidel. That is something that perhaps you don't know; perhaps you do. But if you don't know, I mention it so that the comrades— that is, the Soviets—understand the situation that exists, even within the highest political organization.' . . .

Fleitas speaks: 'In March 1962 Aníbal Escalante went through a political crisis in Cuba, and we consider that since that time the working class has been stripped of power. Aníbal Escalante went to the Soviet Union, and now he is in Cuba. This comrade is the revolutionary leader whom the long-time militants consider one of the firmest in the struggle for giving power to the proletariat, for the proletariat to assume power, alongside the Soviet Union; he is the one who encourages many of us Communists at this time, encourages us to remain firm in our principles,' concludes Fleitas. (This . . . suffices to illustrate the shameful activities of these elements in connection with persons in other countries.)

(I would like, however, to clarify, as a question of elementary justice, that, notwithstanding the conduct of a very small number of advisers, journalists and functionaries of foreign embassies who participated in the activities of members of the microfaction, numerous technicians from the Soviet Union and other socialist countries have worked in our country, demonstrating exemplary conduct and absolute respect for our Revolution. I personally can state that in these years thousands of Soviet officers, including advisers,

---

[1] *Movimiento Popular Dominicano.*

specialists and technicians of all kinds, have worked with us in the Armed Forces; and there is, really, not a single complaint that can be made about them; quite the contrary, we hold pleasant memories of them and are deeply grateful to them.)

196. An 'old Communist' defines what should be the correct relationship towards the Soviet Union: statement by Carlos Rafael Rodríguez, January 1968:[1] excerpt (*p. 57*)

These people[2] have tried to pose as defenders of the Soviet Union and of respect for the Soviet Union. Yesterday we heard some talk about how much they loved and respected the Soviet Union. I think that the Soviet Union should be respected as the first country to undertake and carry through a Socialist Revolution, and I believe that no one can fail to have respect for the party of Lenin.

But it seems to me that the only proper way of loving and respecting the Soviet Union is by criticizing what we consider to be mistakes in her policy, when we openly express our disagreements, and when we say in a fraternal manner just what mistakes we think they are making in the conduct of their international relationships, and how we do not share their attitude.

To act otherwise is subordination; to act otherwise is renunciation of criticism; to act otherwise is not love but opportunism. For in my opinion and I think we are all agreed on this—this group has not tried to *help* the Soviet Union, but *to make use* of the Soviet Union.

And all the manoeuvres which have been described in the report of the Commission show exactly what steps this group has taken to compromise the Soviet Union more and more (and some of her officials, as we have seen, have let themselves be compromised by acting incorrectly) in order to compromise her in these fractional politics, of which ambition is the sole motive.

And this has been admitted, so there is no need to labour the point. The fact is that these gentlemen, say what they will, have reached the point of treason, of wanting the economic position of our country to get worse, in order to allow what they call the 'friendly' political intervention of the Soviet Union, and to get their leader Aníbal called to govern the country, or rather to govern it together with themselves, for they would be given jobs so that they too could take power—as the documents show—in helping to run the country.

... I would like to propose ... that the problem of relations with foreign officials—officials of other Socialist countries—should be the object of an open discussion with those parties.

I believe that we should no longer put up with a state of affairs where a whole series of officials and members of Socialist organizations—Socialist countries—work against the Cuban Revolution here and in their own country.

[1] *Granma*, 1 Feb. 1968.   [2] i.e., the 'microfaction'.

197. Speech by Fidel Castro calling for 'maximum independence' and warning Cubans against over-reliance on help from abroad, 13 March 1968:[1] excerpts (*pp. 56, 57*)

We are a state, and as such we naturally have to observe certain norms, and in the complex and difficult world we live in it is not always possible to discuss each and every problem in public. For lack of confidence in the people? No —never! Simply because there are questions of a diplomatic nature, questions which have to do with inter-state relations and so on, or questions which could do harm if they came to the knowledge of the enemy. . . .

Some questions, such as the problem of the microfaction,[2] have been well publicized, or at least publicized as widely as possible. On that occasion, we explained a series of questions, and our speech was not published, and that for the reasons we have explained. We did consider publishing it in part, but we really preferred to publish all or nothing, in order to avoid partial explanations. We hope, none the less, that 150 years will not have to elapse before someone has the opportunity of reading some of these documents. . . .

Today, we are not going into the problems relating to our international relations. For the moment, there is very little to say, and you are perfectly aware, for instance, of our Central Committee's decision not to send a delegate to the meeting of the Communist Parties which took place in Budapest. . . .

There are questions which have to do with our present situation and the development of the Revolution which, in our opinion, are much more pressing. . . . One has been the tendency towards complacency—the idea that we were being defended, and that this would be the end of our problems. For when mention was made on one or two occasions of the most famous intercontinental rockets, everyone here began at once to talk about intercontinental rockets, and counted on them as if they really had them in their pockets. Anyone making a speech to the peasants or any other meeting had to bring in a reference to these most famous rockets. And we remember that this theoretical use and abuse of the supposed rockets always made us rather uneasy. In our opinion it tended to create a certain mentality of complacency in the sense that 'we are defended—let us sit back with our hands crossed', when really the only right, sensible, and truly revolutionary thing to do was to look to ourselves and our own strength, and never fail to make the greatest effort in case we had one day to face a direct aggression from the imperialist enemy; to look primarily and solely to ourselves, and to be always ready to sell our lives very dearly without expecting anyone to come to our defence.

There was also created a certain mentality of complacency in the economic field, in the use and abuse of the idea that we could expect that help would immediately come for the solution of any problem. This created a certain complacent mentality in the sense that it kept the people from realizing that the decisive and fundamental effort should come from ourselves. . . .

We shall follow our path, we shall build up our revolution and we shall do it fundamentally by our own effort! Great is the effort which we must make! A people which is not ready to exert itself has no right so much as to

[1] *Bohemia*, 15 Mar. 1968.　　[2] See no. 195.

mention the words independence or sovereignty! Let us struggle boldly in order, amongst other things, to reduce to the utmost our dependence on everything that comes from abroad! Let us struggle to the utmost, for we have known the bitterness of having to depend to a considerable degree on things which come from outside and how that can become a weapon and at least create a temptation to use it against our country. Let us struggle to achieve maximum independence, regardless of the cost!

198. Difficulties in reaching a new Soviet-Cuban trade agreement: press statement, March 1968[1] (*p. 57*)

The 1968 trade protocol between the Soviet Union and Cuba was signed yesterday in Moscow. The annual protocol is usually signed in January or February, but this time the signing was delayed because a mid-term trade treaty was being negotiated by both countries, and the two sides had not reached common viewpoints on treaty terms.

199. Speech by Fidel Castro supporting Soviet action against Czechoslovakia but finding his own grounds for criticism, 28 August 1968:[2] excerpts (*p. 58*)

. . . Some of the things that we are going to state here will be, in some cases, in contradiction with the emotions of many; in other cases, in contradiction with our own interests; and, in still others, they will constitute serious risks for our country.

However, this is a moment of great importance for the revolutionary movement throughout the world. And it is our duty to analyze the facts objectively and express the opinion of our political leadership, the opinion that represents the judgement of the members of our Central Committee, of the leaders of our mass organizations, of the members of our Government, and that we are sure is profoundly compatible with the tradition and sentiments of our people. . . .

We, on the other hand, were convinced—and this is very important—that the Czechoslovak regime was dangerously inclined toward a substantial change in the system. In short, we were convinced that the Czechoslovak regime was heading toward capitalism and was inexorably heading toward imperialism. . . . We consider that it was absolutely necessary, at all costs, in one way or another, to prevent this eventuality from taking place.

Bear with me, because I plan to analyze this in the light of our ideas.

Discussion of the form is not, in the final analysis, the most fundamental factor. The essential point to be accepted, or not accepted, is whether or not the socialist camp could allow a political situation to develop which would lead to the breaking away of a socialist country, to its falling into the arms of imperialism. And our point of view is that it is not permissible and that the socialist camp has a right to prevent this in one way or another. . . .

. . . What cannot be denied here is that the sovereignty of the Czechoslovak

[1] *Granma*, 23 Mar. 1968.   [2] *Granma* (Engl. ed.), 25 Aug. 1968.

State was violated. This would be a fiction, an untruth. And the violation was, in fact, of a flagrant nature. . . . From the legal point of view, this cannot be justified. This is very clear. In our opinion, the decision made concerning Czechoslovakia can only be explained from a political point of view, not from a legal point of view. Not the slightest trace of legality exists. Frankly, none whatever. . . .

Gentlemen, is it conceivable that a situation could occur, under any circumstances, after 20 years of communism in our country, of communist revolution, of socialist revolution, in which a group of honest revolutionaries, in this country, horrified by the prospect of an advance—or rather a retrogression—to counterrevolutionary positions and toward imperialism, could find themselves obliged to request the aid of friendly armies to prevent such a retrogression from occurring? . . . No circumstance of this kind will ever present itself in our country. . . . What kind of communists would we be and what kind of communist revolution would this be, if, at the end of 20 years, we were to find ourselves forced to do such a thing in order to save it? . . . Whenever we have thought of outside help the only idea that has ever come into our minds was that of outside help to fight against imperialist troops and against imperialist armies. . . . We cannot conceive of such things within the Revolution.

I do not believe that justification [for Soviet action against Czechoslovakia] can be found in the appeal from top personalities, since the sole justification can only be the simple political fact that Czechoslovakia was moving toward a counterrevolutionary situation and that this seriously affected the entire socialist community. . . .

The communist ideal cannot, for a single moment, exist without internationalism. . . . We can say—and today it is necessary to speak clearly and frankly—that we have seen to what extent those ideals and those internationalist sentiments, that state of alertness and that awareness of the world's problems have disappeared or are very weakly expressed in certain socialist countries of Europe. We would not say in all those countries, but in more than one socialist country of Europe. Those who have visited those countries, including Cuban scholarship students, have often come back completely dissatisfied and displeased and have said to us: 'Over there the youth are not being educated in the ideals of communism and in the principles of internationalism; the youth there are highly influenced by all the ideas and tastes prevalent in the countries of Western Europe. In many places the main topic of conversation is money and incentives of this or that type, material incentives of all kinds, material gains and salaries.' As a matter of fact, an internationalist and communist conscience is not being developed in those places. . . . The sensibilities of many of our men have been injured more than once by such vulgar use of material incentives or such vulgar commercialization of the conscience of men. . . .

A series of opinions, a series of ideas, a series of practices incomprehensible to us, which have really contributed to slackening and softening the revolutionary spirit of the socialist countries: ignorance of the problems of the underdeveloped world, ignorance of the shocking misery which exists, tendencies toward maintaining practices of trade with the underdeveloped world which are the same practices of trade which the developed bourgeois capitalist world maintains. I'm not talking about all the socialist countries, but several of them. . . .

. . . The principal promoter of all that policy of bourgeois liberalism, its principal defender, was the organization of the so-called Yugoslav Communists. They enthusiastically applauded all the liberal reforms. . . . Our country has been a constant accuser of that organization.

Nevertheless, as you know, in recent times, many Communist Parties, and among them the Communist Parties of the Warsaw Pact, began to forget the role and the nature of the League of Yugoslav Communists.

Yugoslavia began to be called a communist country; the League of Yugoslav Communists began to be called a communist party and to be invited to meetings of socialist countries, to meetings of mass organizations and of the Communist Parties. And this is what gave rise to our constant opposition, our constant disagreement, our constant discrepancies—expressed on a number of occasions.

. . . . However, we have disagreed with, been displeased at, and protested against the fact that these same countries have been drawing closer economically, culturally and politically to the oligarchic governments of Latin America, which are not merely reactionary governments and exploiters of their peoples, but also shameless accomplices in the imperialist aggressions against Cuba and shameless accomplices in the economic blockade of Cuba. . . .

. . . We ask ourselves if that policy of economic, political and cultural rapprochement toward these oligarchic governments that are accomplices in the imperialist blockade against Cuba will come to an end. . . .

. . . The TASS statement explaining the decision of the Warsaw Pact governments states in its concluding paragraph: 'The fraternal countries firmly and resolutely offer their unbreakable solidarity against any outside threat. They will never permit anyone to tear away even one link of the community of socialist States.' And we ask ourselves: 'Does that declaration include Vietnam? Does that statement include Korea? Does that statement include Cuba? Do they or do they not consider Vietnam, Korea and Cuba links of the socialist camp to be safeguarded against the imperialists?

In accordance with that declaration, the Warsaw Pact divisions were sent into Czechoslovakia. And we ask ourselves: 'Will the Warsaw Pact divisions also be sent to Vietnam if the Yankee imperialists step up their aggression against that country and the people of Vietnam request that aid? Will they send the divisions of the Warsaw Pact to the Democratic People's Republic of Korea if the Yankee imperialists attack that country? Will they send the divisions of the Warsaw Pact to Cuba if the Yankee imperialists attack our country, or even in the case of the threat of a Yankee imperialist attack on our country, if our country requests it?

We acknowledge the bitter necessity that called for the sending of those forces into Czechoslovakia; we do not condemn the socialist countries that made that decision. But we, as revolutionaries, and proceeding from positions of principle, do have the right to demand that they adopt a consistent position with regard to all the other questions that affect the world revolutionary movement.

Index

Abbes, J., 42 n.
Acosta, Armando, 295
Africa, 54, 289
Afro-Asian-Latin American People's Solidarity Organization (AALAPSO), 28
Afro-Asian People's Solidarity Organization (AAPSO), 28
Aguirre, Severo, 253–4
Aid policy, 24–5, 210
Aksenov, N. V., 31
Alba, Victor, 16 n.
Albov, N., 70
Alekseyev, Aleksandr, 65, 295
Alianza Popular Revolucionaria Americana (APRA), 11, 14–15, 136–40, 142–4, 148–9, 151
Alyabiyev, M. S., 249–51
Amézaga, J. J., 240
Anikin, A., 206–7
Aragonés, Emilio, 49, 271–2
Aramburu, Pedro, 33 n.
Aranha, Osvaldo, 187
Arbenz, Jácobo, 40–1, 226
Arévalo, Julia, 242
Argentina: Slav minority in, 2, 33, 64–5, 176–7; Lenin's view of, 2, 72–3; CP activities in, 8, 10, 12–13, 17, 19 n., 117–18; diplomatic relations, 8, 21, 32–3, 64, 69, 73, 76, 81, 115–16, 174–6; economic relations, 8–9, 22, 24, 32–3, 75–6, 80, 158–60, 168, 170, 180–3; Comintern contacts, 10–13, 117–18; Perón regime, 32, 64, 172–6; moves Soviet expulsion from League, 32, 116–117; UN membership opposed by USSR, 32, 173–4; Onganía regime, 32, 180; Illia regime, 33, 179; attacks on Soviet Embassy, 33, 177–8; fishing dispute, 33–118, 297; denounces Soviet invasion of Czechoslovakia, 33, 180; Frondizi regime, 177–8, 182–3
Arica, 120
Arismendi, Rodney, 30–1, 242–4
Arms: supplied to Guatemala, 40–1; supplied to Cuba, 44–5, 49–50, 271–6
Austine, see Rabaté
Ayora, Isidro, 148

Baccino, Julio, 242

Banderas, see Pestkovsky, S.
Barboza da Silva, E. P., 193
Barrientos, René, 25 n.
Batista, Alfredo, 299
Batista, Fulgencio, 20, 36–7, 43, 48, 216–18
Bay of Pigs (Playa Girón), 47, 263–4
Bazykin, V. L., 234–5
Beals, Carleton, 3 n.
Belo'us, N., 33 n., 38 n.
Belyakov, A. S., 237
Benutti, Ramón, 242
Betancourt, Rómulo, 27, 39
Bofill Pagés, Ricardo, 298–9
Bolívar, Simón: Marx on, 2, 60, 70–2
Bolivia: Comintern contacts, 12 n.; CP activities, 12 n., 26–7, 199–200; diplomatic relations, 25, 39, 73, 199; economic relations, 24–5, 39, 73, 80, 196–9; guerrilla operations in, 54 n.
Bomfim, Antonio Maciel, 154–5
Borah, W. E., 136, 139–40
Borodin, Michael, 3, 60–1
Bramuglia, Juan A., 174
Bravo, D., 27
Bravo, L., 63
Brazil: CP activities in, 9–12, 18–19, 25–6, 33–4, 64, 151–6, 181 186; Comintern contacts, 9, 12, 18–19, 98–114, 151–6; 1935 revolt in, 18–19, 98–114, 151–6; economic relations, 22, 23 n., 24, 34, 75–6, 167, 170–1; Castel Branco regime, 25, 35; Goulart regime, 25, 35, 195; Marshal Dutra attacked, 33, 185, 193–196; incidents and protests, 33–5, 184, 186–8; at UN, 41, 187–8; diplomatic relations: (Tsarist), 69, 187; (with USSR) established, 33, 187; — severed, 34, 186–8; — renewed, 35
Brezhnev, Leonid, 29, 31, 35, 162, 188–91, 198–9, 243
Broadcasting, 21–2
Bukharin, N., 11, 62, 74
Bulganin, N. A., 21, 158

Caccia, Alejandro, 242
Calles, Plutarco Elías, 4–5, 88–92
Camara, A. Arruda, 184
Campos, Hugo, 236
Campos, Roberto de Oliveira, 195